THE DIPLOMACY OF CONSTRAINT

DENIS STAIRS

The Diplomacy of Constraint: Canada, the Korean War, and the United States

UNIVERSITY OF TORONTO PRESS

© University of Toronto Press 1974
Toronto and Buffalo
Printed in Canada
ISBN 0-8020-5282-7
LC 72-95814

For Valerie

Contents

viii

Preface

Canadian troops fought in the Korean War under the auspices of the United Nations and in support of the principle of collective security. So the policy-makers said, and so – along with the vast majority of their domestic constituents – they believed. It was an understandable conclusion, for the 1950 crisis in Korea appeared at first glance to develop along classical collective security lines. Without prior warning, one member of the international community launched a conventional military invasion of another. It thereby committed a breach of international peace and security and a violation of international law. The matter was brought accordingly before the Security Council of the United Nations, an institution established by international agreement for the explicit purpose of ensuring the maintenance of a peaceful world order. The council called upon the parties involved to terminate their hostilities, and asked the invading forces to return peacefully to their own territory. The 'outlaw' government failed to comply, and the council was forced to take extreme measures. Making full use of its constitutional authority, it asked all members of the UN to contribute to the defence of the invaded power and to the restoration of peace and security in the affected area. Ultimately it assigned to one of its members (the United States) the responsibility for establishing a unified military command, to which the forces contributed by other powers, in fulfilment of their obligations under the UN Charter, were asked to report. The armies of the 'aggressor' state were thus confronted by the legally mobilized combat forces of governments which were prepared to take collective military action in defence of international law and order. By so uncomplicated an accounting as this, the affair in Korea achieves the perfection of a textbook case.

On closer examination, however, the experience of the Korean War is suggestive less of the norms of collective security than of the practice of countervailing power. The analogy is not so much to a united community dispatching a posse in search of a lone and predatory outlaw, as to a pair of rival street gangs in a lawless city. Fearful of the consequences of direct confrontation, the two sides nevertheless probe and test one another by skirmishing on the peripheries of their disputed territory. Looking anxiously on is an audience of innocent bystanders (or 'neutrals') who know their interests will be adversely affected if the skirmishing escalates to a full-scale 'rumble.'

The North Korean attack was thus perceived in the west, and especially in the United States, as an aggression authorized, if not actually engineered, by the Soviet Union. Its most telling historical parallel was thought to be the German seizure of Czechoslovakia in 1938-9. In the context of the Nazi menace the doctrine of appeasement had been exposed as bankrupt policy; in the face of the Soviet menace the doctrine of containment had been devised to take its place. In accordance, therefore, with the view that 'communism' had to be firmly opposed wherever and whenever it attempted to expand, the American government unilaterally decided to intervene in the hostilities and counter the North Korean assault. As an important but not crucial adjunct of its policy, it sought to take the United Nations with it, acquiring in the process a substantial measure of international legitimacy for its cause, together with a smaller portion of military support for its forces. But its combat allies in the theatre were for the most part its political allies in the world at large. There was not a communist power among them; there was scarcely evidence even of the non-aligned.[1] In effect, since the 'enemy' was thought to be not the government of North Korea alone, nor later the governments of North Korea and China together, but rather those of the 'communist world' as a whole, the United Nations was being made to perform as an instrument of western security. This was an underlying reality which was inevitable in the context of a world deeply divided by the cold war, but it gave the enterprise in Korea a character very different from the one anticipated for such cases by the founders of the UN Charter.

The American recourse to the Security Council in June 1950 nevertheless had profound implications for Canada, for without this formal involvement of

---

1 In addition to South Korea, the United States, and Canada, Australia, Belgium, Colombia, Ethiopia, France, Greece, Luxembourg, the Netherlands, New Zealand, the Philippines, Thailand, Turkey, South Africa, and the United Kingdom made contributions of combat forces. Medical units were supplied by Denmark, Italy, India, Norway, and Sweden. A few other countries offered small military contingents, but for a variety of practical reasons they were rejected.

the United Nations the government in Ottawa would no more have embroiled itself in the conflict in Korea than it did later in the war in Vietnam. To this extent American policy-makers were very successful in recruiting, through the UN, the active support of a foreign government (Canada's was of course only one among several) that would otherwise have remained aloof. The price the Americans had to pay, and the advantage the Canadians (along with others who were similarly affected) were able to gain, was a measure of participation in the formulation of allied, or 'United Nations,' policy. For a variety of reasons – most of them relating in one way or another to the desire to prevent the Americans from becoming bogged down in Asia at a time when there was a more vital theatre to defend across the Atlantic – Canadian officials felt it was essential to moderate and constrain the course of American decisions. In attempting to do so, they acted in concert with other powers of like purpose, and their instrument was the United Nations itself. They met with only marginal success – they would say now that they did as well as conditions allowed, and that in any case a small advance is better than none at all – but the effort itself was fundamental to their diplomacy throughout the conduct of the hostilities as well as in the political negotiations which preceded them and which later followed in their wake.

This general pattern of Canadian behaviour, in which initiatives were taken on a multilateral basis through the United Nations with a view to moderating the exercise of American power, gives this book its central theme. The analysis begins with a discussion of an American-inspired United Nations attempt, in which Canada was closely involved, to secure an early resolution of the Korean question in 1947-8 (Chapter 1), and it concludes with a treatment of the Canadian role in the Korean phase of the Geneva conference in 1954 (Chapter 8). For the rest, the book is concerned with the history of the origin, substance, and conduct of Canadian diplomacy during the war itself. Since the military aspects of the hostilities have been fully treated in the official histories published under the auspices of the Department of National Defence, they receive only cursory mention here, although some attention is paid in Chapter 6 to the political and diplomatic implications of issues bearing on the organization and command of the Canadian Army Special Force. On the other hand, considerable space is devoted to the activities of policy-makers in Washington and elsewhere whenever this appears necessary in order to establish the context of Canadian policy.

The 'story' of any political phenomenon can of course be told in many different ways, depending on the question one asks and the premises upon which the question is based. One could, for example, undertake an examination of Canada's role in the diplomacy of the Korean War by focussing on the attitudes, perceptions, and beliefs of the secretary of state for external affairs. The result might well be a perfectly coherent account of Canadian policy in which the government's behaviour would be related directly to the basic tenets of Mr Pearson's political philosophy. On the other hand, it would be equally possible to 'explain' the Canadian involvement entirely in terms of Canada's 'place' or 'position' vis-à-vis other powers in the international community, and to do so without any reference whatever to the predilections of Canadian statesmen. Here the behaviour of Canadian policy-makers would be accounted for in terms of Canada's proximity to the United States, the size, structure, and external linkages of its economy, the strength of its military establishment, and other such 'objective' conditions. Many alternative versions of 'what happened' are in this sense possible, each of them having in varying degree its own interest and utility, and surviving without apparent damage in the presence of all, or most, of the others.

In the light of these and related reflections, I have added a final chapter on 'analytical alternatives' which discusses the sorts of conclusions that might ensue if Canada's experience in the diplomacy of the Korean War were examined from a variety of differing perspectives. This chapter is intended for professional teachers of foreign policy analysis, and especially for their students, but I hope it will be of interest to others as well.

With regard, finally, to sources, the principal advantage that can be claimed for this book is that it has been written sufficiently soon after the events it describes to permit interviews at first hand with most of the policy-makers who were centrally involved. Their memories and reflections, not all of which will be fully recorded in the formal correspondence and internal memoranda of the official government community, are the source of much of my information. I am persuaded that this material, taken in conjunction with the written public record, is sufficiently detailed to outweigh the disadvantages of writing the manuscript in advance of the release of official diplomatic files. If future historians prove me wrong, then I hope at least that the book will make a useful addition to the store of documentary evidence which by then will have become available.

DS
Ottawa
January 1973

Acknowledgments

In researching and writing this volume, I have incurred a multitude of debts. I would like in particular to thank Rear Admiral J.V. Brock, Mr Peter G.R. Campbell, Mr M.J. Coldwell, Brigadier A.B. Connelly, Lieutenant-General F.J. Fleury, Professor Douglas V. LePan, Professor R.A. MacKay, Mr Escott Reid, Mr H. Basil Robinson, Lieutenant-General G.G. Simonds, Brigadier Harold E. Taber, and Mr Freeman M. Tovell, all of whom extracted time from their busy schedules to answer questions, and in some cases to engage in follow-up correspondence. The late General Charles Foulkes and Mr A.D.P. Heeney also submitted most helpfully to interviews. The Honourable J.W. Pickersgill read parts of the manuscript, discussed a number of aspects of the project at considerable length both in a personal interview and through the mails, and at an early stage generously allowed me to examine relevant portions of the third volume of *The Mackenzie King Record* before it was published. For his assistance, and that of Professor D.F. Forster of the University of Toronto, who made the necessary arrangements for my viewing this material, I am very grateful.

The Right Honourable Lester B. Pearson was an indispensable source of information, and evidence of the generosity of his assistance can be found everywhere in the following pages. He not only agreed to a lengthy interview with the cheerful good humour for which he was famous, but later dealt with a number of additional questions through the mails, and subsequently in a series of encounters during his last weeks at Carleton University. It is difficult to imagine a more helpful and reflective informant.

Mr Geoffrey Pearson of the Department of External Affairs sacrificed hours of his time to an examination of his father's personal papers in search of answers to a multitude of inquiries, and devoted hours more to a personal interview. He also read and commented most usefully upon an early draft of the manuscript. Miss Mary Macdonald of the Prime Minister's Office, the Honourable Paul Martin, leader of the government in the Senate, Professor F.H. Soward of the University of British Columbia, Professor Dale Thomson, the biographer of Louis St Laurent, and several members of the Department of External Affairs Historical and Information Divisions, and of the Canadian Forces Headquarters Directorate of History – all answered tedious questions by mail, as did the late Mr Blair Fraser, Ottawa editor of *Maclean's* magazine. Mrs Brooke Claxton very kindly agreed to open her husband's personal papers for my inspection, and Mr John B. Claxton generously made the necessary arrangements with the Public Archives of Canada.

Mr John W. Holmes, director general of the Canadian Institute of International Affairs, suggested the topic in the beginning and provided indispensable assistance in the form of interviews, lengthy correspondence, comments on early drafts, and suggestions for further lines of inquiry. Every student of Canadian foreign policy will understand immediately the extent of this debt.

I owe much to a number of university and public libraries, but I am particularly indebted to Mr Ian Wilson of the Douglas Library Archives at Queen's University, and to Mr R.S. Gordon of the Public Archives of Canada for their help in arranging access to certain collections of private papers. I am especially grateful also to the staff of the Canadian Institute of International Affairs in Toronto – not merely for their practical assistance, which was extensive, but also for their unassailable good cheer, through which they dispel more bookworm's gloom than they can possibly imagine.

The libraries of the *Globe and Mail,* the *Toronto Daily Star,* the *Montreal Star,* and the Montreal *Gazette* kindly allowed me to examine their Korean files. Miss Leslie Brent of the Public Service Office, *Chicago Tribune,* and Miss Margaret S. Crabb of the *Vancouver Sun* Press Library searched their respective records for particular items in which I was interested. Miss Byrne Hope Sanders of the Canadian Institute of Public Opinion very generously granted me access to her complete collection of CIPO polls.

I would like also to extend special thanks to my doctoral supervisor at the University of Toronto, Professor James Eayrs, whose comments on early versions of the manuscript were delivered with a delightful combination of instructive clarity and healing tact. I am very grateful both for them and for all his other assistance, much of which he must have found the more tedious to bestow as a result of the need to communicate by post. Professors Richard

Gregor and Stefan Dupré of the University of Toronto offered much at various stages in the way of valuable comment and advice. I am very grateful also for the observations of a number of other authorities who kindly agreed to read the manuscript, in whole or in part. These include Mr Gordon R.S. Hawkins, executive director of the Centre for Foreign Policy Studies, Dalhousie University; Professors Roger L. Dial, Michael MccGwire, and Donald Munton, also of Dalhousie; Mr Alex. I. Inglis, former resident historian with the Department of External Affairs; and Professors Peyton V. Lyon, Lynn Mytelka, and Robert R. Simmons of the Carleton University School of International Affairs. Professor Henry Roper of Huron College, University of Western Ontario, volunteered to help with the Index, and Mrs Doris Boyle of Dalhousie's Centre for Foreign Policy Studies cheerfully saw to its typing.

For financial assistance I am much indebted to the Province of Ontario and to the J.W. Dafoe Foundation for fellowships during my two years of residence and research at the University of Toronto; to the Research Development Committee for the Humanities and Social Sciences at Dalhousie University for a travel grant which enabled me to conduct a number of interviews; and to the Social Science Research Council of Canada for a generous subsidy in support of publication.

To Rik Davidson and Rosemary Shipton of the University of Toronto Press I owe a debt much larger than they will allow me to reveal. Fervently, I thank them both.

DS

THE DIPLOMACY OF CONSTRAINT

1
Rehearsal

Like so many tragedies of international affairs, the war in Korea was ultimately rooted not so much in the politics of those who inhabited the victim state as in the ambitions of foreign powers. More specifically, it emerged in the context of the rivalry which developed between the Soviet Union and the United States after the 1945 defeat of Germany and Japan.

The Japanese had established their authority over the Korean peninsula following the Russo-Japanese War in 1904-5. But their administration was vigorously opposed by Korean nationalists, some of whom organized in 1919 a self-styled provisional government in China and began to propagate the cause of Korean national independence. Neither the Chinese nor the Americans were prepared at first to recognize the legitimacy of this industrious group, but with the outbreak of the Pacific war late in 1941 its objectives acquired a certain political as well as moral currency in Allied capitals. The matter was therefore discussed by Roosevelt, Churchill, and Chiang Kai-shek at the Cairo Conference in the autumn of 1943, and their subsequent declaration included the statement that the 'three great powers, mindful of the enslavement of the people of Korea, are determined that in due course Korea shall become free and independent.' In later discussions the Americans and British secretly secured the agreement also of the Soviet Union, which was not at war with the Japanese. At Yalta in February 1945 it was suggested tentatively that Korea might be administered after the war by a multi-power trusteeship as a prelude to genuine independence. On 28 May of the same year, Harry Hopkins cabled President Truman from Moscow to say that Stalin had definitely agreed 'that there should be a trusteeship for Korea under the United States, China,

Great Britain, and the Soviet Union.'[1] On 8 August the USSR declared war on Japan and in so doing announced that it would adhere to the Potsdam Declaration of 26 July, which included a reaffirmation of the Cairo Declaration of 1943.

As in the case of so many of the plans originating in the diplomacy of World War II, these arrangements were based on the assumption that the unity of the great powers would continue into the postwar period. Of course it did not, and the subsequent political geography of Korea came ultimately to be determined by the temporary *ad hoc* provisions that had been devised for administering its occupation. These were contained in the terms of Japanese surrender agreed upon by the Soviet and American authorities, and they included a stipulation to the effect that Japanese forces in Korea north of the 38th parallel would surrender to the USSR, and south of the parallel to the United States. The division was intended to last only until arrangements for the granting of Korean independence had been concluded by the two occupying powers.

The initial steps were taken at a meeting of the Council of Foreign Ministers in Moscow in the autumn of 1945. By the so-called Moscow Agreement concluded on 27 December, the signatories contracted to set up 'a provisional Korean democratic government' with 'a view to the re-establishment of Korea as an independent state' and 'the creation of conditions for developing the country on democratic principles.' In preparing the appropriate measures, the two occupation commands would form a Joint Commission which would 'consult with the Korean democratic parties and social organizations.' The resulting recommendations of the commission would be presented 'for the consideration' of the Soviet, Chinese, British, and American governments, but the final decision would be taken by the Soviets and Americans alone. Once the provisional government was established, it would be consulted by the Joint Commission in the formulation of proposals for the creation of a 'four-power trusteeship of Korea for a period of up to five years.' In the meantime there would be a conference of representatives of the two occupying powers, to take place 'within a period of two weeks,' in order to discuss 'urgent problems' affecting both zones and to work out arrangements for 'permanent coordination in administrative-economic matters.'[2]

These arrangements were badly received by nationalist and conservative politicians in South Korea, who had hoped for immediate independence, but they appeared to arouse no serious public complaint among the left-wing groups that were predominant in the North.[3] In any event, the Moscow Plan

1 Quoted in Grey, jr, 'The Thirty-Eighth Parallel,' 483
2 The full text of this agreement is reprinted in McCune, *Korea Today*, 275-6
3 See Goodrich, *Korea*, 19

never reached fruition. There were preliminary meetings between the two commands in January and February 1946 to provide for the economic and administrative co-ordination of the two zones, but they accomplished nothing. Discussions by the Joint Commission began on 20 March, but were adjourned on 8 May without agreement. Ostensibly the issue in dispute concerned the interpretation of the clause in the Moscow Agreement providing for consultation with 'Korean democratic parties and social organizations.' In particular, the Soviets took the view that the consultation provision should apply only to those groups which had expressed their support for the five-year trusteeship proposal, while the Americans argued that organizations which had been critical of the plan should be included also. Underlying these opposing positions was the fact that those who had criticized the trusteeship arrangement were conservative nationalists resident in the South, while those who had supported it were left-wing radicals based predominantly in the North. Since each of the occupying powers was anxious to establish a Korean government favourable to its own interests, the outcome of the dispute was regarded as a matter of considerable political significance by both sides.

Bilateral discussions between the two occupying powers continued both in Korea and through conventional diplomatic channels over the next fourteen months, but without productive result. In the meantime, the administrative policies of the authorities within the two zones began sharply to diverge, and the 38th parallel developed into an increasingly impenetrable barrier. The negotiations broke down completely in August 1947, and the Americans then suggested that the dispute be referred for settlement to a conference of the four great powers (Britain, China, the United States, and the USSR). They proposed also that the Moscow Plan be abandoned in favour of an arrangement whereby provisional government elections would be held under the auspices and supervision of the United Nations. The Soviets rejected this initiative and countered with a proposal that both occupying powers withdraw from Korea by 1 January 1948, allowing the Koreans to conduct the elections by themselves. This in turn proved unacceptable to the United States.

By now the situation in Korea had become a matter of serious concern to the American authorities. Their administration of the southern zone had aroused considerable criticism, not least because their own errors of occupation policy and the opposition of the conservative Korean politicians upon whose support they relied had prevented them from introducing effective economic and political reforms. The Koreans themselves were becoming increasingly vociferous in their demands for political independence, and at home there were congressional complaints about the enormous expense which the occupation incurred. The government's anxiety to escape the political, economic, and military costs of its Korean involvement intensified accordingly, although it was still unwilling to abandon the peninsula entirely to the careful ministrations of the USSR.

In order to resolve this dilemma, George Marshall, the American secretary of state, on 17 September 1947 dispatched John Foster Dulles to the General Assembly of the United Nations with a request that 'The Problem of the Independence of Korea' be placed on the agenda. The American proposal, as amended after discussion, was that the Assembly should appoint a United Nations Temporary Commission on Korea (UNTCOK) to supervise an election throughout the peninsula, the polling to take place preferably before the end of March 1948. The popular representatives thus selected could then set up an administration, establish police and security forces, and thereafter accept the transfer of governmental functions from both occupation authorities. By these means Korea would become united and independent, the American Department of State would be relieved of an expensive and embarrassing political problem, and the Joint Chiefs of Staff could withdraw their troops without leaving an inviting vacuum of power in their wake. The supervision of the entire proceedings by the United Nations would have a particular advantage in that it would furnish the new Korean state with a mantle of international legitimacy.[4]

The Soviet Union and its allies argued vigorously that the question of Korea was a matter coming solely within the jurisdiction of the great powers directly concerned, and that any United Nations involvement would therefore be illegal. In spite of their protests, however, the resolution was placed on the agenda on 23 September, and from 28 October to 5 November it was intensively debated in the Assembly's Political Committee. In these discussions the representatives of the Soviet bloc continued to argue that the proposal was illegal, and declared in addition that 'Korea could not establish its Government freely until after the complete withdrawal of foreign troops.' They suggested also that the United Nations should in any case make no decision on the matter until it had consulted with 'elected representatives of Korea, excluding persons nominated by the foreign military authorities.'[5]

These arguments had a cold reception among most of the delegations from countries outside the Soviet bloc, the Canadian included. The Canadian spokesman was J.A. Bradette, Liberal member of Parliament for Cochrane and

4 Gordenker, 'The United Nations, the United States Occupation and the 1948 Election in Korea,' 428
5 United Nations, GAOR (First Committee), A/C.1/SR.116, 251-2 (Mr Gromyko of the USSR)

chairman of the House of Commons Standing Committee on External Affairs, who spoke briefly on two occasions in support of the American position. During a meeting of the Political Committee on the afternoon of 28 October he attacked the Soviet proposal that the committee and General Assembly consult with representatives of the Korean people, pointing out that the disputants were unable to agree on who the representatives should be, and that in any case such consultations seemed unnecessary in view of the fact that both powers were unanimous in citing Korean independence as their final objective.[6] On the second occasion, two days later, he declared that Canada 'was particularly interested in the future of Korea because of its position on the northern Pacific,' and expressed the view that the peninsula 'should not be treated as two separate political units.' To withdraw the forces of occupation before a national government had been constituted, as the Soviets were suggesting, 'would only lead to chaos and disunity.' In any event, the proposed Temporary Commission would ensure that the presence of foreign troops would not hinder free elections.[7]

Mr Bradette's second intervention was to be the source of considerable irritation to Prime Minister Mackenzie King, who had arrived in New York on 31 October to receive an honorary award from the Canadian Club before departing for Great Britain to attend the wedding of Princess Elizabeth and to have discussions with British and European officials. Mr Bradette was not regarded as an authority on foreign policy, and was known to depend for his remarks entirely upon speeches written by the Department of External Affairs. When Mr King noticed a reference to his comments in the 30 October edition of the *New York Times*, he exclaimed to an aide, in derogation as much of the department as of the Liberal MP, 'This United Nations is going to destroy us yet. Just imagine, *Bradette* making speeches about Korea!'[8] Upon his return from Great Britain in December, he was to regard the matter in a light more sombre still.

The events which led to the prime minister's personal involvement seemed to the participants at the time relatively innocuous. After a number of minor

6 Ibid., 258
7 Ibid., 284
8 Pickersgill, interview, 13 March 1968. The quotation is Mr Pickersgill's approximate reconstruction of Mr King's comment. The *New York Times* carried a brief reference to Bradette's remarks in a story published on pages 1 and 17 of the 30 October edition under the title, 'U.S. Urges a U.N. Body on Korea to "Insure" Elections of Delegates.' The general outline of the story is confirmed by Mackenzie King's diary. See Pickersgill and Forster, eds., *Mackenzie King Record*, IV, 135

amendments, the American draft resolution was passed in the Political Committee on 4 November by a vote of 46 to 0 with 4 abstentions (Scandinavian countries), the members of the Soviet bloc refusing to take part. The resolution then went to the General Assembly in plenary session, and after a further two days of fruitless and repetitive debate from which the Canadian delegation remained aloof, it was passed by a vote of 43-0-6.

The significant feature of these proceedings from the Canadian point of view was the fact that Mr Dulles had included Canada among his nominations for UNTCOK membership. Leon Gordenker, the principal historian of the commission, has suggested that the Canadian (and Syrian) delegations 'were taken by surprise when Mr Dulles read out his list,' and that the Canadians refrained from rejecting the proposal only 'in order to save the United States from embarrassment.'[9] It is true that the Canadians had to make their decision quickly, since once it had become clear that the resolution would be accepted, the Americans were in a hurry to obtain a satisfactory list of participants. But their proposal was not considered by the Canadian delegation to be so significant a matter as Mr Gordenker's account implies. Mr Pearson regarded the commission as simply another routine United Nations committee, and although he protested half-jokingly to the Americans that they might have found a nominee with more experience in the Far East, he saw no reason for offering more than token resistance.[10]

The leader of the Canadian delegation was the minister of justice, J.L. Ilsley, who had accepted the assignment to the United Nations as a means of securing a rest from his regular duties,[11] and who was not in attendance until the proceedings had reached their final phase. When he was then approached, he somewhat reluctantly agreed to Canada's inclusion in the list of nominees on the advice of Mr Pearson, and in Mackenzie King's absence from Ottawa he subsequently secured the approval of the secretary of state for external affairs and acting prime minister, Louis St Laurent.[12] None of those involved thought at the time that the commission, at least from the Canadian perspective, was a matter of more than temporary and routine significance.[13]

---

9 Gordenker, *The United Nations and the Peaceful Unification of Korea*, 31
10 Pearson, interview, 18 Oct. 1968
11 Hutchison, *Mackenzie King*, 433. Confirmed by Heeney, interview, 7 March 1968
12 Pickersgill and Forster, eds., *Mackenzie King Record*, IV, esp. 135-6; Hutchison, *Mackenzie King*, 433; Pearson, interview, 18 Oct. 1968
13 This point was reiterated several times by Mr Pearson, interview, 18 Oct. 1968, and was mentioned also by Mr Heeney, interview, 7 March 1968, and by Mr Pickersgill, interview, 13 March 1968. Supporting evidence is provided by Brooke Claxton's subsequent account of the

These views were not shared, however, by the prime minister himself, who still laboured in the grip of his longstanding isolationism, and who in any case resented the decision being taken without his knowledge. By now he was preparing gradually for his disengagement from active politics, but he was determined to retain all his authority as prime minister until the day he actually relinquished office. In this respect, his sensitivity to his personal position tended to reinforce his characteristic hostility towards any Canadian involvement in the affairs of the Far East.[14] As Minister of National Defence Brooke Claxton later observed, King's reactions 'were the last bellows of the leader of the herd before he cashed in his cheques.'[15] They converted a relatively minor foreign policy issue into the subject of a major Cabinet upheaval.

Mr King expressed his concern about the Canadian commitment to serve on the commission in conversation with St Laurent shortly after his return to Ottawa from Great Britain on 4 December,[16] but the disagreement first erupted in significant proportions at a Cabinet meeting exactly two weeks later when the External Affairs minister sought what he thought would be routine approval for an order-in-council appointing Dr George S. Patterson, counsellor of the Canadian embassy in Nanking, as the commission's Canadian representative. The prime minister, as Claxton recorded later, 'blew a gasket' and proceeded to give St Laurent 'a going over as if he was a naughty little school-boy who had committed a sin against the Holy Ghost.' He said he was unable to support the recommendation, and could not 'understand how a matter of such dangerous importance could have been dealt with in this off-hand fashion.'[17] It was a grave error to embroil Canada in Asian and European affairs of which the members of the government had no knowledge, and which involved the conflicting interests of great powers. Given the current state of world politics, war might well break out between the United States and the Soviet Union – indeed, President Truman had once told him that he was particularly worried about the situation in Korea and Manchuria – and Canada could be drawn into such

---

way in which St Laurent raised the subject for the first time in Cabinet, when his 'manner made it obvious that he regarded this of so little consequence that it was hardly worth mentioning.' Notes, Claxton Papers, VI, 1126 (hereafter cited as Claxton notes)

14 Pickersgill, interview, 13 March 1968. See also Thomson, *St. Laurent*, 220-1
15 Claxton notes, 1126
16 Thomson, *Louis St. Laurent*, 221
17 Claxton notes, 1126. The last of these quotations is from Claxton's reconstruction of King's words. Claxton's recollection (pp. 1125 and 1128) was that this meeting of the Cabinet occurred in September 1947, but this would have pre-dated the Korean discussions in the United Nations. King's diary establishes the date as 18 December. See Pickersgill and Forster, eds., *Mackenzie King Record*, IV, 134

a conflict if the government interfered with Soviet-American relations. In the Korean case the risk was especially high because, aside from France, Canada was the most important power among the temporary commission's members, and hence 'would be made the spearhead of whatever arose.' The government 'knew nothing about the situation and should keep out of it.'[18]

St Laurent, who was restraining 'himself with noticeable difficulty,'[19] observed that so long as Canada was a member of the United Nations, the government was obligated to accept such responsibilities. The prime minister commented in reply that, except as a vehicle for Russian propaganda, 'the United Nations counted for nothing so far as any help in the world was concerned.' If the agreement to serve on the commission had been a mistake, the sooner it were corrected, the better. The original decision had not been taken by the Cabinet as a whole, and in any case the proper role of Canada 'was not that of Sir Galahad to save the whole world unless we were in a

18 Ibid. There is a theory that the volatility of the prime minister's reaction was due at least in part to an encounter with a London spiritualist, Miss Geraldine Cummins, during his visit to the United Kingdom earlier in the autumn. Miss Cummins later described the incident in her autobiography, in which King is referred to simply as 'Mr S.' Apparently Miss Cummins and a colleague attended the prime minister one Saturday afternoon at the Dorchester Hotel, Park Lane, where he was confined to his quarters by illness. According to her own account, Miss Cummins acted as Mr King's 'medium' to the spirit world, and among the communicants who were aroused during the session was the late American President, Franklin Delano Roosevelt (identified in the autobiography as 'X.Y.Z.'). Her hand under the control of Roosevelt's spirit, Miss Cummins wrote out a warning which 'greatly surprised' the prime minister. While '[t]roubles in Asia had not begun,' the spirit 'strongly urged attention being given [sic] to Asia. The danger was there and in the Far East ... X.Y.Z. wrote that he thought war likely in a certain year. But no statement was made as to whether it would be localized war or world war.'

   Miss Cummins' account reports that 'Mr S. seemed puzzled and a little shaken by this part of the communication. He then said that he made it a rule to ignore advice thus given: he trusted solely to his own and his advisers' judgment.'

   The account goes on to observe that 'In view of the later success of the Communists in China, and the removal of American troops from Korea, followed by the Korean War, it now seems regrettable that, in this instance, the hint was disregarded.' See Cummins, *Unseen Adventures*, 179. The background details are in Fraser, 'The Secret Life of Mackenzie King.' Mr Pearson subsequently concluded that the 'hint' was not 'disregarded' at all, but in fact explained much of the vehemence of Mr King's reaction to the affair of the Temporary Commission (remarks to seminar on Canadian external relations, Carleton University, 16 Oct. 1972). Whether he was right is a problem for psychiatrists and spiritualists to determine. To the layman it seems probable that communications such as those of 'X.Y.Z.' were taken seriously by their recipient only if they confirmed a position already held; in other cases they were doubtless ignored. Even on this interpretation, however, it is still conceivable that the incident served to strengthen the prime minister's resolve.

19 Claxton notes, 1127

position to do it.'[20] King repeated his position 'over and over and over again,' and with the exception of J.L. Ralston's resignation as minister of national defence in 1944, Brooke Claxton thought it the 'most painful scene' that he had ever witnessed at a meeting of the Cabinet.[21] Ilsley eventually intervened with the blunt declaration that he could see no reason why Canada should not accept service on the Korean commission, and that in any case the government was now obliged to fulfil its commitment. The atmosphere in the room then became electrically intense, and the prime minister postponed further discussion. He left the meeting darkly suspicious that the root of his trouble lay with Mr Pearson and the Department of External Affairs, which he thought was inadequately controlled by ministers of the crown, and which, as he now sadly reflected, was no longer administered by the more experienced hand of O.D. Skelton.[22]

After the Cabinet adjourned, King and St Laurent appear not to have discussed the matter further,[23] but on 21 December the prime minister examined a memorandum which had been prepared by Mr Pearson on the question of Canada's representation on the Korean commission. After reading it, he felt 'more strongly than ever' that the government should not proceed with the assignment of Patterson to the commission's staff. When the matter came up in the Cabinet again on 22 December, he began the proceedings by announcing that he had refused since their last meeting to sign the order-in-council providing for Patterson's appointment. St Laurent then offered a brief account of the commission's background, and observed that Canada had been 'one of the few countries acceptable to everyone' in the search for suitable members. It 'was one of the obligations of membership in the United Nations that a country like Canada must sometimes accept responsibility even where its own interests are not directly involved.'[24]

The discussion then proceeded much as before, although both sides now presented their cases in more coherent and settled form. King relied for support principally upon his argument that it was not in the Canadian interest to become involved in great power quarrels. It was clear that the Americans were eager to have Canada take part, and the inevitable result would be that the Canadian delegation would ally with the United States against the Soviet Union. This was particularly dangerous since the United Nations had no

20 Pickersgill and Forster, eds., *Mackenzie King Record*, IV, 134-5
21 Claxton notes, 1127
22 Pickersgill and Forster, eds., *Mackenzie King Record*, IV, 135-6
23 Claxton notes, 1130
24 Ibid., 1130

power to impose upon the disputants a solution of its own. He therefore would not agree to Patterson's appointment as a commissioner, and Ilsley would have to advise the commission to that effect.

Humphrey Mitchell and James G. Gardiner, the ministers respectively of labour and agriculture, and Wishart Robertson, the government leader in the Senate, all supported King, but the remaining members of the Cabinet were either silent or openly opposed. According to the prime minister's diary, Ilsley was 'dour; hard as a rock.' He said that the External Affairs officials at the time had done everything possible to avoid a nomination, but once it had come he had agreed with them that it would be unwise publicly to decline. He conceded, however, that he had not been present during the preliminary discussions, and that the decision had been taken without the prior approval of the Cabinet or of Mr St Laurent.[25] Brooke Claxton suggested that if Canada refused to take part, the Soviets would make the most of what they would interpret in the United Nations as a lack of unity among those supporting the American resolution. He thought privately 'that an organization for international co-operation in every part of the world could only function if the disinterested countries, the countries with no axe to grind or no particular interest in a specific question, were willing to act as mediators, administrators and even judges regarding points in issue involving other countries,'[26] and he 'defended the action of supporting the Resolution when members of the delegations found themselves in an awkward place.'[27] King's view, however, was 'that no government should surrender its power of issuing instructions as to what was to be done on these matters that involved the possibility of war.'[28] He threatened to resign if his position were not accepted, so that he might then publicize his case in the country. Ilsley countered with a statement which implied that he himself would resign if his original decision and public commitment were now repudiated.

As a temporary solution to this deadlock, it was decided that the Americans would be told that in view of current international developments, of which Mr King had been informed on his recent visit to Europe, the Canadian government felt that the creation of the commission ought to be reconsidered. At the suggestion of Mr St Laurent, King agreed also that General Marshall and President Truman should be advised that the prime minister would not approve the appointment of a Canadian commissioner. The purpose of this

25 Pickersgill and Forster, *Mackenzie King Record*, IV, 136-8. King's account of Ilsley's intervention appears to exaggerate the degree to which Mr Pearson resisted the nomination.
26 Claxton notes, 1130-1
27 Pickersgill and Forster, eds., *Mackenzie King Record*, IV, 138
28 Ibid., 138

arrangement was to relieve the minister of justice of any responsibility for the change in the Canadian position, and Ilsley insisted that he be given an opportunity to examine the dispatch before it was communicated to the State Department.[29] By now Mr St Laurent, too, had begun to think of the possibility of resigning.[30]

According to the terms of these decisions, a message was transmitted to Washington on the following day, 23 December. In the early evening of 27 December, the American ambassador, Ray Atherton, arrived at Laurier House with a reply from President Truman asking King not to make any final decision on the matter until the American under-secretary of state, Robert A. Lovett, had had an opportunity, in the absence from Washington of General Marshall, to make representations. To this the prime minister agreed, and there ensued a lengthy conversation during which King outlined the reasons for his position. He became increasingly convinced, as Atherton talked in reply, 'that Pearson had been thrown into the situation under pressure from the United States and had yielded in order to help them out, so to speak.'[31] Atherton argued, first, that his government wished to withdraw its troops from Korea, that the Temporary Commission would give it an opportunity to do so, and that if the opportunity failed to materialize the troops might have to remain where they were; secondly, that it would be a serious matter for a member of the Security Council to withdraw from the commission; and thirdly, that Canada, as the commission's only strong member, would have the dominant role in determining the course of its proceedings. Subsequent events were to deal harshly with the last of Mr Atherton's arguments, but in any case King remained adamant. He informed the ambassador that under no circumstances could he be persuaded to approve the dispatch of a Canadian representative to Korea, and that he hoped he would not be placed in a position in which he would have to reject an explicit request from the American president or secretary of state.

Mr Lovett's representations, strengthened by the knowledge that not all the members of the Canadian government shared the prime minister's views,

29 Ibid., 139
30 Thomson, *Louis St. Laurent*, 223. Claxton's account suggests (1131) that St Laurent implied during the Cabinet discussion that he would resign if the decision went against him, but there is no evidence of this in the prime minister's diary. Ilsley and St Laurent both made clear their determination to resign, if necessary, in subsequent private conversations with Claxton, who would have joined them. Claxton reports also, however, that when he informed the prime minister of St Laurent's intentions, King was surprised, and said that 'he would have to reconsider the matter.' Claxton knew then that 'we had won.' Claxton notes, 1132-5
31 Pickersgill and Forster, eds., *Mackenzie King Record*, IV, 142

arrived in Ottawa on 30 December, and at mid-day Mr King spent an hour discussing their contents with St Laurent and Pearson. He was now more than ever convinced of the wisdom of his own position. He told them of his conversation with Atherton in which the ambassador had indicated that whether or not American troops were withdrawn from Korea would depend upon the success of the Temporary Commission, which in turn was heavily reliant upon the co-operation of Canada. This was precisely what the prime minister had feared would happen. Canada was now being held accountable, with the United States, for future events in Korea, and for any Soviet response that might result. The commission was being dispatched in any case 'on a fool's errand,' since it was powerless to achieve its objective. If, however, the other members of the Cabinet felt differently – and except for St Laurent and Ilsley, he believed they did not – he would resign immediately and allow them to assume control. In the meantime, so far as Lovett's communication was concerned, he 'did not think it was part of the duties of any official of the United States Government to begin to tell me what should or should not be done by the Canadian Government.'[32]

Mr St Laurent then warned the prime minister that his resignation would compel the formation of a Liberal-Conservative coalition. To this King replied that such a prospect was absurd, given that the subject in dispute was not even of direct concern to Canada. He readily agreed to a suggestion by St Laurent that Mr Pearson be sent personally to Washington to discuss the matter with Marshall and Truman, pointing out that Pearson himself had made a similar proposal during the previous week. If necessary, St Laurent might later go himself. There was some discussion of what Mr Pearson was to say, and King agreed that he should express the government's concern about the extent of American 'interference' in Canadian policy-making, a point which he repeated when briefing him more fully on the following day.

In an anxious mood, the under-secretary departed for Washington on 2 January. He knew that if he were unable to obtain from the president a guarantee that the commission would not be used for purely American purposes, or in any way that would lead to conflict in the Far East, Mr King would remain firm in his position and St Laurent and Ilsley would then both resign – an eventuality which he strongly wished to avoid. His discussions with State Department officials and with President Truman were therefore very frank, and the latter expressed his surprise that the matter should be taken so seriously by the Canadian authorities.[33] The appropriate assurances were obtained,

32 Ibid., 144
33 Pearson, interview, 18 Oct. 1968. See also Thomson, *Louis St. Laurent*, 224

however, and the under-secretary reported them to the prime minister in a long message from Washington on 4 January.

Mr Pearson believed in later years that Mr King was pleased by the outcome of these conversations, but the prime minister's diary indicates that his doubts remained. Other than a suggestion that Canada might play a quiescent rather than a dominant role in the commission's activities, the report in his view contained nothing new and served merely to confirm his belief 'that the State Department was simply using the United Nations as an arm of that office to further its own policies.' Convinced now that Mr Pearson was much 'too ready to be influenced by American opinion,' King remained unaltered in his determination not to approve Canadian participation. He informed Pearson of his reaction in a telephone conversation late that afternoon, and advised him that his department should proceed accordingly. The prime minister complained in particular of a comment in the latest American statement to the effect 'that the Commission would probably get the United Nations to arrange for setting up of independence in one half of Korea [sic].' He observed that if 'they could do that with the aid of a milk and water Commission, they could certainly do it without any such fictitious support.' It was all clearly 'an effort on the part of the United States to put us into sharing the responsibility vis-à-vis Russia in the action taken or against the acceptance of the Russian suggestion.'[34]

Pearson replied that he believed the Americans now regretted the formation of the commission, and were primarily concerned to avoid the Soviet propaganda that might result from Canadian-American disagreement and any consequent failure to proceed with the implementation of the original resolution. But the prime minister was not impressed, and when on 6 January he received additional American representations over the signature of President Truman, he telephoned Pearson in New York to inform him that he was preparing a strong reply. King thought this was the first time that he had 'quite emphatically declined to meet a wish expressed by any President of the United States,'[35] and when Mr Pearson returned to Ottawa on the following day, the prime minister showed him the draft of his letter. The under-secretary inquired whether the letter would be considered by the Cabinet as a whole, and King answered in the negative, although he indicated that before being sent it should be examined by St Laurent. Pearson then expressed concern for the need to advise the United Nations of the prime minister's decision. Asked why he himself had not done so after receiving King's telephone call on the previous

34 Pickersgill and Forster, eds., *Mackenzie King Record*, IV, 146-7
35 Ibid., 148

day, he said that he had not wished then to say anything definite, and that he had only hinted that there were difficulties. From this King concluded 'that External Affairs have made up their mind from the start that they would rather bring pressure on me than agree with a course which I think is full of future embarrassment and defend the position taken at the Assembly of the United Nations where Canada's consent was given without any reference to the Government.'[36]

On leaving the prime minister, Mr Pearson showed the draft of his letter to the secretary of state for external affairs, who after a consultation with Ilsley telephoned King and requested an interview. King invited him to dinner, and following their meal the two men adjourned to the library for serious discussion.[37] St Laurent immediately made it clear that both he and Ilsley would resign if Canada were not represented on the commission, adding later in the conversation that he felt responsible for the original decision to take part. King replied that if anyone were to go, it should be he, but St Laurent protested that this would destroy the government, and went on to agree with the prime minister that the commission probably would accomplish nothing, and that in any case it should act only with the approval of the Soviet Union. His interpretation of the parent resolution was that it authorized the commission to supervise elections in both occupation zones, or not at all. Since the Soviets almost certainly would refuse to co-operate, there was little chance of success.

This observation provided the answer to their difficulties, for if the commission could function only with Soviet-American agreement, there was little danger that it would be compelled to take sides. That is, it would operate with the approval of *both* the occupation authorities, or not at all. King pointed out that he had been worried by an American comment to the effect that if the Russians opposed an election in the North, the commission might act as an electoral supervisor in the south alone. St Laurent assured him that he could honestly say in the House that his understanding of the resolution was that the commission would act only on the condition that it could do so throughout the peninsula and with the consent of both occupation powers. On this basis, King agreed to Canada's participation, observing that the arrangement would have the added advantage of depriving the Soviets of an opportunity for engaging in propaganda attacks. He said that if St Laurent would have the appropriate instructions drawn up for the Canadian representative, he would include them in a letter to President Truman on the following morning. The Americans, he complained, 'were seeking to make the United Nations a politi-

36 Ibid., 149
37 Thomson, *Louis St. Laurent*, 224

cal arm of the Secretary of State's Department,' as Truman's personal intervention in the Canadian-American exchange had demonstrated. They had 'shifted their whole original ground of desiring Canada because she was so prominent and would be so influential, to agreeing to have her stay in the background, and do nothing so long as we did not take her off the Commission.'[38]

With that the conflict was resolved, and Mr St Laurent left for home, stopping on the way at Mr Pearson's house to tell the under-secretary the news. Mackenzie King's distrust, however, of the Department of External Affairs and the American State Department remained, as did his reservations with respect to Canada's involvement in great power quarrels. He was to enjoy some consolation in the fact that the subsequent history of the Temporary Commission was to confirm a few, at least, of his dark suspicions.

The Prime Minister was right, for a start, in thinking that the Americans had tailored the Temporary Commission for use as an instrument of American foreign policy. Canada aside, its remaining eight members included Australia, China, El Salvador, France, India, the Philippines, Syria, and the Ukrainian SSR. Of these (in addition to Canada), Australia, China, El Salvador, and the Philippines 'all had close ties, if not alliances, with the United States and could be expected generally not to take a position completely contrary to American views of international affairs.'[39] The French, moreover, had an interest in common with the Americans in their desire to contain 'communism' in the Far East, while it was clear from the beginning that the Ukrainians would boycott the entire proceedings. India and Syria were the only members who might be expected to take an independent position, but their commitment to the principle of national self-determination seemed to place them firmly on the side of the American interest in an independent Korea.[40]

In sum, the American government had turned to the United Nations as a means of implementing policies which it had been unable to execute through

---

38 Pickersgill and Forster, eds., *Mackenzie King Record*, IV, 152
39 Gordenker, *The United Nations and the Peaceful Unification of Korea*, 31
40 These points were not lost upon the members of the Soviet bloc. After Mr Dulles read out his list of nominations to the Assembly's Political Committee, Mr Manuilsky of the Ukrainian SSR, in observing that his government would not take part in the commission's proceedings, commented that it 'would have been better if the Temporary Commission had consisted of neutral persons, and not of representatives obeying government instructions, in most cases favourable to United States policy.' See United Nations, GAOR (First Committee), A/C.1/SR. 116, 306-7. Later, in the plenary meetings of the General Assembly, he undertook a country-by-country demolition of the commission's membership. See United Nations, GAOR (Plenary Meetings), A/PV.128, 855-7

its own efforts. There was nothing unusual in this – every member of the United Nations regards the organization in one way or another as a potential instrument for the pursuit of its foreign policy and uses it accordingly. But in this case the exercise could work for the United States only if the Temporary Commission shared the American view of the problem in Korea. If it did not, a conflict might easily develop between the commission's members and the American authorities. One way of preventing such difficulties was to ensure that a majority of the UNTCOK membership was comprised of the representatives of governments which were sympathetic to American policy.

Not least because of the efforts of Canada, the plan failed to function as smoothly as the State Department obviously had hoped. The Department of External Affairs had been as aware as Mackenzie King of the need to preserve the commission's independence, not only for the sake of Canada and of Korea, but also for the sake of the United Nations as a whole, which could ill afford a reputation for subservience to the will of a single power. It was partly for this reason that Dr Patterson had been selected as the Canadian representative, for his character was such that he could be relied upon not to succumb to American pressure. Patterson himself had no intention of becoming a tool of American diplomacy, and like the prime minister and the senior officials of the department, he was strongly opposed to any policy which threatened to prolong the political division of the Korean peninsula.[41]

The commissioners held their first meeting at Seoul on 12 January 1948, and it quickly became clear, as St Laurent had predicted, that no co-operation would be forthcoming from the Soviet authorities in the North. The Soviet commander and North Korean political leaders refused even to take part in the preliminary discussions.[42] The commissioners thus confronted their long-expected dilemma. Their terms of reference clearly indicated that they should function in both occupation zones and should have the 'right to travel, observe

41 Pearson, interview, 18 Oct. 1968; Mr P.G.R. Campbell, interview, 20 Oct. 1968. This view of Patterson's suitability for the job was shared by the minister of national defence, who later recorded that he knew 'the Far East exceedingly well. He not only spoke Chinese but he was one of the few westerners who had lived and worked in Korea. By reason of his background he was an exceptionally good man for the job. He also was experienced and cautious. It was unlikely that he would do anything embarrassing if it could be avoided.' Claxton notes, 1129-30
42 The Americans, by contrast, were willing and bountiful helpers: 'During almost all of its life, UNTCOK depended on the American Occupation for a roof, food and transportation.' Gordenker, 'The United Nations, the United States Occupation and the 1948 Election in Korea,' 430

and consult throughout Korea.'[43] Now, however, they were effectively barred from any activity north of the 38th parallel, and were compelled to operate in the southern zone alone or not at all.

Under these circumstances, precisely the conflict which the Americans had hoped to avoid, and which Mackenzie King had predicted during his discussions in the Cabinet,[44] came swiftly to the surface. At their second meeting, the commissioners had approved an Australian resolution stating specifically that steps should be taken 'to guard against any misconceptions which might be placed upon the initial presence of the Commission in South Korea or upon the acceptance by its members of the courtesies extended to them in Seoul,' and 'to make it clear that the sphere of this Commission is the whole of Korea and not merely a section of Korea.'[45] But in the absence of Soviet co-operation, the American occupation commander, Lt-Gen. John R. Hodge, argued on behalf of his government that if necessary the elections should be held in the South alone,[46] thereby compelling the commissioners to consider whether or not they should accept his partisan advice.

The problem was a difficult one, and at first the debate centred on the question of whether or not the commission should make use of a clause in its parent resolution which provided that it might 'consult with the Interim Committee [of the General Assembly] ... with respect to the application of this resolution in the light of developments.'[47] The initial Canadian position, reflecting the understanding between King and St Laurent, was that the lack of Soviet co-operation made impossible the execution of the commission's task, and that accordingly no consultation with the Interim Committee was necessary. Dr Patterson therefore introduced a resolution which merely would have reported the difficulties and have advised the General Assembly that no further steps could be taken. The Australian, Indian, Syrian, and French delegates objected to this proposal, however, on the ground that it would place unnecessary obstacles in the way of Soviet co-operation in the future, and Dr Patterson accordingly withdrew it in favour of a simple statement of the facts.

43 For the text of the resolution, see United Nations, GAOR (First Part of the Report of the United Nations Temporary Commission on Korea, vol. I), A/575, 4-5
44 As he uncharitably reminded his ministers on 5 Feb. See Pickersgill and Forster, eds., *Mackenzie King Record*, IV, 157
45 United Nations, GAOR (First Part of the Report of the United Nations Temporary Commission on Korea, vol. I), A/575, 24
46 Gordenker, 'The United Nations, the United States Occupation and the 1948 Election in Korea,' 432
47 United Nations, GAOR (First Part of the Report of the United Nations Temporary Commission on Korea, vol. I), A/575, 5

On the procedural question of whether the commission should consult with the Interim Committee before making a final decision, the commissioners were sharply divided. China and the Philippines both agreed with the American view that an election in the South should be initiated immediately, and they were supported by France. Australia, Canada, India, and Syria, on the other hand, insisted that the Interim Committee should be consulted first, clearly expecting that the 'Committee would instruct UNTCOK not to attempt to observe elections in the southern zone alone.'[48] El Salvador abstained, and in consequence the UNTCOK chairman, Krishna Menon of India, was dispatched to New York on 14 Feb.

During the resulting discussion at the Interim Committee, the character of the dispute became more obvious and explicit. Philip C. Jessup of the United States argued forcefully that UNTCOK should be advised 'to implement its programme ... in such parts of Korea as are accessible to the Com-mission,'[49] and he and other members of his delegation indulged in several days of careful lobbying on behalf of a resolution incorporating this position. According to Leon Gordenker, the 'American representatives were especially anxious to convince India, Australia and Canada to support the resolu-tion,'[50] but Australia and Canada were the two countries which persevered in their opposition to Mr Jessup's proposal. The final vote on 26 February was 31 to 2 in favour, with 11 abstentions (including Syria).

In essence the Australian view was that the establishment of an elected regime in South Korea alone would tend to harden the 38th parallel into a permanent and therefore disruptive international boundary. Rival govern-ments would result, and in 'the event of threats from the North, the United Nations might be placed in the difficult position of having either actively to support, or else to renounce, all responsibility for the government it had established.'[51] The arguments employed by Dr Patterson in his discussions at Seoul indicate that this was also a primary concern of the government in Ottawa, but in presenting the Canadian case in the Interim Committee, Mr Pearson argued on the more legalistic ground that to supervise elections in the

48 Gordenker, 'The United Nations, the United States Occupation and the 1948 Election in Korea,' 432
49 Quoted in Spencer, *Canada in World Affairs*, 106
50 Gordenker, *The United Nations and the Peaceful Unification of Korea*, 71. The American lobbying took place during a ten-day adjournment designed ostensibly to allow member delegations to study the matter. Mr Pearson among others opposed the delay, doubtless because he knew the Americans would use the time to their good advantage. Ibid., 70
51 Ibid., 74. The United Nations documents from which Mr Gordenker has drawn his quotations have restricted circulation.

South alone would involve changes in the commission's terms of reference which were beyond the power of the Interim Committee to decide. Canada, he said, strongly supported the objective of a free, united, and democratic Korea, and condemned the USSR for preventing its realization. Nevertheless, his government felt 'that it would be unwise to seek to associate the UN with an effort to achieve this desirable objective, by asking its commission in Korea to do things that it has not, under its terms of reference, the power to do.'[52] He also remarked that the Canadian policy 'would at least have the advantage of proving the unwarranted nature of certain allegations to the effect that the Temporary Commission was in the service of the United States of America.'[53]

Mr Pearson's recourse to a legal strategy had been arranged in a discussion with Mackenzie King and St Laurent in Ottawa on 18 February. The prime minister had once again commented upon the danger of allowing the commission to proceed, as the Americans wished, in the South alone, and both the other men had agreed. The under-secretary and his minister suggested that by resting their case on a point of law, they might thereby find 'a way out of having to vote against the United States in their effort to take the further step.' Mr Pearson was especially concerned to avoid a division between Canada and the United States on a matter in which the Soviets and Americans were at odds.[54]

He failed to achieve his objective. Before the vote on the resolution was taken, and when it was obvious that it would go in Mr Jessup's favour, Mr Pearson made a final statement in which he announced that the Canadian delegation would vote against it:

We do so on the understanding that it is, in any event, merely advice to the commision.

If the commission should accept that advice, and that is for the commission to determine, a new and serious situation would be created which would have to be taken into consideration by the governments who are members on the commission, and who feel that the advice from this committee is unwise and unconstitutional.[55]

From the American point of view, the failure of Mr Pearson's campaign was a fortunate development. Had it succeeded, the Americans would have

---

52 Quoted by Prime Minister St Laurent in Canada, House of Commons, *Debates*, 10 March 1948, 2075
53 Quoted in Gordenker, *The United Nations and the Peaceful Unification of Korea*, 73
54 Pickersgill and Forster, eds., *Mackenzie King Record*, IV, 159-60
55 Quoted by Prime Minister St Laurent in Canada, House of Commons, *Debates*, 10 March 1948, 2075

suffered what one authority on United States policy in the United Nations has described as 'a major setback.'[56] In particular, they would not then have been able to arrange for the election in the south of a national regime having UN approval, and this in turn would have complicated enormously the problem posed by their desire to withdraw their occupation forces.

But the battle was not quite over, and Mr Pearson's act of defiance was not Canada's last. The commission still had to decide whether or not to accept the Interim Committee's advice. When news of the success of the American resolution reached UNTCOK headquarters in Korea, Dr Patterson was occupied with other business in Tokyo, and on 28 February the seven remaining members met on an informal basis without him. By now the growing impatience of nationalist political groups in South Korea had reached alarming proportions, and with a view to forestalling public demonstrations the seven representatives decided unanimously to announce on 1 March that elections would be held in the American zone not later than 10 May. Lt-Gen. Hodge promptly issued a declaration setting Sunday, 9 May as the precise date. Dr Patterson was not consulted, 'although he had left his telephone number with the principal secretary of the commission on his departure from Seoul, with the request that he be called should any important matter arise.'[57]

Ottawa immediately instructed the Canadian representative 'to seek clarification' regarding the 1 March announcement and 'to maintain the position taken at Lake Success, namely, that the commission should not accept the advice given to it in the United States resolution or associate itself with the conduct of elections in South Korea only.' He 'was further instructed that, if the commission did not support the Canadian view on this matter, he was to state that he could not participate further in its activities until he had received further instructions from his government.'[58]

Dr Patterson on 6 March accordingly journeyed to Korea to protest the commission's announcement. In particular, he 'requested the Commission to clarify its position with respect to certain public statements made by the Commanding General, United States Army Forces in Korea, regarding the elections to be held on 9 May 1948.' He 'considered that the Commission had not yet officially reached a decision concerning the observation of elections and had therefore taken no action which substantiated the statements of the Commanding General.' The decision of the informal meeting of 28 February could not be regarded as official. He warned that 'unless a clarifying statement were

56 Goodrich, *Korea*, 50
57 Prime Minister St Laurent in Canada, House of Commons, *Debates*, 22 March 1948, 2452
58 Ibid., 10 March 1948, 2076

issued, he would be compelled to abstain from participation in the activities of the Commission pending receipt of further instructions from his Government.'[59]

The meeting produced no constructive result, and it was therefore decided as an interim measure to have the commission secretariat draft a press release stating that the Canadian delegation had questioned the election declaration and that in consequence the commissioners were still considering whether it would be officially confirmed. A second meeting was held later on the same day, 9 March, to consider three versions of the release. After one of them had been selected and a vote taken, it was discovered that it had failed to receive the required majority, two of the commissioners having voted against and three having abstained. Dr Patterson thereupon withdrew from the room pending 'further instructions' from Ottawa, and the commission adjourned for thirty minutes. After informal discussions, it reconvened and voted 4-0-3 to accept a modified version of the press release after all. For the time being the Canadian had scored a point: UNTCOK had to consider again the 'advice' of the Interim Committee, and General Hodge's plans for a 9 May election were once more placed in jeopardy.[60]

There is evidence that Dr Patterson's activities had aroused considerable concern both in Korea and elsewhere. The American diplomatic authorities were infuriated,[61] and when news of the Canadian reaction to the 1 March election announcement reached General Hodge, a spokesman for the Military Government was ordered to issue a brusque declaration to the effect that the decision had been 'cleared with the proper authorities.'[62] In Canada, Dr Patterson's subsequent withdrawal from the commission's proceedings was reported in the press on 10 March as a 'walk-out,' and for a time the secretary of state for external affairs had difficulty in finding an explanation for his behaviour that would satisfy the House of Commons.[63] The Canadian representative's maneouvre also produced considerable anxiety among Korean politicians, and stimulated speculation in the South Korean press.

These fears were unnecessary, however, for Dr Patterson's efforts, and those of his Australian colleague, proved to be in vain. When the commission

59 United Nations, GAOR (First Part of the Report of the United Nations Temporary Commission on Korea, vol. I), A/575, 27
60 Gordenker, *The United Nations and the Peaceful Unification of Korea*, 78-9
61 Campbell, interview, 20 Oct. 1968
62 Gordenker, *The United Nations and the Peaceful Unification of Korea*, 77
63 When the matter was raised in the House on 12 March, Mr St Laurent implied that Patterson's 'walk-out' had been no more than a response to a natural call. Certainly it 'had no international connotation.' (Canada, House of Commons, *Debates*, 12 March 1948, pp. 2147-8)

turned again a few days later to the substance of its problem, the Canadian delegate reiterated his government's view that the Interim Committee was entitled only to advise, and not to instruct, and that the advice it had given was 'completely contrary to the judgment of the Commission, shared almost unanimously by its members and conveyed to the Interim Committee by Mr. Menon.' An examination of the situation left him, moreover, with

the terrible doubt that the one and only purpose for which the Commission is in Korea will not be furthered one step but rather perhaps disastrously set back if the advice of the Interim Committee is accepted. If the argument of unity fails, the basis for United Nations participation in the election vanishes, the Commission is left floundering unsupported by any conviction of a moral or political kind [sic]. If elections in South Korea alone contribute nothing to the unifying of Korea, then the United Nations Commission has no right to participate in them.

Dr Patterson argued also that a United Nations commission could not be expected to do what 'one great power' had failed to do, and that it could not carry out a United States responsibility. The commission should act only in circumstances which made constructive action possible. In the event that the commission decided to proceed with elections in the South alone, Canada would have to reconsider her participation in the commission's activities.[64]

With the exception of Australia, however, the other delegations took the view that to continue with the elections was the only sensible course in the light of political realities in Korea, although Syrian support was qualified by the condition that the voting must be conducted in a genuinely free atmosphere. On 12 March, therefore, the original decision was confirmed by a vote of 4 to 2 (Canada and Australia) with 2 abstentions (France and Syria).[65] Dr Patterson accordingly withdrew once more from the proceedings to await further instructions from Ottawa, and refused to take active part until 23 March, a period of eleven days. By then he had received orders to co-operate in the observation of the elections, and thereafter the Canadian government offered no serious opposition. Officially, however, it still held to the view that 'the responsibility for running the elections rests with the United States military government authorities and any action towards the establishment of a government in Korea following the elections will not be on the strength of the resolution of the General Assembly but on the legal position of the occupying military authorities.'[66]

64 Gordenker, *The United Nations and the Peaceful Unification of Korea*, 81-2
65 For the complete text of the resolution, see United Nations, GAOR (First Part of the Report of the United Nations Temporary Commission on Korea, vol. I), A/575, 29
66 Prime Minister St Laurent in Canada, House of Commons, *Debates*, 22 March 1948, 2453

The rest of the story is easily told. The election was held on 10 May after a violent political campaign in which 589 persons were killed. Of these, 44 died on polling day, but on 24 June the commissioners unanimously decided, in view of the very high voter turn-out (an estimated 75 per cent of potential voters), that the election had been 'a valid expression of the free will of the electorate in those parts of Korea which were accessible to the Commission.'[67] At the same time, the Canadian, Australian, and Syrian delegates 'all continued to hold grave doubts about the activities of UNTCOK in the election,' thereby reflecting their 'real concern that the course chosen in Korea would make permanent the division of the country and make worse the relations between the two parts.'[68]

Following the elections a new 'Government of the Republic of Korea' was established under the leadership of Syngman Rhee, and on 12 August the United States declared that in its view the new regime was entitled to be regarded as the 'Government of Korea' as envisaged in the Temporary Commission's parent resolution. Recognition by China and the Philippines swiftly followed. On 14 August the commission agreed by a vote of 4-2-1 to accede to Dr Rhee's request for consultation in regard to the transfer of governmental functions from the occupation authorities and the withdrawal of foreign troops. The Canadian delegate would make no statement on Canadian recognition of the regime until the commission's reports had been filed with the General Assembly.

On 25 August the North Koreans responded to these developments in the South by holding elections of their own and by establishing a 'People's Democratic Republic.' Subsequently, the Czech delegation at the United Nations succeeded in placing a resolution on the Assembly's agenda which would have provided for North Korean participation in the discussion of the commission's reports. Mr Pearson voted against this proposal on the ground that in the absence of United Nations supervision it was natural to assume that the elections in the North 'had not been held in a democratic manner.' It was therefore 'quite impossible to accord the representatives of North Korea the same status as the representatives of South Korea.'[69] The Czech resolution was defeated, and in its place the Political Committee adopted a Chinese resolution which invited only representatives of the South to participate in the debate.

Thereafter, the attention of the Political Committee was directed to the reports of the Temporary Commission. A draft resolution approving them was

---

67 Quoted in Spencer, *Canada in World Affairs*, p. 108
68 Gordenker, 'The United Nations, the United States Occupation and the 1948 Election in Korea,' 449
69 United Nations, GAOR (First Committee), A/C.1/SR.236 Part I, 948

introduced by Australia, China, and the United States, and it eventually passed the General Assembly on 12 December by a vote of 48 (including Canada) to 6, with 1 abstention. In addition to approving the UNTCOK reports, the resolution declared

> that there has been established a lawful government (the Government of the Republic of Korea), having effective control and jurisdiction over that part of Korea where the Temporary Commission was able to observe and consult and in which the great majority of the people of all Korea reside; that this Government is based on elections which were a valid expression of the free will of the electorate of that part of Korea and which were observed by the Temporary Commission; and that this is the only such Government in Korea.

The resolution also recommended that the occupying powers withdraw their forces 'as early as practicable,' and authorized the establishment of a new United Nations Commission on Korea (UNCOK) to continue the work of the Temporary Commission, observe the withdrawal of occupation forces, and otherwise assist in the problems of political transition and unification.[70]

Mr Pearson did not take an active part in the discussions of the Political Committee. When his turn came to speak, he offered to forego the privilege on the ground that the committee was running out of time.[71] Somewhat later in the proceedings, however, he seized the opportunity presented by the American proposal that the new commission should have the same composition as its predecessor to extract his government from its involvement in the Korean morass. In the General Assembly he introduced an amendment providing for the reduction of the size of the commission from nine members to seven. His government, he said, although sharing the confidence expressed by the assembly in the work of the Temporary Commission, felt nevertheless that a smaller body might be more effective. Since the Ukrainian SSR had signified once again that it would boycott the commission's proceedings, its membership had already been effectively reduced to eight, an awkward number for voting purposes. His amendment therefore provided for the withdrawal of Canada as well, so that the new commission would comprise only seven. The proposal was carried by 42 to 0 with 3 abstentions, the Soviet bloc boycotting the vote.[72]

---

70 The text of the resolution is reprinted in McCune, *Korea Today*, 306-8
71 United Nations, GAOR (First Committee), A/C.1/SR.236 Part I, 1017
72 Department of External Affairs, *Canada and the United Nations, 1948*, 71. The text of Mr Pearson's statement is on pp. 227-8.

In December 1948 the Soviets announced that they had withdrawn all their forces from North Korea. Six months later the last of the American forces, with the exception of a small contingent of military advisers, had departed also. Early in 1949 the Republic of Korea filed an application with the Security Council for admission to the United Nations, and after preliminary discussion the matter was referred to the Committee on the Admission of New Members. In this committee the Canadian delegation supported the application with the observation that it was 'satisfied that the claim of the Government of the Republic to be a peace-loving State is a valid one and has confidence that it will be able to carry out the obligations imposed on member nations by the United Nations Charter. The representatives of the Republic of Korea, in presenting their application for admission to the United Nations, have already given proof of their willingness to comply with the requirements of the Charter.'[73]

The committee reported in favour of admission, but on 8 April the application was vetoed in the Security Council by the Soviet Union. On 14 July Mr Pearson informed President Rhee that Canada's affirmative vote on this occasion was 'to be regarded as full recognition by the Government of Canada of the Republic of Korea as an independent sovereign State with jurisdiction over that part of the Korean peninsula in which free elections were held on May 10, 1948, under the observation of the United Nations Temporary Commission.'[74]

By now it had become clear that the new United Nations Commission on Korea could do very little to further the cause of Korean unification. As tension mounted in the border areas, therefore, it was authorized in a resolution supported by Canada on 3 October 1949 to appoint at its own discretion observers to assist in reporting 'developments which might lead to or otherwise involve military conflict in Korea.'[75] Such observations proved subsequently to be UNCOK's chief contribution to the history of postwar international affairs.

In the meantime the Canadian role in Korea had come to a temporary end. But the initial skirmishing had given a taste of what was to come. The United States had resorted to the United Nations as an instrument in the pursuit of its foreign policy. Once, however, the United Nations had become involved, some of its more active members – Canada among them – came to view the

73 Department of External Affairs, 'Canada and the United Nations,' *External Affairs*, I, 3, March 1949, 14-15
74 The Rhee-Pearson exchange of letters is reproduced in Department of External Affairs, 'Canadian Recognition of the Republic of Korea,' *External Affairs*, I, 8, Aug. 1949, 19-20
75 Department of External Affairs, *Canada and the United Nations, 1949*, 74-5

problem of Korea from a perspective somewhat different from that of the American government. This in turn produced a conflict between certain members of the Temporary Commission and decision-makers in the United States.

The Canadians, in particular, resented any implication that UNTCOK 'was in the service of the United States of America.' In the case of the prime minister this was principally because he wished to isolate Canada from embroilment in the volatile quarrels of the great powers, and because he was determined to preserve the integrity of Canadian foreign policy from the manipulations of the American Department of State, which by now had replaced Downing Street as his *bête-noire* in international affairs. The second of these two concerns was a factor also in the attitudes of St Laurent, Lester Pearson, and their senior subordinates in the Department of External Affairs, but their greater preoccupation lay with protecting the integrity not so much of Canada, which they hardly saw as threatened, as of the United Nations, which they thought in this context to be much more vulnerable to great power abuse.

But whatever the disagreements within the Canadian decision-making community, the external effects of the policy that emerged were both clear and explicit. In expressing their opposition to proposals that the Temporary Commission act upon American advice in supervising elections only in the southern zone, Canada's representatives employed legal arguments the express implication of which was that the commission was subject solely to the resolutions of the United Nations as a whole, and was completely independent of the American authorities. When these views failed to sway the UNTCOK majority, the Canadian government co-operated in implementing its decision, but only on the understanding that it retained its opinion that the elections were under American, and not under United Nations, auspices. In short, if the Americans wished to have United Nations assistance in solving their problems, they would have to recognize that they must grant in return a degree of decision-making authority to the United Nations organization as a collective body. Since this was not, in fact, the American intention, the inevitable result in the context of a substantive policy disagreement was a conflict between the more independent members of the commission on the one hand, and the United States and its more subservient allies on the other.

The same patterns were subsequently to recur throughout the course of the Korean war, although the government in Ottawa was not on that occasion internally divided. There was then, however, an added complication in the form of an emerging contradiction between the government's aspirations on the one hand for the establishment of a 'collective' world order, and on the other for the achievement of regional and selective security goals.

2

The first days

On Sunday, 25 June 1950, at approximately 4:00 AM local time,[1] artillery and mortar units of the Korean People's army opened fire on targets south of the 38th parallel, and the war in Korea was under way. Following a co-ordinated two-hour barrage, the invading North Korean forces engaged in a general advance along the full length of the border, with their main line of attack directed towards Seoul, the South Korean capital. By 9:00 AM their troops, supported by a large but as yet undetermined number of tanks and other heavy equipment of Soviet manufacture,[2] had occupied Kaesong. Six hours later they claimed to be in control of a band of territory extending ten to fifteen miles south of the parallel across the full breadth of the peninsula. At 11:00 AM Radio Pyongyang explained to its listeners that the government of the Democratic People's Republic of Korea had declared war on the South Korean regime because 'the bandit traitor Syngman Rhee' had launched an invasion of the North.

Among policy-makers in the West, the outbreak of the hostilities in Korea generated a shock of such proportions as to transform in an instant their perceptions of the scope and intensity of the Soviet threat. The growth of

1 Clock time in both Korea and Japan is fourteen hours ahead of clock time in Ottawa, Washington, and New York. Hence, when it was 4:00 AM in Korea on Sunday, 25 June 1950, it was 2:00 PM in Ottawa and Washington on Saturday, 24 June. Times and dates are given throughout this study in terms of the time zones in which the events described actually occurred. In cases where the time factor is important, it has been treated explicitly in the text.
2 The South Korean military authorities later estimated that the initial invading forces included 110,000 troops, 1400 artillery pieces, and 126 tanks. See Paige, Korean Decision, 81

mutual distrust and suspicion between West and East had been persistent throughout the late 1940s, but notwithstanding the extremities of the Berlin blockade and the Czech *coup*, it had somehow been assumed that the 'communist' challenge would fall short of conventional military invasion.[3] Very little Western rearmament had been stimulated even by the establishment of the NATO alliance, the initial purposes of which were more political and psychological than military. But the assault in Korea suggested that the Soviets were following in fact a different and more ominous set of rules. The implications of this perception were quickly to dominate the preoccupations of allied policy-makers, and they were to continue to do so for at least two decades of 'cold war.'

The first American authorities to learn of the attack were the military advisers in Seoul.[4] At 5:30 AM they received reports of fighting along the parallel, and a half-hour later were informed by their personnel in the field that the Seventeenth Regiment of the South Korean army was about to be overrun by North Korean units on the Ongjin peninsula. The time then in Washington and Ottawa was 4:00 PM on Saturday, 24 June. For some hours there was confusion about the scale and intensity of the North Korean assault, and the American ambassador, John J. Muccio, was not advised that it was in progress until 8:00 AM, four hours after it had begun. By the time he had reached his embassy, analysed the available information, and dispatched a coded report over his mission's official circuits to Tokyo for relay across the Pacific, it was 9:30. The cable arrived at the State Department about two hours later, at 9:26

---

3 There is some evidence, however, of speculation among policy-makers in Washington very early in 1950 that some sort of limited conflict with communist forces might soon be forthcoming, although Korea was not identified as a probable location. See Hammond, 'NSC-68: Prologue to Rearmament,' 265-378. It has been argued that in these quarters the outbreak of hostilities in Korea was to some extent welcomed because it made an expansion of the American defence budget politically feasible. See Simmons, 'The Korean War: Containment on Trial'

4 Several accounts of the activities of American officials during the early hours of the Korean War are available. The most detailed analysis is in Paige, *The Korean Decision*. The best general history of the war is Rees's *Korea: The Limited War*, and a discussion of the early phases of American policy-making is contained in Chapter II. An amazingly accurate account by a journalist which appeared while the conflict was still in progress is Warner, 'How the Korea Decision Was Made,' 100. Details can also be obtained from the memoirs of participants. See in particular Truman, *Memoirs.* II: *Years of Trial and Hope*, 377 ff; Acheson, *Present at the Creation*, 402 ff; Kennan, *Memoirs: 1925–1950*, 484 ff; Collins, *War in Peacetime*, passim; Douglas MacArthur, *Reminiscences*, 372 ff; Ridgway, *The Korean War*, especially Chapter II; and Lie, *In the Cause of Peace*, 323 ff. See also George, 'American Policy-Making and the North Korean Aggression,' 209-32; and Neustadt, *Presidential Power*, especially 123 ff

PM Washington time. It notified the department that hostilities were in progress, and that the North Korean attack appeared to constitute an 'all-out offensive against ROK.'[5] An officer of the department's Bureau of Far Eastern Affairs, already alerted by an inquiry from the United Press news agency, immediately began the process of informing senior officials of the American foreign policy community.

The tranquillity of their counterparts in Canada was not so quickly disturbed, and since students of decision-making have a particular interest in the processes by which policy-makers are informed of the development of unexpected events, there may be value as well as interest in a detailed account of the movements of Canadian officials during the early hours of the crisis. There was not in 1950, as there is now, an external affairs 'Operations Centre,' monitoring the course of global politics on a round-the-clock basis and providing instant intelligence for the benefit of the minister and his senior advisers. On quiet weekends the department was manned instead by a lonely duty officer whose job it was to keep an eye on incoming cables while his colleagues sensibly retired to their sundry recreations. Partly because Canada had no official representatives in Korea, these relaxations on the occasion of the North Korean attack continued for some time without interruption. Three Canadian citizens were employed on the secretariat of UNCOK, but reported directly to UN headquarters. Most of the department's senior staff therefore came ultimately to be informed of the conflict not by their own diplomatic service, but by the public press. The majority were away from Ottawa, and many were initially inaccessible even to the ubiquitous emissions of radio. Mr St Laurent, the prime minister, was vacationing at his summer home in St Patrice, Quebec.[6] Mr Pearson, the secretary of state for external affairs, was spending the weekend with his family at their cottage at Burnet, fifteen miles north of Ottawa on the Gatineau River. The under-secretary, A.D.P. Heeney, and the clerk of the Privy Council and secretary to the Cabinet, Norman Robertson, were both in New York on government business which had nothing whatever

---

5 The text of Muccio's cable is reprinted in Truman, *Years of Trial and Hope*, 379-80, and in Paige, *The Korean Decision*, 91.

6 Except where otherwise indicated, the following reconstruction of the movements of Canadian officials in the early hours of the crisis is based on correspondence and interviews with Campbell (interview, 20 Oct. 1968); Heeney (interview, 7 March 1968); Holmes (interview, 1 March 1968 and letters to the author, 20 Aug. 1969 and 9 June 1970); LePan (interview, 5 March 1968); Macdonald (letters to the author, 28 Oct. and 19 Nov. 1968); G.A.H. Pearson (interview, 18 Oct. 1968); Lester B. Pearson (interview, 18 Oct. 1968); Reid (letter to the author, 20 June 1968 and interview, 9 June 1969); Robinson (interview, 5 May 1970); and Tovell (interview, 5 May 1970).

to do with the affairs of the Far East. In Mr Heeney's absence the department's senior official in Ottawa was Escott Reid, and like Mr Pearson he was spending the weekend in the country with his family, in this case at their farm on Lac Gauvreau in the Gatineau Hills. Arthur Menzies, the head of the department's Far Eastern Division, was away on holiday, and his acting replacement, Peter G.R. Campbell, had left the capital for his Gatineau cottage on Friday evening. The head of the United Nations Division was John W. Holmes, but in this period he was serving as acting permanent representative of Canada to the United Nations. On the weekend of 24-25 June he was enjoying his role as host to his sister and brother-in-law, who were visiting him at his apartment in New York. Of Mr Holmes' two advisers, H.H. Carter and George K. Grande, the latter was out of the city for the weekend, and the former, like Mr Holmes himself, had no reason to think that his services would be required before the regular working week began on Monday morning.

In this weekend atmosphere, therefore, the first Canadian diplomatic official of senior rank to become actively involved in the crisis was Douglas V. LePan, who in Mr Holmes' absence from Ottawa was acting as head of the United Nations Division of the Department of External Affairs. His first knowledge of the fighting in Korea came, as he now recalls, about mid-morning on Sunday, 25 June when he was sleeping late and was aroused by a telephone call from the duty officer at the department, who advised him of the outbreak of hostilities. It was unusual to be disturbed in this way at home, and Mr LePan accordingly realized that the conflict must have reached comparatively serious proportions. He therefore prepared immediately to leave for his office, although he was not yet certain whether the matter fell within his own bailiwick or within that of the Far Eastern division. As it subsequently developed, the conflict was to affect the workings of almost every policy-making division in the department, but during the early months, partly as a result of the initial absence of Mr Menzies, the main responsibility for Canada's Korean War diplomacy was to be lodged with the division devoted to United Nations affairs.

Mr LePan arrived in his office around noon, there to be joined by his assistant in charge of political affairs, H. Basil Robinson. He was shortly advised that the Security Council was scheduled to be called into emergency session at 2:00 PM. Accordingly, he telephoned to inquire of Mr Holmes in New York whether he was aware of this development, and whether he planned to observe the proceedings. Holmes was nearly caught by surprise. In entertaining his relatives, he had pleaded with his brother-in-law, who had an enthusiastic interest in international affairs, to keep the radio turned off during their stay, so that he might enjoy a brief respite from the trials of world politics.

His injunction was not obeyed, and his brother-in-law heard some early reports of the developing crisis on a news broadcast to which he had listened in another room. Mr Holmes at first had dismissed the matter as merely another in a series of incidents that had been plaguing the Korean border in recent months, and it was not until his chauffeur telephoned to inquire whether he wished to be driven to the Security Council to observe the afternoon's proceedings that he realized that something much more serious was involved. A few moments later he received Mr LePan's call, and was able to say that he was fully aware of the latest developments, and that he had already made preparations to go to the United Nations. LePan and Robinson then began the task of briefing Canadian diplomatic missions abroad, and of organizing the preliminary arrangements for the administration of Canada's response to the crisis.

As they started their work, the weekend vacationers in the Gatineau Hills were still blissfully unaware of the hostilities which were to monopolize so much of their attention during the ensuing weeks. In the end their quiet was to be broken not by the Department of External Affairs, but by Mr Pearson's secretary, Mary Macdonald, who had at her disposal the information services of the CBC. Like the Reid family, she was at a cottage on Lac Gauvreau, but it was her regular custom to listen on Sunday afternoons to the CBC's 2:00 PM 'Capital Report.' The afternoon of Sunday, 25 June was no exception, and she was accordingly informed by the announcer that fighting had broken out in Korea, that the Security Council had been called into emergency session, and that Mr Holmes had been dispatched to observe its proceedings. Miss Macdonald at first thought this rather strange, since Canada was not at that time a member of the council, but she decided in any case that Mr Reid ought to be informed. The acting under-secretary was in a boat on the lake with his son, who was celebrating a birthday, and she therefore had to row out to tell him the news.

Mr Reid was surprised to hear that an invasion was underway, although initially he doubted whether it would produce an American military response. He had no telephone at his cottage, and after deliberating on the possibility of calling Ottawa from nearby Ste Cecile de Masham, he decided to return to the capital on Sunday evening. In the meantime it was agreed that Miss Macdonald would drive the sixteen miles to Burnet to inform Mr Pearson. She arrived at the Pearson cottage later in the afternoon, almost twenty-six hours after the start of hostilities in Korea. Since the minister had no telephone either, Miss Macdonald drove him another two miles to the nearest public booth, in Larrimac, where he called his department. After being briefed on developments, he decided to place another call to Mr St Laurent in St Patrice. The prime minister agreed at once that if any effective military action were to be taken, it would have to originate with the Americans, since the United Nations lacked readily available forces. On the other hand, it was important that the United Nations be made the vehicle for whatever response was to be made, since 'there was a serious danger that if the Americans acted unilaterally, the conflict might be turned into a global struggle between the Communists and the non-Communists.'[7]

Having thus advised the prime minister, and having reflected so soon upon what was to become his principal preoccupation throughout the first phase of the war, the secretary of state for external affairs returned to his cottage, and later that evening drove back to Ottawa with Mrs Pearson.

The acting head of the Far Eastern Division, Mr Campbell, was like Pearson and Reid in having no telephone at his cottage. Unlike them, he was able to complete his weekend break in peace, and did not return to his office until his regular hour on Monday morning. Long before then, reports had begun to flow into the Department from Mr Holmes in New York and from Hume Wrong, the Canadian ambassador in Washington.

The first of Mr Holmes' messages was a sombre account of the Sunday afternoon discussions in the Security Council, which he telephoned to Ottawa on the same evening. He had attended the proceedings in a severe depression, wondering whether the harshest among the cold war warriors had not been proved right after all. The mood was not dispelled by the information that he acquired from the council's emergency session, and since the situation at the front continued to deteriorate in the days that followed, it remained with him for a considerable time thereafter.[8]

The secretary-general, Trygve Lie, had opened the session by reading a report from the United Nations Commission on Korea (UNCOK), which warned that the situation was developing into a 'full-scale war' and a potential threat to 'the maintenance of international peace and security.' The Commission suggested that he consider bringing the matter to the attention of the Security Council.[9] Lie was easily persuaded. As he wrote later:

I resolved to take up the Commission's suggestion, not only because the United Nations organ most immediately involved so advised, but because this to me was clear-cut aggression – apparently well calculated, meticulously planned, and with all the elements of surprise which reminded me of the Nazi invasion of Norway – because this

7 Thomson, *Louis St. Laurent*, 292
8 Holmes, interview, 1 March 1968
9 Department of External Affairs, *Canada and the Korean Crisis*, 17

was aggression against a 'creation' of the United Nations, and because the response of the Security Council would be more certain and more in the spirit of the Organization as a whole were the Secretary-General to take the lead. My determination to speak out was hardened by the feeling that Moscow ... had been building up a peaceful atmosphere well suited to the surprise attack in Korea.[10]

He might have added that he called the Council into session not least of all because the Americans had asked him to do so. The possibility of raising the matter in the United Nations had first been discussed in the State Department late on Saturday evening. The assistant secretary of state for far eastern affairs, Dean Rusk, and the assistant secretary for United Nations affairs, John D. Hickerson, had been summoned to the department along with other senior officials after the arrival of Ambassador Muccio's cable from Seoul. In a telephone conversation with the Secretary of State, Dean Acheson, they had suggested 'that as a general policy the United States should react to the attack through the United Nations.' The matter should therefore be called to the attention of the Security Council through an emergency session.[11] The secretary had tentatively approved and agreed that Trygve Lie should be appropriately forewarned. Acheson himself telephoned the president, who was at his home in Independence, Missouri. Truman immediately agreed with the recommendation to raise the matter in the Security Council, but reserved his final decision until more specific proposals were ready.

Hickerson in the meantime called the secretary-general to advise him of what was happening in Korea, and of the action which was now under consideration by the Department of State. On the basis of Hickerson's account of Muccio's cable, Lie concluded that the fighting amounted to 'much more than a border skirmish,' and that it 'sounded like a major violation of the Charter's ban on military aggression.' He assured Hickerson that he 'was prepared to bring the Security Council together at once,' and subsequently telephoned his executive assistant, Andrew W. Cordier, to ask him to cable the United Nations commissioners in Korea for an immediate report.[12]

By 2:00 AM the officials in the State Department had become more certain of their information from the front, and had crystallized their proposals for raising the matter in the United Nations. Acheson therefore called Truman once again, and with the president's approval, the deputy United States representative to the UN, Ernest A. Gross, telephoned Trygve Lie at 3:00 AM with

10 Lie, *In the Cause of Peace*, 328-9
11 Paige, *The Korean Decision*, 92. See also Acheson, *Present at the Creation*, 402
12 Lie, *In the Cause of Peace*, 327-8

a formal request for an emergency session. The secretary-general scheduled the meeting for two o'clock on Sunday afternoon and went back to his much-interrupted sleep.[13] Gross and his colleagues meanwhile continued with the preparation of their case.[14]

Mr Holmes was not aware of the details of these feverish activities when he began to listen to the secretary-general's opening statement in the Security Council that afternoon. Nor was he informed then of the relief with which the American delegation had learned of the arrival at mid-morning of the report from the United Nations Commission on Korea that Lie was now citing as evidence in support of his view that the North Koreans were guilty of aggression. As one student of the subject has recently observed, the Americans could have used the report from Ambassador Muccio as the factual basis for the preamble of their resolution, but 'it was considered far more preferable to have a report from the United Nations body at the scene of the fighting,' since entire 'reliance on American sources might have meant trouble with some members of the Council.'[15]

In the event, both Mr Lie and Mr Gross made good use of this impartial resource. In presenting the UNCOK report to the council, the secretary-general told the members that, taken together with information from other sources, it made 'it plain that military actions have been undertaken by Northern Korean forces,' that these actions were in violation of earlier United Nations resolutions as well as of the Charter itself, that they constituted 'a threat to international peace,' and that he considered 'it the clear duty of the Security Council to take steps necessary to reestablish peace in that area.'[16]

The American representative then presented his draft resolution. In the ensuing discussions an attempt by uninstructed delegations to have the proceedings adjourned was overruled, but Mr Gross was compelled to accept a number of minor modifications designed to reduce the provocation in the wording of his draft.[17] Nevertheless, in its final form the resolution closely resembled the initial American proposal. It called for an immediate cessation of hostilities and for the withdrawal of North Korean forces to the 38th

---

13 Paige, *The Korean Decision*, 102-3; and Lie, *In the Cause of Peace*, 328. The American ambassador to the United Nations, Warren R. Austin, was on vacation in Vermont.

14 For a full account of these preparations, see Paige, *The Korean Decision*, 105-8

15 Ibid., p. 107

16 Quoted in Lie, *In the Cause of Peace*, 330

17 For example, the phrase 'Armed invasion' was changed to 'armed attack,' and the call 'for the immediate cessation of hostilities' was addressed to both sides, and not, as the Americans had at first intended, to the North Koreans alone. See Hoyt, 'The United States Reaction to the North Korean Attack,' 51

parallel. It also requested the United Nations Commission on Korea to 'communicate its fully considered recommendations on the situation with the least possible delay,' to 'observe' the North Korean withdrawal, and to 'keep the Security Council informed on the execution of [its] resolution.' Finally, it called 'upon all Members to render every assistance to the United Nations in the execution of this resolution and to refrain from giving assistance to the North Korean authorities.'[18] The resolution was passed by a vote of 9-0, with the USSR absent and Yugoslavia abstaining.[19]

From the point of view of the 'western' powers, the absence of the Soviet Union was a particularly fortunate circumstance. Since 13 January the USSR had been boycotting Security Council proceedings ostensibly on the ground that they were illegal so long as China was represented by a Formosan rather than a mainland delegation. Had Yakov Malik, the Soviet representative, been present, there is little doubt that he would have exercised his right of veto, bringing the United Nations involvement in the Korean War, temporarily, at least, to a full stop. That the Americans were relieved by the continuing absence of the Soviet delegate has been amply documented by Trygve Lie, who in his memoirs recalls having personally invited Mr Malik to attend the session of the Security Council scheduled for the afternoon of Tuesday, 27 June. Malik declined, and Ernest Gross, who had witnessed the exchange, later gave vent to his relief. 'Think,' he told Lie, 'what would have happened if he had accepted your invitation.' The secretary-general agreed that 'it would have been difficult. We would have had to fight it out, and move on to the General Assembly.'[20]

During the morning of 25 June, in preparing for just such a contingency, Mr Gross had expressed his belief that it would be possible to call the assembly into action within twenty-four hours,[21] but this would have involved serious delays. There would have been procedural obstacles to overcome, and the Soviets doubtless would have used them to good advantage. In the interval, the American authorities would have been confronted with the choice of either

18 For the full text of the resolution see Department of External Affairs, *Canada and the Korean Crisis*, 17-18
19 The members of the Security Council included the five permanent members, plus Cuba, Ecuador, Egypt, India, Norway, and Yugoslavia. The Yugoslav delegate lacked instructions from his government.
20 Lie, *In the Cause of Peace*, p. 333. The reasons for the continued absence of the Soviet Union from the Security Council in June and July continue to mystify western observers. For a review of the most commonly accepted theories, together with some new speculations, see Simmons, 'The Strained Alliance.'
21 Paige, *The Korean Decision*, 106

taking military action without official United Nations support, or resigning themselves to the loss of South Korea. From the Canadian point of view the significance of the crisis would then have been very different.

But all this is hypothetical history. As it happened, the Americans were able without difficulty to obtain the necessary support for the first of their resolutions, and after setting three o'clock on the afternoon of Tuesday, 27 June as the tentative time for the council's next meeting, its president, Sir Benegal N. Rau of India, brought the session to a close. Joining the crowd as it milled from the room, John Holmes hurried to his apartment to compose his report to the Department of External Affairs.

There had been several reasons for the alarm with which American officials had viewed the North Korean attack. In spite of repeated intelligence reports which for some time had pointed to the probability of an outbreak in the Korean theatre, Washington policy-makers, like their counterparts in Ottawa, had been taken completely by surprise.[22] Stunned by the scope of the invasion, and by its calculated efficiency, they perceived it immediately as a clear challenge to their policy of containment, the viability of which depended, they believed, upon their allowing no exceptions to the general rule. The Republic of Korea was in any case an American foster child, and the government had never relinquished entirely the responsibility for its security.[23] Above all, there was a certainty throughout the high places of American politics that this was aggression in the Hitler style, and that it had to be dealt with accordingly. No one has expressed this grim conviction with more effective clarity than President Truman, who later recorded his thoughts during the flight from Independence to Washington, while the Security Council was in session on Sunday afternoon:

In my generation, this was not the first occasion when the strong had attacked the weak. I recalled some earlier instances: Manchuria, Ethiopia, Austria. I remembered how each time that the democracies failed to act it had encouraged the aggressors to keep going ahead. Communism was acting in Korea just as Hitler, Mussolini, and the Japanese had acted ten, fifteen and twenty years earlier. I felt certain that if South Korea was allowed to fall Communist leaders would be emboldened to override nations closer to our own shores. If the Communists were permitted to force their way into the Republic of Korea without opposition from the free world, no small nation would

22 See Truman, *Years of Trial and Hope*, 377; Paige, *The Korean Decision*, passim; and Higgins, *Korea and the Fall of MacArthur*, 15-16. The North Korean invasion is discussed as a failure of American intelligence in DeWeerd, 'Strategic Surprise in the Korean War,' 435-52.

23 For a statement of this argument, see Spanier, *Truman-MacArthur Controversy*, 26-7

have the courage to resist threats and aggression by stronger Communist neighbors. If this was allowed to go unchallenged it would mean a third world war, just as similar incidents had brought on the second world war. It was also clear to me that the foundations and the principles of the United Nations were at stake unless this unprovoked attack on Korea could be stopped.[24]

In thus so stark a fashion did the experience of the recent past impose itself upon perceptions of the current crisis. The resulting evaluation of the stakes at issue led irresistibly, as the week progressed, to the military intervention of United States forces.

It was not insignificant that the American president in his catalogue of preoccupations should place the survival of the United Nations last. The Canadian secretary of state for external affairs thought of it first, and his concern for the organization's welfare did not diminish thereafter. At the same time, however, there was an awareness throughout the Canadian policy-making community that the parameters of the crisis would be determined in the final analysis by decisions taken, not in Ottawa, but in Washington,[25] and there is evidence that at first there was considerable doubt whether the Americans would actively intervene.[26] In the case of Mr Pearson, this suspicion was reinforced by the recollection of a speech delivered by Secretary of State Dean Acheson to the National Press Club on 12 January, in which he had defined the American defence perimeter in the Pacific as extending from the Aleutians to Japan through Okinawa to the Philippines, and had indicated that areas falling outside the line, such as Korea and Formosa, would have to depend for their defence upon themselves and upon the United Nations.[27] In the following February Mr Pearson had stopped in Tokyo on his way home from the Colombo Conference, and had been briefed by General MacArthur. The American commander had shown him a large wall map, and with his finger had drawn upon it a line beyond which, he said, the communists would not be allowed to expand. The line had excluded Korea from the American protective umbrella, for reasons which were related to the strategic disutility of the

24 Truman, *Years of Trial and Hope*, pp. 378-9
25 Holmes, interview, 1 March 1968; LePan, interview, 5 March 1968; Pearson, interview, 18 Oct. 1968
26 Pearson, interview, 18 Oct. 1968; letter to the author, 20 June 1968; and interview, 9 June 1969
27 Rees, *Korea*, 18. Acheson's address was not a declaration of new policy, however, but a reaffirmation of a long-standing position. See Collins, *War in Peacetime*, 28-31. For an attempt to explain the apparent reversal of American policy, see May, 'The Nature of Foreign Policy,' 653-67.

peninsula as a base for American forces. The External Affairs minister had been impressed both by MacArthur's person and by his arguments, and as he later recalled, he thought this particular judgment 'very sensible.'[28] There seemed little reason to expect the Americans now to change their minds.

In any case, Canadian External Affairs officials on Monday devoted themselves primarily to keeping a close watch over developments in Korea and in Washington with a view to assessing their implications for Canadian policy. The department was rife with speculation. Some of its members felt that South Korea was for practical purposes already lost, and that the real significance of the invasion was that it signalled the beginning of a more violent and volatile phase in the 'cold war' which would require a greater commitment to military defence. There was some possibility that the attack in Korea was merely the first stage of a two-edged assault, the second of which might well occur in Europe. Even if this were not the case, did the Americans really possess the military capabilities required for effective intervention? Was there any possibility that the invasion might be repulsed by air power alone? If military counteraction were taken, would the Soviet Union respond in kind? Would it be possible to separate the conflict in Korea from the quarrel over the two Chinas? If the Americans revealed an inclination to react on a unilateral basis, how could they be persuaded to resort instead to United Nations decision-making machinery?[29]

The answers to most of these questions were still unknown by Monday evening, and the intentions of the American administration remained a subject for speculation. Earlier in the day, Mr Pearson had had long telephone conversations with John Holmes in New York and Hume Wrong in Washington. Neither of them had thought that the Americans would take any concrete military action.[30] Mr Pearson had agreed with their estimate, and his Monday

---

28 Pearson, interview, 18 Oct. 1968. See also Fraser, *The Search for Identity*, 95-6. This appears to have been standard MacArthur routine. In the summer of 1949 Lt-Gen. G.G. Simonds visited the American commander in Tokyo, and MacArthur showed him a map of Korea with the locations of clashes with communist troops marked in red. Simonds recalls now that it 'looked like a rash of scarlet fever.' MacArthur told him that he had advised Washington that they should either reinforce their troops in Korea or get out altogether; in their present strength they amounted to a provocation without being really effective. Simonds, interview, 9 June 1970

29 Holmes, interview, 1 March 1968. The minister of national defence and his advisers had no faith in the view taken by some American staff officers that air and naval support would be sufficient. They 'regarded the whole operation as extremely difficult and serious,' and were convinced from the beginning 'that soldiers would be required, particularly infantry.' Claxton notes, 1142

30 Pearson, interview, 18 Oct. 1968

statement to the House of Commons reflected the general shortage of information. He told the House that he could not provide a full report because the government was awaiting further details of the developing crisis from the Canadian representative at the United Nations and from friendly governments which had sources of intelligence in the theatre. Parliament therefore had to be satisfied with an account of the resolution passed in the Security Council the day before, together with Mr Pearson's opinion that it would 'commend itself to all members of the House' and his hope 'that as a result of the intervention of the United Nations some effective action may be possible ... to restore peace.' The North Korean attack, he said, constituted 'a breach of the peace' and 'an action of unprovoked aggression.'[31] Nothing more of substance was to be heard in the Commons for another forty-eight hours.

That evening the minister held a press conference, partly off-the-record, in which he made it clear that he did not expect military sanctions to be applied either by the United States or by the United Nations. Korea was a special case, and one that the Soviets had obviously picked because its significance for the strategic and political balance of cold war affairs was ambiguous (as, for example, it would not have been had the aggression taken place across clearly defined international boundaries in a vital area like the North Atlantic). He thought an intervention might be ill-advised, given that it could lead to the direct participation in the hostilities of the USSR, and perhaps also of the Communist Chinese.[32]

But at the very moment Mr Pearson was advising Canadian newsmen of his belief that the North Koreans would be allowed to complete their operations relatively unopposed, President Truman and his senior advisers in Washington were making precisely the decisions that would prove him wrong. The reactions of American decision-makers, even on Sunday, had been very different from the ones that were predicted of them in the forecasts of Mr Wrong and Mr Holmes. The president had arrived in Washington late Sunday afternoon, and had proceeded immediately to a dinner conference at Blair House. The officials who were gathered there to meet him included the four chiefs of staff, the three armed services secretaries, Dean Acheson, John Hickerson,

31 Canada, House of Commons, *Debates*, 26 June 1950, 4116-17
32 Pearson, interview, 18 Oct. 1968. See also Fraser, *The Search for Identity*, 96, and Barkway, 'Korea,' 11. This expectation in Ottawa that the Americans would not intervene militarily adds credence to the view that the Soviet authorities failed to send their ambassador back to the UN Security Council for the same reason – that is, because they assumed that the council would not take substantive action. If the Canadians – so closely familiar with the American policy-making community – were surprised by the American response, it is not difficult to imagine the Soviets making a similar mistake.

Dean Rusk, Ambassador Philip C. Jessup, and the under-secretary of state, James E. Webb. The information from the front was still incomplete, and there was a general belief that, unless the invaders had received extensive external assistance, the South Koreans would be able to contain the assault by themselves. Nevertheless, after discussion the president made three major decisions: first, that an order be issued to MacArthur to evacuate American nationals from Korea, using whatever air protection south of the parallel as was necessary to achieve this objective; second, that another order be dispatched instructing him to transport ammunition and other supplies to the ROK forces; and third, that the United States Seventh Fleet be placed under MacArthur's operational control, and that it be sent immediately to the theatre from its base in the Philippines.[33]

There was some discussion of possible further assistance to South Korea through the United Nations, and President Truman indicated 'that he would wait until the Security Council resolution was flouted [by the North Koreans] before taking any action additional to that already decided upon.'[34] He authorized the Joint Chiefs of Staff to prepare the orders necessary to make American forces available should their services be requested by the United Nations. He has since testified in his memoirs to 'the complete, almost unspoken acceptance on the part of everyone that whatever had to be done to meet this aggression had to be done. There was no suggestion from anyone that either the United Nations or the United States could back away from it. This was the test of all the talk of the last five years of collective security.'[35]

Meanwhile, the military situation in Korea was deteriorating rapidly, and on Monday, 26 June, Washington received an urgent message from General MacArthur which included the following dramatic paragraph: 'South Korean units unable to resist determined Northern offensive. Contributory factor exclusive enemy possession of tanks and fighter planes. South Korean casualties as an index of fighting have not shown adequate resistance capabilities or the will to fight and our estimate is that a complete collapse is imminent.'[36]

At a second Blair House conference that evening, therefore, the Truman administration escalated the intensity of its response. After general discussion, the president instructed his secretary of defence, Louis Johnson, to call MacArthur on the scrambler telephone and order him to give air and naval

33 For a full account of this meeting, see Paige, *The Korean Decision*, 124-41. See also Truman, *Years of Trial and Hope*, 380-2
34 Paige, *The Korean Decision*, 139
35 Truman, *Years of Trial and Hope*, 381
36 Quoted ibid., 383, and in Paige, *The Korean Decision*, 162

support south of the 38th parallel to the ROK forces, and to dispatch the Seventh Fleet to the Formosa Strait. According to Truman, the purpose of the latter manoeuvre 'was to prevent attacks by the Communists on Formosa as well as forays by Chiang Kai-shek against the mainland, this last to avoid reprisal actions by the Reds that might enlarge the area of conflict.'[37] The president also approved measures to strengthen American forces in the Philippines and to provide increased aid to the French fighting in Indo-China. It was agreed that the 'action in Korea would be reported to the United Nations in whose name it would be taken.'[38]

During the night, State Department officials drafted a statement announcing these decisions to the American public, intending it for delivery by the president at 12:30 PM on Tuesday, 27 June. The draft received minor alterations at a meeting in the White House at eight o'clock on Tuesday morning,[39] and one and a half hours later the American ambassador in Ottawa, Stanley Woodward, called upon Mr Pearson to discuss its contents. The meeting had been arranged on the previous day, but Mr Woodward's revelations now took the minister completely by surprise. After the ambassador's departure, he telephoned Mr Wrong in Washington, and indicated that his main concern was to ensure that the American action would be brought under the United Nations umbrella.[40]

In principle, Mr Pearson's view was fully coincident with that of the American government. At the Blair House meeting on Monday evening there had been 'full agreement that whatever action the United States took in Korea would be carried out within the framework of the United Nations,'[41] and Dean Acheson had argued in an atmosphere of consensus 'that the whole moral basis of American policy, and the confidence of the world in the United States, in the United Nations, and in the whole collective security system was at stake.'[42] The difference of opinion, therefore, had to do not with the content of American policy, but with its timing. In particular, Mr Pearson thought that

37 Truman, *Years of Trial and Hope*, 384. The manoeuvre may, however, have had a significance more symbolic than real, for the Seventh Fleet in 1950 was not a very formidable force. See Simmons, 'The Korean War,' 18-19
38 Paige, *The Korean Decision*, 178
39 Ibid., 186
40 Pearson, interview, 18 Oct. 1968. Mr Pearson's recollection is confirmed by Freeman M. Tovell, who was then a member of the Minister's staff, and was in his office at the time the call was placed (interview, 5 May 1970).
41 Paige, *The Korean Decision*, 169
42 James Reston, quoted ibid., 177. Acheson's own account does not give this particular emphasis, however. See *Present at the Creation*, 407

President Truman ought to withhold his announcement until authorization for military action had been obtained from the Security Council.[43] The American view, by contrast, was that the 25 June resolution could be 'stretched' to cover the decisions taken on Monday night. In any case the State Department was sure that the enabling resolution which they were planning to present to the council on Tuesday afternoon would have the necessary consensual support.[44]

Canadian and American officials in Washington had an opportunity on the same morning to exchange their respective points of view. At 11:30 the ambassadors of the NATO powers, including Mr Wrong, were called to the State Department for a briefing on American policy and the forthcoming presidential announcement by George Perkins, the assistant secretary for European affairs, and Counselor George F. Kennan. The Americans made it clear that the meeting was to be regarded as an informal discussion among the ambassadors of friendly countries, and not as an official gathering of the representatives of NATO per se. They also apologized for the lack of advance consultation, indicating that the American decisions had been worked out over a prolonged period of time, and only after co-ordinating the efforts of a large number of governmental agencies. Mr Perkins commented that even now there was some doubt whether the intervention would come in time to prevent the successful completion of the North Korean invasion. He also announced that MacArthur had been given his military instructions during the night, and that Chiang Kai-shek had been informed of the decision to place the Seventh Fleet in the Formosa Strait.[45]

Mr Kennan's responsibility was to inform the ambassadors of the reasoning behind the American response to the crisis, and to identify the administration's objectives. It was for him a hazardous assignment, since he had not participated in the decision-making process, and was himself inadequately briefed. After presenting a personal estimate of the international significance of the North Korean attack, he 'confidently and innocently assured [the ambassadors] that we had no intention of doing more than to restore the *status quo ante*.'[46] He said that a distinction had to be drawn between the local conflict on the Korean peninsula and any intervention that might be forthcoming from the Soviet Union, since this would alter the character of the crisis and would probably require a different response. He emphasized that the decision to

43 Pearson, interiew, 18 Oct. 1968; and Tovell, interview, 5 May 1970
44 Pearson, interview, 18 Oct. 1968. See also Paige, *The Korean Decision*, 169
45 Holmes, interview, 5 March 1968; Kennan, *Memoirs*, 487; Paige, *The Korean Decision*, 191-2
46 Kennan, *Memoirs*, 487. See also Paige, *The Korean Decision*, 191

occupy the Formosa Strait had been taken to reduce the danger of a wider war, and he pointed out that the United States, by virtue of its commitments in Japan and its special military capabilities, naturally had responsibilities in meeting the aggression which differed to some extent from those of other United Nations members.[47] When Hume Wrong, fresh from his telephone conversation with Mr Pearson, raised the question of the timing of President Truman's announcement, Kennan acknowledged that he was aware of the problem, and that the legality of the American decisions might be questioned, but he was of the view that the resolution passed on Sunday had provided all the authorization required. Privately, Kennan believed that the decision to respond to the invasion through the United Nations had been an unnecessary error, but he was the only senior American official involved to take this view.[48]

At 12:30 PM President Truman issued his statement to the press, adding that he knew 'that all members of the United Nations will consider carefully the consequences of this latest aggression in Korea in defiance of the Charter of the United Nations. A return to the rule of force in international affairs would have far-reaching effects. The United States will continue to uphold the rule of law.' He announced also that he had 'instructed Ambassador Austin, as the representative of the United States to the Security Council, to report these steps to the Council.'[49]

That afternoon the Canadian Cabinet met for an hour and a half to discuss the crisis, and according to a report for the Canadian Press news agency by Douglas How, its members dealt 'largely with a resume of official reports.'[50] Among them was Hume Wrong's account of his morning briefing in Washington, the contents of which had already reassured senior officials in the Department of External Affairs, who considered the American reaction, on the whole, to be quite sensible, and certainly necessary to the maintenance of a viable United Nations security system. Whether their satisfaction was universally shared among the members of the Cabinet, who had their domestic publics to consider, it is impossible to say. In any case, when the Cabinet had completed

---

47 Paige, *The Korean Decision*, 192
48 Kennan, *Memoirs*, 490; Paige, *The Korean Decision*, 98 n74, 284. Later, however, such attitudes became more prevalent and extended into other branches of government. Senator Hickenlooper, for example, subsequently told Arnold Heeney that the United Nations had 'let the United States down' over Korea. See Heeney, *The things that are Caesar's*, 126-7
49 Quoted in Truman, *Years of Trial and Hope*, 386. The statement is also contained in Department of External Affairs, *Canada and the Korean Crisis*, 20-1.
50 Douglas How, 'Canada May State Position on Korea Today,' *Globe and Mail*, 28 June 1950

its survey, Prime Minister St Laurent called opposition party leaders into a conference which lasted a further half-hour – a measure in itself of the gravity with which the government was now regarding the developing crisis.[51]

While these deliberations were in progress in Ottawa, at Lake Success the Security Council had convened at 3:00 PM for its second emergency session. Mr Malik of the Soviet Union was still absent, and Ambassador Austin introduced a resolution recommending 'that the Members of the United Nations furnish such assistance to the Republic of Korea as may be necessary to repel the armed attack and to restore international peace and security in the area.'[52] General discussion ensued, and at 5:12 PM the council president, Sir Benegal Rau, recessed the proceedings for one hour while the representatives of India and Egypt sought to obtain instructions from their governments. In the event, neither delegation was successful, and the vote was therefore taken later that evening without their participation. The result was 7 to 1 in favour of the resolution, with Yugoslavia opposed, India and Egypt not voting, and the Soviet Union still absent. Later, at a council meeting on 30 June, the Indian delegate announced that his government had accepted the 27 June resolution, and Fawzi Bey reported that Cairo would have ordered him to abstain.

The news of the safe passage of the American resolution reached the Department of External Affairs on Tuesday night, not long after the arrival of reports that Seoul had fallen to the advancing North Korean forces.[53] Escott Reid and Douglas LePan began immediately to work on statements for Mr Pearson dealing with its implications for Canadian policy.[54] Similar activities were also in progress in other capitals. On Wednesday, 28 June, the chairman of the Canadian Joint Staff in London, Major-General S.F. Clark, reported to Ottawa that the British chiefs of staff had begun to emphasize the

---

51 Such procedures were not very common. On 25 Oct. 1962, at the height of the Cuban missile crisis, the then leader of the opposition, Lester Pearson, was invited by Prime Minister Diefenbaker to attend a meeting of the Cabinet Defence Committee, and *Time* magazine was able to report that this was the first such occasion since the Korean War. See 'Direct & Immediate Menace,' *Time*, Canada Edition, LXXX, no 18, 2 Nov. 1962, 9. M.J. Coldwell, the leader of the CCF at the time, does not recall that it happened again during the hostilities in Korea. On this occasion he was away from Ottawa, and his place at the meeting was taken by Stanley Knowles. Interview, 10 July 1970

52 For the text of the resolution, see Department of External Affairs, *Canada and the Korean Crisis*, 21

53 The government was not formally in receipt of a copy of the resolution for some time, however. On 28 June Mr Pearson reported to the House that he did not have an official copy, although he had seen the text. Canada, House of Commons, *Debates*, 28 June 1950, p. 4253. Seoul fell about 5:00 PM Tuesday, Ottawa time.

54 Reid, interview, 9 June 1969

importance of 'showing the U.S.S.R., its satellites and Japan that the North Atlantic Treaty and Commonwealth powers are solidly behind the actions taken by the United States in Korea.' They were 'studying the whole Far Eastern situation with a view to determining whether or not land forces could be made available from Hong Kong.'[55]

On the same day Mr Pearson made his first lengthy statement to the House. In it he observed that the North Koreans had ignored the Security Council resolution of 25 June, and that the council itself had been unable to take direct military action because the United Nations forces envisioned in the Charter had never been established. In consequence, if any steps were to be taken to deal with the crisis, they would have to be taken by individual council members 'acting within the terms of the Charter, but on their own initiative.' In the Korean case, the United States had 'recognized a special responsibility which it discharged with admirable dispatch and decisiveness.'

The minister then read into Hansard President Truman's press statement of the previous day announcing the commitment of American air and naval forces to the support of the ROK, commenting that he felt sure that all members of the House would 'applaud and support this act of high courage and firm statesmanship on the part of the government of the United States.'[56]

The members did indeed applaud,[57] but as their desk-thumping died away and Mr Pearson continued his remarks, it became clear that the American reaction was not so firmly identified with United Nations decision-making as the minister would have liked. He felt obliged to tack it down. 'I should like to point out,' he told the House, 'that although the United States government has taken this step on its own authority, it is acting not only in accordance with the spirit and letter of the Charter of the United Nations, but also in pursuance of the resolution which was adopted by the Security Council on Sunday. This resolution ... called on all members of the United Nations to render every assistance in regard to its execution.' The United States had special responsibilities for the maintenance of peace and security in the Far East, particularly in Japan, and this no doubt had contributed to the decision 'to come at once to the aid of Korea.' If further international authorization were required, it had been provided by the resolution of 27 June, which recommended 'that the members of the United Nations furnish such assistance to the Republic of Korea as may be necessary to repel the armed attack and to restore international peace and security in the area concerned.'[58]

55 Quoted in Wood, *Strange Battleground*, 10
56 Canada, House of Commons, *Debates*, 28 June 1950, 4251
57 As Howard Green reminded the House on the following day. See ibid., 29 June 1950, 4389
58 Ibid., 28 June 1950, 4251-2

Since the 25 June resolution had called only for a cease-fire and for the withdrawal of North Korean forces, and since the 27 June resolution had been passed long after the American decision to intervene had been reached, Mr Pearson's argument in terms of international law was somewhat tenuous, as his senior advisers knew very well. It was necessary, however, if the response to the North Korean invasion was to be viewed as having been collectively rather than unilaterally derived, and if American policy was to be brought within the United Nations arena.

The minister concluded his remarks by expressing the government's hope that the action already taken would soon bring the war to an end and make possible a permanent settlement of its underlying causes. Asked by Gordon Graydon what practical steps the government had taken to implement its support of the Security Council resolutions, he said merely that he and his colleagues were not yet formally in receipt of the text of the 27 June measure, although they had seen a copy of it the night before, but they would 'be conferring, through the United Nations, with other members of the United Nations as to which part we in Canada can and should take in any future action that may be necessary.'[59]

This reply is interesting in view of the fact that on the following day Dean Acheson reported to President Truman that Canada, together with Australia, New Zealand, and the Netherlands, had already offered to assist in the crisis.[60] On Wednesday afternoon there had been some discussion of this question in a conversation involving Hume Wrong and American officials at the Department of State. The Americans had said that they appreciated Canada's moral support, but they wanted to know whether more concrete contributions would be forthcoming. Mr Wrong speculated on the possibilities, but made it quite clear that as yet he had no instructions regarding any Canadian commitment. On the advice of Brooke Claxton, the Cabinet earlier in the week had tentatively approved the contribution of three destroyers and the services of an air transport squadron should these prove to be of potential assistance in the crisis.[61] For now, however, the government was biding its time. At its meeting on Wednesday afternoon, the Cabinet had decided to instruct Mr Holmes in New York to find out what the other members of the United Nations who were supporting the American resolutions were going to do. Air Vice Marshal Campbell, the chief of the Canadian staff in Washington, was similarly asked to inquire of the Americans what they would regard as an

59 Ibid., 4253
60 Truman, *Years of Trial and Hope*, 389. By this time, too, the British had placed their naval forces in Japanese waters under General MacArthur's control. See Rees, *Korea*, 24-5
61 Claxton notes, 1141

acceptable offering, and in particular whether they could make use of two or three Canadian destroyers.[62] This explains part of Mr Pearson's report to the House of Commons on the following day, when he remarked that

we have been discussing not only at Lake Success but in Washington with United States authorities what action Canada, as another member of United Nations [sic], might appropriately take to help the government of South Korea maintain itself in the face of this aggression. Also our High Commissioner in London is meeting with the Prime Minister of the United Kingdom and with representatives of other Commonwealth governments to see what can be done, to exchange views with these governments on what they are preparing to do.[63]

Also on Wednesday, the United Nations Secretariat had asked the Canadian government to supply one or two military observers to join the United Nations Commission on Korea, which was now hard-pressed to find trained military personnel. The Cabinet had immediately agreed, and in due course two officers were dispatched to the theatre, arriving in Korea on 24 July. They comprised the first concrete Canadian contribution to the United Nations cause in the Korean War.[64]

In the light of Mr Pearson's dissatisfaction with the timing of the American intervention decision, it is worth commenting at some length on the significance of the foregoing chronicle. Albert Warner, among others, has observed that the vote on the 27 June resolution took place almost eleven hours after the president's statement to the press, and a full twenty-four hours after he had ordered the commitment of American armed forces to the defence of South Korea.[65] This circumstance subsequently became the source of considerable criticism, since it suggested that the Truman administration had usurped from the United Nations the responsibility for initiating collective security action,

62 Pearson, interview, 18 Oct. 1968
63 Canada, House of Commons, *Debates*, 29 June 1950, 4384
64 Pearson, interview, 18 Oct. 1968. See also Canada, House of Commons, *Debates*, 29 June 1950, 4384. The two officers were Lt-Col. F.E. White and Wing Commander H. Malkin. Wood, *Strange Battleground*, 12, note. George Drew, the leader of the opposition, thought the two men would be good sources of intelligence. He told the House that through 'those observers the Canadian government will be kept in touch with all information which the United Nations Commission obtains as to the actual conditions on the spot. Undoubtedly through that advice the government will be able to formulate its plans with the advantage of direct knowledge from Canadian observers as to what the situation is.' Canada, House of Commons, *Debates*, 29 June 1950, 4384
65 Warner, 'How the Korea Decision Was Made,' 104. See also Goodrich, 'Korea,' 143-4

and in so doing had placed the Security Council in the awkward position of having either to support a *fait accompli* or oppose the United States. In his announcement to the press, Truman had attempted to legitimize the decision by arguing that it fell within the terms of the resolution of 25 June, which had called upon 'all Members to render every assistance to the United Nations in the execution of this resolution.' As explained above, however, this resolution provided only for the cessation of hostilities and the withdrawal of North Korean forces. To view it as authorizing military intervention was therefore to distort its meaning.

On the other hand, it could also be argued that the Americans knew in advance from their diplomatic consultations with other Security Council members that the 27 June resolution would be approved, and that accordingly they could proceed with their military deployments without worrying unduly about matters of form. Warner, for example, considered the whole question 'largely academic since the American delegation had assurances of support for a resolution specifically calling on members of the UN to give military assistance in repelling the North Koreans.'[66] Trygve Lie took a similar view, arguing later that the United States action was 'fully within the spirit of the Council's resolution of June 25 and did not anticipate its resolution of June 27 so much as it seemed to do, for diplomatic consultations before the issuance of the [American] order had made it clear that there were seven votes – the required majority – in the Council for authorizing armed assistance to the Republic of Korea.'[67] But even if this interpretation of the scope of the 25 June resolution were valid, the strength of the argument was predicated on the assumption that the USSR would continue to boycott the Security Council, an eventuality of which no one could be certain in advance.

These observations are not intended as debating points, or even as illustrations of the niceties of international law. Their purpose is rather to demonstrate that the response to the North Korean attack had already become enmeshed in a confused overlapping of unilateral and collective sources of decision. The United Nations, representing the collective element, had certainly become involved, but in many important respects its role was merely to act as an adjunct to the unilateral policies of the United States. Rightly or wrongly, the fact remains that the decision to repel the North Korean invasion by force was an American decision, just as the decision to refer the crisis to the Security Council was at American behest and in the American interest. The United Nations did not itself decide collectively to condemn the aggression and then

66 Warner, 'How the Korea Decision Was Made,' 104
67 Lie, *In the Cause of Peace*, 332

to obligate its members, including the United States, to take action to stop it; rather, the United States decided to oppose the aggression and then to ask the members of the United Nations for moral and material support.[68]

This is not to say that the majority of the United Nations' members were opposed to a UN intervention in the crisis, or that they were being forced to support it against their will. Indeed, Canadian decision-makers had been aware from the beginning that any effective measures would have to originate with the United States, since no other non-Communist power was sufficiently well equipped to intervene, and they were pleased that the American decision had made United Nations action possible.[69] To the extent that the 38th parallel was generally recognized as an international border and the Republic of Korea as an independent sovereign state, the North Korean attack did constitute an 'aggression' within intelligible definitions of the term. To that extent, therefore, the interests of the United Nations as an international institution dedicated to the maintenance of world peace and security coincided with those of the United States as a powerful nation determined to contain 'communism' everywhere. In any case, there is every evidence that in June 1950 the Americans were as eager as their allies to sustain the viability of the United Nations as a collective security agent. Although motivated above all by a determination to avoid any appeasement of what he perceived as communist aggression, President Truman felt also that 'the foundations and the principles of the United Nations were at stake unless this unprovoked attack of Korea could be stopped,'[70] and the sense of a commitment to 'the ideal of collective security and the desire to strengthen the United Nations as an instrument of peace' was widely shared among the senior members of his administration.[71] The decision to conduct the American response through United Nations machinery was never at any time seriously debated in Washington, and for all practical purposes it was an automatic reaction.

By acquiring United Nations auspices for their policies, however, and by soliciting the moral and material support of their allies, the Americans exposed themselves to a series of external pressures and constraints which they would have avoided had they chosen to act on a unilateral basis. In resorting to United Nations mechanisms, they could hope to sustain the principle of collec-

---

68 As Lincoln Bloomfield has put it, 'the Korean action [of the United Nations] was of chief utility to the American national interest by legitimizing and broadening the political and moral base of a military counterdemonstration the United States felt it imperative to make' (*The United Nations and* U.S. *Foreign Policy*, 61).

69 Holmes, interview, 1 March 1968, and several others

70 Truman, *Years of Trial and Hope*, 379

71 Paige, *The Korean Decision*, 99. See also Acheson, *Present at the Creation*, 402-13

tive security, to legitimize the conduct of their operations, and to acquire the military assistance of friendly governments. But the price of this multilateral involvement was that it gave those, like the Canadians, who were obliged to contribute to the military campaign a licence to intervene in the decision-making process, and thereby 'to impose constraints on American policy-making, some of which seemed at the time irksome.'[72] But as General Ridgway has since conceded, they 'also laid a restraining hand on military adventures that might have drawn us into deeper and deeper involvement in Asia.'[73]

By 27 June it had already become clear that the coincidence of interest between Washington and Lake Success did not extend to the full range of American policy in the crisis, and that in the area where the coincidence came to an end, the possibility of conflict began. Take, for example, President Truman's controversial decision to 'neutralize' Formosa by deploying the Seventh Fleet in the Formosa Strait. As Leland Goodrich has pointed out:

This action was not directed against the North Korean armed attack, except on the assumption, which the Security Council had not up to this time accepted, that world communism, and not just North Korea, had committed the breach of the peace. It was directed against the Communist regime in China, which many members of the United Nations, including some of the more faithful adherents of the cause of freedom had recognized as the government of China. It involved other members in the consequences of a course of action on which they had not been consulted and which they would probably not have approved had they been consulted. It may have seemed necessary to the United States government, forced as it was to consider its own national security and the demands of influential domestic groups, but it weakened the United Nations character of the collective action and quite possibly was a contributing factor in later developments which jeopardized the success of the initial undertaking.[74]

In the case of this particular decision, the Canadian authorities were not unduly alarmed. Indeed, Pearson, Heeney, Holmes, and LePan, among others, thought it was well calculated to limit the scope of the hostilities, not only because it would place constraints upon the behaviour of the regime in Peking, but also because it would inhibit Chiang Kai-shek, who might otherwise be tempted to take advantage of the situation in order to renew active operations against the Chinese Communist forces.[75] Nevertheless, the general question of

72 Bloomfield, *The United Nations and* U.S. *Foreign Policy*, 61
73 Ridgway, *The Korean War*, 230
74 Goodrich, 'Korea,' 144-5
75 Pearson, interview, 18 Oct. 1968; Heeney, interview, 7 March 1968; Holmes, interview, 1 March 1968; LePan, interview, 5 March 1968

the conflict between the more limited concerns of the United Nations in Korea on the one hand, and the wider interests of the United States as one pole in a bipolar world on the other, was to plague the course of allied diplomacy throughout the war. In the case of Canada, the tensions were aggravated by the fear that the Americans might lose their sense of perspective, and escalate the conflict into an ideological crusade against communism.[76] Every attempt by the American authorities, therefore, to extend the objectives or the conduct of the hostilities beyond the limits which defined the United Nations role in the crisis produced a conflict between Ottawa and Washington. For the Canadians most directly involved, the politics of the Korean War consisted largely in the attempt to make the collective, or United Nations, aspect of the crisis the dominant one, and since to succeed in this was to constrain the United States, friction in their official relations with their American counterparts was the result. It was in consequence of such trials that General J. Lawton Collins, then chief of staff of the United States army, was later moved to recall the advice of one of his War College instructors: 'If you have to go to war, for God's sake do it without allies.'[77]

But while this pattern of conflict was already perceptible, its outline became distinct only in the second week of the crisis. In the meantime the military situation in the field continued to deteriorate, and the American involvement intensified accordingly. On 29 June Korean time, General MacArthur made a personal reconnaissance of the battle area.[78] When he returned to Japan he wired a report to the Pentagon in which he described in detail the rout of the South Korean troops and declared that the intervention of American ground forces had become essential. Without them, he warned, 'our mission will at best be needlessly costly in life, money and prestige. At worst, it might even be doomed to failure.'[79]

In the early hours of the crisis there had been some concern in Washington that the North Korean attack might be no more than a diversionary exercise on the part of the Soviet Union, and that a large-scale commitment of American troops might therefore leave the 'containment front' vulnerable to attack in other areas – for example, in Yugoslavia. By the time the general's wire arrived in the Pentagon on Friday, 30 June, however, the State Department had already exchanged communications with Moscow. The American note, delivered shortly after the commitment on Tuesday of air and naval forces to

76 Holmes, communication with the author, Aug. 1969
77 Collins, *War in Peacetime*, 35
78 See MacArthur, *Reminiscences*, 377-9, for the general's account of this trip.
79 Quoted in Higgins, *Korea and the Fall of MacArthur*, 26-7

action in support of South Korea, had contained the following curt passage: 'In view of the universally known fact of the close relations between the Union of Soviet Socialist Republics and the North Korean regime, the United States Government asks assurance that the Union of Soviet Socialist Republics disavows responsibility for this unprovoked and unwarranted attack, and that it will use its influence with the North Korean authorities to withdraw their invading forces immediately.'[80]

On the assumption that Pyongyang was acting on Soviet orders, the Americans had hoped that this communication, together with an initial show of force, would encourage the Soviets to withdraw from their enterprise. This hope was not fulfilled; the Soviet reply merely blamed the South Koreans and their supporters for the outbreak of hostilities. In addition, however, it also stated that the Soviet government regarded the crisis as a matter internal to Korea, and that it opposed the intervention of foreign powers in the domestic concerns of other nations.[81] This was interpreted in Washington to mean that the USSR would not play a direct military role in the conflict, although it might provide ancillary assistance, and that accordingly the danger of an outbreak of war on a world-wide scale was not very great.[82]

Immediately after the arrival of the Soviet reply, therefore, the president authorized the removal of restrictions which had confined the operations of the United States air force to targets south of the 38th parallel, retaining only the stipulation that activity in the air was not to extend beyond the borders of the Korean peninsula. When General MacArthur's report reached the president early on Friday morning he authorized the commitment of a Regimental Combat Team, and at 8:30 AM he held a conference at the White House to discuss the possibility of dispatching larger forces still. At this meeting it was agreed, with Truman at first reluctant, that an offer from Chiang Kai-shek of 33,000 men would be declined, since the Formosan troops were inadequately equipped and in any case were needed for the defence of the island. The president 'then decided that General MacArthur should be given full authority to use the ground forces under his command.'[83] At the suggestion of Admiral Sherman, he also ordered a naval blockade of the entire Korean coast. The United States of America was in fact, if not in law, at war.

80 Quoted in Spanier, *Truman-MacArthur Controversy*, 32
81 Ibid., 33. The complete text of the Soviet reply is in Paige, *The Korean Decision*, 247
82 Spanier, *Truman-MacArthur Controversy*, 33; Truman, *Years of Trial and Hope*, 389; Rees, *Korea*, 26
83 Truman, *Years of Trial and Hope*, 391. For a full account of this meeting, see Paige, *The Korean Decision*, 257-61

Policy-makers in Canada, meanwhile, confined their efforts for another day or so to a continuing assessment of the developing conflict. The politicians among them contributed to the cause by delivering stout declarations of piety and goodwill, and they were joined in this undertaking by all three parties of opposition in the House of Commons. Such, indeed, was the unanimity of opinion in Parliament that it placed a damper on serious debate. One academic commentator was moved later to the dry observation that such important issues as the co-ordination of United States and United Nations policies, and Canada's relation to both, were 'ignored in the inexorable processes of prorogation and railway schedules to Canada's far-flung constituencies.'[84] So time-consuming were these momentous matters that according to one press gallery witness, the Korean discussions in the House were attended by 'barely a quorum throughout and most of the time the galleries were empty.'[85]

There was only one discordant note to clash upon this gentle harmony. It came from Jean-François Pouliot, the veteran Liberal member for Temiscouata, whose long political career had been nourished in part by his devotion to French-Canadian isolationism, and who at this late hour had no intention of deserting so politically rewarding a philosophy. Honourable members were discussing Korea, he told the House on 29 June, merely 'because of the yellow press that has magnified the incident.' The secretary of state for external affairs had said that Canada was ready to support the Security Council, but the precise character of this institution needed close examination. By itself it was totally without the power to impose sanctions because the establishment of a United Nations military force had never received the unanimous support of its permanent members. The council was therefore 'something hypothetical and theoretical.' It was 'a meeting of nations who follow where the United States and the United Kingdom lead.' In this case, they were leading to Korea, but, he asked, 'what interest do we have in Korea? There may be a few Canadian missionaries of various denominations in that place, but how many Canadians are there in South Korea? If Canada is going to support the Security Council's decision regarding Korea, what form will that support take? ' Mr Pearson should not have volunteered Canada's assistance. We were 'supposed to receive a call for help. It was not our duty to run after it. If they need us, let them say so. If they do not need us, we shall be left alone – not alone in the sense of being abandoned, but alone in the sense of enjoying peace. Sir, the desires of all are for peace. I hope that the Canadian people will be in a position

84 Harrison, *Canada in World Affairs, 1949-1950*, 272
85 I. Norman Smith, 'The Commons Backs UN,' *Ottawa Journal*, 1 July 1950

to breathe after the excitement about Korea is over. We need it because the Canadian people suffered so much during the last war ... '[86]

M. Pouliot's analysis of the United Nations was not without merit, but there is no evidence that his sentiments were shared by other members present. He was to suffer, in fact, a most unkind cut, for the inevitable rebuff came not only from Anglo-Saxon Protestants on the front bench, but also from a representative of French Canada. Maurice Boisvert (L: Nicolet-Yamaska) rose from his seat to say that he had not intended to take part in the debate, but the speeches thus far had made it clear that the country was facing a difficult situation. In such circumstances, it was 'the duty of members of this parliament to endeavour to get everyone in the country to back the policy of the government to deal with the conditions that arise.' He wanted the House 'to know that we from the province of Quebec will be like brothers with those from other provinces in our readiness to support the government and to make it strong in the presence of conditions which none of us want but which must be faced.'[87]

On hearing this, M. Pouliot stalked from the House, thus removing from the chamber its only serious malcontent.[88] The remaining speakers seemed actually to compete for opportunities to support the government's position. Howard Green, for the Progressive Conservatives, even argued that Canada should be doing more. He reminded the House that the minister had said that Canada was going to supply two military observers: 'Well, that is not in line with the position Canada occupies in the world today. I plead with the minister and with the government that a clear-cut statement be made to this parliament, and through this parliament to the Canadian people, to the effect that Canada stands now beside the United Kingdom and the United States in this great crisis.'[89]

Mr Pearson replied that of course the government stood beside the United Kingdom, the United States, and all the members of the United Nations who accepted the Security Council resolution. But, 'As to what we should do to carry out this resolution or to participate in its carrying out is something which cannot be decided in an hour or a day ... The situation is changing in Korea from hour to hour. Naturally any participation by ourselves in this collective effort – because that is the only encouraging feature about this whole tragic

86 Canada, House of Commons, *Debates*, 29 June 1950, 4386-8
87 Ibid., p. 4392
88 Smith, 'The Commons Backs UN.' In an editorial in the same issue entitled 'The Pity of Mr. Pouliot,' the *Journal* complained that the MP had been talking 'nonsense,' and that he was 'living in a world which died when an atomic bomb fell on Hiroshima.'
89 Canada, House of Commons, *Debates*, 29 June 1950, 4390

situation, that it involves for the first time, genuine, effective collective effort – must be guided by events.'[90]

Given that the military campaign in Korea was to be conducted only by countries who were allies in the cold war, the suggestion that 'genuine, effective collective effort' had become truly characteristic of the crisis seems in retrospect a dubious claim, but the fact that the government was being urged by democratically elected legislators to take a more active part in an ominously expanding conflict was intriguing, especially in the light of Canada's diplomatic past. As Norman Smith reported in the *Ottawa Journal* a few days later,

It would have seemed a strange debate to Laurier and Borden and Meighen and Lapointe. Even Mr. King might have found it strange, though he showed no hesitation September 3, 1939.

There was the Canadian Parliament begging its executive ministers to send ships or troops or planes to fight in a far-off mountainous land where no Canadians are and whose economic interest to Canada is less than that of Smiths Falls.

And the begging was being done though nobody had declared war on anybody. It was being done, too, without any speeches of appeal or pressure having been made by the executives.[91]

The pressure, in fact, was moving the other way. When the Department of External Affairs drew up its 'Analysis of Canadian Editorial Comment' for the week of 26-30 June, it observed that 'Almost without exception editorial writers regard the forceful action by the United States on behalf of the United Nations as having been necessary to bolster the waning strength of the United Nations as an effective world organization.' The official who compiled the analysis complained, however, that 'From a purely Canadian point of view, the most noticeable absence among the considerable volume of editorial opinion examined is the lack of detailed attention given by editorial writers to what Canada's role should be. Canada's responsibilities to the United Nations are recognized but few writers go beyond that to suggest how Canada can practically implement her responsibilities.' Nevertheless, there was no doubt that the bulk of the English-language press agreed 'that Canada must face up to her responsibilities as a member of the United Nations and align herself firmly with the United States and the democracies to resist Russian expansionism.'[92]

90 Ibid., 4391
91 Smith, 'The Commons Backs UN.' Canada's formal declaration of war in 1939 did not, however, come on 3 September, but a week later, on 10 September. See Eayrs, *In Defence of Canada*. II: *Appeasement and Rearmament*, 185
92 Department of External Affairs, 'Korean War: Analysis of Canadian Editorial Comment – (26–30 June),' 1-2, 4

The reaction in French Canada, to which in a document containing five pages of text the analyst devoted only a half-page, was somewhat different, although editorial opinions there were not always expressed with settled conviction. Some gave evidence of cross-pressures, doubtless resulting from a conflict between a traditional commitment to isolationism on the one hand, and a hostility to communism on the other. For example, *L'Action Catholique,* after analysing the implications of the North Korean attack for the prestige of the United Nations, the objectives of the Soviet Union, and the position of the United States, emphasized the danger of escalation, and urged public opinion to fight against it by 'refusing to play into the hands of the war propagandists whether on one side or the other.' *Le Canada* agreed that a firm stand was required, but urged that the democracies not allow themselves to be swept into a war hysteria. *La Presse,* more cautious still, described the conflict as 'a local affair, a civil war,' and urged the government to adopt an attitude of 'prudence joined with optimism.'[93]

Some papers, however, were bluntly opposed to Western intervention. Of these, the most strident was *Le Devoir,* which complained that the Security Council, in the absence of the Soviet representative, had been 'transformed almost into a western council of war.'[94] Those who supported a Canadian contribution were 'like little dogs who are impatient to show their master [the United States] that they adore him, who need but a gesture and they will throw themselves into the water.'[95] 'Combien de Canadiens,' the editors asked on 30 June, 'il y a dix jours auraient pu trouver la Corée sur la carte? Probablement dix pourcent. Alors pourquoi cette croisade? Allons-nous payer les bêtises des Américains?'[96] *La Tribune,* taking a similar view, could not see why Canada 'should become blindly involved in the Asiatic conflict and espouse that quarrel simply because its natural sympathies are with the victims of aggression,' and *Le Soleil* wanted to know why the government 'should be caught in the trap of alliances which commit this country to more than the defence of its territory.' Canadians regarded war as a crime, and 'the best way to avoid it is not to meddle in the affairs of foreigners.'[97]

But the editors of the isolationist press in French Canada had no more than a handful of allies in the House of Commons. When Prime Minister St Laurent

---

93 Ibid. Translations are those of the department
94 Ibid.
95 Translated and quoted in Thomson, *Louis St. Laurent,* 293
96 Quoted in Wood, 'Canadian Foreign Policy and Its Determination During the Korean War,' 22, n25
97 Department of External Affairs, 'Korean War: Analysis of Canadian Editorial Comment – (26–30 June)'

announced on 30 June – the last day of the session – that the government had diverted naval units into Western Pacific waters, where they 'would be closer to the area where they might be of assistance to the United Nations and Korea if such assistance were required,' the House 'burst into shouting applause.'[98]

It is clear from the prime minister's statement, however, that the government was becoming increasingly fearful that under American direction the war was taking on the character of an anti-communist crusade. Mr St Laurent was careful to emphasize at the beginning of his speech that Canadian 'responsibility in this matter arises entirely from our membership in the United Nations and from our support of the resolution of the Security Council passed on Tuesday last.' He went on to say:

Any participation by Canada in carrying out the foregoing resolution – and I wish to emphasize this strongly – would not be participation in war against any state. It would be our part in collective police action under the control and authority of the United Nations for the purpose of restoring peace to an area where an aggression has occurred as determined under the charter of the United Nations by the security council, which decision has been accepted by us. It is only in such circumstances that this country would be involved in action of this kind. The house, I think, has already approved this position.

In the event that a Canadian contribution to a United Nations operation under a United Nations commander was 'important to achieve the ends of peace,' the government 'would immediately consider making such a contribution.' This might take the form of destroyers to operate with other United Nations naval units, but if the situation in Korea deteriorated further after Parliament had been prorogued, and more extensive action by Canada proved necessary, the members would 'immediately be summoned to give the new situation consideration.'[99]

Leaders of the three opposition parties reiterated once again their support for the government's policy. George Drew, for the Progressive Conservatives, argued that the crisis had shown the need for a strengthening of the armed forces. Like Mr Pearson and Prime Minister St Laurent, he seemed to feel the need of defending the American initiative. As the only country with effective military forces in the Far East, the United States had taken action which had 'already produced significant results,' but it had done so 'on behalf of the United Nations.' 'What is of vital importance and vital concern to every one

98 Canada, House of Commons, *Debates*, 30 June 1950, 4459; Smith, 'The Commons Backs UN'
99 Canada, House of Commons, *Debates*, 30 June 1950, 4459

of us,' he went on, 'is that more than the use of military force has been committed within these past few days. The whole prestige of the United Nations has been committed. Our prestige and the prestige of every member nation are committed by these events. On the outcome of this issue in Korea depends the future effectiveness of the United Nations. For that reason it is not only the fate of South Korea that hangs in the balance; it is the fate of the United Nations, the fate of that organization upon which the hope of peace in the years ahead now rests.'[100] No more effective statement could be found anywhere of the significance for Canada of the American decision to respond to the situation in Korea through the United Nations. By committing Lake Success, Washington had committed Ottawa, too.

Mr Drew's remarks were followed by affirmations of the justice of the United Nations cause from Stanley Knowles for the CCF[101] and Solon Low for Social Credit. But it was the redoubtable M. Pouliot who had the last word, commenting to Mr Speaker with a sour irony that 'if I did not rely upon the wisdom and the foresight of my leader, the Prime Minister, I would make now a longer speech than that of the Leader of the Opposition.'[102] Shortly thereafter Parliament was prorogued for the summer, and the elected representatives of the Canadian people hurried to their waiting trains.

100 Ibid., 4460
101 Knowles' action was later approved by the party leader, M.J. Coldwell, who was away from Ottawa. It subsequently developed that some CCF supporters were critical of the party's official position because the United States had acted in advance of the United Nations. The parliamentary party was united, however, and Coldwell thought the critics were unrealistic, given the circumstances. M.J. Coldwell, interview, 10 July 1970
102 Canada, House of Commons, *Debates*, 4461

3
The call to arms

In his last statement to the House of Commons before prorogation, Prime Minister St Laurent had remarked that 'the attitude of the house in the last two days' had given the government a 'mandate' to 'do its full duty, within the measure of its power and ability, as a member of the United Nations, in common with other members, to make the collective action of the United Nations effective, and to restore peace in Korea.'[1] George Drew, the leader of the opposition, had been in complete agreement with this interpretation of the Commons consensus, and had observed that there seemed 'little doubt that the sentiment expressed in this house is the sentiment of the people of Canada whom we represent.'[2] Hence, as the parliamentarians departed eagerly from the capital, their minds intent as much upon the nursing of constituencies and the casting of trout flies as upon the problems of international affairs, the makers of Canada's foreign policy were left with considerable freedom to chart whatever course they wished in response to the crisis in Korea.

External Affairs officials thus far had confined their attention for the most part to the elaboration of an intelligence assessment. By now their analysis embraced at least three broad propositions: first, that the United Nations, which customarily enjoyed Canada's enthusiastic support, was irrevocably committed to playing an active role in the crisis in Korea; second, that there was nevertheless a serious danger that what was ostensibly an exercise in collective security would in fact become a general manoeuvre in the 'cold war'

---

1 Canada, House of Commons, *Debates*, 30 June 1950, 4459
2 Ibid., 4460

under the control and direction of the United States, and that special care would therefore be needed to preserve the United Nations character of the operation and to limit, if possible, the range, intensity, and duration of the hostilities; and third, that within broad limits the government was free to make whatever contribution it thought necessary or appropriate, since in doing so it would receive multipartisan support from Parliament and probably also from the majority of its attentive publics. The government had decided already to dispatch two military observers to the theatre, and it had prepared for a possible naval deployment by ordering three destroyers on the Pacific coast to equip themselves for duty in the Far East. For the rest, it possessed a blank cheque with which to make almost any contribution that it liked to the resolution of the military conflict.

Even blank cheques, however, must be covered by sufficient funds, and while still preoccupied with their watch over the unfolding politics of the war, Canadian policy-makers by now were also examining their Defence Department's assets. They cannot have found their investigation very encouraging, for like other countries in which political destinies are ultimately determined by taxpayers, Canada had welcomed the peace of 1945 with a miserly zeal. Indeed, the reduction of defence expenditures after World War II had proceeded at such an enthusiastic pace that by fiscal 1947-8 they had dropped to a mere $195,000,000 from a wartime peak of $2,963,000,000.[3] In 1946 the government had established active personnel ceilings for the three armed forces as follows: army, 25,000; navy, 10,000; air force, 16,000. Only in the case of the RCAF, however, were these levels ever attained, and as of 31 March 1950, less than three months before the outbreak of the Korean War, enlistments stood at 20,652 for the army, 9259 for the navy, and 17,274 for the air force, providing a total active force of 47,185.[4] This entire establishment amounted to less than one-half the size of the infantry forces committed to the invasion of South Korea by the government in Pyongyang. In all, it was a paltry measure in the balance of international military affairs.

Nor was the training and disposition of these forces calculated to make them very useful for the kind of enterprise which the crisis in Korea would probably require. The entire Canadian defence programme as it had been developed during the postwar years was predicated on the assumption that Canada's responsibility in any future outbreak would be to participate, under world war conditions, in the defence of North America and/or of Western

3 Stacey, 'Canadian Military Policy, 1928-1953,' 54-5
4 Department of National Defence, Canada's Defence Programme, 1952-1953, 8

Europe.[5] Even this possibility was not anticipated in the early part of the period, when the prospects for more or less permanent great power amity still seemed good, and by March 1948 the total strength of the three regular forces had dropped to about 35,000. On the other hand, this was also the year of the Czech *coup* and the Berlin airlift, and the ensuing political gloom led inevitably to increased military precautions. But the resulting increments in military strength were still nominal, and they tended to demonstrate that Canadian military planners, ever loyal to the reputation of their profession, were industriously preparing themselves for the previous war. Witness, for example, Mr Claxton explaining his policies to the House of Commons on 24 June 1948:

... the fact is that by themselves our forces could never deter the Russians, nor in a general conflict could they deliver a knock-out blow. What we want are forces which can defend Canada and enable us to play such part as Parliament and the people may support in any efforts for common defence with other countries.

Against this background it is now possible to set down Canada's present defence aims and objectives. They are: (1) to provide the force estimated to be necessary to defend Canada against any sudden direct attack that could be or is likely to be directed against it in the near future; (2) to provide the operational and administrative staffs, equipment, training personnel and reserve organization which would be capable of expansion as rapidly as necessary to meet any need; and (3) to work out with other free nations plans for joint defence based on self-help and mutual aid as part of a combined effort to preserve peace and to restrain aggression.[6]

The culmination of the third of these objectives was the NATO Pact, but for the rest, Canadian policy amounted to a modicum of territorial defence plus an elasticized military infrastructure. In the eyes of the Department of National Defence even NATO took on the character of a bonus-for-nothing, as it triumphantly revealed in its White Paper of 1949:

It is still too early to spell out the consequences of the pact in terms of men and dollars. One thing must be emphasized: the North Atlantic Treaty is a pact for peace. Its final result will not be to increase the expenditures which every nation on our side must take. By pooling resources, the effect of the pact should be to reduce the total expenditures which each of the twelve countries would have found necessary for their

---

5 There had been consideration as early as 1946 of the possibility of making a brigade of the army available for use by the Military Committee of the United Nations Security Council, but the committee was never effective. Foulkes, interview, 7 March 1968
6 Canada, House of Commons, *Debates*, 24 June 1948, 5784

security had there been no pact. However, that result is some distance off and in the meantime, Canada will have to make such modifications of her plans as may be found necessary to meet the situation. While the North Atlantic Treaty makes for security, it will only be effective as it represents a pooling of strength rather than a dilution of strength.[7]

A large portion of allied co-operation together with a small dash of internal adjustment, and the world would indeed be safe for democracy.

It is true that defence appropriations mounted steadily over the following months and that expenditures in fiscal 1949–50 were almost double those of the post-1945 low.[8] But the qualitative allocations were designed to increase Canadian military capabilities in the event of a general war, rather than to develop a highly mobile force suitable for small conflicts in remote theatres. As late as 11 November 1949 Mr Claxton was still telling the Commons that any future war involving Canada 'would be a world war involving all western peoples,' and according to Lt-Col. Wood, the official army historian of the Korean War, this was 'the consensus of military opinion at the time.'[9] Indeed it must have been, for the same views were expressed with almost religious conviction in the department's White Paper of 1949: 'The only kind of war which would involve Canada would be a war in which Communism was seeking to dominate the free nations, in other words, a war in which we would be fighting for the one thing which we value more than life itself, and that is our freedom as a nation and our freedom as a people – freedom to speak and meet and vote and worship as we like. Such a war would be a war for survival ...'[10]

This having been established, the department went on to draw the prudent conclusion that so wretched a conflict would be best fought 'as far away from Canada as possible.' It is clear, however, that they had the luckless Europeans and not the Asians in mind, for they were relying on NATO to keep the hostilities at a distance, and NATO's front lines lay on European soil.

Here, then, was the rationale for Canada's postwar Active Force, which in 'addition to its familiar duties of assisting the civil power and training the military,' as one admiring observer has written, 'was assigned the task of operating and maintaining the Northwest Highway and the North West Territories and Yukon radio system, and of developing equipment and techniques

---

7 Department of National Defence, *Canada's Defence Programme, 1949-1950*, 8
8 About $385 millions, as compared with $195 millions in 1947-8
9 Wood, *Strange Battleground*, 16-17
10 Department of National Defence, *Canada's Defence Programme, 1949-1950*, 11

for use in ground operations in the North.'[11] And here, too, the judgment of
the director of Military Operations and Plans, who early in July 1950 reported
to Mr Claxton that if all the units of the Active Force Brigade Group were
brought up to strength and permitted to concentrate on training, they would
be reasonably efficient after a period of six months.[12]

As Canadian policy-makers considered their predicament in the first days
of July, therefore, they quickly realized that they had rather few bolts to
throw.[13] They could, of course, throw none at all, and leave the war to pursue
its ugly path without interference from Canada. But such a policy confronted
a number of serious objections. For one thing, they had already satisfied
themselves that they wanted to support any action which would serve to
strengthen the United Nations as a security agent in the international community. Now that the organization had been embroiled in the crisis by the
United States, to refrain from giving it substantive assistance would operate
against this objective in two ways: first by denying the UN in a time of serious
international crisis the support of one of its most vociferously enthusiastic
members, and second, by making the opposition to the invaders from North
Korea even less 'collective' than it already was. While the government, moreover, was taking great pains to view the Korean outbreak as a local breach of
the peace, they believed nonetheless that the invasion was Soviet-inspired. It
followed that its defeat would contribute generally to the security of the
western powers. It might be true that the progress of the war could not be
significantly altered by anything that Canada would be able or prepared to do,
but at the very least Canadian participation would allow Ottawa's diplomatists
to speak virtuously in the councils of the 'western world.' At best, it might also
expand their influence over the conduct of American policy in the war.

Without a substantive Canadian contribution, certainly, such influence as
they now possessed would steadily diminish, as their discussions with American officials in Washington were already beginning to show. Mr Pearson and
his departmental subordinates had been conscious from the beginning that the
inevitable preponderance of American forces in any United Nations response
would mean that the most significant decisions, particularly in the area of

11 Stanley, *Canada's Soldiers*, 387. The emphasis on Arctic defence was due in part to the
government's desire to take over from the Americans the administration of the Alaska highway
and staging route. The United States had to be sure in return that the route would be properly
defended and maintained. Washington also wanted assurances that the Eldorado uranium
deposits would be effectively secured. Foulkes, interview, 7 March 1968
12 Wood, *Strange Battleground*, 19
13 General Charles Foulkes, among others, has remarked upon the limitations of Canada's
military capabilities in this period. Interview, 7 March 1968

military operations, would be made by the United States government.[14] Nevertheless, they were not thereby inhibited from attempting to shape the course of American policy, as can be seen in their initial forays in this exercise, conducted while the question of a Canadian contribution was still under review.

It will be recalled that on 30 June, the same day the Canadian Parliament prorogued, President Truman authorized General MacArthur to make full use of the ground forces under his command in dealing with the North Korean invasion, and ordered a naval blockade of the entire Korean coast. Shortly thereafter he 'approved a proposal prepared jointly by the Departments of State and Defense to introduce in the UN a resolution creating a unified command in Korea' and asking the Americans to name a commander.[15] This manoeuvre by the United States, although perfectly consistent with Washington's dominant military role in the crisis, collided immediately with the Canadian desire, shared by the UN secretary-general,[16] to maximize the 'collective' element in the United Nations response. According to an informed journalist based in Ottawa at the time, 'the very difficult task of working out a procedure for United Nations command of the Korean operation ... caused more work and worry than anything else in the opening weeks of the crisis.'[17] The United Nations Charter had originally provided that the five permanent members of the Security Council would establish a Military Staff Committee, comprised of their respective chiefs of staff, which would 'advise and assist the Security Council on all questions relating to the Security Council's military requirements for the maintenance of international peace and security, the employment and command of forces placed at its disposal, the regulation of armaments, and possible disarmament' (Article 47). It has often been lamented that the great powers were never able to agree upon the effective execution of this provision, although in view of the circumstances surrounding the Korean War the presence of a Soviet staff officer on the UN Command might well have proved embarrassing. In any event, such a command now had to be improvised, and, as Blair Fraser put it, it was 'absolutely vital' in the Canadian view that 'the combined forces under MacArthur ... be a United Nations force and not just the US and her allies.' This was so 'for two separate reasons:'

14 Campbell, interview, 20 Oct. 1968; Holmes, interview, 1 March 1968; Pearson, interview, 18 Oct. 1968 and others
15 Truman, *Years of Trial and Hope*, 394-5
16 Lie, *In the Cause of Peace*, 336
17 Fraser, 'Backstage at Ottawa,' *Maclean's*, 15 Aug. 1950, 54. These views have been confirmed by Mr Pearson. Interview, 18 Oct. 1968

Domestically, it had to be made clear that Canada [was] acting as a loyal member of the UN and not as the tail to an American kite. As one External Affairs man put it, 'We can't jump from an imperial frying pan into an American fire.'

Even more important, the combined force had to be limited to objectives defined by the United Nations and not by the US high command in Washington. Suppose, for example, that Washington decided MacArthur's force was needed in a hurry to defend Formosa? Defending Chiang Kai-shek is no part of Canada's foreign policy.

That's why it was so essential, in Ottawa's opinion, to find a mode of operation that would be legally unassailable under the terms of the United Nations Charter. And that's why Canada, though no longer a member of the Security Council, played such an active role in framing the key resolution that set up a United Nations Command.[18]

'Active' the Canadians certainly were. Effective, they were not. This, however, was not for want of trying. As early as 30 June Hume Wrong began his discussions with State Department officials on the substance of the American proposals. The conversations were continued at intervals over the next seven days. They were supplemented by consultations at the United Nations with Andrew Cordier and other Secretariat officials, who shared Ottawa's belief in the need to link the operation in Korea as closely as possible to the UN organization.[19] During this period, Trygve Lie had even proposed to members of the Security Council that military operations be supervised by a 'Committee on Coordination of Assistance for Korea.' But the American Joint Chiefs of Staff had 'offered strong objections.' As General Collins has recalled,

We pointed out that to place a United Nations committee in the chain of command could seriously interfere with the strategic and tactical control of operations by General MacArthur and his commanders of army, navy and air forces in the field. We favored a command arrangement somewhat comparable to our own executive-agency system, that is, one in which the United States would act as executive agent for the United Nations, with no one interposed between MacArthur and the United Nations. Our suggestions were followed. The resolution as adopted by the Security Council called simply for periodic reports from the United Nations commander.[20]

Most of the Canadian diplomatic activity, although equally unsuccessful, was directed to the more modest objective of changing the wording of the

18 Fraser, 'Backstage at Ottawa,' 54. These views have been repeated by Mr Pearson, interview, 18 Oct. 1968
19 Pearson, interview, 18 Oct. 1968
20 Collins, *War in Peacetime*, 34

American text in such a way as to reinforce the impression that the United Nations was the genuine parent of the response to the North Korean attack, and hence to establish that the command really was a United Nations agent. The government's second preoccupation – the isolation of Formosa from the sphere of UN operations – was also very much in evidence, and on 6 July Ottawa instructed the Canadian ambassador in Washington (and Mr Holmes in New York) to raise the possibility of including in the forthcoming Security Council resolution a provision which would have defined territorially the area around Korea within which UNC forces would be acting on United Nations authority. Such a provision would have had the practical effect of excluding the United Nations from any responsibility for military activity relating to the island of Formosa or to the territory of mainland China. It would have helped also to establish a clearly-defined boundary, visible to both sides, within which the conduct of hostilities could be confined. In other words, it would have tacitly communicated to the enemy the message that the states supporting the United Nations action had no intention of deliberately escalating the war beyond its immediate geographic limits.[21]

The proposal was offered at too late a stage in the deliberations, however, to have any effect, and the American resolution was introduced in the Security Council on the following day under the combined auspices of Britain and France. In any case, Hume Wrong, by now thoroughly exasperated with the ceaseless demands of his superiors in Ottawa that he raise new issues with an already harrassed Department of State, had been reluctant to suggest such an addition to the United States authorities at a time when the result might well be a serious delay in the UN's proceedings. This view was shared by Mr Holmes in New York. The Americans, moreover, had already made it clear that they regarded the neutralization of Formosa as an aspect of their own policy quite separate from that of the United Nations, and Mr Wrong believed they would not take kindly to a recommendation that by implication would cast doubt upon the sincerity of their motives and the reliability of their guarantees. Furthermore, the wording of the resolution as it now stood made it very plain that the United Nations was involved only in the defence of the Republic of Korea.[22]

The third Security Council resolution on Korea was therefore passed under the sponsorship of Britain and France on the following day, 7 July, without the benefit of the proposed Canadian alteration.[23] The vote was 7 to 0, with

21 Details from confidential source
22 Ibid.
23 The Americans apparently arranged to have the resolution presented by the British and French in order to broaden the range of important countries that could be identified with the United Nations response

Egypt, India, and Yugoslavia abstaining, and the Soviet Union still absent. The resolution is worth quoting in full:

The Security Council,

Having determined that the armed attack upon the Republic of Korea by forces from North Korea constitutes a breach of the peace,

Having recommended that Members of the United Nations furnish such assistance to the Republic of Korea as may be necessary to repel the armed attack and to restore international peace and security in the area,

1 *Welcomes* the prompt and vigorous support which governments and peoples of the United Nations have given to its Resolutions of 25 and 27 June 1950 to assist the Republic of Korea in defending itself against armed attack and thus to restore international peace and security in the area;

2 *Notes* that Members of the United Nations have transmitted to the United Nations offers of assistance for the Republic of Korea;

3 *Recommends* that all Members providing military forces and other assistance pursuant to the aforesaid Security Council resolutions make such forces and other assistance available to a Unified Command under the United States;

4 *Requests* the United States to designate the commander of such forces;

5 *Authorizes* the Unified Command at its discretion to use the United Nations flag in the course of operations against North Korean forces concurrently with the flags of the various nations participating;

6 *Requests* the United States to provide the Security Council with reports as appropriate on the course of action taken under the Unified Command.[24]

While the contents of this resolution were being formulated in Washington, Hume Wrong had protested strongly against some of the phrases employed. In particular, the Canadian authorities disliked the expression 'in the area,' which appeared in the second paragraph of the preamble and the first paragraph of the body of the resolution, and which they felt gave inadequate definition to the scope of United Nations operations. Mr Wrong had objected also to the words 'under the United States,' which were included in Paragraph 3, and in general he had argued on instructions from Ottawa that references to the United States occurred too frequently throughout the text.[25] None of these protests, however, had produced a positive result.

24 Department of External Affairs, *Canada and the Korean Crisis*, 27
25 Details from confidential source. On being reminded of them, Escott Reid told the author that 'later events demonstrated the unwisdom of the "in the area" clause since the Americans used this as part of their justification for crossing the 38th parallel. The resolution should have spoken only of the restoration of the *status quo ante bellum*.' Interview, 9 June 1969, and letter to the author, 21 Nov. 1972

Meanwhile, at three o'clock on the afternoon of 5 July, the three Canadian destroyers, *Cayuga*, *Sioux*, and *Athabaskan*, had sailed from their berths in Esquimalt, British Columbia, bound initially for the American naval base at Pearl Harbor. It will be recalled that their departure for the western Pacific had been ordered on 30 June on a contingency basis only – they were to be available in the theatre in case they were needed – and the instructions received by the commanding officer, Captain J.V. Brock, reflected the general uncertainty surrounding their mission. Captain Brock had just been appointed the senior officer of the destroyer division on the Pacific coast, and had expected his first operational assignment to be a European cruise by way of the Panama Canal. Now, suddenly re-routed to the Far East, he had no idea of what to expect. His only terms of reference were those included in personal letters from Brooke Claxton and Lester Pearson. Claxton's amounted to a personal letter of credit. It merely wished him good luck, promised that he would be kept fully informed, advised him that the details of logistical support would be worked out later, and authorized expenditures up to a specified limit. Pearson's similarly expressed good wishes and encouragement, adding that the government knew little about the operation or how it would turn out. It reminded the captain that he would be representing Canada in the theatre, and said that the government had every confidence in him. The minister's only specific injunction was that Brock be sure to avoid embroilment in any action involving Formosa. For the rest, he had a free hand.[26]

It was not until 12 July, two hours after the destroyers had reached their destination in the Hawaiian Islands, that Captain Brock received instructions from Rear Admiral F.L. Houghton, vice chief of the Naval Staff in Ottawa, transferring his ships to General MacArthur's Unified Command and authorizing them to fly the United Nations flag. On orders from General MacArthur in Tokyo they then proceeded to the Far East and arrived in Sasebo, Japan, to take up active duty on 30 July.[27]

The Cabinet had made its final decision to commit the destroyers at a meeting on 12 July,[28] and while Rear Admiral Houghton was sending his signals to the fleet, John Holmes in New York was executing instructions to inform the United Nations secretary-general of the Canadian naval contribution. He was asked to include with this official diplomatic communication a copy of the text of Mr St Laurent's statement to the House of Commons on

26 Brock, interview, 23 July 1969
27 Thorgrimsson and Russell, *Canadian Naval Operations in Korean Waters, 1950-1955*, 4-5, and note 38
28 Pearson, interview, 18 Oct. 1968; confirmed in interview with Geoffrey A.H. Pearson after reference to his father's personal notes, same date

30 June. This has been significant primarily for its unequivocal enunciation of the principle that any action taken by Canada would be pursued only as part of a 'collective peace action under the control and authority of the United Nations' and not as an act of 'war against any state.'[29]

The UN Secretariat was then occupied with the task of preparing cables to be sent to the fifty-three member states of the United Nations which had announced their approval of the Security Council resolutions. These were dispatched to their destinations on 14 July, sufficiently late for the telegram to Mr Holmes to contain an acknowledgment of the contribution of Canadian destroyers. What was of particular concern to Ottawa, however, was the following embarrassing request:

I have been informed that the Government of the United States which, under the resolution of 7 July 1950 has been given the responsibility for the Unified Command, is now prepared to engage in direct consultation with your Government with regard to the co-ordination of all assistance in a general plan for the attainment of the objectives set forth in the Security Council resolution. In this connection I have been advised that there is an urgent need for additional effective assistance. I should be grateful, therefore, if your Government would examine its capacity to provide an increased volume of combat forces, particularly ground forces. Offers of military assistance should be communicated to the Secretary-General in terms leaving detailed arrangements for subsequent agreements between your Government and the Unified Command (USG).[30]

The request was embarrassing partly because the Canadian authorities had very little in the way of suitable ground forces to send, partly because they were not yet certain that they wanted to send them even if they had, and partly because the secretary-general's communication had been released to the press and therefore required a public reply. This had the effect in turn of making it even more difficult for Ottawa to refuse to supply additional forces, not only because such a refusal would arouse criticism among attentive publics in the United States and elsewhere, but also because it might have damaging political repercussions at home. One of the intended advantages of the decision to begin Canada's active participation by contributing only a small fleet of destroyers was that it would give the government time to consider more carefully its

29 Department of External Affairs, *Canada and the Korean Crisis*, 27-8; and Canada, House of Commons, *Debates*, 30 June 1950, 4459
30 Department of External Affairs, *Canada and the Korean Crisis*, 28. See also Lie, *In the Cause of Peace*, 337-8

position with respect to a possible contingent of forces on the ground.[31] Now, however, this dividend was being threatened by a public plea for an army contribution which emanated from precisely the organization whose welfare and integrity the government was committed to support and defend. In any case, there was a suspicion in Ottawa that Trygve Lie was working in league with the Americans, an assumption for which his memoirs provide some support.[32]

The arrival of the secretary-general's request was therefore not entirely welcome in the Canadian capital. Nor was its reception improved by the fact that accounts of its contents appeared in the mass communications media a full twenty-four hours before Ottawa was advised that an original copy of the message had been officially presented to the Canadian mission in New York. A minor diplomatic skirmish ensued, and according to Blair Fraser, one Cabinet minister complained bitterly at the time that Lie's action was 'unthinkable,' adding, 'You don't just spring things like that on member governments. Lie should at least have consulted those countries, like Canada, who were already taking an active part.'[33]

In fairness to the secretary-general, however, it is worth noting that while the decision to release the message to the press was taken as a matter of deliberate policy, it was not intended that it should appear in the news media before the official version arrived in the diplomatic offices of member governments. In the Canadian case, the original copy of the communication had been delivered to Mr Holmes' office on Fifth Avenue in New York while he was taking part in the proceedings of the Interim Committee at Lake Success. A duplicate copy was delivered to him in the General Assembly, and after reporting its contents to Ottawa, he returned directly to his apartment later that evening without stopping at his office. In the meantime the under secretary, A.D.P. Heeney, had called him from the External Affairs Department to inquire whether he had seen the original version of the secretary-general's message, and he had replied in the negative. He was then instructed to raise the matter of timing with Andrew Cordier. Next morning he was dismayed

31 Campbell, interview, 20 Oct. 1968
32 See, for example, Lie, *In the Cause of Peace*, 336-9. H. Basil Robinson has pointed out that the 'specific gravity of the UN was very different from what it became soon after. Western influence was dominant, and Lie was a reflection of that, just as Hammarskjold reflected a new balance later on. In this sense, we were all very partisan.' Interview, 5 May 1970. In this case, however, the secretary-general's close co-operation with the United States was not entirely welcomed by Canadian authorities.
33 Fraser, 'Backstage at Ottawa,' *Maclean's*, 1 Sept. 1950, 4. Confirmed by Pearson, interview, 18 Oct. 1968; and by Holmes, interview, 1 March 1968

to discover the original lying on his desk, and immediately telephoned Mr Heeney to explain that it had been there for some time. He had not been advised of its arrival because his office had known that he had received a duplicate copy at Lake Success, and had assumed – quite rightly, in Mr Holmes' view – that the distinction between the copy and the original was an unimportant formality. The under-secretary subsequently informed the prime minister, but in the meantime Mr Holmes, to his own embarrassment and irritation, was obliged to discuss the question with Mr Cordier. Cordier apologized for the confusion, and by way of excuse pointed out that his office was both under-staffed and under pressure – an explanation which did not entirely satisfy Holmes' superiors.[34] The deed, however, was done, and a response still had to be devised.

As it happened, the three most important decision-makers were out of town. Prime Minister St Laurent was away fishing, Defence Minister Brooke Claxton was in Newfoundland consulting with American officers on problems of North American defence, and External Affairs Minister Lester Pearson was in Toronto to deliver an address before a joint meeting of the Engineering Institute of Canada and the American Society of Civil Engineers.[35] The remarks of the latter, however, betrayed something of the government's preoccupations. After commenting with contempt upon the current flurry of 'peace campaigns' in the Soviet bloc, Mr Pearson defended both the legality and the necessity of Security Council's action, and pointed out that it had received the support of fifty-three states. These included 'many countries, and Canada is one of them, who resent and repudiate the charge that in doing our duty to the international community, and to peace, we are merely following the orders of a single member of the United Nations which has particular interests to safeguard in Korea. This is not the case. The people of Canada know that it is not the case.' Canada's position was 'dictated by the necessity of supporting United Nations action.' That was 'our only obligation,' and it was being discharged 'from considerations both of national honour and national safety.' Some might argue that Canada had no interest in a country so remote as Korea, but 'There could be no reasoning more false than this. The terrible events of the last twenty years have shown us that there is no country far away from Canada and that there is no Canadian interest which matches our interest in peace. If that interest in peace is risked in Korea, or any other place, it becomes a matter of immediate concern to the Canadian people; for Canada,

---

34 Holmes, interview, 1 March 1968; Pearson, interview, 18 Oct. 1968
35 Fraser, 'Backstage at Ottawa,' *Maclean's*, 1 Sept. 1950, 4. For the text of Mr Pearson's address, see Department of External Affairs, *Statements and Speeches*, no 50/26

in this jet-propelled, atomic, interdependent age, cannot by itself remain secure and at peace in a warring world.' Peace, then, was indivisible. But so also was the defence of Canada, for the minister reproved those who felt that the government should undertake a large-scale mobilization and dispatch all the country's forces to the Pacific theatre. Such a course 'might give some satisfaction to those who would like to trouble the waters elsewhere so that they could fish in them.' We had, therefore, to 'be resolute,' but also 'cool and far-sighted.' In the meantime, the government had dispatched three destroyers to operate in Korea under the United Nations flag: 'This is no mere token assistance. Nor is it assistance to any one state. It is a contribution to the United Nations for the restoration of peace in Korea.'[36]

The minister's speech was notable, then, for its emphatic reaffirmation of the view that the operation in Korea was an enterprise in genuine collective security, and that the principal entrepreneur (if not the largest investor) was the United Nations, not the United States. These remarks did not go unobserved in Washington, where the propagation of such an opinion served well enough the needs of political legitimacy. In Washington also, however, there was a desire to improve upon its credibility – a desire which Canada's contribution of three naval destroyers did little to assuage. 'No mere token,' Mr Pearson had called them, and an unidentified American State Department official was reported later to have commented, 'Okay, let's call it three tokens.'[37] The American authorities were alleged by the press to be irritated by what they regarded as a 'holidays-as-usual' atmosphere in Ottawa,[38] and more than once in this period they pressed the government to supply an army contingent.[39] It was the appeal from Lake Success, not the appeal from Wash-

36 Department of External Affairs, *Statements and Speeches*, no 50/26
37 Fraser, 'Backstage at Ottawa,' *Maclean's*, 1 Sept. 1950, 4
38 Ibid. Their views found an echo in the American press. In their issue of 18 July, the editors of the *Chicago Daily Tribune* delivered a succinct assessment: 'That Canada, one of our allies in the North Atlantic pact, should drag its feet in a war in the Pacific demonstrates that the practical effect of the pact is that we shall have the privilege of rescuing the British Empire in any new European war, but when the imperial interest is not directly engaged, the privilege of killing and being killed will be ours alone.' Quoted in Wood, *Canadian Foreign Policy and Its Determination During the Korean War*, p. 32, n8
39 Campbell, interview, 20 Oct. 1968; Foulkes, interview, 7 March 1968; Holmes, interview, 1 March 1968; R.A. MacKay, interview, 7 March 1968; and, with somewhat less positive recollection, Robinson, 5 May 1970. In general, perceptions of the intensity of American pressure varied according to one's place in the bureaucracy. Escott Reid, for example, recalls that in July 1950 it was 'intolerable – the worst arm-twisting I ever saw.' Interview, 9 June 1969. A.D.P. Heeney, on the other hand, could remember that there was pressure, but did not regard it as remarkable. Interview, 7 March 1968

ington, however, that had the most significant impact on Canadian decision-makers, although outwardly the secretary-general's message failed to ruffle their official calm.[40] The prime minister interrupted his vacation to consider the matter briefly in Ottawa, but collective discussion by the government as a whole was postponed until the regularly scheduled Cabinet meeting on Wednesday, 19 July and it was brought to an end in time for the ministers to catch their trains.[41]

The day before the Cabinet was to meet, the minister of national defence was briefed by the chiefs of staff of the three armed services in a conference which included Rear Admiral F.L. Houghton of the navy, Air Marshal W.A. Curtis of the air force, and the chief of the General Staff, Lt-Gen. Charles Foulkes of the army. An account of this meeting by the official army historian indicates that the three senior officers were in some disagreement over the kind of military role Canada was capable of playing, their points of view reflecting the capacities and interests of their respective services. Admiral Houghton argued that the three destroyers already committed to the UN Command comprised a 'fair contribution' for Canada, and that in any case the other available naval units, stationed in the Atlantic, had as their first responsibility the fulfilment of commitments to NATO. Air Marshal Curtis announced in turn that he could supply an RCAF transport squadron of five North Stars, which he thought might be expanded later to ten.[42] He explained that the RCAF already had made a tentative offer to the United States air force of a small air combat unit, but the Americans had turned the offer down and had asked for transport aircraft instead.[43] Transport Squadron 426 had been placed on alert for a possible Pacific airlift, pending a decision by the government.[44]

But ground contingents were the main concern, and General Foulkes suggested that there were four possible ways of using the currently available Active Force, although he was not enthusiastic about any of them. The least of his four evils would be the contribution of an infantry brigade consisting of three infantry battalions and a minimal logistics tail, all of which would operate within the context of a Commonwealth division. The reason for his preference for this particular arrangement was that it would allow the Canadi-

---

40 Holmes, interview, 1 March 1968. All the Canadian officials interviewed were agreed that American pressure was not a major consideration for Canadian decision-makers on this issue. The point was stressed not only by Mr Holmes, but also by Pearson, interview, 18 Oct. 1968, and by Heeney, interview, 7 March 1968 and letter to the author, 26 March 1968.
41 Fraser, 'Backstage at Ottawa,' *Maclean's*, 1 Sept. 1950, 4
42 Wood, *Strange Battleground*, 19-20
43 Wood, 'Canadian Foreign Policy and Its Determination During the Korean War,' p. 39
44 James A. Oastler, 'Cabinet Continues Air Study,' *Montreal Star*, 19 July 1950

an contingent to make use of British sources of supply and thereby avoid needless and expensive supply-line duplication. His other three alternatives 'were variations of larger formations of brigade group size which could operate independently, if necessary,' but it was pointed out that even the more modest plan that he preferred 'would take almost every trained infantry soldier in the Army.'[45] The only way to make a ground force contribution without denuding Canada's defences entirely appeared to be the adoption of a fifth and very different course – that is, the recruitment of a special force designed specifically for service in Korea, although still functioning within the context of a Commonwealth division. The general thought in any case that the government should wait to see whether the British were planning such a division before taking any action. Mr Claxton was not confident at first that such a contingent could be raised on short notice, especially under current conditions of high employment, but at this point the discussions were terminated pending a meeting of the Cabinet Defence Committee on the following day.[46]

The fact that none of the reports had conveyed a very impressive picture of Canada's military capabilities reflected the pattern of postwar Canadian defence policy described earlier. It also reflected the conviction of senior armed forces personnel that the main strategic front in the 'cold war' was in Europe, and that Korea comprised a peripheral engagement which must not be allowed to drain Canada's strength from more important theatres. Lt-Gen. G.G. Simonds had believed initially that the North Korean attack was a diversionary manoeuvre designed to attract attention away from some other area of planned Soviet attack,[47] and his views for a time had been shared by the President of the United States.[48] But the Americans were in a position to guard the home front and dabble in the Far East, too, while Canada had a choice in the short run of doing either one or the other, but not both. In such circumstances, Canadian commanders were unwilling to embroil themselves too deeply in a conflict so remote from their home base. Hence the remark of an unidentified Cabinet minister, who told Blair Fraser that he was 'convinced that public opinion wouldn't allow us to send away all our operational defence forces. But even if the public would tolerate it our chiefs of staff would not. They'd all resign.'[49]

These strong feelings were fortified also by the belief that Canadian forces in Korea might be unnecessary. Before the 18 July meeting with Mr Claxton,

45 Wood, *Strange Battleground*, p. 20
46 Ibid.
47 Wood, 'Canadian Foreign Policy and Its Determination During the Korean War,' 21, n22
48 Truman, *Years of Trial and Hope*, Chap. XXII, passim.
49 Fraser, 'Backstage at Ottawa,' *Maclean's*, 1 Sept. 1950, 55

the chiefs of staff had obtained an intelligence report drawn up by their Joint Intelligence Committee and entitled, 'The Imminence of War.' The report agreed with the view taken by military authorities in Britain that some six divisions would be required to repel the invaders in Korea and that the United States was the only country capable of providing them. The estimate predicted also that the Americans would succeed in establishing a defence perimeter around the port of Pusan, that with the assistance of their superiority in the air they would then be able to build up their strength in the field, and that accordingly they could be expected to undertake an offensive within two or three months.[50] Since the currently available Canadian Active Force would require six months of intensive training before being ready for operations, and since the development of a special force would take even longer, there seemed to be little time left for Canada to make a useful contribution.

Nevertheless, the government was now under considerable pressure to provide tangible evidence of its support for the United Nations cause, and the problem therefore still had to be faced. Early on Wednesday, 19 July, prior to the scheduled full-dress meeting of the Cabinet, the chiefs of staff conferred for some two hours with the Cabinet Defence Committee. In addition to the three service officers, those present included Mr St Laurent (prime minister and chairman of the committee), C.D. Howe (minister of trade and commerce), D.C. Abbott (minister of finance), Lester Pearson (secretary of state for external affairs), C.M. Drury (deputy minister of national defence), and Robert Bryce (assistant deputy minister of finance).[51] The discussions were conducted in secret, but according to the army historian Mr Claxton informed the committee that no 'authoritative' request for Canadian ground forces had yet been received. By that he presumably meant that no such request had been received from the United Nations Command, since there obviously had been one from the UN secretary-general, and the State Department on several occasions had made quite explicit appeals. This was confirmed by General Foulkes, who reported that the American JCS had advised the chairman of the Canadian Joint Staff in Washington that they 'had not been consulted on the matter of assistance from UN nations, nor were they clear as to how the ground

---

50 Wood, 'Canadian Foreign Policy and Its Determination During the Korean War,' 36; Wood, *Strange Battleground*, 10. Brooke Claxton's account confirms that the Canadian chiefs of staff were convinced that a considerable commitment of infantry would be required. Claxton notes, 1142

51 The army historian implies that only the CGS attended this meeting (Wood, *Strange Battleground*, 20), but James Oastler reported to the *Montreal Star* that all three chiefs of staff were present ('Cabinet Continues Air Study,' *Montreal Star*, 19 July 1950), and this was the usual practice. See Eayrs, *The Art of the Possible*, 15

force would be integrated into General MacArthur's organization.' The general reiterated to the Defence Committee his view that any Canadian contribution should come within the context of a Commonwealth division.[52]

It is impossible from the available evidence to describe in detail the discussions which ensued in this meeting and in the full session of the Cabinet which followed, but the decisions that were taken are a matter of public record. They were mimeographed in the form of a statement by the prime minister and distributed to the press within a half-hour of the end of the deliberations.[53] After a brief comment to the effect that Canada had obligations not only to the United Nations but also to the North Atlantic Treaty and to the joint defence of the North American continent, the statement noted that the Cabinet had 'given full and earnest study to the Secretary-General's request for assistance in the light both of the needs of the Korean situation and of the other interests and responsibilities of Canada.' The statement reminded its readers that three Canadian destroyers were already on their way to Korea, and announced that in order to be 'prepared for other eventualities' the navy had been authorized 'to place additional ships in commission, to bring others up to full complement, and to recruit whatever additional men are needed.' But the request for ground forces had been turned down:

Having in mind the other obligations for the employment of Canadian ground forces, the Cabinet has reached the conclusion that the despatch, at this stage, of existing first line elements of the Canadian Army to the Korean theatre would not be warranted. However, with a view to strengthening the Canadian Army to meet future requirements the Cabinet has authorized recruiting above present ceilings and the acceleration of other aspects of the Army programme.[54] Should a decision be taken by the Security Council of the United Nations to recruit an international force for service, under the UN Commander, in Korea, the Canadian Government will give immediate consideration to Canadian participation in such an undertaking. Any participation of this nature would require approval by Parliament in accordance with my statement made in the House of Commons on 30th of June.[55]

---

52 Wood, *Strange Battleground*, 20
53 Fraser, 'Backstage at Ottawa,' *Maclean's*, 1 Sept. 1950, 4. Mr St Laurent refused to make any informal comment, confining his remarks to reporters to the following succinct summary of his immediate plans: 'well, gentlemen, I hope to be out fishing again the day after tomorrow.' It was to be a bad summer for vacations.
54 Brooke Claxton and Hugues Lapointe went on radio next day, 20 July, to appeal for recruits. See Fraser, 'Backstage at Ottawa,' *Maclean's*, 1 Sept. 1950, 55. The results were poor.
55 Department of External Affairs, *Statements and Speeches*, no 50/28. The reference to a specially recruited 'international force' seems to have been inspired by a proposal made by

The statement went on, however, to say that the government had been notified that there was a need for air transport assistance and that accordingly Canada would provide 'a long range RCAF transport squadron for service in the Pacific air lift.'[56] Aircraft production and the recruitment of RCAF personnel were also going to be accelerated. And once again the global view:

> The Korean situation cannot be viewed in isolation. The attack on the Republic of Korea has increased the cohesion of resistance to aggressive Communism in other parts of the world. The measures which the United States Government have taken and are taking are far-reaching and significant. Here in Canada we also shall press on with measures which will increase the preparedness of this country. We are increasing immediately our defence effort and expenditure. We are also giving consideration to further measures of aid by this country to our North Atlantic partners.[57]

Trygve Lie in mid-July. He had suggested that 'in order to secure the maximum effective military forces,' the 'Unified Command should find a way of using all capable volunteers from foreign countries. An international brigade which would be organized by the United States, but at the disposal of the Security Council, might be the device.' The brigade 'would bear the United Nations name and wear United Nations uniforms and be enlisted for a term of two to three years.' Lie 'anticipated that the number of volunteers would be large, but felt that the only practical way of organizing the brigade was to entrust the responsibility – and the expense – to the United States.' The Americans, however, gave the idea 'a mixed reception.' They agreed that it would 'facilitate the participation of small countries in the United Nations effort. But special United States legislation would be required; perhaps the job might better be left to Canada' (Lie, *In the Cause of Peace*, 339). According to one student of Canada's involvement in the Korean campaign, the Canadian government for a time thought this might be an easy way to fulfil its UN responsibilities and satisfy Canadian public opinion, but became less enthusiastic when it became clear that Lie felt that Canada should take the lead in making the organizational and administrative arrangements (Wood, 'Canadian Foreign Policy and Its Determination During the Korean War,' 42). Few of the Canadian decision-makers can now recall this proposal, however, although it was discussed briefly by Mr Pearson in Washington on 29 July, when it was dismissed as impractical (Pearson, interview, 18 Oct. 1968)

56 John Holmes informed Trygve Lie officially of the offer of aircraft on 21 July. See Department of External Affairs, *Canada and the Korean Crisis*, 30. This was to be the chief contribution of the RCAF to the conduct of the war, although some twenty fighter pilots and a number of technical officers took part in the hostilities on individual assignment to the USAF and were credited with more than twenty enemy jet fighters destroyed or damaged. No 426 Transport Squadron completed its task in June 1954. By then it had flown over 600 round trips, carrying more than 13,000 passengers and 7,000,000 pounds of cargo without loss. Additional air contributions were made in the form of regular chartered flights by Canadian Pacific Airlines. See Wood, *Strange Battleground*, 179-80, and Prime Minister St Laurent in Canada, House of Commons, *Debates*, 24 Nov. 1952, 37. John Holmes notified the secretary-general of the decision to provide the CPA charter flights on 11 August 1950. See Department of External Affairs, *Canada and the Korean Crisis*, 35

57 Department of External Affairs, *Statements and Speeches*, no 50/28

These increments in defence spending were merely the first of several which were stimulated by the outbreak of the war in Korea. Indeed, the conflict was in large degree responsible for the subsequent arming, in earnest, of the entire NATO pact.[58] But with respect to Korea itself, the government had decided to increase its contribution by no more than a small and risk-free portion. The five North Stars would not be flying in the combat zone, and of Canadian ground forces there was still no sign. The cost, it seemed, of sending them independently, equipped with their own logistics base, would be unrealistically high. To meet this difficulty, the senior army adviser had suggested dispatching them to the theatre as part of a British Commonwealth division, but thus far no such division was in sight. In any case the available troops were six months short of being combat-ready, and if new units were recruited, their training would take longer still. Above all, to send the currently available Active Force to the Far East would denude entirely Canada's already paltry defences, and just at a time when the importance of retaining such defences seemed greater than on any other occasion since the end of World War II. The conflict with the Soviet bloc was global, and it would never pay to strengthen one sector of the front to the point of incapacitating a more important sector somewhere else. Canada, Mr Pearson had said, could not 'by itself remain secure and at peace in a warring world.'[59] Peace to that extent was indivisible. But by the same token, so, potentially, was any 'communist'-inspired war. The prime minister had called the North Korean aggression 'a breach in the outer defences of the free world,' and each member of the free world had its own responsibilities. Canada's included those of the NATO pact and home defence, as well as those of the United Nations,[60] and it was well in times of crisis to pay due heed to them all – in short, to 'be cool and far-sighted.'

If all this produced a loud and indignant howl from important organs of the press, the government had only itself to blame, for from the beginning it had based its public policy very largely upon the view that the North Korean attack constituted a selective aggression for which the appropriate response was a selective collective security action. Since the United Nations could be effective in this role only to the extent that it received the moral and substantive support of its component members, it was incumbent upon Canada – a loyal and enthusiastic adherent – to play an active part. The difficulty was that the Canadian authorities were not really certain that they could safely regard the

58 Holmes, interview, 1 March 1968; Reid, interview, 9 June 1969; Simonds, interview, 9 June 1970; and others
59 Department of External Affairs, *Statements and Speeches*, no 50/26
60 Ibid., no 50/28

North Korean assault as a merely regional breach of the international peace. It had erupted, after all, in the context of a much larger and far more ominous confrontation, and it followed that no decision relating to it could be taken without considering conditions elsewhere in the world – and closer to home. Hence General Simonds' preoccupation with the possibility that the North Korean attack was a feint designed to draw 'Western' attention and strength away from theatres upon which the Soviets had more serious designs. Hence too the reluctance of Canadian military authorities to contribute to the United Nations action in Korea at the price of weakening their already inconsequential defences in North America. The government's dilemma was that it believed on the one hand that the practice of collective security ought to be upheld, but was uncertain on the other whether this was a situation in which the practice could be safely pursued. The *legal* prerequisites for the initiation of a collective security engagement had obviously been fulfilled – the Security Council had acted in accordance with the provisions of the United Nations Charter.[61] It was on this assumption that the government and its supporting publics had legitimized their entire approach to the war. But the *political* preconditions upon which the actual maintenance of a collective security system depended – notably the unity of the great powers, and their willingness to combine in opposition to an 'aggressor' irrespective of his identity and of the time and place of his aggression – were absent. To act as if they were otherwise seemed at the time dangerous and foolhardy. Thus, the government was in the unhappy position of being morally and politically committed to a course of action which its defence establishment regarded as strategically unwise, given the current level of Canadian military capabilities.

It was therefore not surprising that the prime minister's statement should be regarded in almost every quarter as an outrage. Press and publics from coast to coast fulminated against the government's circumspect response to what was regarded as a fundamental Canadian obligation. At best the reluctance of the authorities in Ottawa to take firm and decisive measures indicated the dire state of disrepair into which the Canadian defence establishment had fallen; at worst it demonstrated Canada's unwillingness to stand behind freely accepted international responsibilities. The *Globe and Mail*, which on 18 July had accused the government of being 'secretive and stupid' in its refusal to give 'an

---

61 Of course the Soviet bloc disputed this contention, and a small body of legal analysis resulted. See, for example, Kunz, 'Legality of the Security Council Resolutions of June 25 and 27, 1950,' 132-42; Potter, 'Legal Aspects of the Situation in Korea,' 709-12; and Yoo, *The Korean War and the United Nations*

accounting of our military strength,' complained now (20 July) of the 'Penalties of Unpreparedness.' Western military planners, the editors observed, 'have been thinking in terms of a struggle with Russia, to be won with atomic bombs and guided missiles. Korea shows that Russian policy is to avoid involving the Soviet Union directly in war while providing satellite armies with the means of subduing and annexing territory. This strategy clearly calls for much greater all-round preparedness than the Western Nations have been buying.' The *Toronto Telegram* warned on the same day that we 'must not be caught again in a state of unpreparedness,' and the Montreal *Gazette* on 21 July ran an editorial to the same effect under the title, 'Korea Shows Us What We Haven't.' The *Winnipeg Free Press* similarly remarked on 4 August that the 'Korean crisis revealed the total inadequacy of our defences like those of the United States and other free nations.' Support for an expansion of Western defence capabilities found vigorous expression in almost every English-language daily from Halifax (*Chronicle-Herald*, 21 July 1950) to Victoria (*Daily Colonist*, 27 July 1950). 'By its carefree holiday spirit in this time of world crisis,' the *Toronto Telegram* complained on 24 July, 'the federal cabinet has displayed a shocking lack of leadership to the country.' The *Telegram*'s editors compared the relaxed summer schedules of Canadian Cabinet ministers unfavourably with the intense activity of political leaders in the United States, and argued the 'need for clear statements of policy and leadership.' The attack was renewed in editorials on 31 July and 2 August.

Even in Quebec there was little editorial opposition to Canadian participation in the United Nations campaign, although most of the French-language newspapers were reasonably satisfied with the programme announced by Mr St Laurent, and refrained from pressing actively for a larger contribution (for example, *Le Canada*, 20 July). Only *Le Devoir* and *Montréal Matin* remained firmly hostile to any form of Canadian military embroilment, and they based their arguments less on principles of isolationism *per se* than on the view that the Western intervention, far from being an exercise in collective security, was really an enterprise in American foreign policy. *Le Devoir*, in particular, took the view that in supporting the United Nations action, which had been possible only because of the absence of the Soviet Union from the Security Council, the government was becoming a slavish supporter of the American role in world affairs. The editorialist, Gerard Filion, advocated the pursuit of a neutralist policy after the pattern of Nehru's India.[62] With these exceptions, however,

---

62 *Le Devoir*, 22 July 1950. See also Soward and McInnis, *Canada and the United Nations*, 126; French-Canadian Observer, 'French-Canadian Opinion on NATO and Korea,' 102-3; and Wood, 'Canadian Foreign Policy and Its Determination During the Korean War,' 45-6. A

the editors of French-language newspapers either supported the government or confined themselves to expressing cautious reservations. Their views therefore did nothing to counterbalance the heavy pressure in favour of greater involvement which was issuing from editorial columns elsewhere in the country.

Meanwhile, the United Nations operation was still receiving the support of the opposition political parties. George Drew of the Progressive Conservatives and M.J. Coldwell of the CCF both issued statements in mid-July in which they gave their sanction to the government's decision to provide naval and air transport assistance. Their remarks, in the enthusiastic view of the *Montreal Star*, proved 'not only to the nation but to the outside world that Canada is united, that no internal dissensions weaken Parliament's possible action.'[63] On 27 July the Annual National Convention of the CCF passed a resolution approving by a vote of 115 to 25 the measures taken by the United Nations Security Council, and pressing the government to dispatch Canadian ground forces to the theatre.[64]

Confronted by so loud a public clamour, the members of the Cabinet might well have reflected upon the irony of their position. Had they maintained a high level of armament in the immediate postwar years, they would have been thought wasteful and immoral; now that they were without such armament at a time of international crisis, they were accused in some quarters of irresponsible incompetence. In the unkindest cut of all, *Saturday Night* was soon to call for the replacement of Mr Claxton, the executor of defence 'consolidation and retrenchment,' by Mr Howe, the 'synonym both here and abroad for driving energy.'[65]

The Canadian officials most closely involved in the decisions of the summer of 1950 seem now to be unanimous in holding the view that such domestic pressures exerted upon the government a permissive rather than a causal influence, although Mr Pearson still recalls the sting of editorial pens.[66] It

systematic discussion of foreign policy attitudes in post-1945 French Canada is contained in Gow, 'Les Québécois, la guerre et la paix, 1945-60,' 88-122. For an analysis of the press, see especially 96-103
63 *Montreal Star*, 19 July 1950
64 'CCF Resolution Asks Canada Join Korean Conflict,' *Globe and Mail*, 28 July 1950. The divisions on this issue within the party's ranks may have been more severe than was suggested by the actual vote. See Wood, 'Canadian Foreign Policy and Its Determination During the Korean War,' 45, n36
65 'Change Needed at Defence,' *Saturday Night*, LXV, 43, 1 Aug. 1950, 5
66 Campbell, interview, 20 Oct. 1968; Heeney, interview, 7 March 1968; Holmes, interview, 1

seems probable, nonetheless, that Cabinet ministers had already begun the nursing of second thoughts, when the news came on 22 July of the death at seventy-six of the Right Honourable W.L. Mackenzie King. It was a small caprice of Canadian history that on the day he died, leaders of opinion among the populace whose isolationist views he had nurtured for so long were clamouring to send troops to an obscure and ugly war in the Far East. It was also a melancholy commentary on the short-lived influence of departed politicians that some of Mr King's former colleagues used the train-ride back to Ottawa from his funeral in Toronto as the occasion to reach agreement on the principle of a Canadian ground force contribution to the conflict in Korea.[67]

The meeting was held in Mr St Laurent's private railway car on 27 July, the day after the British announced their intention of sending a self-contained brigade group to Korea and the Australians made public their decision to contribute a still undetermined quantity of forces on the ground. It began therefore to appear that General Foulkes might not have to wait very long for the formation of his Commonwealth Division. In any case, the ministers without difficulty now agreed in principle to the idea of contributing a Canadian army unit, and much of their discussion was devoted not to the decision itself, but to the question of when it should be announced. Some of those present were in favour of notifying the press immediately, in order thereby to bring an end to domestic criticism. But others argued that no commitment should be made publicly until the Defence Department was ready to supply the precise specifications of the Canadian contingent, and was in a position to indicate in exact terms how it would be raised. Those with the second opinion won the day, and no immediate change in policy was announced.[68]

After the arrival of the train in Ottawa, Mr St Laurent immediately departed to resume his shattered vacation at St Patrice, leaving Mr Pearson to cope with the diplomatic implications of the Cabinet's decision, and to combat the mounting pressure from abroad. The latter had become severe. During the 27 July Cabinet meeting the External Affairs minister had advised his colleagues that the American embassy in Ottawa had delivered a note from Washington asking the Canadian government to supply a brigade group for operations in

March 1968; LePan, interview, 5 March 1968; Pearson, interview, 18 Oct. 1968; Robinson, interview, 5 May 1970; and Simonds, interview, 9 June 1970

67 'Ottawa View,' *Saturday Night*, LXV, 44, 8 Aug. 1950, 2. The meeting was held, however, during the return trip to Ottawa rather than on the way to Toronto, as this story suggests. See Fraser, *The Search for Identity*, 98. Confirmed by Pearson, interview, 18 Oct. 1968

68 Pearson, interview, 18 Oct. 1968; 'Ottawa View,' *Saturday Night*, LXV, 45, 15 Aug. 1950, 2; Robert Taylor, 'Send No Korea Troops Cabinet Decides, Meets on King Funeral Train,' *Toronto Star*, 27 July 1950; and Fraser, *The Search For Identity*, 98-9

the theatre.[69] Since the note had arrived on 26 July, when the Americans were perfectly aware that Ottawa was about to reconsider its position, it had not received a very warm welcome. Mr Acheson was subsequently informed that such interventions were irritating and unnecessary, and as a result of this protest they were discontinued thereafter.[70]

But there were other, somewhat less direct, pressures, many of them by way of example. On 24 July Thailand, as a case in point, had offered a contingent of 4000 men, and the Turks had followed suit on 26 July with a promise of 4500. Somewhat later, on 3 August, the Australians had made more explicit the character of their contribution by announcing that their infantry force in Japan would be fitted for combat and dispatched as soon as possible to the theatre. By then the New Zealanders had also joined the parade, with an undertaking to raise a regiment of field artillery, and on 4 August South Africa announced the contribution of an air fighter squadron replete with ground support. The Panamanians on 7 August offered a corps of volunteers, and on 8 August the Dutch made public a decision to raise two combat companies. Still other offers appeared later in the month.[71]

These embarrassing displays were accompanied not only by the forthright appeals of the American Department of State, but also by the more subtle proddings of officials in Whitehall. On 28 July the chairman of the Canadian Joint Staff in London cabled Ottawa that the War Office had already requested information about the size of the expected Canadian contribution, and on the same day the British liaison officer in Canada made similar inquiries through Major-General H.D. Graham, the Canadian vice chief of the General Staff.[72]

On Saturday, 29 July Mr Pearson flew to Washington and New York for discussions with Acheson, Lie, Wrong, Holmes, and other officials at the State Department and the United Nations.[73] The main purpose of his trip was to advise the American authorities of the plans being developed by the Canadian government, and to discuss in general terms the conditions under which the contingent would be made available. He was anxious in particular to secure guarantees that Canadian troops would not be used in combat before they were adequately trained – there was to be no repetition of Hong Kong – [74] and that

69 Wood, *Strange Battleground*, 22
70 Confidential source
71 Department of External Affairs, *Canada and the Korean Crisis*, 13-4
72 Wood, *Strange Battleground*, 22-3
73 Pearson, interview, 18 Oct. 1968. See also 'The Dominion,' *Time*, Canada edition, LVI, 7, 14 Aug. 1950, 30; and Mr Pearson's report to the House of Commons in Canada, House of Commons, *Debates*, 4 Sept. 1950, 221-2
74 Pearson, interview, 18 Oct. 1968

under no circumstances would they be involved in any way in the defence of Formosa.[75] These assurances were given, and the Americans indicated that the Canadian ground force would be of great value militarily, but more importantly would have enormous significance politically, not least of all within the United States, where public opinion was demanding to know why other countries were giving so little concrete help. They also agreed, after Mr Pearson indicated his annoyance with their previous interventions, not to pester Ottawa again for further military assistance.[76]

Mr Pearson's was not the only temper in the Canadian capital to fray under the weight of external pressures. *Time* magazine in a current issue quoted an irritated official as saying, 'We'll make this decision quite well enough by ourselves,'[77] and even if this was a paraphrase, it gave a fairly accurate portrayal of the atmosphere in the East Block. The government was already committed to making a ground force contribution, and its members needed no further encouragement. Their problems at this stage were entirely instrumental in nature, and it was part of Mr Pearson's task in Washington to obtain information which would help to resolve them. According to the official army historian,

those in authority were finding it difficult to discover just what the United Nations wanted Canada to do. The need for speed was obvious, but this very need would of necessity limit the size of any force Canada might send, since it would have to come from the understrength Mobile Striking Force. The CGS recorded that after further discussions with the Minister and Deputy Minister he was left with the distinct impression that any Canadian contribution would be restricted to a specially organized battalion group. While undertaking to provide such a unit from the Active Force, he continued to recommend the recruitment of a special force, saying he was sure that there were enough people in Canada of the 'soldier of fortune' type to organize at least one brigade. There would have to be a guarantee of service overseas, and a short engagement, say eighteen months, since the Army would not wish to retain this type of soldier on a long term basis. The staff at Army Headquarters was directed to consider the implications of raising such a force.[78]

The idea of sending a small battalion group to show the Canadian flag early in the UN operation was popular among a number of officials in the Depart-

75 Canada, House of Commons, *Debates*, 4 Sept. 1950, 221-2. See also Wood, 'Canadian Foreign Policy and Its Determination During the Korean War,' 46-7
76 Pearson, interview, 18 Oct. 1968
77 'The Dominion,' *Time*, Canada edition, LVI, 7, 14 Aug. 1950, p. 30
78 Wood, *Strange Battleground*, 23

ment of External Affairs.[79] General Foulkes, however, disliked the proposal for three reasons: (1) a battalion is a very small military unit, consisting of about 800 men, and so tiny a force would win little credit for Canada; (2) any such battalion would have to function as part of an American combat team, whereas all the previous experience of the Canadian army had been with the British; and (3) the identity of the Canadians would be lost in a sea of American troops, with the result that there would be no public indication of a uniquely Canadian role. Since the general believed there would be no difficulty in recruiting a special force from the veterans of World War II, he saw no reason for accepting the disadvantages of the battalion alternative, however more readily available it might be.[80]

General Foulkes' directive to Army Headquarters to consider the implications of raising a special force was issued as late as 31 July. In the meantime the politicians continued to suffer from editorial attacks in every sector of the country except French Canada, and even in Quebec there was little evidence that a voluntary ground force commitment would be very vigorously opposed, at least by the daily press. On 3 August, however, the Canadian Institute of Public Opinion released the results of a poll of Canadian attitudes vis-à-vis the Korean War, its first since the start of the hostilities.[81] The poll showed that 75 per cent of the sample interviewed supported the American decision to send both equipment and troops to the Korean theatre, while only 12 per cent disapproved. The remaining 13 per cent were undecided.[82] More important from Ottawa's point of view was the fact that 59 per cent of the sample thought Canada should contribute by sending equipment to the theatre, and 34 per cent favoured a contribution of fighting men. The figures were not high, but on the other hand only 23 per cent of those interviewed were positively opposed to Canada's supplying equipment, and only 39 per cent were against a contribution of both equipment and troops. The remainder held qualified or undecided opinions. In Ontario only 28 per cent signified their opposition to a Canadian contribution of both men and equipment. In Quebec, where the question

---

79 Notably Escott Reid, who recalls 'feeling at the time ... that it was a pity we did not act sooner and send fewer men. My motto in this sort of thing is "Get there fastest, with the fewest". We would have got more credit with the United States for sending a battalion almost immediately than sending a big brigade group after a considerable delay.' Letter to the author, 20 June 1968, and repeated in interview, 9 June 1969
80 Foulkes, interview, 7 March 1968
81 'Special Release,' 3 Aug. 1950
82 A similar poll in the United States found 81 per cent of respondents to be in support of Truman's intervention decisions. See Canadian Institute of Public Opinion, 'Special Release,' 3 Aug. 1950

inevitably raised the spectre of conscription (it was phrased to read, 'Would you approve or disapprove if Canada sent men to fight in the war?' and hence failed to specify how the troops would be raised), the figure was much larger (62 per cent), suggesting that the general public in Quebec was more hostile to Canadian involvement than were the editors of French-language newspapers.[83] Even so, as many as 21 per cent of the Quebec sample were in favour of a contribution of troops, and only 36 per cent were opposed to the possibility of supplying equipment.[84]

A Cabinet meeting was held on the same day these results were released, but it produced no immediate decision. On 4 August, however, the prime minister informed inquiring reporters that they could expect an announcement shortly after the Cabinet ministers who were still on vacation had returned to the capital.[85] The detailed arrangements for the conduct of a recruiting campaign were finally completed on 7 August,[86] and on the same day, a Monday, Prime Minister St Laurent at last announced in an address broadcast over CBC radio that the government had decided to send ground forces to Korea, or at least to raise a special force which would be available for that purpose if required.[87]

The prime minister's speech was a masterly performance in the tradition of the pastor-to-his-flock. 'I would like to talk to you tonight,' he began, 'about recent serious international developments [and] of the relationship of our country to them.' With that he embarked on a simply-phrased resume of Canada's Korean policy. In retrospect, his words highlight very clearly the difficulties of the government's position. The Korean operation was not a war, he declared, but a 'police action intended to prevent war by discouraging aggression.' Hence it had Canada's full support. But the prime minister's accompanying analysis was suggestive more of a conflict of alliance systems than of an exercise in collective policemanship. Both the United Nations and the NATO pact, he said, had been established for the same purpose: 'to avoid

83 For an analysis of this point, see Gow, 'Les Québécois, la guerre et la paix, 1945-60,' especially 114-17
84 Unfortunately the ethnic composition of the Quebec sample is not specified. It is possible that the supporters of a contribution of troops included a substantial number of English-speaking residents of the province.
85 Wood, 'Canadian Foreign Policy and Its Determination During the Korean War,' 48. Among those who were absent were Douglas Abbott, James Gardiner, Alphonse Fournier, Gordon Bradley, and Wishart Robertson. See 'Ottawa View,' *Saturday Night*, LXV, 45, 15 Aug. 1950, 2
86 Wood, *Strange Battleground*, 24
87 The text of the prime minister's address is reproduced in Department of External Affairs, *Canada and the Korean Crisis*, 31-5

war.' The current international situation was like that of the late 1930s, when one 'successful act of Fascist aggression followed another, until the Fascist tide of conquest could be stopped only by a world war.' This must not be allowed to happen again. If 'the Communist aggressors' were stopped in Korea, they might also be discouraged in other theatres.

Yet the Korean action by itself would not be enough. It was a matter of equal urgency 'to make the free world as strong as collective efforts can make it to resist aggression anywhere.' In the Korean theatre the main burden had fallen upon the Americans because they alone had the necessary forces immediately available. Canada had provided three destroyers and later also an RCAF transport squadron, but everyone knew 'that ground forces trained and ready for immediate action' would be helpful. In view of 'other obligations for the employment of Canadian ground forces and the uncertainties of the whole world stituation,' however, the government had earlier concluded that it should not send 'existing first line elements of the Canadian army' to Korea, and this remained its position. Canada's post-war military policy had been designed to provide 'for our immediate territorial defence and for a basic training establishment,' but it had not been aimed at maintaining 'a fully trained expeditionary force available for immediate action outside Canada.' Before 'the aggression in Korea,' moreover, 'no definite plans [had] existed for the creation of a United Nations force,' so that the current action was the UN's 'first effective attempt to organize an international force to stop aggression.'

Given all these circumstances, the government had wondered how it might contribute to the United Nations 'police action' in Korea on the one hand, and to what extent it could increase its 'ability to participate in other common efforts, either under the United Nations Charter or the North Atlantic Treaty' on the other. After considering a number of possibilities, it had decided that its best recourse was to recruit an additional army brigade – the Canadian Army Special Force – to 'be specially trained and equipped ... for use in carrying out Canada's obligations under the United Nations Charter or the North Atlantic Pact.' With 'the approval of Parliament,' the brigade would 'be available for service in Korea as part of United Nations forces, if it [could] be most effectively used in that way when it [was] ready for service.'[88]

The prime minister went on to make an appeal for volunteers – 'young men, physically fit, mentally alert, single or married, particularly, just as many veterans of the Second World War as possible' – and announced that recruit-

---

88 John Holmes advised Trygve Lie officially of the CASF contribution on 14 Aug. 1950. See Department of External Affairs, *Canada and the Korean Crisis*, 35

ment in the three regular services and in the reserves would also be expanded. Production of the new all-weather jet fighter, the 'Canuck' CF-100, would be accelerated, and the first F-86 Sabre jets manufactured in Canada would be tested within a week. Canadian capacity to produce Orenda jet engines would also be increased, as would the manufacture of naval vessels, armament, ammunition, radar equipment, and other military items. In order to maximize Canada's production capabilities, an effort would be made to link Canadian production as fully as possible with that of the United States, and the Joint United States-Canada Industrial Mobilization Planning Committee would meet in Ottawa on the following day to consider this question.[89]

Mr St Laurent reminded his listeners of his promise to recall Parliament in the event further action were needed in Korea or elsewhere, and noted that the expansion and acceleration of the defence programme would require parliamentary action. The members would therefore 'be summoned as soon as it is possible to gather the fuller information and to formulate the specific plans we will wish to lay before [them].' This would probably be in about six or seven weeks, unless international developments made an earlier session necessary. In the meantime the members of the government were doing their 'best to prevent war.'

It was clear from the prime minister's address that the government would continue to hold publicly to its view that the action in Korea comprised the response of a collective security policeman to a breach of the international peace. It was clear also, however, that it believed the Korean challenge to be symptomatic of a far more significant and general threat to the states of the 'free world' than this interpretation, taken by itself, would imply. While the authors of the threat might be chastened and made more circumspect by a rebuff in Korea, that by itself would not deter them. Hence, while it was both wise and virtuous to fight for the United Nations cause everywhere, it was both necessary and prudent to look to one's own safety first: security, like charity, begins at home. In making a contribution to the battle in Korea, therefore, it was important to undertake a more general review of Canadian defence policy and where necessary to expand the size and effectiveness of Canada's military establishment. Korea had shown that the world was unsafe for democracy, and even if the democrats won the skirmish, the war – however cold – would still be on.

On the whole, this was received with immense satisfaction by the writers of newspaper editorials. A few – for example, the *Montreal Star* on 8 August

---

89 The American delegation comprised Stuart Symington, chairman of the United States National Security Resources Board, and Hubert E. Howard, chairman of the United States Munitions Board. See 'Ottawa View,' *Saturday Night*, LXV, 43, 1 Aug. 1950, 2

and the *Calgary Herald* on 9 August – complained that the Special Force was too modest a contribution and that it had come too late. Some thought, too, that it was unwise to recruit the Canadian contingent on a 'Special Force' basis, arguing that this would have a detrimental effect upon the morale and prestige of the regular Active Force.[90] The Montreal *Gazette* (8 August) pointed out that the prime minister's speech had revealed – as indeed it had – how ill-equipped were the Canadian armed forces to cope with the challenges of the era. Such observations, however, were mustered in most cases for the purpose of defending the government's plans for rearmament. Even the newspapers of French Canada, with the notable exception of *Le Devoir* (8 August 1950), offered their support, albeit with varying degrees of enthusiasm. In general, therefore, the Cabinet could now look forward to a period of domestic political relief, and the community of foreign policy decision-makers could turn its full attention to the intricacies of international politics.

90 For example, the *Globe and Mail* on 9 August and the *Toronto Telegram* of the same day. The *Globe and Mail* had first raised this objection as early as 31 July.

4

Containing America

On 7 August 1950 the Canadian Joint Chiefs of Staff were in receipt of Order-in-Council PC 3860/50 commanding them to establish a Canadian Army Special Force of brigade strength for service overseas. General Foulkes accordingly embarked upon his search for Canadian 'soldiers of fortune' who were prepared to fight under the banner of the United Nations in defence of their country, their allies, and the principle of 'collective security.' He was to encounter in the course of this undertaking a considerable battery of tribulations,[1] but with the general's hardships the politicians were not primarily concerned. While the army dealt feverishly with the military consequences of the government's decision, the ministers of the crown could bask for a time in its political rewards – and contemplate, no doubt, its diplomatic implications.

For Canadian diplomatists the most significant feature of the government's decision to send ground forces to Korea was that it made more urgent the need to strengthen and to emphasize the 'collective' element in the United Nations role in the conflict. John Spanier's view that 'the Korean War was undertaken by the United States and her allies to protect their *selective security*, to preserve the global balance of power against the Soviet Union, and to prevent the disintegration of ... the North Atlantic Alliance'[2] is convincing as far as it goes, but in the Canadian as in other cases the moral and political legitimacy of the operation had been founded upon the fact that it was to be conducted under

1 See Chapter 6
2 Spanier, *Truman-MacArthur Controversy*, 38-9 (italics his)

United Nations auspices. Even with the authority of the Security Council's resolutions behind it, the Canadian government had mustered its substantive contribution with obvious caution, and the pace of its decisions had been quickened only under serious internal and external pressure. If the United Nations had not become involved in the confrontation, it seems probable that the Department of National Defence would still have undertaken a reassessment of its military capabilities, and that in the light of its findings it would have endorsed the need for an increased armed forces establishment. But whether it also would have provided a military contingent for action in Korea – simply because on the one hand the enemy was a Soviet satellite, and on the other the United States was an ally of Canada in theatres elsewhere in the world – is much more open to doubt. In any case, Ottawa placed a higher value upon the defence of the 'free world' in Europe and in North America than in the Far East, and now that Canada was embroiled militarily in such a remote quarter of the globe, it had become very much a part of the national interest to limit as fully as possible the intensity, duration, and territorial scope of the hostilities. In concrete terms, this meant (a) limiting the conduct of the war to the Korean peninsula; (b) making every effort to prevent the allies of North Korea – notably Communist China – from being driven by strategic or other considerations to participate in the hostilities; (c) ensuring in particular that the question of Formosa did not become linked to the outcome of the conflict in Korea; and (d) concluding at the earliest possible opportunity a satisfactory cease-fire in the theatre.

Because the United Nations effort in the war was so totally dominated by the United States, and because many influential Americans – among them the United Nations commander – regarded the conflict in global strategic and ideological terms, favouring a now-or-never, all-or-nothing approach to its resolution, the obstacles in the way of achieving these objectives were bound on the allied side to emanate from the American authorities. It followed that if Canadian diplomats wished to guide the development of 'United Nations' policy in Korea in the direction of their own limited goals, they had to sway the opinions of decision-makers in Washington. Given the comparative modesty of the Canadian military contribution to the war, however, there was little likelihood that Ottawa could exert by itself much influence within the American capital. If, on the other hand, the United Nations were to play an active role in the formulation of the relevant decisions, the possibility of success would be substantially improved, for the organization's other members (the Soviet bloc aside) tended to share Ottawa's limited view of the UN's proper role in the conflict, and could be expected to join in the task of restraining the Americans.

Canadian policy-makers therefore had three reasons for maximizing United Nations authority in the conduct of the war, the first idealistic, the second political, and the third diplomatic and military. The idealistic reason was that they hoped that the UN response to the North Korean attack could be shaped into a genuine example of collective security enforcement, thereby strengthening the collective security principle. The political reason was that if the authority of the United Nations in the crisis could be clearly established and maintained, it would reinforce at home the legitimacy of the Canadian military contribution. The diplomatic and military reason was that a dominant United Nations role would have the effect of strengthening Canadian influence over the conduct and purposes of the hostilities and thereby reduce, in the Canadian view, the danger of uncontrolled military escalation.

Given the fortuitous conditions under which the Security Council had originally been able to act, and given also the fact that the military operations in Korea were conducted by powers which in effect were allies of the United States, the first of these objectives was totally unrealistic, and reflected a failure to recognize the political conditions upon which a system of collective security must rest. The United Nations campaign in Korea was bound to be *sui generis,* and the hope of making it otherwise was soon abandoned by Canadian officials, although it remained for some time a part of their rhetoric.

By contrast, the second objective met with spectacular success. With a very few exceptions – notably the editors of *Le Devoir* – attentive Canadian publics continued to regard the war as a justifiable exercise in international policemanship and to be proud of Canada's participation in it.

With respect to the third, the government ultimately was able to argue that the war had indeed been limited, although not as fully as it had originally hoped. While allied diplomatic ministrations, including those of Canada, may have contributed to this outcome, however, the most significant sources of restraint upon American policy were located within Washington itself, and not at Lake Success or in foreign capitals. A by-product of the diplomacy by which the Canadian government pursued this objective, on the other hand, was that it not infrequently disturbed the quiet harmony which normally prevailed over Canadian-American relations.

The government's preoccupation with the problem of establishing a degree of multilateral control over American policy had been reflected in its objections to the wording of the Security Council resolution of 7 July, which authorized the Americans to organize the United Nations Command. The fears of Canadian officials were not allayed by the ensuing forays of the UN commander into international (and domestic) politics. As Supreme Commander for Allied

Powers (SCAP) in Japan, MacArthur 'was solely responsible for the implementation of allied occupation policy,' which meant in turn that he 'was the real ruler of 83,000,000 Japanese.'[3] His office was the source of considerable inconvenience to the representatives of Canada and other powers interested in the Korean crisis even before his appointment to the UN Command. The head of the Canadian Liaison Mission in Tokyo, E.H. Norman, complained to Ottawa a full ten days after the North Korean invasion had begun that he was still unable to reach the general to obtain a first-hand report on what was happening in Korea, and other allied diplomats were having the same difficulty.[4]

The fact that Canadian officials were concerned from the beginning about American policy in the Far East explains not only their suggestions for modifications of the 7 July resolution of the Security Council, but also Mr Pearson's insistence upon obtaining assurances, when he visited Washington at the end of July, that Canada's military contingent would not be involved in the defence of Formosa. Earlier in the month, on 19 July, President Truman had delivered a message to Congress explaining his response to the North Korean attack, and in it he had expressed his desire to ensure that Formosa did 'not become embroiled in hostilities disturbing to the peace of the Pacific and that all questions affecting Formosa be settled by peaceful means as envisaged in the Charter of the United Nations.' But Mr Pearson had been only partially satisfied, for the president had gone on to add that with 'peace reestablished, even the most complex political questions are susceptible of solution. In the presence of brutal and unprovoked aggression, however, some of these questions may have to be held in abeyance in the interest of the essential security of all.'[5] These remarks implied that the settlement of the dispute over Formosa was not unrelated to the resolution of the conflict in Korea, and this was precisely the impression that Ottawa wished to avoid.[6]

3 Ibid., 65
4 Confidential source. Admiral Brock, who had better luck, now recalls that in Tokyo MacArthur 'appeared to be a god; not to be *like* a god, but to *be* a god.' The veneration and awe with which the general was regarded were the result of 'an attitude of mind which had prevailed there for many years.' He was surrounded by 'soul-less figures, who were themselves part of the myth,' (interview, 23 July 1969). This view was shared by Dean Acheson, among others. Acheson records in his memoirs that General Marshall once told him of a conference he had had with MacArthur during World War II, 'at which the latter began a sentence with the phrase, "My staff tells me ... " General Marshall interrupted him, saying, "General, you don't have a staff; you have a court" ' (*Present at the Creation*, 424)
5 United States, Department of State, *Department of State Bulletin*, XXIII, 578, 31 July 1950, 166
6 Pearson, interview, 18 Oct. 1968

Mr Pearson had received his assurances in Washington at the end of July, but his anxieties soon returned. Just two days before his arrival in the American capital the Joint Chiefs of Staff had recommended at a meeting of the National Security Council that the United States provide extensive aid to the Chinese Nationalists in order to increase their capacity to cope with an attack by the mainland regime. As a result of this recommendation President Truman had 'approved three specific proposals: the granting of extensive military aid to Nationalist China; a military survey by MacArthur's headquarters of the requirements of Chiang Kai-shek's forces; and the plan to carry out reconnaissance flights along the China coast to determine the imminence of attacks against Formosa.[7] General MacArthur had suggested earlier that he himself might make the visit to Taipeh, but in relaying to Tokyo the decisions taken at the 27 July meeting, the joint chiefs advised him to send a senior officer instead, since the State Department was still worried about the political repercussions of placing the Seventh Fleet in the Formosa Strait. The advice was ignored, and on 31 July the general flew to Taipeh in the company of Generals Almond, Whitney, Willoughby, and Stratemeyer.[8]

The resulting talks with Chiang Kai-shek were more than amicable, and when MacArthur returned to Japan he released a statement expressing his admiration for the Nationalist leader's 'indomitable determination to resist Communist domination,' and suggesting that it paralleled 'the common interests and purpose of Americans, that all people in the Pacific should be free – not slaves.'[9] This view of the outcome of the meeting was confirmed by Chiang Kai-shek himself, who announced on 1 August that the conference had laid the groundwork for the joint defence of the island, and praised General MacArthur 'for his determined leadership in the common fight against totalitarianism in Asia and for his deep understanding of the menace of communism.'[10]

These declarations received considerable attention in Canadian as well as foreign newspapers, and the Canadian secretary of state for external affairs began now to follow the general's exploits with increasing dismay. It was a measure of the government's anxiety that shortly after this incident Mr Wrong was instructed to raise with the State Department the possibility of their establishing a separate command in charge of the defence of Formosa. This,

7 Truman, *Years of Trial and Hope*, 397
8 Rees, *Korea: The Limited War*, 73
9 Quoted in Spanier, *Truman-MacArthur Controversy*, 71
10 Quoted ibid.

it was argued, would substantially reduce the danger of the China question becoming embroiled in Korea.[11]

Nothing came of the suggestion, and Mr Pearson's confidence was not improved when General MacArthur on 10 August issued still another statement reiterating his conviction that the discussions with Chiang Kai-shek had been 'limited entirely to military matters' and 'had no connection with political affairs.' The general complained that the visit to Taipeh had 'been maliciously misrepresented to the public by those who invariably in the past have propagandized a policy of defeatism and appeasement in the Pacific.'[12]

From the point of view of America's NATO allies, these were bleak and ominous sentiments, coming as they did from the commander of the United Nations forces in Korea. Mr Pearson felt the need to add to the private exhortations of Hume Wrong[13] a mild public rebuke. He did so in an address in Victoria, BC, on 21 August:

In order to get the strong and vigorous support of free Asia for United Nations action in Korea, and, indeed, for United Nations action wherever aggression has to be met, we must also continue to emphasize that the United Nations, in its recent decisions, is concerned only in defeating aggression in Korea, and is not concerned, for instance, with the re-conquest by the National Chinese Government in Formosa of the mainland of China. There is nothing that the USSR would like better than to confuse the Korean and Formosan issues.[14] There is nothing that the democracies should be more careful to avoid than such confusion. If we do not, we play right into the hands of the communist propagandists, make anxious and uneasy those who wish to maintain a strong and united front against aggression in Korea.[15]

Mr Pearson might have taken some comfort from the fact that the Truman administration was no less alarmed than he. As early as 3 August Truman had dispatched Averell Harriman to Tokyo to discuss the government's Far East

---

11 Pearson, interview, 18 Oct. 1968; confirmed by Geoffrey A.H. Pearson after reference to his father's personal notes, interview, 18 Oct. 1968

12 Quoted in MacArthur, *Reminiscences*, 386

13 In this period the State Department was receiving repeated pleas from Ottawa to make more explicit the separation of the Korean and Formosan affairs. Pearson, interview, 18 Oct. 1968. At one stage Mr Wrong exclaimed in exasperation to a colleague, 'I can't see the Secretary of State every day!' Holmes, interview, 1 March 1968

14 The USSR was attempting to do precisely this in the Security Council throughout the month of August, and the potential effectiveness of their arguments had been a matter of considerable concern to Canadian officials. Pearson, interview, 18 Oct. 1968

15 Department of External Affairs, *Statements and Speeches*, 50/31

policy with MacArthur. On his return, Harriman had filed what Dean Acheson has since described as 'an ambivalent report.'[16] 'For reasons which are rather difficult to explain,' he wrote, 'I did not feel that we came to a full agreement on the way we believed things should be handled on Formosa and with the Generalissimo.' MacArthur would act according to the president's wishes, 'but without full conviction.' He had 'a strange idea that we should back anybody who will fight communism.'

In defending the president's position, Mr Harriman had deployed an argument which shows in retrospect that the restraints imposed by allied powers on the conduct of American policy, however irritating in other contexts, were sometimes useful to the Washington administration in its negotiations with the field commander. According to his report, he 'explained in great detail why Chiang was a liability, and the great danger of a split in the unity of the United Nations on the Chinese-Communist-Formosa policies; the attitude of the British, Nehru and such countries as Norway, who, although stalwart in their determination to resist Russian aggression, did not want to stir up trouble elsewhere. I pointed out the great importance of maintaining UN unity among the friendly countries, and the complications that might result from any missteps in dealing with China and Formosa.' MacArthur, however, had not appeared to recognize all the difficulties.[17]

Harriman's uncertainty notwithstanding, Truman was 'reassured' by the report, and to 'make doubly sure' he approved on 14 August a Joint Chiefs of Staff directive to the general limiting United States action in the defence of Formosa 'to such support operations as would be practicable without committing any forces to the island itself.' He then 'assumed that this would be the last of it.'[18] It was a false assumption. On 17 August MacArthur was asked to send a statement to be read to the annual convention of the Veterans of Foreign Wars, scheduled for 28 August. He took the opportunity, 'as a matter of routine,' to express his 'personal opinion of the strategic importance of Formosa and its relation to our defensive position in the Pacific.' There was, he wrote later, 'nothing political in it.'[19]

16 Acheson, *Present at the Creation*, 422
17 For the text of Harriman's report, see Truman, *Years of Trial and Hope*, 397-403. Harriman's reference to the need to maintain allied unity was matched on MacArthur's side with a demand that the allies should enlarge their contributions to the conduct of the war. The general, Harriman reported, 'feels the British should send a brigade from Hong Kong or Malaya; thinks it could be replaced from the United Kingdom. The French could send some forces from Indochina. A brigade from Pakistan and Turkey would be most welcome. Canada should send some troops ... ' Ibid., 399-400
18 Ibid., 404
19 MacArthur, *Reminiscences*, 387

The general's conception of the 'political' was somewhat eccentric, to say the least. His statement argued that the retention of Formosa in non-communist hands was essential to the maintenance of American security in the Far East, and that if the island fell to Peking, the defences of the United States would be driven back to the American coast. In such a case, war would be 'inevitable': 'Nothing could be more fallacious than the threadbare argument by those who advocate appeasement and defeatism in the Pacific that if we defend Formosa we alienate continental Asia. Those who speak thus do not understand the Orient. They do not grasp that it is in the pattern of the Oriental psychology to respect and to follow aggressive, resolute and dynamic leadership ... '[20]

President Truman first heard of this new pronouncement on 26 August, two days before its scheduled delivery, but by then it was too late to prevent its publication in the press, which had been issued advance release copies. 'The damage,' Truman wrote later, 'had been done.' MacArthur's statement

could only serve to confuse the world as to just what our Formosa policy was, for it was at odds with my announcement of June 27 ... There can be only one voice in stating the position of this country in the field of foreign relations. This is of fundamental constitutional significance. General MacArthur, in addition to being an important American commander, was also the United Nations commander in Korea. He was, in fact, acting for and on behalf of the United Nations. That body was then debating the question of Formosa, and its members – even those outside the Soviet bloc – differed sharply in their views regarding Formosa. It was hardly proper for the UN's agent to argue a case then under discussion by that body.[21]

The administration's embarrassment was accentuated by the fact that 'only the day before Ambassador Austin had restated to Trygve Lie, Secretary General of the United Nations, the limited purposes of our action regarding Formosa.'[22] The general's message accordingly was discussed in a meeting of the National Security Council, and the upshot was a curt order that the statement be withdrawn on the ground that its 'various features with respect to Formosa are in conflict with the policy of the United States and its position in the United Nations.' Truman gave 'serious thought' to relieving MacArthur of his responsibilities for Korea and Formosa, but eventually decided that this would be unnecessarily harsh.[23]

20 Quoted in Spanier, *Truman-MacArthur Controversy*, 74
21 Truman, *Years of Trial and Hope*, 404-5
22 Acheson, *Present at the Creation*, 423
23 Truman, *Years of Trial and Hope*, 405-6. For an account of this meeting, see also Acheson,

In the meantime, the suspicions and anxieties of the allies had once again been aroused, and Mr Wrong was among those who filed representations with the State Department. Mr Pearson and his senior advisers in the Department of External Affairs by now had become genuinely alarmed,[24] and their unease was to intensify in subsequent weeks. Even those allied diplomats who cared little about the substance of the issue could reflect upon the fact that their already meagre influence in Washington would become a diminishing asset should the Truman administration lose control over the actions of the senior commander in the field.

The authority of the United Nations was threatened in addition by the return to the Security Council on 1 August of Yakov Malik, the representative of the USSR, whose turn it was to preside for a month-long period over the council's proceedings. It was a wretched month:

Although thirteen out of a total of fourteen sessions held in August were devoted to the question of Korea, the Security Council became so entangled in procedural discussions that no substantive resolutions were approved despite constant pressure by the majority and a stream of reports from the Commander-in-Chief of the United Nations Command in Korea (MacArthur), indicating continued if slower advances of North Korean forces. Four sessions were needed to adopt the agenda, eight for arguments as to whether the representative of the Republic of Korea (Chang) – who had participated in the discussions during June and July – should be seated, and two more sessions to decide whether the Council should place on the agenda a complaint by the People's Republic of China that the United States had invaded Formosa.[25]

The precise record of this desultory performance has been summarized elsewhere,[26] and the details in the present context are unimportant. That the Soviet Union was opposed to the United Nations action in Korea had been obvious from the beginning; that its delegate to the United Nations would attempt to obstruct the council's proceedings was natural in the light of the

Present at the Creation, 423-4. The secretary of defense, Louis Johnson, was reluctant to issue the order, apparently because he was fearful of the general's reaction. At one stage he asked Acheson whether they 'dare' send it.

24 Campbell, interview, 20 Oct. 1968; Heeney, interview, 7 March 1968; Pearson, interview, 18 Oct. 1968. For allied reaction generally, see Spanier, *Truman-MacArthur Controversy*, 76

25 'International Organizations: Summary of Activities,' *International Organization*, IV, 4, Nov. 1950, 631

26 Ibid. See also Department of External Affairs, 'The Korean Crisis,' *External Affairs*, II, 9, Sept. 1950, 319-25

USSR's interpretation of its national interest. The experience nevertheless drove home the fact that the response to the North Korean invasion was an enterprise in 'collective security' only in form. Its political reality was that it was an act of containment initiated by western allies under the leadership of the United States. Only through fortuitous circumstances had the American government managed to acquire for its decisions the official stamp of United Nations approval. Except as a place for marshalling friends and irritating enemies, the United Nations as a collective body was not in itself a significant actor in the crisis. No 'United Nations tags or flags could cover up the stark fact of American aggression in Korea,' Malik argued in the Security Council in August,[27] and beneath the rhetoric could be discerned a valid case. Aside from permitting Mr Malik to issue such remarks, as the Department of External Affairs ruefully observed,

The Soviet return to the Security Council had also served several subsidiary purposes of Soviet policy: the striking unity which the free world had displayed in the early stages of the Korean crisis had been broken several times during the lengthy Security Council debates. A dangerous attempt had been made to drive a wedge between the countries which had recognized Communist China and those which had not. And to add to the problems thus created, the Soviet Union, by returning to the Security Council, had served notice that the Council's difficulties in dealing with any future Communist aggression would be substantially increased.[28]

In the meantime Mr Malik was making it very difficult for the United Nations to maintain even the appearance of control over American policy in the Korean theatre. Allied diplomatists, Canadians among them, could still remonstrate with American officials in the lounges, corridors, and dining rooms of their profession, but the fiction of 'collective security' which in Canada had made a virtue of the South Korean cause was nevertheless in danger of being exposed. In the same 21 August speech in which by implication he had chastised the UN commander for his ill-chosen interventions in politics, Mr Pearson felt obliged to answer the Soviet case:

The communists will try to represent anything the United Nations does now in Korea as assistance to American imperialists against an Asian people struggling to be free. Mr. Malik is already doing his vicious best at Lake Success, through this technique of the big and constantly repeated lie, to create this fiction. With devilish ingenuity and

27 Quoted in Department of External Affairs, ibid., 322
28 Ibid., 322

energy worthy of a better cause, this 'big lie' is being drummed into the minds of the Asian millions day and night, and may have some success. The fact is that in Korea, we are not helping the United States. The United States itself has been the first country to insist on this. We are discharging our obligation as a member of the United Nations in defence of peace. The Canadian Government has been determined from the beginning to make this principle the basis of its policy in respect of Korea.

The government had taken this position partly 'to make it clear to the Asian people that this conflict is not one of the East versus the West; the white man against the yellow man.' Rather, it was 'the rallying of all those from all the free world – East *and* West – who would defend peace against an aggressor, and who are determined to make it clear in quarters where it needs to be made clear, that aggression does not pay.'[29]

Canada, then, had been discharging an 'obligation as a member of the United Nations in defence of peace.' All the more embarrassing, therefore, to discover that the return of the Soviet Union to the Security Council, together with the disproportionate and not always predictable role played in the crisis by the United States, had converted the UN organization into a largely innocuous arena in which the deadlocked diplomats of the great powers could do little more than conduct a propaganda war. In view of this embarrassment, Canada's support for Mr Acheson's Uniting for Peace Resolution later in the year is easily understood, but in the meantime, with the opposing armies locked in stalemate around the perimeter of Pusan, and with the remedies of diplomacy exhausted, Mr Pearson could do little but continue to propagate the ideology of Canada's commitment.[30]

But if wars are sometimes bad for diplomacy, they are often good for business, and from the perspective of businessmen not all the events of August were so gloomily unproductive as those in the Security Council. In North America the stimulus to industry that flows from the expansion of armed forces results not merely from the placing of defence orders *per se*, but also from the rationalization of productive effort. More specifically, the governments of Canada and the

---

29 Department of External Affairs, *Statements and Speeches*, 50/31
30 He may have been enjoying moderate success. A release of the Canadian Institute of Public Opinion on 23 August showed that 36 per cent of an interview sample were 'satisfied' with 'progress made to date by the United Nations,' as compared with 30 per cent in July 1949. In the same period, however, those who were 'dissatisfied' also increased – from 19 per cent to 24 per cent. Only those falling into the category of 'Not Familiar' and 'No Opinion' decreased as a proportion of the total, from 51 per cent to 40 per cent. The war in Korea was dealing a blow at least to indifference.

United States, when confronted by common external enemies, are prone to shedding parts, at least, of the apparatus of peacetime protectionism in order to make the most efficient use of their combined productive capacities. The consequences in terms of continental economic integration can sometimes be profound. In announcing on 7 August the government's plans for increasing general expenditures on defence, Mr St Laurent had indicated that the Joint Industrial Mobilization Planning Committee of Canada and the United States would meet in Ottawa on the following day to discuss the co-ordination of defence production. Stuart Symington and Hubert E. Howard, the chairmen respectively of the United States National Security Resources Board and of the United States Munitions Board, duly arrived in the Canadian capital for negotiations with government officials. Their deliberations, stimulated by a new conflict, were part of an old tradition. It had begun with an agreement concluded by Mackenzie King and Franklin D. Roosevelt at Hyde Park in April 1941, which had provided for American purchases of military commodities in Canada as a means of countering the wartime drain upon the Canadian store of American dollars. It also laid the foundation for the co-ordination of Canadian-American defence production programmes, and by the end of World War II orders approximating one and a quarter billion dollars had been placed in Canada by the United States.[31] An exchange of notes in May 1945 had provided for the extension of the principles of the Hyde Park declaration to cover the period of transition from wartime to peacetime economic activity, but the agreement had had little practical significance. As late as 3 February 1948 the secretary of state for external affairs, Louis St Laurent, was unaware even of its existence.[32]

With the beginning of modest rearmament programmes later in the year, however, the possibility of deriving real advantage from a renewal of the practice of co-ordination once again became obvious, and in June the two governments agreed that they 'should exchange information on problems of mutual interest concerning the industrial mobilization planning activities of the two countries.' Ten months later this general principle received institutional expression in the form of an exchange of notes establishing a Joint United States-Canada Industrial Mobilization Planning Committee. There followed several months of administrative exploration of the possibilities for defence production co-ordination, accompanied by high-level Canadian lobbying for

---

31 See Pickersgill, *Mackenzie King Record.* I: *1939–1944*, 180-204; McLin, *Canada's Changing Defense Policy*, 174; and Dziuban, *Military Relations Between the United States and Canada*, 292
32 'North American Defense: Coordination in Canada and the USA,' 329

American contracts. The latter enterprise bore modest fruit in May 1950, when the American secretary of defense, Louis Johnson, advised Mr Claxton that he would spend between $15 million and $25 million on defence orders in Canada during the 1950-1 fiscal year.[33]

With the outbreak of the war in Korea, the problems of defence production acquired a new urgency, and it was with this in mind that the committee held its second meeting in Ottawa on 8 August 1950. It was there decided 'that studies should be made of the basic industrial programmes of the two countries and of the steps necessary to meet the production and supply requirements involved.' It was also agreed that the two countries would 'establish a set of principles which would define and motivate the joint use of materials and resources by Canada and the United States.'[34]

The immediate consequence of this agreement was an exchange of notes signed by Hume Wrong and Dean Acheson in Washington on 20 October 1950 and released to the press six days later. The notes signified the approval of the two governments of a 'Statement of Principles for Economic Cooperation,' which reaffirmed the general concepts embodied in the Hyde Park Declaration of 1941, and went on to say that for the purpose of achieving 'an optimum production of goods essential for the common defence, the two countries [would] develop a co-ordinated programme of requirements, production and procurement.' As necessary, and after appropriate consultation in each case, they would 'institute co-ordinated controls over the distribution of scarce raw materials and supplies.' There would be free exchange, 'where feasible,' of 'technical knowledge and productive skills' in the affected fields. Such barriers as impeded 'the flow between Canada and the United States of goods essential for the common defence effort' would, 'as far as possible,' be removed, and the appropriate government agencies would 'consult concerning any financial or foreign exchange problems' arising from the implementation of the agreement.[35]

The concrete results of these arrangements were substantial, although they were not in the early years sufficient to offset entirely Canada's deficit in defence commodity trade with the United States. During the early phase this was due largely to the fact that Canadian industry lacked the capacity to take advantage of the American market potential, a problem which C.D. Howe's Department of Defence Production, established early in 1951, did much to

33 Ibid., 330-2
34 Department of External Affairs, 'Joint Canada-United States Industrial Mobilization Planning Committee,' *External Affairs*, III, 1, Jan. 1951, 21
35 Department of External Affairs, 'Canada-United States Economic Co-operation,' *External Affairs*, II, 11, Nov. 1950, 414-15

resolve. Nevertheless, the imbalance continued for some time even after the war in Korea was over, when the volume of trade diminished in both directions as a result of reduced political incentive.[36] Between 1 April 1951, when the new department first began to keep records, and 31 December 1952, American defence purchases in Canada amounted to approximately $300 million, but Canada in the same period spent a corresponding $857 million in the United States.[37] In 1953, the net value of American prime defence contracts and subcontracts placed in Canada dropped to $47.8 million, and in 1954 it fell to $19.2 million. Thereafter it fluctuated at comparatively low levels: $28.5 million in 1955, $20.5 million in 1956, $58.7 million in 1957, and $37.9 million in 1958.[38] Canadian purchases in the United States did not again rise to the heights of 1951-2, and they declined substantially after 1954. They totalled $61.3 million in 1953, $110.6 million in 1954, $16.2 million in 1955, $2.0 million in 1956, $34.8 million in 1957, and $10.0 million in 1958.[39] Thereafter, the system was replaced by the more elaborate Defence Production Sharing Agreement negotiated by the Diefenbaker government.

Canadian nationalists might now complain of the implications of these arrangements for their country's independence, and opponents of American foreign policy would doubtless quarrel with the links they established with the Washington defence community. But at a time when American economic largesse was highly coveted in Canada, and when Canadians and Americans were in basic accord on the fundamental issues of world politics, there was little opposition to such rational utilization of the continent's defence production capacity. Indeed, given the 'buy American' propensities of politically sensitive Congressmen, the agreement constituted a considerable achievement for Canadian diplomacy, and the communications media of the business community were not displeased. The editors of *The Financial Post*, motivated, one suspects, by a mixture of avarice and patriotism, had demanded of the government in August 1950 that it 'Let Industry Know Its Defense Job.' Time was being lost because Canadian industries were ignorant of what would be expected of them in the forthcoming rearmament programme. The Joint Industrial Mobilization Planning Committee was therefore importuned to decide quickly

36 McLin, *Canada's Changing Defense Policy*, 175-6
37 Calculated from data presented to the House of Commons by the minister of defence production, Raymond O'Hurley. See Canada, House of Commons, *Debates*, 28 January 1960, 456. See also McLin, *Canada's Changing Defense Policy*, 175
38 See 'Summary of Production Sharing Type United States Contracts and Subcontracts Placed in Canada, 1953 – 1959,' in Canada, House of Commons, *Debates*, 9 Feb. 1960, 916
39 Compiled from the annual *Reports* of the Department of Defence Production, appropriate years.

upon the kinds of equipment that would be required, and to make available 'specific "get-ready" assignments for specific plants.'[40] Within a month the same journal, in a story headed 'Looking for Defense Orders? Here's What to Expect, How You Can Sell to Ottawa,' was offering advice to its readers on the procedure for submitting tenders for the supply of war materiel.[41] Thereafter, the *Post*'s editors confined themselves to expressions of the need for an even greater rationalization of Canadian-American defence production, and to descriptions of the horrific results that would ensue should the government attempt to infringe upon the free enterprise of defence commodity producers.[42]

The initial decisions upon which the new-found treasure of Canadian industry was based were approved by Parliament in a session which began on 29 August 1950, and which gave Mr Pearson an opportunity once again to publicize his government's concept of its role in the Korean War. Thanks largely to the aspirations of Canada's non-operating railway workers, who were on strike, the members were summoned, as the Throne Speech put it, 'to meet somewhat earlier than was anticipated.'[43] Professor W.E.C. Harrison remarked some years later that in 'view of the danger we were in that summer, the judgement of History may be harsh on the principals in that ill-timed [railway] dispute.'[44] In retrospect it hardly appears that Canadian security was in so dire a condition as this prognostication would suggest. But Parliament, in any case, assembled on 29 August for a Special Session which was to last for two and one-half weeks, and the secretary of state for external affairs had access once again to an important public forum.

He made good use of it. The Speech from the Throne had informed the members that they would 'be asked to give urgent consideration to the measures for increased national security and international co-operation required by the fighting in Korea and the increasingly grave international situation which that struggle reflects,' and on Friday, 31 August Mr Pearson delivered so forceful a survey of foreign affairs that he stunned both politicians and press. The themes, however, were old. He began with an assessment of the 'world-

---

40 'The Nation's Business: Let Industry Know Its Defense Job,' *Financial Post*, 5 Aug. 1950

41 Ibid., 2 Sept. 1950

42 See 'The Nation's Business: Not Time Yet for Controls,' ibid., 3 March 1951; 'No Need Yet for Desperate Measures,' ibid., 31 March 1951; and 'The Nation's Business: Did Well to Resist This Clamor ... ,' ibid., 14 April 1951

43 Canada, House of Commons, *Debates*, 29 Aug. 1950, 4

44 Harrison, *Canada in World Affairs*, 269. The strike created problems for the army in handling recruits for the CASF. See Wood, *Strange Battleground*, 31-2

wide scale' of 'soviet communist imperialism,' and drew once again the conclusion that while the focus of the conflict was now in Korea, there were 'other
critical points where the flames may break out.' Military aggression, moreover,
was not Soviet communism's only weapon; it employed 'conspiracy, subver-
sion and mass agitation,' too, feeding on the misery of those who lived 'in
distress and privation, offering them the hope of a better life.' It followed that
'the west, while laying bare the trickery and malice of soviet protestations,
must at the same time provide some real satisfaction for those everlasting
hungers for bread, security and freedom to which the communists pretend to
cater.'

The minister went on to review at some length the course of post-1945
Korean history and to dismiss the Soviet allegation that the conflict had begun
with an aggression by South Korea against the North. The truth was otherwise, and Canada's 'obligation under the Charter of the United Nations' was
clear. That obligation, however, was 'to the United Nations alone, and to our
own security.' It concerned 'nothing beyond the restoration of peace and the
defeat of aggression in Korea.' The government in the early days of the crisis
had pressed very hard for the principle of a unified command operating under
United Nations auspices, and had 'welcomed' the resolution of 7 July 'because
it established the United Nations character' of the enterprise 'without limiting
unduly the military authority which any commander must have if he is to be
successful.'

This expression of satisfaction with the July resolution did not entirely
square with Mr Pearson's reservations at the time, but in any case he now went
on to outline the steps Canada had taken thereafter in fulfilment of the government's obligations. One of the reasons Parliament had been called into session
was to make good Mr St Laurent's 30 June pledge to summon the House if
additional measures were necessary. In the meantime the United States, as the
only non-communist power with a substantial military establishment in the
Far East, had shouldered on UN authority 'the chief responsibility, outside that
of South Korea itself, for repelling the North Korean forces.' The possession
of mobile ground units for action in remote theatres was, of course, a normal
accoutrement only of the largest powers, and since the Soviet veto had rendered inoperative the articles of the UN Charter providing for military sanctions, the government had not expected to 'be called upon ... to contribute to
collective military action against aggression many thousands of miles away.'
The 'rather fortuitous absence' of the Soviet Union from the Security Council
together with the 'initiative and leadership' of the United States had 'changed
the whole character of the United Nations, at least for the time being, and
changed it for the better.' But this had not been foreseen:

Canadian defence policy, therefore, until June of this year, had been based on the concept of providing a small, highly-skilled regular army, charged with responsibility for doing its immediate share of North American defence, especially in the Arctic, and designed to be capable of rapid expansion in the event of a general war which might require Canada to be defended outside of Canada. The furnishing to the United Nations on short notice of expeditionary forces capable of quick deployment in distant areas wherever acts of aggression might take place had not, I admit, entered into our planning as it had not entered into the planning of any other country.

Mr Pearson concluded from his analysis, not that the action in Korea was *sui generis* and unlikely to be repeated, but that the United Nations had shown itself to be a potentially effective instrument of collective security after all. In the circumstances of the day, the United States was simply the most prominent of its many loyal servants. Canada had set 'a valuable example and precedent' by earmarking a portion of her armed forces as a special contingent available for deployment under the UN when required. If other countries followed suit, 'there would be ready throughout the free world national contingents for a United Nations force which could be quickly brought together in the face of a future emergency.' The CASF had to be prepared for 'collective defence' operations under NATO as well, but only because there was a danger of 'communist-inspired attacks elsewhere,' especially in Germany. In the world of 1950 the equation of the purposes of the United Nations with the security interests of the western powers thus tripped easily off the tongue.

At the end there was a rebuke for General MacArthur. The conflict in Korea must be 'confined and localized,' and no one must be given 'an excuse for extending it.' Otherwise 'the risk of a world-wide war' would be increased, 'the high degree of unanimity which had been obtained in the United Nations' would be threatened, and the 'close co-operation between the free countries of Asia and the Western world' might be lost. The government had been upset by reports of military measures in Taiwan and by Chiang Kai-shek's statements concerning Sino-American 'military co-operation.' It had been disturbed also 'by statements that seem in our minds to confuse the defence of Korea, which has been assumed by the United Nations, with the defence of Formosa, which has not; statements that have even implied – somewhat mistakenly I think – that those who wish to draw at this time a distinction between the two operations are defeatists and appeasers.' The government was 'concerned solely with carrying out our United Nations obligations in Korea or elsewhere,' and these did not include anything that could 'be interpreted as the restoration of the nationalist Chinese government to the mainland of China, or an intervention in Formosa.'[45]

This, by customary standards of Canadian diplomacy, was powerful stuff, although its force was somewhat weakened by the fact that the government still had no troops in the field. Nonetheless, it was well received by the House, whose members responded with 'a prodigious round of applause.'[46] In spite of Mr Pearson's admission that the UN action in Korea had been possible only because of fortuitous circumstances, they apparently perceived no difficulty in accepting his argument that it was a genuine and viable precedent for collective security.

But if the reasoning had been tortuous, it had also been useful, for its logic gave Mr Pearson a foundation upon which to admonish those American policy-makers who suggested that the conflict in Korea – a UN enterprise – should be extended to include the protagonists in the dispute over Formosa – a quarrel in which the United Nations was not involved. In such circumstances, the Americans, although comprising the major ingredient of the UN's military effort, could be said to have no business dragging the question of Formosa into the Korean affair.

Finally, just as the cause of the United Nations in general was also the cause of the NATO Pact, so the challenge in Korea – 'communism' – was also the challenge in Europe and in North America. It was true that it had a capacity to feed upon social and economic misery, and that it therefore posed in some ways a greater threat in Asia than it did elsewhere, but that was a poor reason for arguing that Canada should concentrate her military strength in the Far East. The guards should hold the most vital fort.

By now these were old themes. But they were presented with global sweep, and the conflict they described held the perennial fascination of all wars between Virtue and Sin. 'Know your enemy,' Mr Pearson had advised the House, and proceeded to describe him as 'insidious,' 'oppressive,' 'degrading,' 'perverted,' 'malicious,' and 'diabolic.' 'Believing as they do,' [he went on], 'that their slave system is in inevitable opposition to the free systems of government of other peoples, the masters of the Kremlin survey every part of the world in their calculations ... To get the better of such an enemy, active in all parts of the world with propaganda and espionage, relying ultimately

45 For Mr Pearson's address, see Canada, House of Commons, *Debates*, 31 Aug. 1950, 90-7. For the origins of his references to statements by Chiang Kai-shek, and to allegations of defeatism and appeasement, see above, 000.

46 Wilfrid Eggleston, 'Capital Comment: A Great Address by Pearson,' *Saturday Night*, LXV, 48, 12 Sept. 1950, 3

upon the brute weight of 170 powerful divisions but making also its crocodile appeal to real needs and honest longings, we will have to show ourselves resourceful and imaginative as well as strong.'[47]

This was the combative oratory of the grimmest phase of the Cold War, and it was not without effect. One of the 'great moments of recent years,' 'an historical occasion,' an enthusiastic newsman called it later. Before 'a tense House' and 'a large and growing Gallery,' the minister had 'said just as plainly as men can say how diabolical is the menace with which the free world is faced.' The address had been 'disturbing, but left the hearer with a sense of elation.'

Messrs. St. Laurent and Howe followed him with rapt attention. Had they been wondering who was coming along in the party, in Parliament, to fill the places of the veterans? ... If they were, they must have been enheartened. On such addresses as that of August 31, Lester B. Pearson involuntarily lays claim to consideration for still greater responsibilities, in due course.[48]

While the members of the press were thus prophetically overcome, the members of the parties of opposition were somewhat less impressed. But they did not quarrel with the minister on fundamentals. Indeed, they may have thought more of them than did Mr Pearson himself. Their complaints, rather, were confined on the Progressive Conservative side to lamentations over the government's lack of military preparedness,[49] and among CCFers to regrets that it had failed to include in its defence programme 'substantial economic aid for underdeveloped countries.'[50] Social Crediters unabashedly supported the government. So stifling was the underlying consensus that during the defence debate on 2 September one member complained that in spite of the importance of the issue, half the representatives were absent from the House.[51]

47 Canada, House of Commons, *Debates*, 31 Aug. 1950, especially 90-1
48 Eggleston, 'Capital Comment: A Great Address by Pearson,' 3
49 The Conservatives moved the following amendment to the address: 'We regret that Your Excellency's advisers have failed to provide adequately for the defence of Canada and have failed to take steps to deal with inflation and the rapidly rising cost of living.' Canada, House of Commons, *Debates*, 1 Sept. 1950, 116
50 The CCF moved the following amendment to the Conservative amendment: 'By the imposition of price controls and the provision of necessary subsidies; we regret further that Your Excellency's advisers have failed to include in Canada's defence programme substantial economic aid for underdeveloped countries, for it is the opinion of this house that the spread of communism cannot be prevented by military action alone, but only by the provision, in addition, of all possible assistance to bring about social and economic progress in such countries.' Ibid., 124
51 J.M. Macdonnell (PC: Toronto-Greenwood), ibid., 2 Sept. 1950, 180

There was one development of interest, however, in that Jean-François Pouliot had by now acquired a small band of vociferous supporters. In retrospect, some of their observations appear surprisingly perceptive. Among the most articulate of their number was Raoul Poulin (Ind.: Beauce), who told the house that he was 'all for helping our allies, or avoiding isolationism,' but he thought that from 'the humane point of view the invasion of South Korea by the people of North Korea might be regarded simply as a sort of brutal reuniting of two members of the same family whose guardians had felt able to keep asunder in order to exploit them more thoroughly.' This 'would then be a civil war.' He argued that 'clever and well managed propaganda' had done much to show that communist Russia was lurking behind the North Korean aggression, making the war one of 'communist ideology against democracy and freedom.' It was important to notice that the United States had undertaken military action several hours before being authorized to do so by the United Nations Security Council. In this instance the American decision might be 'timely,' but in future cases the interests of the United States could well conflict with those of the UN. Under these circumstances the Korean precedent might compel us 'to carry on against our will, against common sense, and against our own interests.' Canada in any event should look to her own defences, and not send soldiers overseas. Otherwise the government might be forced into conscription, which was strongly opposed by the people of Quebec.[52]

M. Poulin was roundly rebuffed by the Liberal member for Gaspé, J.G.L. Langlois, who pointed out at length that his views were not shared by *Le Droit* and *L'Action Catholique*, and these publications were known to be 'leaders of public opinion in my province and other French-speaking centres.'[53] But M. Poulin had allies of his own. Paul Gagnon (Ind.: Chicoutimi) observed with some indignation that the 'charitable dispositions with which our leaders seem to be overflowing lately should first of all be applied to Canada.' The volunteer brigade was 'but the prelude to that dire course called conscription.' He would fight as well as anyone for the defence of Canada, but was the country 'to become involved in all conflicts between the followers of the USSR and those of the United States?' A few years before, the government had taken its orders from the British. Now it took them from the Americans.[54]

Henri Courtemanche (PC: Labelle) agreed entirely. The enterprise would lead 'inevitably' to conscription. Nothing in the conflict justified Canada's intervention. Having followed 'in the wake of London' in the past, the govern-

52 Ibid., 177-80
53 Ibid., 189-91
54 Ibid., 4 Sept. 1950, 198-202

ment was 'now tied to Washington's apron strings.' French-speaking members of the Liberal Party might be silent, but this was 'the general opinion of the French Canadian people.'[55]

But these were lone voices, and M. Courtemanche's claim to speak for French Canada was greeted with jeering laughter. Nor was M. Langlois the only French-speaking member to retaliate. Maurice Boisvert (L: Nicolet-Yamaska) heard the speeches of Messrs Poulin and Gagnon 'with surprise and astonishment';[56] Pierre Gauthier (L: Portneuf) thought Mr Pearson's speech 'was quite right,' and pledged that both he and his son, who was old enough to go to war, would 'fight communists everywhere and anywhere';[57] and while Philippe Picard (L: Bellechasse) thought that the government should guard carefully against American pressure, he nevertheless fully supported its decision to fulfil its obligations under the United Nations Charter and the NATO Pact.[58] The views of the Progressive Conservative member for Three Rivers, Leon Balcer, were essentially the same.[59] The renegades were thus deprived of a broadly based spectrum of support, and their position was not widely shared among editors of the French-language press. That being the case, their utterances could safely be discounted – a fate which they did not entirely deserve.

The main course of debate, however, involved few such fundamental differences as these, and in general the government was criticized only for its lack of adequate defence preparedness and for being sluggish in rectifying its mistakes. When the special session prorogued on 15 September, the ministers had general support for their interpretation of the crisis and for the measures they had taken to meet it. In addition, they had secured an authorization to spend a further $142,200,200 on defence in the current fiscal year. This would cover unexpected expenditures 'due to the destroyers being in Korean waters; to the airlift to Japan organized by the RCAF; to the charter of aircraft from Canadian Pacific Airlines; and to the raising, training, equipping and use of the Canadian Army special force.'[60] They were authorized also to undertake commitments involving defence expenditures in future years up to a total of $414,567,821 over and above already existing schedules, and to float loans to help defray these various expenses up to a maximum of $300,000,000.[61]

55 Ibid., 249-51
56 Ibid., 214
57 Ibid., 5 Sept. 1950, 257-60
58 Ibid., 12 Sept. 1950, 617-20
59 Ibid., 4 Sept. 1950, 240-3
60 Ibid., 5 Sept. 1950, 298
61 Figures compiled from the Defence Appropriation Bill read to the House of Commons by Douglas Abbott, the minister of finance. See ibid., 4 Sept. 1950, 195. The purpose of the bill

Finally, the Commons had passed an Essential Materials (Defence) Act providing for the 'Control and Regulation of Production, Distribution and Use of Essential Materials and Services.' Under this legislation the government was empowered broadly 'to take action to avert possible disruption of defence preparations requisite for the safeguarding of national security and to assist the United Nations in accordance with Canada's obligations; also to prevent economic disorder and hardship on a national scale; with authority to appoint and fix the remuneration and expense of assistants and advisers to the minister.'[62]

After viewing the effect of Korea upon the fortunes of their profession, the members of the armed forces, if not the non-operating railway workers, could be forgiven if they thought the June invasion not such an ill wind after all. But as Parliament prorogued, their attention was riveted elsewhere – on the landings at Inchon.

On 4 September Mr Pearson had observed in the House of Commons that there had been suggestions that Canada should have made further efforts to use mediation and other pacific measures to settle the Korean dispute. This, he said, was unrealistic, for 'even when it was tried – and it was tried in the early days of this dispute – the aggressor treated that suggestion with contempt. What we are doing on this occasion is to try to make it clear – and by 'we' I mean the members who have accepted the security council resolution – that this time the aggressor will not be able to destroy his victims one by one, as he was able to do in 1938 and 1939.'[63]

In sum, political negotiations would have to wait upon military success, and the United Nations and South Korean forces thus far had managed to maintain only a small bridgehead around the port of Pusan. Just a few hours before the prorogation of Parliament, however, the situation began swiftly to change, as General MacArthur launched an amphibious landing behind enemy lines at Inchon on the west coast of Korea approximately twenty miles from Seoul. The wisdom of this manoeuvre has been the subject of much controversial discussion,[64] but of its success there can be no doubt. The port of Inchon was

was outlined in detail by Brooke Claxton, the minister of national defence, on 5 Sept. See ibid., 298-305

62 Ibid., 4 Sept. 1950, 196

63 Ibid., 220. The reference to early mediation attempts reflected diplomatic initiatives undertaken by Britain and India. See Acheson, *Present at the Creation*, 416-20

64 See, for example, Acheson, *Present at the Creation*, 447-8; Collins, *War in Peacetime*, 114-42; Rees, *Korea: The Limited War*, 77-97; Commander Malcolm W. Cagle, 'Inchon – The Analysis of a Gamble,' *United States Naval Institute Proceedings*, LXXX, 1, Jan. 1954, 47-53; Lt-Col.

itself in United Nations hands within twenty-four hours, and the advance toward Seoul began the following morning. By 20 September, five days after the first assault, American Marines were within 5000 yards of South Korea's government buildings. The North Korean forces began at this point to put up a more determined resistance, and it took another seven days of devastating combat to occupy the city. In the meantime elements of the forces landed at Inchon had linked up on 26 September with units of General Walker's Eighth Army, which had broken out of the Pusan perimeter. Large portions of the North Korean Army were thereby cut off from their source of command and supply, and the military situation was reversed within a matter almost of hours. By 30 September Syngman Rhee had been reinstalled in his government headquarters, and the invaders had been driven back to the 38th parallel with total losses amounting to an estimated 335,000 men. Only 25-30,000 are thought to have reached North Korea.[65]

According to a later account by Blair Fraser, the initial Canadian reaction to the Inchon operation was one of pique because Ottawa had not been consulted in advance. The issue involved matters more weighty than those of diplomatic courtesy, since the success of the manoeuvre had serious implications for the planning of the future of the Canadian Army Special Force. Yet on Mr Fraser's report, and in spite of the presence in the theatre after 24 July of two Canadian military observers, 'the first any Canadian knew about the Inchon landing was when it appeared in the newspapers.' In consequence, 'External Affairs Minister L.B. (Mike) Pearson protested to Washington and was told it had been a military secret. True – but the press reported it later as "the worst kept secret in military history." Apparently it was open gossip in half the bars of Tokyo days before it happened. But nobody thought to tell the Canadians.'[66]

If this was really the reaction of Canadian diplomatic officials, few of them can remember it now, although they recall their admiration for General MacArthur's command of the operation, and their exhilaration in response to the resulting alterations in the fortunes of the war.[67] Some now go so far as

James F. Schnabel, 'The Inchon Landing: Perilous Gamble or Exemplary Boldness?' *Army*, IX, 10, May 1959, 50-8. General MacArthur had to press very hard for approval of his plan; for his own account, see his *Reminiscences*, 393-400. An interesting feature of his case was that it drew upon Wolfe's victory at Quebec in 1759 as a precedent for the action he hoped to undertake at Inchon. Captain Brock nevertheless thought at the time that the venture was too hazardous. Brock, interview, 23 July 1969

65 For an account of these operations, see Rees, *Korea*, 89-94

66 Fraser, 'Win or Lose, the Russians May Get Korea,' *Maclean's*, LXIV, 1, 1 Jan. 1951, 38

67 Campbell, interview, 20 Oct. 1968; Heeney, interview, 7 March 1968; Holmes, interview, 5 March 1968; LePan, interview, 5 March 1968; Pearson, interview, 18 Oct. 1968

to say that advance consultation would not have been welcome in any event, since it would have embroiled Ottawa in the responsibility for the purely military aspects of the hostilities, a responsibility which was well enough left to the Americans.[68] In any case, the government was not forewarned of the enterprise. Captain Brock, whose destroyers played a role in the initial assault, naturally perceived it as a purely military manoeuvre coming solely within his own responsibility.[69] Known among newsmen in Tokyo as 'Operation Common Knowledge,' the attack came as a complete surprise even to the Canadian military attaché in Washington.[70]

The real significance of the Inchon victory, however, was that it compelled the government to consider whether or not it would support a United Nations crossing of the 38th parallel. Until now Canada's official view of the UN's objectives in Korea had not been defined very clearly, except for declarations of the government's interest in supporting the United Nations generally, resisting the aggressor, and confining the scope of the hostilities. The Security Council resolution of 27 June had recommended merely that member-states 'furnish such assistance to the Republic of Korea as may be necessary to repel the armed attack and to restore international peace and security in the area.' This seemed to indicate that the minimum objective was the expulsion of the invaders from South Korean territory, but beyond that it was not very precise.

Mr Pearson's 31 August speech in the House of Commons had been no more enlightening. The job of Canada, as he had defined it, was 'to play our part, a part determined by ourselves, but worked out in consultation with our friends, in the collective effort of the free countries to prevent aggression if possible, by showing that it cannot succeed; or to defeat it if it occurs.' But what in such a case constituted 'defeat' of the aggressors? He did not say. He thought in any event that it was 'too early to see clearly what might be the shape of a just and lasting settlement in Korea.' Any such settlement would have 'to remove the possibility of a repetition of the recent attack ... commend itself to the inhabitants of Korea ... command support from Asian opinion, and ... recognize the progress which has already been made under the auspices of the United Nations in establishing an independent government in Korea.'[71]

68 Brock, interview, 23 July 1969; Foulkes, interview, 7 March 1968; MacKay, interview, 7 March 1968; Taber, interview, 7 June 1969
69 Brock, interview, 23 July 1969. See also Thorgrimsson and Russell, *Canadian Naval Operations in Korean Waters*, 17-18
70 Taber, interview, 7 June 1969
71 Canada, House of Commons, *Debates*, 31 Aug. 1950, 95-6

Principles so general as these could hardly be regarded in themselves as concrete policy decisions. The government had been decisively forthright upon one point only: that the hostilities in Korea must not be allowed to spread to the conflict over Formosa. As the department had put it in its monthly publication, *External Affairs*, 'It is a cardinal principle of Canadian policy in the Korean crisis that Canada's immediate obligation does not go beyond the restoration of peace and the defeat of aggression in Korea. It had been frequently emphasized by Government leaders that the United Nations action covers Korea and nothing else: that it does not, for example, extend to Formosa.'[72] But what precisely was involved in 'the restoration of peace and the defeat of aggression in Korea' had never been explicitly defined. In the first weeks of the conflict, the government had simply assumed that the operation would be confined to a restoration of the *status quo ante bellum*, without considering in detail what this would mean. The assumption was in line with the statement of objectives offered to the NATO ambassadors in Washington by George Kennan on 27 June.[73]

This is not to say that the issue had never been raised. In the House of Commons as early as 4 September Angus MacInnis (CCF: Vancouver East) had suggested to those who wanted the forces of the United Nations to cross the 38th parallel

that if we want to start a third world war that would be the best way to start it. The Soviet Union may not move into this fight until an attempt is made – if it is made – to cross that boundary. But surely no one can be so naive as to expect that the Soviet Union would give up any jurisdiction or any influence it considers it has by arrangement or by treaty, and allow the forces of the United Nations to go beyond the 38th parallel. I suggest that point should be made clear, and that the government should state where it stands in the matter. It should be made clear before we ask our soldiers to enlist.[74]

It was the interest of China, not of the Soviet Union, that was in need of careful examination, but in any case the government thus far had made no decision. In this it was not alone. The matter had not been discussed in Washington until the middle of July, and the tentative deliberations among American military and diplomatic officials which had developed in subsequent

72 Department of External Affairs, 'Canadian Policy in the Far East,' *External Affairs*, II, 9, Sept. 1950, 329
73 See above, 44
74 Canada, House of Commons, *Debates*, 4 Sept. 1950, 229

weeks had shown that on the question of crossing the parallel the policy-making community was internally divided.[75] Only General MacArthur seems at the beginning to have had no doubts. He had informed General Collins, the army chief of staff, as early as 13 July that his intention was to destroy the North Korean forces entirely, and not merely to drive them back across the border.[76] General Collins and Admiral Sherman had indicated their agreement with these objectives during discussions with the UN commander late in August, and on 7 September the joint chiefs had recommended officially that ground operations should be carried 'beyond the 38th parallel as necessary to achieve' the destruction of North Korean military forces.[77]

The political authorities in Washington reached a decision after a meeting of the National Security Council on 11 September, when they agreed to authorize MacArthur to extend his operations into North Korea. Subject to there being 'no indication or threat of entry of Soviet or Chinese Communist elements in force,' he was to make preparations for its occupation. A directive to this effect was forwarded to Tokyo on 15 September.[78] Twelve days later the general received more detailed instructions:

> Your military objective is the destruction of the North Korean Armed Forces. In attaining this objective you are authorized to conduct military operations, including amphibious and airborne landings or ground operations north of the 38th parallel in Korea, *provided that at the time of such operations there has been no entry into North Korea by major Soviet or Chinese Communist Forces, no announcement of intended entry, nor a threat to counter our operations militarily in North Korea.* Under no circumstances, however, will your forces cross the Manchurian or USSR borders of Korea and, as a matter of policy, *no non-Korean Ground Forces will be used in the northeast provinces bordering the Soviet Union or in the area along the Manchurian border.* Furthermore support of your operations north or south of the 38th parallel will not include Air or Naval action against Manchuria or against USSR territory.[79]

General MacArthur promptly replied with a battle-plan for the advance into North Korea. This was duly approved by President Truman on the advice of the joint chiefs and the secretary of state, and on the following day – 1

75 See Acheson, *Present at the Creation*, 450-2, and Collins, *War in Peacetime*, 143-71
76 Collins, *War in Peacetime*, 144
77 Quoted in Rees, *Korea*, 99
78 Truman, *Years of Trial and Hope*, 410
79 Quoted in Acheson, *Present at the Creation*, 452-3 (italics mine). The first of the two italicized passages is excluded from the version appearing in MacArthur's *Reminiscences*, 407. For Truman's summary, see *Years of Trial and Hope*, 411

October in Korea – the general directed the following message to the commander-in-chief of the North Korean forces: 'The early and total defeat and
complete destruction of your armed forces and war-making potential is now
inevitable. In order that the decisions of the United Nations may be carried
out with a minimum of further loss of life and destruction of property, I, as
the United Nations Commander-in-Chief, call upon you and forces under your
command, in whatever part of Korea situated, forthwith to lay down your
arms and cease hostilities under such military supervision as I may direct
... [80] There was no reply, and a few hours later units of the South Korean army
advanced across the 38th parallel. 'Containment,' as one historian of the
Korean War has written, 'predicated on a calculated return to the *status quo
ante* in cold war and limited war engagements between East and West, was
the chief policy casualty of Inchon.'[81]

There remained for the Americans only the problem of gaining for these
new policy decisions the approval of the international body upon whose behalf
they were ostensibly made. After the termination of Mr Malik's presidency of
the Security Council at the end of August, the chair had passed to Sir Gladwyn
Jebb of the United Kingdom, and the sessions had been conducted with
improved efficiency thereafter. Nevertheless, each of a series of resolutions
proposed respectively by the principal opponents – the Soviet Union and the
United States – failed to pass in the voting, which regularly found Mr Malik
in a minority of one. These proceedings, as the Department of External Affairs
remarked sadly at the time, 'showed the Security Council's inability to act
effectively in the face of Great Power disagreement.'[82]

A solution did not become possible until the opening of the Fifth Session
of the General Assembly on 19 September. Article 12 of the UN Charter
provides that while 'the Security Council is exercising in respect of any dispute
or situation the functions assigned to it in the present Charter, the General
Assembly shall not make any recommendations with regard to that dispute or
situation unless the Security Council so requests.' But there had been a precedent in the Palestine case in which the assembly had dealt with the long-term
political aspects of a dispute while the Security Council had been preoccupied
with the short-term pacification of the belligerents. Moreover, the assembly's
agenda already included consideration of an UNCOK report which involved the
question of the independence and unification of Korea, and this gave the
Americans an opportunity to suggest informally that the assembly during the

80 Department of External Affairs, *Documents on the Korean Crisis*, 3
81 Rees, *Korea*, 100
82 Department of External Affairs, 'The Korean Crisis,' *External Affairs*, II, 10, Oct. 1950, 364

course of its proceedings might wish to signify its approval of their decision to advance into North Korean territory.

The Americans argued at first that a formal resolution would not be necessary, since the Security Council in its resolutions of June and July had authorized the restoration of 'international peace and security *in the area*,' without further defining the geographic limits of the operation.[83] This was precisely the ambiguity which had worried the Department of External Affairs at the time, and its senior officials were not now prepared to interpret the meaning of the earlier authorizations so broadly. Nevertheless, they were still in need of an explicit and clearly formulated policy.

The policy discussions which ensued in the department were concerned less with ends than with means. It was generally agreed that the immediate objectives of the UN operation were to end the hostilities, to compel the North Koreans to withdraw from the South, and to restore peace and security in Korea. In addition, there was a long-term objective, dating back to 1947, of establishing a unified, independent, and democratic government throughout the whole of the peninsula. The essential question now was whether all of these objectives ought to be pursued by military means. Clearly there was a danger that the Soviets or Chinese might be drawn into the hostilities if the United Nations Command attempted to achieve unification by force, especially if military operations were conducted in areas immediately adjacent to their borders. On the other hand, the opportunity seemed almost too good to miss, and given the heavy UN casualties already incurred, there might be widespread public disappointment if the advance were stopped at the 38th parallel. It was therefore decided that the official Canadian position would be to suggest that the assembly pass a resolution re-stating the short-term objectives of the United Nations in the war and providing for emergency relief for the much-abused Korean populace. The question of the crossing of the parallel would be left open in the hope that before it became necessary the North Koreans would agree to terminate the hostilities.[84] The government was definitely 'not in favour of UN forces crossing the parallel unless North Korea continued to wage war or unless there was a need to supervise all-Korean elections.'[85]

The immediate result of these initial deliberations was an address delivered to the Plenary Session of the General Assembly by Mr Pearson on 27 Septem-

83 Pearson, interview, 18 Oct. 1968
84 Ibid.; confirmed by Geoffrey A.H. Pearson after reference to his father's personal notes, interview, 18 Oct. 1968
85 Pearson, letter to the author, 13 Nov. 1968

ber. In it he outlined the Canadian position in the form of five basic principles which he thought should be embodied in an assembly resolution:

In the first place, the general objective as we see it of the United Nations in Korea should be to fulfil now the purposes which have repeatedly been stated at previous Assemblies – a united Korea, a free Korea, a Korea which the Korean people themselves govern without interference from outside. *This should be achieved by United Nations action and not through decisions reached by certain of its members.*

Secondly, the United Nations must assist the people of Korea to establish peace and order *throughout their territory* as the firm foundation for democratic institutions and free government. It is our hope that the people of Northern Korea, having been forced into a perilous and disastrous venture by their communist rulers, will now themselves repudiate these rulers and co-operate with the United Nations in bringing to Korea the peace and unity which its people desire. This is the time for the aggressors to cease fire, to admit defeat. *If they do, it may not be necessary for United Nations forces in Korean territory to advance far beyond their present positions. The United Nations must, however, leave its forces free to do whatever is practicable to make certain that the communist aggressors of North Korea are not permitted to re-establish some new base in the peninsula from which they could sally forth again upon a peaceful people.*

Third, the Korean people – once peace has been restored – must be assured that no nation will exploit the present situation in Korea for its own particular advantage. This of course means a Korea without foreign bases and free of foreign military domination; it means a Korea which will be responsible for its own defence within the framework of our collective security system. *Above all, it means a Korea which will not be divided and disturbed by subversive communist elements directed from outside Korea.*

The fourth principle should be that nothing shall be done in the establishment of a united, free Korea which carries any menace to Korea's neighbours ...

My fifth principle is that the free governments of Asia should take a major share of the responsibility for advising the Korean people upon methods of government which they should adopt and procedures which they should follow in establishing these methods of government ... [86]

If a distinction could, in fact, be drawn between the short-term and long-term purposes of the United Nations in Korea, the enunciation of such principles as these must surely have obscured it, for together they comprised an ambitious, belligerent, and self-contradictory set of objectives. They were ambitious because they included in the United Nations purpose in Korea not merely the securing of the *status quo ante bellum*, but also an extravagant

[86] Department of External Affairs, *Statements and Speeches,* 50/34 (italics mine)

programme for the unification of the Korean people and territory and for the democratization of their political process. They were belligerent – or must have seemed so to the North Koreans – because in principle two they contained what was in effect an ultimatum to the Communist forces in the North either to admit total defeat and repudiate their political leadership, or suffer a shattering military disaster at the hands of a (reluctantly) unleashed United Nations army. They were self-contradictory – in fact if not in logic – because in principle three they provided for a unified Korea entirely free from external political or military influence, and in particular from the influence of Communists, while at the same time stipulating in principle four that these objectives should be achieved without giving the peninsula's Communist neighbours cause for alarm. It was improbable that either the Soviet Union or Communist China would regard the conquest of Korea by an American-dominated United Nations force as an eventuality devoid of menace.

Canadian officials were not unaware of these difficulties, and they were much more reluctant to support a crossing of the 38th parallel than either their public statements or their voting at the United Nations would appear to suggest. M.J. Coldwell, who was acting as an observer of the General Assembly's proceedings, recalls that the opposition of the Canadian delegation to an advance into North Korea was very strong, and Mr Pearson was peppered with messages from Escott Reid and Norman Robertson in Ottawa advising him not to support an American initiative.[87] Nevertheless, after several days of feverish informal discussions in New York with Commonwealth and other delegations, a resolution based on a draft drawn up by the American secretary of state was presented to the Political Committee on 30 September.[88] The Americans had succeeded in attracting as sponsors Great Britain and seven other countries, including Australia, Brazil, Cuba, the Netherlands, Norway, Pakistan, and the Philippines. The resolution recommended:

(a) That all appropriate steps be taken to ensure conditions of stability throughout Korea,
(b) That all constituent acts be taken, including the holding of elections, under the auspices of the United Nations for the establishment of a unified, independent and democratic Government in the sovereign state of Korea,

---

87 Coldwell, interview, 10 July 1970; Reid, interview, 9 June 1969
88 Rees, *Korea*, 102. The American role is confirmed by Lie in his *In the Cause of Peace*, 345. Dean Acheson's account, displaying a modesty not entirely characteristic of its author, notes only that the resolution 'had been drafted with our participation.' *Present at the Creation*, 454

(c) That all sections and representative bodies of the population of Korea, South and North, be invited to co-operate with the organs of the United Nations in the restoration of peace, in the holding of elections and in the establishment of a unified Government, (d) That United Nations forces should not remain in any part of Korea otherwise than so far as necessary for achieving the objectives specified at (a) and (b) above, (e) That all necessary measures be taken to accomplish the economic rehabilitation of Korea.

The resolution provided also for the appointment of a United Nations Commission for the Unification and Rehabilitation of Korea (UNCURK) to take the place of UNCOK in representing the United Nations in the fulfilment of the recommendations, and in arranging for such relief and rehabilitation as would be approved by the General Assembly on the suggestion of the Economic and Social Council. UNCURK's member states were to include Australia, Chile, the Netherlands, Pakistan, the Philippines, Turkey, and Thailand.[89] The ambivalence of the wording of the resolution, as Dean Acheson has since acknowledged, gave encouragement 'to General MacArthur's adventurism,'[90] but it was precisely this ambiguity of meaning that allowed it to pass the General Assembly. Mr Pearson told the Political Committee on 3 October that his government thought the resolution 'both moderate and constructive in its approach,' and that it had found 'the same moderation in the proclamation issued on Saturday last to the North Korean Forces by the United Nations Commander-in-Chief.'[91] With respect to the conduct of hostilities, it was obvious 'that no resolutions of this Assembly should interfere with military action which is considered essential to repel, extinguish and prevent the recurrence of aggression in Korea.' Of course, the use of UN forces in the theatre 'must be restricted to the restoration of peace and security,' but then, no one had ever contemplated using them for any other purpose. The resolution itself provided for the political unification and economic rehabilitation of the Korean people, but there was 'no thought of establishing anything in the nature

89 The complete text of the resolution is in Department of External Affairs, *Documents on the Korean Crisis*, 5-6. Subsequently, on 1 December, the General Assembly passed a resolution establishing under UNCURK's auspices an aid organization entitled the United Nations Korean Reconstruction Agency (UNKRA), to which Canada ultimately contributed $7,500,000. Otherwise, Canada did not play an active part. For a brief study of the difficulties faced by the agency, see Lyons, 'American Policy and the United Nations' Program for Korean Reconstruction,' 180-92. For a full-dress analysis, see the same author, *Military Policy and Economic Aid.*
90 Acheson, *Present at the Creation*, 454
91 See above, 118

of a continuing protectorate, or, indeed, a protectorate of any kind, over Korea, either by the United Nations or any of its members.' The Korean people would be 'new to democratic political life' and might make mistakes, but they would not be the first to do so and their fate at least would be 'in their own hands.'

A five-power resolution sponsored by the Soviet bloc was also before the committee. It recommended an immediate cease-fire and the withdrawal of American and other foreign troops from Korea, to be followed by the election of a 'parity' commission by a joint meeting of the Assemblies of North and South Korea, to organize and conduct elections for an all-Korean national assembly.[92] But Mr Pearson argued in reply to this that the Security Council had already called for a cessation of hostilities, and pointed out that withdrawal of foreign troops would have the effect of leaving the North Koreans free to resume their aggression. In any event he was suspicious of the parity commission proposal because it would involve an interim government composed equally of communist and non-communist members. 'We know,' he said, 'from experience in other parts of the world what happens when that kind of constitutional set-up is decided upon.'

The Indian delegate had agreed with the fundamental objectives of the eight-power resolution, but was opposed to the provisions which gave the UN commander tacit authority to carry his operations into North Korea. This, he thought, would increase tensions in the area, and he therefore recommended the appointment of a sub-committee to work out a compromise solution.[93] But Mr Pearson doubted whether this could produce any positive result in view of a Soviet statement to the effect that there was no possible compromise between the two opposing positions.[94]

Mr Pearson and the prime minister for a time had contemplated the possibility of arranging for modifications in the eight-power resolution which would have made it more palatable to the Indians, whose alienation from the United Nations they were particularly anxious to avoid, but the quick pace of events in the assembly deprived them of the opportunity.[95] On 4 October the Indian and Soviet proposals were both defeated in the Political Committee, Canada voting negative in each case, while the eight-power resolution favoured by the United States was approved by a count of 47 to 5, with 7 abstentions. Since it was now too late to hope for substantive alterations in the eight-power draft,

92 Department of External Affairs, *Canada and the United Nations, 1950*, 4 and 6
93 Ibid., 6
94 For the complete text of Mr Pearson's address, see Department of External Affairs, *Statements and Speeches*, 50/38
95 Pearson, interview, 18 Oct. 1968

Mr Pearson suggested privately to the American secretary of state that its passage in plenary session might be postponed 'until diplomatic contact was made with the North Koreans.'[96] Certainly it ought not to be brought to a vote before the North Korean government had been given an opportunity to respond to an advance warning.

Acheson appeared at first to be impressed by this proposal, and on Friday, 6 October, he agreed informally to a postponement of a few days pending the initiation through the United Nations of a diplomatic approach to the North Korean authorities in which they would be asked to lay down their arms. On the following morning, however, Mr Pearson attended the plenary proceedings of the General Assembly only to discover that these arrangements had been abandoned, and that the eight-power resolution was moving rapidly to a vote. It soon passed by the same count as in the Political Committee – that is, by 47 to 5 (Soviet bloc), with 7 abstentions (several of the Arab powers, together with India and Yugoslavia). Not having been informed in advance of the change in American plans, Mr Pearson was 'horrified' and 'very angry.' In what was for him a foul temper, he stalked from the assembly's proceedings while they were still in progress and sought a diversion with which to 'cool down.' Not uncharacteristically, he chose a world series baseball game. Later the same weekend, he received a telephone call from Dean Acheson in Washington, who apologized for breaking their understanding and explained that on the night before the assembly's vote, he had raised the matter with President Truman only to be overruled at the last minute by the president on the advice of the military.[97]

This may have been adequate explanation, but it was poor comfort. The Canadian delegation had given the eight-power resolution their formal support, but as Mr Pearson wrote later, they had 'regretted the haste with which the Resolution was passed and the disregard of India's objection to it.' In the absence of Canadian ground forces in the theatre, however, the minister believed that in the final analysis he was not in sufficiently strong a position to press his case to the point of withholding Canada's affirmative vote.[98] Even so, at least one senior official in the department of external affairs argued strenuously against the decision, and still thinks that it was a mistake.[99] He

96 Pearson, letter to the author, 13 Nov. 1968
97 Pearson, comments to seminar on Canadian external relations, Carleton university, 16 Oct. 1972
98 Pearson, letter to the author, 13 Nov. 1968, and interview, 18 Oct. 1968. Mr Pearson told Norman Robertson shortly afterwards that it was impossible in the circumstances to persist in opposing the United States on the border-crossing issue. Reid, interview, 9 June 1969
99 Reid, letter to the author, 20 June, 1968; and interview, 9 June, 1969

has since inquired searchingly of his conscience whether or not he could 'have done more in the autumn of 1950 to persuade the Canadian delegation to the United Nations not to vote in favour of a resolution which could be interpreted by General MacArthur as authorizing him to advance to the Yalu.'[100]

The question itself has no public answer, but the accuracy of its estimate of the danger is a matter of record. By the time of Acheson's telephone call to Mr Pearson, American units under MacArthur's command, bent now upon the transportation of war and democracy to the doorsteps of China, had already crossed the 38th parallel.

'China,' as a Canadian historian has observed, 'proved to be as unwilling to admit such a plan for Korea as the United States might have been if United Nations forces, mostly Chinese, had been about to arrange for a people's democracy in Mexico.'[101] The Communist Chinese intervention, which developed on a small scale within a month and escalated to major proportions a few weeks later, not unnaturally became the source of much recrimination within and among the capitals of the UN states most intimately concerned. In particular there was extensive *post mortem* analysis of the intelligence failure. Why had the intervention not been foreseen?

In what is perhaps the definitive western study of Chinese policy in the Korean War, Allen S. Whiting has argued that the government in Peking in the early stages probably did not expect to become directly involved. The primary concern of the Chinese authorities was the consolidation of their still-unstable regime on the mainland, and the extension of their jurisdiction to include the island of Formosa. Except for its vituperative reaction to President Truman's decision to neutralize Formosa, the mainland press appeared in June and July to treat the conflict in Korea as a matter of secondary importance. Large numbers of armed forces had been moved into the Manchurian area as early as April 1950, and these continued to increase until well into the middle of July, but Whiting concludes that the Peking government did not give up the possibility of avoiding embroilment until Warren Austin delivered a statement on 17 August to the effect that the United Nations objective in Korea was the conquest and political reorganization of the entire peninsula. The Chinese thereafter began to issue protests with respect to various aspects of the UN's conduct of the war, and the quality of anti-American propaganda appearing in their press became more stridently mili-

---

100 Reid, 'The Conscience of the Diplomat,' 583
101 Harrison, *Canada in World Affairs*, 293

126 Canada and the Korean War

tant.[102] Following the Inchon landings, the statements emanating from Peking assumed a tone more sombre and threatening still. On 22 September the Chinese Ministry of Foreign Affairs admitted that it had transferred some troops of Korean ethnic origin from its own forces to those of North Korea, and announced: 'We clearly reaffirm that we will always stand on the side of the Korean people ... and resolutely oppose the criminal acts of American imperialist aggressors against Korea ... '[103]

Three days later K.M. Panikkar, the Indian ambassador in Peking, dined with General Nieh Jung-chen, the acting Chinese chief of staff. The general told him 'in a quiet and unexcited manner that the Chinese did not intend to sit back with folded hands and let the Americans come up to their border.' Panikkar 'tried to impress on him how destructive a war with America would be; how the Americans would be able to destroy systematically all the industries of Manchuria and put China back by half a century, how China's coastal towns would be exposed to bombardment and how even the interior could be bombed. The general only laughed. "We have calculated all that," he said. "They may even drop atomic bombs on us. What then? They may kill a few million people. Without sacrifice a nation's independence cannot be upheld." He gave some calculations of the effectiveness of atomic bombs and said: "After all, China lives on the farms. What can atom bombs do there? Yes, our economic development would be put back. We may have to wait for it." '[104]

'This conversation,' Panikkar reports, 'left me very depressed.' But it must have been more depressing still for him to discover that his subsequent warnings to foreign governments were destined, like the prophecies of Cassandra, not to be believed – not, at least, in the chancelleries of the western world which counted most in the conduct of the war. Allen Whiting has pointed out how difficult it is in such situations to convey a credible threat,[105] and the Chinese on this occasion had no more luck that most. Panikkar's warnings were received in Washington *via* London, Moscow, Stockholm, New Delhi, and other capitals, but as President Truman later wrote, 'the problem that arose in connection with these reports was that Mr Panikkar had in the past played the game of the Chinese Communists fairly regularly, so that his statement could not be taken as that of an impartial observer. It might very

---

102 Whiting, *China Crosses the Yalu*, 46, 57-8, 78-9, and 103
103 Quoted in Rees, *Korea*, 100. There is some evidence that the North Korean regime concluded a bilateral treaty of mutual defence with the communist Chinese forces as early as March 1949. See Simmons, 'The Strained Alliance', 70-2.
104 K.M. Panikkar, *In Two Chinas*, 108
105 Whiting, *China Crosses the Yalu*, 110

well be no more than a relay of Communist propaganda.'[106] Even when the ambassador cabled that he had been aroused from his bed in the middle of the night of 2-3 October for a 12:30 AM meeting with Chou En-lai – there to be told that if American troops crossed the 38th parallel, China would intervene in the war – his urgent messages for the most part were not taken seriously in the West.[107] 'Panikkar,' as the Americans were wont to reassure their allies at Lake Success, 'is panicking.'[108]

Even in the Canadian Department of External Affairs, where there was a genuine disposition to sympathize with New Delhi's position and an anxiety to ensure that the Indians were not antagonized by western ventures in Asia, Mr Panikkar's despatches were not considered as hard evidence. They were treated more soberly in Ottawa than in Washington, not least because Canadian officials were unsure in any case of the wisdom of advancing too far into North Korea. But New Delhi officials were themselves doubtful about the degree to which the reports accurately reflected Chinese intentions, and they were therefore treated as inconclusive.[109] The Department was not even convinced when, on 10 October, the Chinese Ministry of Foreign Affairs, in terms strangely reminiscent of a famous declaration by Franklin Roosevelt many years before, issued a final, unequivocal warning: 'Now that the American forces are attempting to cross the thirty-eighth parallel on a large scale, the Chinese people cannot stand idly by with regard to such a serious situation created by the invasion of Korea ... and to the dangerous trend towards extending the war. The American war of invasion in Korea has been a serious menace to the security of China from its very start.'[110]

This announcement was made the day after General MacArthur had issued a second surrender ultimatum to the North Korean commander-in-chief,[111] And as Mr Pearson later conceded to the House of Commons, 'We ourselves did not think it a sufficient reason for refusing the United Nations commander permission to complete the task which had been assigned to him; but many

---

106 Truman, *Years of Trial and Hope*, 413
107 Panikkar, *In Two Chinas*, 109-10. See also Acheson, *Present at the Creation*, 452
108 Reid, interview, 9 June 1969
109 Confidential sources
110 Quoted in Whiting, *China Crosses the Yalu*, 115. In August 1938 at Kingston, Ontario, President Roosevelt announced in the context of the rising Nazi menace 'that the people of the United States will not stand idly by if domination of Canadian soil is threatened by any other empire.' See 'Relations with Canada. Address of President Roosevelt at Queen's University, Kingston, Ontario, Canada, August 18, 1938,' in Jones and Myers, eds., *Documents on American Foreign Relations*, 25
111 For the text of this ultimatum, see Department of External Affairs, *Documents on the Korean Crisis*, 7

delegations, including our own, considered it to be a good reason for conducting military operations in North Korea with, shall I say, great circumspection.'[112]

The second of these conclusions, if not the first, was sound. Chinese troops secretly crossed the Yalu River into North Korea in the middle of the month, and on 26 October they conducted their first engagements against South Korean troops.

Reactions in the West were slow in coming, for the intervention began on a minor scale and early intelligence reports from MacArthur's headquarters were confused and speculative. The first indication that Chinese troops were actually in the battle area arrived in Washington as late as 31 October.[113] President Truman immediately requested 'an up-to-date estimate of the situation from General MacArthur,' who complied on 4 November with a report to the effect that while a fully fledged Chinese intervention was among the possibilities, 'a final appraisement should await a more concrete accumulation of military facts.'[114] On the following day the UN commander-in-chief submitted a special report to the United Nations advising that his forces 'in certain areas of Korea' were 'meeting a new foe,' and listing a series of intelligence reports of exchanges with 'Chinese Communist military units.'[115] With that the news was out, and the reports which followed in subsequent weeks describing the escalating scale and significance of the Chinese intervention served only to deepen and intensify the gloom which pervaded Ottawa and other capitals.

The Canadian government now realized what it had half-suspected from the beginning – that the attempt to unify Korea by force of arms was incompatible with Peking's view of the requirements of Chinese security. The result was that Mr Pearson began to de-emphasize his interest in the general objective of a unified Korea, and to concentrate instead on the immediate need to reassure the Chinese and prevent a further extension of the hostilities. In a public address in Windsor, Ontario, ten days after the arrival of MacArthur's first report on the intervention, he reminded his audience that Canada from the beginning had worked to keep the war 'confined and localized,' and that one of the principles that he had advanced in the General Assembly was 'that nothing should be done in the establishment of a united and free Korea which would carry the slightest menace to Korea's neighbours.' This might 'in certain

112 Canada, House of Commons, *Debates*, 2 Feb. 1951, 56
113 Truman, *Years of Trial and Hope*, 424. For Dean Acheson's reflections on the uncertainties of this period, see *Present at the Creation*, 463 ff
114 Quoted in Truman, *Years of Trial and Hope*, 425
115 For the full text of this report, see Department of External Affairs, *Documents on the Korean Crisis*, 9-10

circumstances complicate the immediate problems which face the United Nations Commander,' but it was essential as long as there was 'any chance of preventing the war from spreading.'[116] This passing reference to the problems faced by General MacArthur was the result of an earlier dispute with Washington regarding the bombing of bridges on the Yalu River. On 5 November MacArthur had ordered the American Air Force to destroy the twin spans from Sinuiju, Korea, to Antung, Manchuria, in an effort to reduce the flow of supplies and personnel flowing across the border from China. Truman, reluctant to undertake such a provocative measure unless there was 'an immediate and serious threat to the security of [American] troops,' immediately countermanded the order pending further explanations from Tokyo.[117] The General regarded this as 'the most indefensible and ill-conceived decision ever forced on a field commander in our nation's history,'[118] and cabled an impassioned protest on the following day, 6 November. In it he argued that bombing the bridges was the only way to stop the reinforcement of the enemy, and that such a measure was 'entirely within the scope of the rules of war and the resolutions and directions which I have received from the United Nations and constitutes no slightest act of belligerency against Chinese territory, in spite of the outrageous international lawlessness emanating therefrom.' He could not 'overemphasize the disastrous effect, both physical and psychological,' that would result from a bombing restriction.[119]

On receiving this message President Truman changed his mind. MacArthur was authorized to proceed with his plan, on the condition that this was still necessary for the safety of his forces, and 'that extreme care be taken to avoid [a] violation [of] Manchurian territory and airspace and to report hostile action from Manchuria.'[120] The bridge was bombed on 8 November, although by this time most of the Chinese forces were already in Korea.

The bombing aroused considerable anxiety in the Department of External Affairs, whose ambassador in Washington had been instructed earlier to suggest to the State Department that United Nations forces be kept well away from the Yalu River.[121] Mr Pearson was concerned in particular about the safety of nearby power installations,[122] and he and his senior advisers were

116 Ibid., 12-13
117 Truman, *Years of Trial and Hope*, 426-7
118 MacArthur, *Reminiscences*, 423
119 Quoted in Truman, *Years of Trial and Hope*, 427-8
120 Quoted ibid., 428-9
121 Pearson, interview, 18 Oct. 1968. See also above, note 98
122 Pearson, letter to the author, 13 Nov. 1968

horrified by the American air attack.[123] Hence his advocacy of military restraint, both privately through Hume Wrong in the United States and publicly
in his 15 November address in Windsor.

The minister conceded to his audience on the same occasion that the
Chinese might 'demonstrate by their future actions that what they intend is
an unlimited aggression against Korea. If unhappily that turns out to be the
case, it will be necessary for the United Nations to take knowledge of the fact
and to enlarge the field of action of the United Nations Commander. The
aggressor may have to be met where he comes from. The Canadian Government could hardly, however, be party to any action which has not been
sanctioned by the United Nations or support within the United Nations any
action to extend the field of operations unless and until it is clear that Chinese
Communist forces have been sent to Korea on more than a protective and
border mission.'[124]

Mr Pearson's hope that the Chinese 'Volunteers' might be engaged only in
'a protective and border mission,' so that an extension of the field of operations
would not be necessary, was based on the possibility that 'the Chinese might
think it in their interests to limit hostilities and that their primary motive was
to protect the Yalu dam.' He was therefore in favour of an attempt by the
United Nations 'to get in touch with the Chinese to find out about their
intentions,'[125] and for a time it did in fact appear as if their objectives might
be very limited. On 7 November, the day before the Yalu bombings, enemy
forces had withdrawn from action along the entire front, and the subsequent
lull in the fighting lasted for nineteen days. In the interval, on 24 November,
General MacArthur launched his famous 'home by Christmas' offensive,
which was designed to end the war and to carry South Korean and United
Nations forces to the banks of the Yalu River. Two days later, the Chinese
counterattacked on a massive scale in every sector, and within hours the
offensive had turned into a rout. On 28 November MacArthur announced to
the world the beginning of 'an entirely new war,' and by 15 December, after
a chaotic withdrawal of 120 miles, a good part of General Walker's Eighth
Army was stationed once again along the 38th parallel.

In Canada these ill winds blew at least some good if they only served to
force home at last the contradictions of Mr Pearson's 28 September programme. With reports of fresh military disasters pouring in from the front, the

123 Campbell, interview, 20 Oct. 1968; Heeney, interview, 7 March 1968; Holmes, interview, 5
    March 1968; LePan, interview, 5 March 1968; Pearson, interview, 18 Oct. 1968; Reid, inter-
    view, 9 June 1969
124 Department of External Affairs, *Documents on the Korean Crisis*, 13
125 Pearson, letter to the author, 13 Nov. 1968

External Affairs minister told a conference of provincial premiers in Ottawa on 4 December that

The Chinese Communists have now made it abundantly clear that they regard United Nations action in Korea as something that menaces their interests so greatly that they are willing to risk a general war in challenging it. Therefore, as soon as circumstances make it possible, we must take up again the effort to reconcile on the one hand the determination of the United Nations to resist aggression, and on the other whatever legitimate interests the Chinese may have in the future of Korea and the adjacent area. I am not sure that we *can* reconcile these two – our interests in world peace with the purposes behind their intervention – but we must try; and we must try by some more practical and effective means than mere public statements of good intentions and pious hopes.[126]

Mr Pearson did not on this occasion explicitly indicate just what these 'practical and effective means' of reconciliation would be, but quite clearly they ruled out the possibility of a Korea unified by force of arms. If the war was to be limited, so also must be the objectives.

The intervention of the Chinese comprised in one sense a tragic vindication of the government's diplomacy in New York and Washington during October and November. When it had become clear in the United Nations early in October that the Americans would eventually obtain without difficulty a resolution – however ambiguous – which could be interpreted as authorizing the advance of UN troops into North Korea, Canadian officials had pursued a 'second-best' policy in seeking to obtain from the United States a commitment not to allow MacArthur to proceed too far into North Korean territory. No explicit agreement was obtained, but verbal assurances were given by the Americans both in New York and in Washington, and it was partly on this understanding that the Canadian delegation had voted in support of the eight-power resolution when it came – prematurely in their view – to a vote in plenary session on 7 October.[127] By now, however, there was some suspicion in the department that decisions in Washington were being made under the influence not so much of the Department of State as of the armed forces in

---

126 Department of External Affairs, *Statements and Speeches*, no 50/50. Excerpts also in Department of External Affairs, *Documents on the Korean Crisis*, 13-15
127 Pearson, letter to the author, 13 Nov. 1968. The view that this was a second-best policy, pursued only after it had become clear that the UN Command would be authorized to cross the parallel, emerged in interviews with Heeney, 7 March 1968; Holmes, 1 March 1968; and MacKay, 7 March 1968

the field,[128] a view which was reinforced by the bombing of the Yalu bridges on 5 November, and by increasing evidence of MacArthur's intention of carrying his campaign all the way to the Manchurian border. The impression was heightened by the fact that State Department officials, in attempting to explain to their allies why their assurances had not been kept, used as an excuse their difficulties in keeping the general under control. In the Department of External Affairs, such explanations served only to intensify the 'nightmarish quality' of events in the theatre, which seemed to have developed a wild momentum of their own.[129]

Canadian 'misgivings' over MacArthur's intention of advancing to the Yalu were expressed 'confidentially to the United States authorities in Washington as early as November 6,' and in subsequent 'private discussions at the United Nations' the Canadian delegation supported a widely examined 'proposal that a buffer state should be left along the northern boundary of Korea in order to avoid giving any excuse for suspicion on the part of the Chinese Government that its legitimate interests might be in danger.'[130] The proposal was favoured also by Britain, France, and a number of other powers. The British chiefs of staff advised the Americans on military grounds to halt their advance at the narrow waist of the Korean peninsula roughly half-way between the 38th parallel and the Manchurian border, and British, French, and Canadian representatives in Washington together discussed with the State Department the possibility of establishing a buffer zone to the north of this line.[131] As Escott Reid subsequently put it, 'It made political sense to stop at the 38th parallel, and military sense to stop at the waist, but it was nonsense to go any further.'[132]

The intensity of this diplomatic activity was confirmed by the American secretary of state on 5 June 1951, during the MacArthur Hearings. Asked whether any of the allies had suggested that American forces stop short of the Yalu River, he acknowledged that suggestions for a demilitarized zone south of the Manchurian border had been advanced in the United Nations in October and November with a view to preventing 'clashes' between UN and Chinese or Soviet forces. The proposal, he said, had been 'pretty extensively discussed' by 'the British and the French and the Canadians and maybe three or four others.'[133]

128 Campbell, interview, 20 Oct. 1968; Pearson, interview, 18 Oct. 1968
129 Reid, interview, 9 June 1969
130 Canada, House of Commons, *Debates*, 2 Feb. 1951, 56
131 Truman, *Years of Trial and Hope*, 449; Rees, *Korea*, 145; and Higgins, *Korea and the Fall of MacArthur*, 72
132 Reid, interview, 9 June 1969
133 United States, Senate, *Military Situation in the Far East*, 1957-8

In fact, of course, the Americans had themselves imposed limitations on MacArthur's freedom to advance into the northern half of North Korea. His orders of 27 September had provided explicitly that 'no non-Korean Ground Forces will be used in the northeast provinces bordering the Soviet Union or in the area along the Manchurian border.'[134] But on 24 October the general, without first advising Washington, had ordered his officers to 'drive forward with all speed and full utilization of their forces,' in spite of the fact that they were already stationed along the line of maximum authorized advance. The Joint Chiefs of Staff had then dispatched what Dean Acheson has since called 'a timorous inquiry' requesting an explanation. MacArthur's reply argued in essence that the removal of the restriction had been 'a matter of military necessity,' and that in any case it had not originally possessed the status of an order, but was only a general statement of policy and subject to amendment.[135] By now American forces were already in the restricted area, and the joint chiefs 'at least tacitly accepted MacArthur's defense of his order and made no move to countermand it.'[136] Having been 'proven' wrong in their opposition to MacArthur's plans for an amphibious assault upon Inchon in September, the chiefs were still suffering from the loss of confidence which so often afflicts the vanquished. As one of their number has recently confessed, 'The success of Inchon was so great, and the subsequent prestige of General MacArthur was so overpowering, that the Chiefs hesitated thereafter to question later plans and decisions of the general, which should have been challenged.'[137]

The uncertainties of the joint chiefs were matched by the doubts of the politicians. In a meeting with General Marshall and the JCS on 21 November, just four days in advance of MacArthur's 'home by Christmas' offensive, Dean Acheson gave voice to his preoccupations. 'General MacArthur,' he said,

seemed to have confused his military directive (to follow and destroy the remnant of the North Korean Army unless Chinese intervention in force made it evident that he could not succeed in this task) with his civil affairs directive intended to follow military success (helping the UN Commission establish a government for a united Korea). At this point our object was not 'real estate' but an army. An attempt to establish a united

---

134 See above, 117
135 Quoted in Acheson, *Present at the Creation*, 462
136 Collins, *War in Peacetime*, 180
137 Ibid., 141-2. Dean Acheson has since ascribed this phenomenon to 'uneasy respect for the MacArthur mystique,' *Present at the Creation*, 467. The view that the success of the Inchon operation expanded MacArthur's confidence while diminishing that of his superiors is shared by General Simonds. Interview, 9 June 1970

Korea by force of arms against a determined Chinese resistance could easily lead into general hostilities, since both the Chinese and the Russians, as well as the Japanese, had all regarded Korea as a road to somewhere, rather than an end in itself. Very definitely the policy of our Government was to avoid general war in Asia.

Nevertheless, it appeared that 'General MacArthur could not determine the degree of Chinese intervention without some sort of a "probe" along his line,' and he therefore 'did not oppose that.' 'Going on to diplomatic methods of easing the dangerous showdown that might be coming by such a method as Bevin favored – a cease-fire and a demilitarized zone along the border – or as others had urged by falling back to the neck of Korea, concentrating our forces, as was thought to be Government policy at the end of September, I was sure that General MacArthur would frustrate any such efforts until he had felt out Chinese strength. Accordingly, I had persuaded the British to hold up any initiative in the United Nations.'[138]

That MacArthur would indeed have attempted to frustrate such efforts is evident from his memoirs. According to the General's account:

At about this time [the second week of November], the British Labour government suggested a strange solution to the problem of combating Red China's intervention – give the Communists a slice of North Korea to serve as a 'buffer' area and as evidence of the United Nations' good intentions.

In protesting the short-sightedness of the British proposal, I compared it with the ceding of the Sudetenland to Germany in 1938. Besides violating the spirit of the United Nations decision of June 25, this so-called 'buffer' zone would be a signal to further aggression on the part of the Chinese, and perhaps most important, would bankrupt our political, military and psychological position in the Far East.[139]

During a luncheon meeting with MacArthur, his wife, and a small party of other officers in this period, Captain Brock of the Canadian destroyer division had expressed his personal view that the Canadian government would probably regard the immediate purpose of the UN action in Korea as having been accomplished with the expulsion of the invaders. Would it not be wise to halt the advance at the narrow waist of the peninsula? MacArthur had replied that there was nothing to worry about; there was not the slightest chance of the Chinese coming in. Brock protested that he knew the Chinese were there – his ships had been at the mouth of the Yalu and had seen them.

138 Acheson, *Present at the Creation*, 467
139 MacArthur, *Reminiscences*, 421-2

MacArthur agreed, but repeated his conviction that they would not actively intervene. The United Nations, as the Chinese well knew, had complete control of the air, and under these circumstances the Chinese army could achieve nothing. The captain was unconvinced, and observed that they had sufficient numbers to come in with sticks and rifles if they so desired. The general was unmoved. 'Brock,' he said, gesturing with his fist, 'I have them in the palm of my hand. In the palm of my hand!' Asked what would happen if the Chinese received air support from the Russians, he repeated the gesture: 'They won't get it. I have complete air and sea superiority. I have them in the palm of my hand.'[140]

As Dean Acheson has himself admitted, the American president in dealing with so determined a commander was entitled to better service from his advisers at home.[141] In its absence, the field officer was given free rein. In a private interview with Richard E. Neustadt, Truman reflected later that, 'What we should have done is stop at the neck of Korea right here [pointing to a globe] ... That's what the British wanted ... We knew the Chinese had close to a million men on the border and all that ... But [MacArthur] was commander in the field. You pick your man, you've got to back him up. That's the only way a military organization can work. I got the best advice I could and the men on the spot said this was the thing to do ... So I agreed. That was my decision – no matter what hindsight shows.'[142]

As late as 22 November, just four days before the start of the Chinese counter-offensive, the British were still hoping that Peking might be persuaded not to intervene in strength. On that day the foreign secretary, Ernest Bevin, conveyed a message to Chou En-lai through the British and Indian embassies in Peking assuring him that the UN action entailed 'no hostile intent' toward China, and emphasizing that its only purpose was the creation of a 'free and independent' Korea. The Chinese border would be respected.[143] The British were thus not yet entirely convinced of the fundamental incompatibility of United Nations and Chinese objectives in Korea, and their uncertainty may have reduced the impact of their views upon decision-makers in Washington (who were similarly ignorant of Chinese intentions, and hence were not prepared to force MacArthur to abandon his 'probe').

In the final analysis the failure of the allies to restrain the Americans during the northern advance was probably unimportant. The question of China's

140 Brock, interview, 23 July 1969
141 Acheson, *Present at the Creation*, 466
142 Quoted in Neustadt, *Presidential Power*, 128
143 Rees, *Korea,* 146-7; and Panikkar, *In Two Chinas,* 114-15

participation may well have been decided much earlier – on 7 October, when the General Assembly passed its resolution and American troops first crossed the 38th parallel. Certainly this was the view that the Chinese attempted to convey. Premier Chou En-lai told Panikkar on 3 October that while the 'South Koreans [already in North Korean territory] did not matter ... American intrusion into North Korea would encounter Chinese resistance.'[144] In late November, when the Indian representative raised the 'strange British idea of a neutralized zone, meaning thereby the annexation of the rest of Korea by Syngman Rhee,' the proposal 'was naturally brushed aside as irrelevant by the Chinese.'[145] Panikkar himself believed that the issue had been settled as early as 8 October. He thought also that the Americans and the British were 'well aware' that the Chinese would resist 'a military settlement of the Korean issue' and that their armies would 'intervene decisively in the fight.'[146] This latter suspicion, however, is not supported by the evidence. Indeed, it was precisely because they were without this certain knowledge that the Americans acceded to MacArthur's pressure. On the other hand, once the consequences of their decision had become clear, they were no less fearful than the Indian ambassador of the prospect of a 'nightmare' war in Asia, and to prevent just such a disaster was the principal preoccupation of Canadian statesmen, among others, for the next three months.

Before turning to their activities, however, it is worth emphasizing that this preoccupation produced among the allies of the United States an even greater determination than before to wield influence and impose restraints upon the conduct of American policy. Early in November, for example, MacArthur had requested permission to bomb air bases in Manchuria and to engage in 'hot pursuit' of enemy aircraft fleeing to this 'privileged sanctuary' from Korea. According to President Truman, 'The State Department and the Joint Chiefs of Staff were in agreement that it would be desirable to have UN approval for such a policy and therefore, with my approval, inquiries were made of all United Nations countries that had forces in Korea. Without exception, they indicated strong opposition. Indeed, they also stressed their wish that no non-Korean units should be placed in the area immediately adjacent to the Yalu River if our offensive should carry us that far.'[147]

This inquiry was despatched from Washington on 13 November, and it arrived in Ottawa on the following day. It advised the government

144 Panikkar, *In Two Chinas*, 110
145 Ibid., 115
146 Ibid., 111
147 Truman, *Years of Trial and Hope*, 435

that it may become necessary at an early date to permit UN aircraft to defend themselves in the air space over the Yalu River to the extent of permitting hot pursuit of attacking enemy aircraft up to 2 or 3 minutes' flying time into Manchuria air space.

It is contemplated that UN aircraft would limit themselves to repelling enemy aircraft engaged in offensive missions to Korea.

We believe this would be a minimum reaction to extreme provocation, would not in itself affect adversely the attitude of the enemy toward Korean operations, would serve as a warning, and would add greatly to the morale of UN pilots ... [148]

The Department of External Affairs signified Canada's opposition to this proposal within 'two hours of their request for our opinion.' [149] The Americans were urged at the very least to wait until there had been an opportunity to warn the Chinese that such action might be taken in the event that their aircraft became engaged over Korea, and not to proceed in any case without having obtained authority first from Lake Success. [150] As Mr Pearson told the House of Commons in April 1951, the State Department was advised that 'though a strong case could be made under international law that the United Nations commander in chief had the right to retaliate against any air attacks launched from Manchuria, we considered it important, as indeed did other governments, that no military operations take place outside Korean borders without specific authority from the United Nations.' He conceded that it was 'possible to visualize a situation where immediate retaliatory action, without consultation, might be unavoidable in pursuing enemy bombers back to the Manchurian air base from which they came.' But the 'decision on the spot to take such immediate retaliatory action would presumably be based on overriding considerations of military security.' It would also 'have to balance very carefully local military considerations against the risk of precipitating a further extension of the war and the effect of such an extension on the security of the United Nations forces in Korea, and the accomplishment of United Nations aims there.' [151]

148 Quoted in Cottrell and Dougherty, 'The Lessons of Korea,' 48
149 Reid, 'The Conscience of the Diplomat,' 584. This view of the Canadian reaction has been confirmed in more general terms by Campbell, interview, 20 Oct. 1968; Foulkes, interview, 7 March 1968; Heeney, interview, 7 March 1968; LePan, interview, 5 March 1968; and Pearson, interview, 18 Oct. 1968. General Foulkes, however, was strongly opposed to the Canadian diplomatic response and sent a memorandum to Mr Pearson in protest. The general took the view that the first concern of a field commander is the security of his operation, and that to deny 'hot pursuit' to MacArthur was to tie his hands.
150 Pearson, letter to the author, 13 Nov. 1968
151 Canada, House of Commons, Debates, 26 April 1951, 2396-7

The allied protest was effective for the time being in restraining the American hand, much to General MacArthur's disgust and chagrin.[152] Not long after Mr Pearson's April report to the Canadian House of Commons, however, the Americans and the British agreed that airfields in Manchuria might be struck 'if they were used to attack the Eighth Army.'[153] There is evidence in any case that the restrictions against 'hot pursuit' were systematically violated by pilots and middle-ranking American air force officers in the field, who sometimes went so far as to destroy combat films in order to conceal the fact that action had taken place north of the Yalu River.[154]

A more lasting product of allied concern over American policy was the creation late in November of the so-called Committee of Sixteen, which included representatives of all the members of the United Nations with armed forces operating in Korea, Canada included. The committee began meeting regularly in Washington in January 1951, twice a week at first, on Tuesdays and Thursdays, and later once a week, usually on Thursdays after lunch.[155] Its primary purpose was to provide the Allies with briefings on military and political developments relating to the conduct of the war, but there has been scepticism in the literature about the degree to which it actually comprised an effective vehicle for the exercise of allied influence. It has been argued in particular that the committee did not receive information in sufficient detail, nor far enough in advance, to permit the effective presentation of alternative views.[156] The Canadian representatives nevertheless found the proceedings extremely useful. The sessions were attended throughout by the second secretary of the Canadian embassy in Washington, P.G.R. Campbell, and when matters of special significance were discussed, by the ambassador, Hume Wrong. They normally began with a military briefing on conditions at the front by a Pentagon officer, usually a captain or major. These reports were highly detailed, and included descriptions of military actions in individual front line locations, often with reference to particular hills or outposts. In itself, the information thus acquired was of use primarily to the Joint Intelligence Board and to the military staffs in Ottawa, but on the political side its chief significance derived from the fact

---

152 The general later complained that 'step-by-step my weapons were being taken away from me.' *Reminiscences*, 415
153 Rees, *Korea*, 373
154 See Mahurin, *Honest John*, 68-72, 83-9, for a first-hand account of how this was done.
155 Campbell, interview, 20 Oct. 1968 and letter to the author, 12 Nov. 1968
156 Goodrich, 'Korea: Collective Measures Against Aggression,' 167-8. This interpretation is shared by Bowett, *United Nations Forces*, 42; and by Yoo, *The Korean War and the United Nations*, 40

that the military engagements in question sometimes had political implications. The political aspects were generally handled by the assistant secretary of state for United Nations affairs, John D. Hickerson, or by the assistant secretary for Far Eastern affairs, Dean Rusk.

Once the briefings were concluded, the discussions ranged widely over the full spectrum of the military and political aspects of the war. Often the American State Department officer would specifically request the opinions of those present with respect to issues that he had raised, but it frequently happened, too, that a major policy question or protest would originate with one of the other nationals in attendance. The Canadian delegate might decide as an alternative to pursue a matter at issue with the State Department later on a bilateral basis. This was particularly the case in the final phases of the war, when a representative of South Korea was added to the committee's membership and when the questions in dispute often concerned Washington's handling of its relations with Seoul.

There was considerable *esprit de corps* among the non-American participants, but there was never advance collusion against the American officials. The Canadians, British, and Australians were especially close and often lunched together beforehand for general discussion, but the views even of these three were seldom unanimous. The principal Canadian participant can recall only one occasion on which there was advance agreement upon a tactic to be adopted during a committee session, and this was merely in support of a request for further information on a specific issue.[157]

The general Canadian view was that the meetings comprised not a forum for coming to grips with issues in dispute, but an important source of information, which facilitated the department's formulation of effective bilateral action.[158] When Mr Pearson was asked in the House of Commons, at the height of the MacArthur controversy, about the problem of maintaining United Nations control over the military in the field, he pointed out that so far as UN forces were concerned, the Americans were doing 'about 95 per cent of the actual fighting,' which naturally meant that they would 'exercise a preponderating influence.' Canada would 'be the last to criticize that,' and 'on the whole' the government had 'very little to complain about the consultation which we have managed to achieve at Lake Success and in Washington on this matter.' It was true that the 'translation of the results of that consultation to the commanders across the Pacific' was 'not always as effective or as easy as

157 Campbell, interview, 20 Oct. 1968
158 Ibid. A similar view of the utility of the committee has been expressed by Heeney, interview, 7 March 1968; Holmes, interview, 1 March 1968; and Pearson, interview, 18 Oct. 1968
159 Canada, House of Commons, *Debates*, 20 March 1951, 1444

we would like it to be,' but this was 'largely because of the nature of the operation.'[159] Some weeks later, he told the House of Commons Standing Committee on External Affairs that reports from the UN commander-in-chief were conveyed first to the United States chiefs of staff, acting as the unified command, and through them to the United Nations and its members, who could offer comments as they saw fit. In addition, the representatives of the contributing powers received regular briefings from State and Defense Department officials in Washington. Canada, he added, had 'influence on general policy as a member of the United Nations with forces in Korea,' but of course the government did not 'interfere in the conduct of military operations.'[160]

In other areas of policy, however, Mr Pearson during the weeks following the Chinese intervention was to apply his entire store of diplomatic energy in an attempt to influence through the United Nations the course of American behaviour.

160 Canada, House of Commons, Standing Committee on External Affairs, *Minutes of Proceedings and Evidence*, 25 May 1951, 30

5

In pursuit of peace

While Canadian and like-minded diplomatists from other countries were attempting to restrain the executors of policy in Washington, their colleagues at Lake Success were trying to temper the consequences of the Chinese intervention. In the pursuit of this objective they were ultimately to collide again with decision-makers in the United States, who in the Korean context were ostensibly United Nations agents. The causes of this collision were complex, but at bottom they were rooted in the fact that the appearance of the Chinese Volunteers produced a reaction among allied delegations at Lake Success very different from the one it generated in the Department of State. At Lake Success it immediately reinforced the supporters of United Nations action in Korea in their original view that the proper function of the UN in the theatre should be limited to repelling the aggressor and preventing him from acquiring his intended spoils. There was a prevailing belief that the 7 October resolution constituted a gross error in judgment which should have been obvious to everyone, and had been obvious to some, from the beginning. The Chinese intervention was unwarranted, perhaps, but not, in the circumstances, difficult to understand. In any case, now that the damage had been done every effort must be made to redefine the United Nations purpose in the theatre and to convince Peking that its security was not under threat. At all costs a major escalation of the political and territorial scope of the hostilities must be avoided, since for various reasons associated with their respective national interests, the last thing desired even by the closest of America's allies was a large-scale Asian war.

In Washington, on the other hand, Chinese participation tended to magnify the importance of the crisis as a 'cold war' challenge which could not safely be ignored. It also had the effect of intensifying the pressures of the American 'Right' upon Truman's administration – pressures which had already been strengthened by Democratic losses in the November mid-term Congressional elections.[1] In addition, it made even more difficult than before the task of maintaining the fiction that the war in Korea was an engagement undertaken on behalf of the principle of 'collective security' and subject to police force limitations. The Communist Chinese, without (in the American view) just cause, had tossed a gauntlet at MacArthur's feet; to make apologies or concessions in the face of such a challenge was politically and strategically as well as morally indefensible. President Truman and his advisers were no more willing than the delegates at Lake Success to embark upon a major war with China or to carry the hostilities beyond their present geographical limits. But the difference in the American perspective nevertheless gave rise to a conflict of views which was reflected in the administration's subsequent relations with allied members of the UN. Canada was among the states most immediately affected by the ensuing diplomatic melee.

The first official notification to the United Nations of Chinese involvement at the front was General MacArthur's special report of 5 November, which arrived at Lake Success on the following day. Although the initial UN response did not directly involve the Canadian delegation, it demonstrated almost immediately the pattern of conflict which was soon to develop between Lake Success and Washington, and which was so frequently to frustrate Canadian policy-makers in their desire to protect the viability of the United Nations without at the same time placing undue strain upon their relations with the United States.

The first of the UN manoeuvres was undertaken at the behest of Great Britain and it consisted of a Security Council resolution inviting Peking to send a representative 'to be present during discussion by the Council' of MacArthur's special report. The resolution was passed on 8 November by a count of 8-2-1, with Nationalist China and Cuba voting against and Egypt abstaining. The American delegate, Warren Austin, had cast his vote in favour of the invitation, but not with enthusiasm. His government, it became clear, thought the wording of the resolution much too courteous and restrained: 'The present facts which are before us could be interpreted as a provocation to general war ... [and] there might be gained some information from witnesses from the Chinese Communist regime which might guide us toward prevention of a

1 See Caridi, *The Korean War and American Politics*, especially Chapter 5

general war ... [However] I believe that this regime should not be invited, but rather they should be summoned to appear.'[2]

Mr Austin did not, however, press the point too vigorously. His restraint was due at least in part to the fact that a public display of diplomatic moderation had become the prerequisite for maintaining the international support upon which the legitimacy of American policy had been based. As President Truman later acknowledged, among the most important of his government's preoccupations throughout the month of November was the need 'to reassure our allies in Europe, especially the British and French, that we had no intention of widening the conflict or of abandoning our commitments in Europe for new entanglements in Asia,' and at the same time to secure in the United Nations 'the maximum support for our resistance against the Chinese intervention in Korea, without, however, pushing the UN toward military sanctions against Peiping – which would have meant war.'[3] Both these endeavours required that Washington refrain from placing obstacles in the way of a UN peace initiative, however futile it might appear to be.

Similar considerations were evident two days later, on 10 November, when six members of the Security Council, including the United States, Britain, France, Cuba, Ecuador, and Norway, introduced a resolution which in effect called upon the Chinese to withdraw from Korea. While the resolution reaffirmed the 7 October objective of a unified, independent, and democratic government throughout the peninsula, it also provided (a) that 'United Nations forces should not remain in any part of Korea otherwise than so far as necessary for achieving' this purpose, (b) that 'no action be taken which might lead to the spread of the Korean conflict to other areas and thereby endanger international peace and security,' and (c) that it was 'the policy of the United Nations to hold the Chinese frontier with Korea inviolate and fully to protect legitimate Chinese and Korean interests in the frontier zone.'[4] The fundamental incompatibility between these guarantees to China and the objective of a 'unified, independent and democratic' Korea was thus still unresolved, but the tone of the resolution was moderate and clearly designed to mollify as well as to warn the authorities in Peking. It was followed by public statements and diplomatic initiatives on the part of Britain, the United States, and other countries, all directed to the same, and as it turned out, futile purpose.[5] The

---

2 Quoted in Department of External Affairs, 'The Korean Crisis,' *External Affairs*, II, 12, Dec. 1950, 429. For the text of the resolution, see Department of External Affairs, *Documents on the Korean Crisis*, 10

3 Truman, *Years of Trial and Hope*, 434

4 Department of External Affairs, *Documents on the Korean Crisis*, 11

5 Department of External Affairs, 'The Korean Crisis,' *External Affairs*, II, 12 Dec. 1950, 430-1

six-power resolution itself was subsequently vetoed in the Security Council by the USSR on 30 November, and the issue was then taken to the General Assembly. On 6 December the assembly voted 51 to 5 (Soviet bloc) in favour of placing the matter before its Political Committee.

On 11 November, meanwhile, the Chinese had announced that they would not accept the Security Council invitation of 8 November on the ground that the scope of the proposed discussions included only the subject of MacArthur's special report and did not extend to the 'question of armed intervention in Korea and aggression against China by the United States Government.' In a separate communication, however, the mainland regime did agree to accept an earlier invitation to consider Peking's own complaint of an American 'armed invasion of Taiwan.'

The Chinese delegation, led by General Wu Hsui-ch'üan, arrived in New York on 24 November, the same day MacArthur launched his 'end-the-war' offensive in Korea. Substantive discussions did not begin in the Security Council for another four days, however, and by then news had arrived of the Chinese counter-offensive and of MacArthur's ominous warning that his forces now faced 'an entirely new war.' These events naturally had an impact on the course of the proceedings, and in particular the United States appeared to take the view that the confrontation with China had progressed beyond the point of negotiation. 'It now appears doubtful,' Warren Austin told the Council, 'that the war in Korea can be quickly concluded. It also appears clear beyond any doubt that what all the free world hoped was an intervention for limited purpose is, in fact, aggression – open and notorious.'[6]

General Wu was no more conciliatory. In proposing a resolution which called for the withdrawal of foreign troops from both Formosa and Korea, he declared that China could not 'afford to stand idly by in the face of this serious situation brought about by the United States Government's aggression against Korea and the dangerous tendency toward the extension of the war.' The Chinese people had 'witnessed with their own eyes Taiwan fall prey to this aggression, and the flames of the United States war of aggression against Korea leap towards them,' and 'stirred into righteous anger,' they were 'volunteering in great numbers to go to the aid of the Korean people.' His government saw no reason for stopping them.[7]

These opening statements by the principals in the dispute set the pattern for the ensuing debate, and except for the consequent deterioration of their respective tempers, no change in the position of either protagonist could be

6 Quoted ibid.
7 Quoted ibid., 432

discerned throughout the duration of General Wu's stay in New York. This display of mutual intransigence accordingly aroused the anxiety of America's allies, among them Britain and Canada. Until the development of the Chinese counter-offensive, these powers had clung to the hope that massive intervention by Peking might be avoided. Now that this hope had been crushed, and with the looming prospect of a major Sino-American conflict in Asia reflected in the desultory exchanges in New York, they began a desperate search for a peaceful solution.

The search was to be complicated by the reluctance ot the American authorities to agree to the initiation of diplomatic inquiries with Peking. On 2 December Warren Austin, Ernest Gross, and Dean Acheson met in Washington to formulate policy recommendations for the president. According to Acheson's account, 'Suggestions of approaching the Chinese or the Russians with proposals for a cease-fire, either through Sir Benegal Rau or Sir Girja Bajpai of India or the Russians directly through our embassy, were vetoed.' The Chinese intervention was clearly designed 'to make the US-UN position in Korea untenable,' and the public attitude and military preparations of the Chinese regime 'indicated an appreciation of the risk of general war with the United States.' 'It was unlikely that the Chinese would have run this risk without some assurances of support from the Soviet Union.' The Soviet government

probably saw advantages to it in the US-Chinese war flowing from the diversion, attrition, and containment of US forces in an indecisive theatre; the creation of conflict between the United States and her European allies and the obstruction of NATO plans; the disruption of UN unity against the original aggression in Korea, thus also aiding Communist objectives in Southeast Asia. If, however, the United States should decline the gamble of war with China and withdraw from Korea, the USSR might be counting on collecting the stakes in Korea and Indochina. In any event, the United States Government should expect aggressive Soviet pursuit of its attack on the world position of the United States. Other aggressions in Asia and Europe were not to be counted out.[8]

Later in the day, in the light of such observations, President Truman directed his advisers to place the question of the Chinese intervention before the General Assembly. They should not, however, recommend any particular course of United Nations action until they had consulted with Prime Minister Clement Attlee of Great Britain, who was arriving in Washington within

8 Acheson, *Present at the Creation*, 473-4

thirty-six hours. They might then suggest to the British leader that the six-power resolution which had been vetoed in the Security Council on 30 November[9] could be taken before the General Assembly under the new 'Uniting for Peace' doctrine.[10] The resolution, which had combined assurances to the Chinese with an appeal that they withdraw from Korea, was 'not wholly appropriate to the changed fortunes of war, but it had the advantage of keeping our own position steady and calm and holding our UN allies together for a while, at least.'[11]

The problem of how to maintain an uncompromising posture vis-à-vis the Chinese, without at the same time alienating the allies, thus became the principal preoccupation of American diplomacy during the ensuing weeks. Since the two objectives were not entirely compatible, and since the Americans attached more importance to the first than to the second, tensions between American and allied officials were the almost inevitable result. They became explicit during the meetings between Truman and Attlee early in December.

These discussions had been arranged as a result of statements made by President Truman during a press conference in Washington on 30 November. In his opening remarks, the president had expressed his regret that mainland China had intervened in the war, had indicated that the United Nations would have to resist the attack, and had announced that his government would support it in doing so. The Chinese 'aggression,' he said, was 'only a part of a world-wide pattern of danger to all the free nations,' and reinforced the need for western rearmament.[12] But what aroused concern abroad, and especially in London, was an apparently casual exchange with one of the reporters during the general discussion which followed the formal statement. Truman had said that the United States would 'take whatever steps are necessary to meet the military situation, just as we always have.' Asked whether this would include the atomic bomb, he had replied that it included 'every weapon that we have.' Did this mean there was 'active consideration of the use of the atomic bomb?' 'There has always been active consideration of its use.'[13]

---

9 See above, 143-4
10 The 'Uniting for Peace' resolution, or 'Acheson Plan,' was advanced by the Americans as a means of activating the General Assembly in contexts in which the Security Council was unable to perform its peace and security functions effectively because of the repeated application of a great power veto. The resolution was approved by the assembly on 3 November 1950 by a vote of 53-5-2. Canada was one of seven co-sponsors. For the full text, and for a statement of the Canadian position, see Department of External Affairs, *Canada and the United Nations, 1950*, 167-72
11 Acheson, *Present at the Creation*, 474
12 Quoted in Truman, *Years of Trial and Hope*, 442-4
13 Quoted ibid., 450

A statement of clarification issued after the conference to the effect that 'consideration of the use of any weapon is always implicit in the very possession of that weapon'[14] made little impression upon the reports which appeared subsequently in the press, and there ensued among other reactions an anxious debate in the British House of Commons. According to one historian of Anglo-American affairs, Truman's 'rash statement ... almost certainly marked the lowest point in the graph of Anglo-American good relations since Pearl Harbour,'[15] and the American embassy in London reported to the president that this was 'the most serious, anxious, and responsible debate on foreign affairs conducted by the House of Commons since the Labor Party came to power in 1945.'[16] Officials in the Canadian Department of External Affairs were also concerned, Mr Pearson having reflected already on the possibility that the Americans would over-react militarily to the difficulties their forces were now facing in the theatre.[17] But it was the government in Whitehall that was under the greatest pressure. Confronted with a letter signed by one hundred Labour members of Parliament protesting any possible use of the atomic bomb in Korea, and fearful himself of an extension of the hostilities to mainland China, Prime Minister Attlee at the end of the debate announced amid cheers from all quarters of the House that he had decided to fly to Washington for talks with President Truman.

After discussions with the premier and foreign minister of France, who were then visiting London, and being 'also in close touch with opinion in the Commonwealth,'[18] Attlee arrived in the American capital on 4 December. The resulting four days of discussions ranged widely over Far East and 'cold war' affairs. President Truman and Dean Acheson have described the progress of the talks in some detail in their respective memoirs,[19] and it is unnecessary to recount the proceedings here. In sum the two parties agreed that military resistance to the Chinese would have to be maintained, that care should be taken to confine operations if at all possible to the Korean theatre itself, and that the western powers in future would have to strengthen appreciably their military defences vis-à-vis the Soviet bloc. At the same time, however, they

---

14 Quoted ibid., 451
15 Allen, *Great Britain and the United States*, 971
16 Quoted in Truman, *Years of Trial and Hope*, 451
17 Campbell, interview, 20 Oct. 1968; Heeney, interview, 7 March 1968; Holmes, interview, 5 March 1968; LePan, interview, 5 March 1968; and the Pearson, interview, 18 Oct. 1968
18 Attlee, *As It Happened*, 200
19 See Truman, *Years of Trial and Hope*, 451-69; and Acheson, *Present at the Creation*, 478-85. Unfortunately, Attlee's memoirs are not helpful, and the available accounts therefore give a one-sided impression.

disagreed on the question of admitting Peking to the United Nations and on the degree to which Chinese policy could be regarded as originating in the USSR. The British in particular did not subscribe to the American monolithic interpretation of Communist bloc politics, and like the Canadians they therefore tended to regard the Chinese intervention as a parochial manoeuvre designed to support what Peking considered to be a vital national interest. The Americans, by contrast, interpreted the Chinese counter-offensive as a 'cold war' initiative emanating ultimately from Moscow, and they consequently believed it to be a matter of far more general – and ominous – significance.

From the Canadian vantage point, the important feature of the Anglo-American exchange concerned the attitudes taken respectively by the two powers on the question of negotiations with the Chinese. Mr Pearson's position on this issue had much in common with that of the British, a fact which became clear in two policy statements which he delivered publicly during the Attlee-Truman talks. Although they were not the product of direct collusion with the British authorities,[20] Prime Minister Attlee may well have found them useful during the course of his discussions with the president. Walter O'Hearn, then the United Nations correspondent of the *Montreal Star*, reported later that

The strength that Canada has shown on Britain's side is not to be underestimated; the British certainly don't undervalue it. The activity shown by Lester Pearson, Canada's External Affairs Minister, during the crisis – an activity which went far beyond two public statements – was the most important backing Attlee received during his talks in Washington.

In the crisis, Commonwealth unity has been tighter than at any time since 1945 – a considerable gain from the British view and one which the sensitive barographs at Lake Success were quick to note.[21]

The first of Mr Pearson's two statements was delivered to a federal-provincial fiscal conference in Ottawa on 4 December, the same day Attlee arrived in Washington. In it the minister made it very clear once again that the Canadian government wished at all costs to avoid an unlimited conflict with the Chinese. Speculating on the 'risk of a major war,' he argued that the

20 Campbell, interview, 20 Oct. 1968; Heeney, interview, 7 March 1968; Holmes, interview, 5 March 1968; Pearson, interview, 18 Oct. 1968. The same sources confirm, however, that *consultation* between the British and Canadian authorities was full and continuous throughout the discussions.
21 O'Hearn, 'The Allies and the War,' 9

conduct of 'military operations against the territory of China itself ... might well result in Soviet assistance to the Chinese forces' and thereafter in an 'open war' with the USSR. For the time being the key to avoiding such an eventuality was 'to find a solution to the grave and menacing problem that has arisen' in Korea. To do this, it was necessary first to stabilize the military front, but not at the cost of a major Asian war, which would divert attention from the more vital theatre in Europe, and certainly not at the cost of using the atomic bomb. Among the dire consequences of the latter policy there might well be included the destruction of 'the cohesion and unity of purpose of the Atlantic community,' and a dangerous weakening of 'the links that remain between the Western world and the peoples of the East.' At the very least, 'a decision of such immense and awful consequence' should not be taken without consultation at the United Nations with the governments principally concerned, of which Canada, as 'a partner in the tri-partite development of atomic energy,' was one. [22]

President Truman's press conference remark was clearly regarded in Ottawa as a blunder. Much more important, however, was the fact that Mr Pearson shared with the British the view that priority should be given in the 'cold war' (as in World War II) to the European rather than to the Asian front, and the conviction that the conflict in Korea should not be allowed to siphon the defensive capabilities of the West away from more vital theatres elsewhere in the world. This meant in turn that the United Nations must avoid at all costs an armed conflagration extending beyond what still could be regarded as a parochial war designed to counter a parochial aggression.

This desire to limit the scope of the hostilities was of course shared by the Truman administration, if not by General MacArthur. Where they differed was in their estimate of the means. The eagerness of the British and the Canadians to bring the war to a speedy end led them to avoid policies which carried a risk of military escalation, and to advocate instead an attempt to open cease-fire negotiations as soon as possible with the Chinese. The Americans, on the other hand, felt that any such endeavour would be foolhardy so long as United Nations forces were on the defensive at the front, and they therefore argued that the military situation had to be improved first.

Mr Pearson's 4 December address made no specific mention of negotiations, and indeed its implication was that the front had to be stabilized (although not necessarily advanced) before they could begin. But in Washington on the same day Prime Minister Attlee began his presentation on the Far East crisis by raising just this possibility, and by asking the Americans what price

22 Department of External Affairs, *Statements and Speeches*, no 50/50

they thought the Chinese would demand in return for a negotiated cease-fire. He told Truman that opinions in the United Nations and in the countries of Europe, Asia, and America had to be considered, together with those of the Asian members of the Commonwealth with whom he had been 'in close touch.' He conceded that the Chinese price for negotiations might go up if Peking detected a 'spirit of accommodation' among the UN powers involved. That would be distasteful, but 'we had to bear in mind that the West [i.e., Western Europe] could not be given up, that it was still the vital point in our line against Communism.'[23]

Acheson was not 'optimistic about prospects of negotiations with the Chinese Communists.' Given that their forces were on the offensive, they would have little to gain from accepting a cease-fire. They would therefore demand a price, which would probably include 'recognition of their government,' 'a seat in the United Nations Security Council,' and 'concessions on Formosa.' It was possible that they would 'even insist that any Japanese peace settlements had to have their assent.'[24]

This was the crux of the disagreement. The Americans maintained that if concessions were made, the Chinese would become more, not less, aggressive in the future, and that in any case a settlement of this kind would be unacceptable to the American public. Truman himself hoped to 'hold the line in Korea until the situation improved the chances for negotiation,' and he read out to Attlee an American policy memorandum which he had approved and which stipulated that while a cease-fire 'might insure full support of the United Nations,' it 'must not impose conditions which would jeopardize the safety of United Nations forces nor be conditioned on agreement on other issues, such as Formosa, and the Chinese seat in the United Nations.' If the Chinese rejected a reasonable cease-fire offer and crossed the 38th parallel into South Korea, 'the United Nations must take immediate action to declare Communist China an aggressor and must mobilize such political and economic measures as are available to bring pressure upon Peiping and to affirm the determination of the United Nations not to accept an aggression.' There was also the possibility of 'military action which would harass the Chinese Communists and of efforts which could be made to stimulate anti-Communist resistance within China itself, including the exploitation of Nationalist capabilities.'[25]

These were precisely the sorts of measures which the British feared would harden rather than soften the Chinese position, and carry in addition the risk

23 Truman, *Years of Trial and Hope*, 452
24 Ibid., 453
25 Ibid., 454-6

of escalating the war. When the discussions were resumed after lunch on the following day, 5 December, therefore, Attlee reiterated his view that the Chinese should be approached in a spirit of accommodation, adding that he thought 'the Chinese Communists were potentially ripe for "Titoism" ' and that the West had everything to gain by wooing them away from the Russians, who were their 'natural rivals in the Far East.' In the course of his presentation, the prime minister pointed out that 'it would be difficult to get UN action on any move that might appear directed against Peiping or likely to result in retaliations,' and later in the same meeting told Truman 'that he knew that I would have to consider public opinion about Chiang Kai-shek and Formosa but that he hoped I would also remember that whatever we did would have to be done through the UN, and it could not be done there by the efforts and votes of just the United States and the United Kingdom, "important as we are." '[26]

The prime minister thus utilized the attitudes prevalent at Lake Success as a bargaining lever for influencing decision-makers in Washington. Such strength as it possessed acquired its force from the desire of the Americans to retain as far as possible the moral support of the United Nations in the pursuit of their policies in the Far East. The merchants of legitimacy were attempting to exact a full price for their wares.

Conspicuous among them, in addition to Mr Attlee, was the Canadian secretary of state for external affairs. On the same evening, 5 December, Mr Pearson broadcast over the CBC an address from Lake Success in which he announced his support for negotiations with the Chinese Communist regime. Several days earlier his department had forwarded a message to Prime Minister Nehru suggesting that he appeal directly to Peking for a cessation of hostilities. Nehru had replied that he was reluctant to undertake any such initiative unless it held a reasonable chance of success, a precondition which he thought was absent, given the positions taken respectively by the American and Chinese governments.[27] Now Mr Pearson was taking an initiative of his own. Beginning with a brief account of the global proportions of the 'cold war' confrontation, he went on to say that the Canadian government from the start had believed that the United Nations action in Korea 'should be directed solely towards defeating the aggression and thereby halting the chain reaction which might have followed its success.' After the successful landings at Inchon, the problem had arisen of determining precisely where the UN 'would attempt to re-establish the political position in the Korean area.' There had been different

26 Ibid., 458-60
27 Pearson, interview, 18 Oct. 1968

opinions, but Canada throughout had 'consistently urged that moderation and a sense of global strategy, both military and political, should be our guide in deciding at what point military operations should be broken off and the work of pacification and reconstruction begun.' The Chinese had now entered the war in very large numbers. 'Their final purpose is not yet beyond doubt, but certainly they have committed themselves to an incursion far in excess of any that might be explained by nervousness over local Chinese interests along the border between Manchuria and Korea. In this dangerous situation, it remains our view that if and when the military position is stabilized, we should try to begin negotiations with the Chinese Communists by every means possible.' Mr Pearson was 'aware of the difficulties' but believed that 'nothing should be left undone which might conceivably result in an honourable and peaceful settlement in Korea.' 'If, for example, providing the military situation is stabilized, there could be a cease-fire followed by negotiations – possibly covering more subjects than Korea – in which the Chinese Communists would participate, there might still be hope of reaching such a settlement. At least, we would have done our best and the responsibility for failure would be placed where it would belong.' He knew that this policy might be called 'appeasement,' but it was 'the function of diplomacy to seek accommodation which can be the basis for stable relations between differing countries and systems.' Care should of course be taken not to weaken the unity or resolve of the countries of the 'free world,' and there would be difficulties in reconciling political and military considerations. For example, there would be a military temptation to use the atomic bomb, but this temptation would have to be resisted. It might well be that negotiation would become impossible in the days ahead, or would be tried and fail, and force would then have to be met only with force. But in the meantime, 'we must guard freedom by wisdom, as well as by arms.'[28]

In one respect the Canadian position seemed closer to the American than to the British, for Mr Pearson's advocacy of negotiations was still predicated upon a stabilization of the military front. It later became clear, however, that he was making a distinction between cease-fire negotiations on the one hand and negotiations for a political settlement on the other. In the following February, in explaining the 5 December address to the House of Commons, he recalled that he had

insisted that a cease-fire must precede and not follow peace negotiations, and that is the position from which we have never wavered. I believe we in this government, in this house and in this country are as anxious as anyone to secure a peaceful settlement

28 Department of External Affairs, *Statements and Speeches*, no 50/51

in Korea, but I think we know that such a settlement would be bought at too high a cost if it denied and betrayed the obligations we as a member of the United Nations had already undertaken in respect to Korea.

In my view it would have been such a betrayal if we had entered into political negotiations, as distinct from cease-fire negotiations, with the Peking Government while its troops were still attacking United Nations forces. We have been willing to have the United Nations discuss with the Chinese Communists a settlement in Korea and throughout the Far East, but we have not been willing at any time to ask members of the United Nations to participate in such discussions under duress while their men were being killed in Korea.[29]

Of the three positions – British, American, and Canadian – two, the British and the Canadian, were unrealistic, the first because it underestimated the intransigence of the Americans, and the second because it underestimated the intransigence of the Chinese. The Canadian view was that progress should be based upon the following sequence of events: (a) stabilization of the military front; (b) initiation of cease-fire negotiations; (c) conclusion of a cease-fire; and (d) general political negotiations to settle a number of outstanding Far East problems, including the future of Korea, the status of Formosa, and the seating of Communist China in the United Nations. The British view was that the Chinese, given the conditions at the front, would not undertake cease-fire *or* political negotiations unless they were granted a number of political concessions in advance, and they therefore advocated a sequence something like the following: (a) American recognition of the Peking regime and the admission of mainland China to the United Nations; (b) initiation of cease-fire negotiations; (c) conclusion of a cease-fire; and (d) negotiations for a general political settlement of the Korean, Formosan, and other outstanding problems in the Far East. The Americans agreed with the British that the Chinese would require political concessions as a precondition for cease-fire negotiations, but disagreed that such concessions should be made; they therefore advocated: (a) improvement of the United Nations bargaining position vis-à-vis the Chinese through an increase in the strength of UN forces in the theatre and through the application of moral and economic sanctions directly against mainland China; (b) initiation of cease-fire negotiations under conditions in which the Chinese, as a result of (a), would be suffering grave military and economic deprivations; (c) conclusion of a cease-fire; (d) initiation, if possible, of negotiations for the settlement of other outstanding Far East issues. In the event, the Canadian policy was attempted – only to fail precisely because the Chinese

29 Canada, House of Commons, *Debates*, 2 Feb. 1951, 56-7

fulfilled British and American expectations in demanding political concessions in advance of a cease-fire; the British policy was never tried because the Americans refused to make the necessary concessions; and therefore in the end a modified progress through steps (a), (b), and (c) of the American programme was completed, the modification consisting essentially of a reduction in the intensity of pressure which was implied in the original American version of (a). Phase (d) was never effectively achieved.

To return to the discussions between Attlee and Truman in Washington, and to the relation of Canadian policy to them, it is of course important to recognize that Mr Pearson's was not the only UN voice advocating a diplomatic initiative. Indeed, on the very same day that he delivered his radio address, an appeal had been signed by thirteen Asian and Middle Eastern powers, including India, and dispatched to Peking *via* General Wu. In it, the Chinese and North Koreans were asked to declare that their forces would not cross the 38th parallel into South Korea. The petitioners argued that this would 'give time for considering what further steps are necessary to resolve the conflict in the Far East, thus helping to avert another world war.'[30]

Two days later Attlee and Truman returned to the subject of Far Eastern affairs, and when it became clear that the American position was unchanged, the British dealt their UN card once again, fortified this time by Mr Pearson's 5 December address and by the thirteen-power petition. Sir Roger Makins, the British deputy under secretary of state, argued that 'any policy our governments followed ought to be a United Nations policy,' and that it therefore 'would have to be one that could command a majority in the General Assembly.' 'As he saw it, there was a very strong sentiment in the United Nations for a negotiated settlement. That feeling, he thought, was so strong that if we had not been so careful in the past to negotiate everything pertaining to Korea through the United Nations we would now be having real trouble trying to keep other nations with us. He thought that perhaps we ought to let the United Nations find the way to some settlement.'[31]

The result was a communiqué, composed on 8 December and issued the following day, which indicated among other things the readiness of both governments 'to seek an end to the hostilities by means of negotiation.' It conceded also, however, that there had been disagreement on the question of a seat for mainland China in the United Nations.[32] In practice this was to

30 Quoted in Department of External Affairs, 'The Korean Crisis,' *External Affairs*, II, 12, Dec. 1950, 433
31 Truman, *Years of Trial and Hope*, 463
32 Ibid., 467-8

amount to a victory – albeit a delayed victory – for the Americans, since the Chinese ultimately indicated that they would reject any initiative that was not prefaced by recognition of their right to hold the UN seat occupied by Formosa. The Americans were prepared to allow the United Nations to attempt a negotiated cease-fire because they agreed with the British that this was necessary for continued UN support for military resistance in the theatre. They believed, nonetheless, that the attempt would be futile unless and until there was an improvement at the front – an improvement which would probably require a considerable intensification of pressure upon the Peking regime. Hence, although they agreed that every effort should be made to prevent the hostilities from escalating into a general war with mainland China, they were at the same time convinced that within this limitation the maximum moral and economic pressure should be exerted upon the Chinese in order to augment the purely military effort on the battlefield itself. If, as the Americans expected, the Chinese rejected the cease-fire initiative, the United Nations should then call them by their true name, and label them as aggressors.

In securing American approval of a United Nations attempt to arrange cease-fire negotiations, the most effective bargaining instrument in the British arsenal had been the demand voiced at Lake Success for precisely such an initiative. The Americans had accepted neither Attlee's interpretation of mainland China's motivations in Korea and elsewhere, nor his views of what constituted the most appropriate Western response. They did not agree either that cease-fire proposals would have much chance of success. But they did want continued United Nations moral support, and for this an attempt at negotiation had become the prerequisite.

After consulting in New York with Commonwealth delegations at the United Nations, Prime Minister Attlee at the invitation of Mr St Laurent briefed Canadian officials in Ottawa during a short stopover on his way back to London. Both premiers appeared happy with the discussions, and in a radio broadcast Mr Attlee claimed to be 'comforted and inspired once more by the acknowledgement that the desires of [Canada] are identical with our own.'[33]

The immediate consequence of the Attlee-Truman compromise was the transfer to the United Nations of the responsibility for an approach to Peking, to be initiated along lines similar to those suggested by Mr Pearson on 5 December. But the fundamental incompatibility between the China policy of the United States and Peking's preconditions for negotiation was to convert this

33 Quoted in Department of External Affairs, 'The Korean Crisis,' *External Affairs*, III, 1, Jan. 1951, 4

initiative into an exercise in futility – illustrating once again the difficulty of reconciling the reality of American preponderance in the conduct of the war with the ostensible requirement that it be placed ultimately under United Nations control. Since Canada was to play a prominent part in the UN initiative, Canadian diplomatists were to bear, as much as any, the burdens and frustrations of this unhappy collision.

It will be recalled that the six-power resolution requesting the Chinese to withdraw from Korea had been introduced in the General Assembly following a Soviet veto in the Security Council on 30 November, and that the assembly on 6 December had overruled the Soviet bloc in voting to place the question of the Chinese intervention before its Political Committee. By now the original resolution had been overrun by events in the theatre, where the rapid advance of the Communist forces quickly dispelled all hopes that the Chinese might be induced to withdraw their troops once the threat to their borders had been cleared. Meanwhile, in answer to the Asian-Arab appeal of 5 December for a declaration from Peking to the effect that the Chinese would not cross the parallel into South Korea, General Wu had reported that the matter was under careful consideration by his government, which he said wanted to 'bring the fighting to an end as soon as possible.'[34] With their hopes thus fortified, the thirteen nations on 12 December introduced to the Political Committee through Sir Benegal Rau of India a resolution requesting 'the President of the General Assembly to constitute a group of three persons, including himself, to determine the basis on which a satisfactory cease-fire in Korea can be arranged and to make recommendations to the General Assembly as soon as possible.' Rau also tabled a second resolution, which was sponsored by twelve of the same powers (the Philippines endorsed only the first), and which provided for the establishment of a committee to meet as soon as possible to 'make recommendations for the peaceful settlement of existing issues in accordance with the purposes and principles of the United Nations.'[35] The first resolution was given priority and was passed in the Political Committee on 14 December by a vote of 52-5-1, with the Soviet bloc opposed and Nationalist China abstaining. The president of the Assembly, Nasrollah Entezam of Iran, selected Lester Pearson and Sir Benegal Rau to work with him on the Cease-Fire Group.

Mr Pearson remarked later to the Canadian House of Commons that 'in taking on that work I was no volunteer. I was the victim of conscription,

---

34 Quoted in ibid., II, 12, Dec. 1950, p. 433
35 The texts of both resolutions are in Department of External Affairs, *Documents on the Korean Crisis*, 19

because it was not a job which anyone would willingly choose.'[36] In spite of his own support for a cease-fire initiative, he was not in fact very optimistic about the prospects for success. Trygve Lie reports in his memoirs that when the Cease-Fire Group discussed with him on 15 December the cease-fire terms of the Unified Command, all three of its members 'seemed to be depressed,' not least because General Wu, who until then had been on relatively good terms with the Indian delegation, 'had lately turned cool toward Sir Benegal Rau.' Wu had hold the secretary-general as early as 9 December that 'the Indian views don't count for much since, among other things, they have no soldiers in Korea,'[37] and his utterances in public were no less depressing. John Holmes can still recall his 'blood being chilled' by the sound of the general's speeches, which were delivered in a staccato, machine-gun style at so fast a pace that the translators were defeated and few of the delegates could follow their meaning.[38]

Mr Pearson was depressed also by the position taken by the Americans, who 'were sceptical and were pressing for action by the UN against China.'[39] The American position was more evident in their private than in their public pronouncements, however, and the minister tended outwardly to discount its importance. In describing the history of the Cease-Fire Group's efforts to the House of Commons, for example, he observed that in 'some quarters it has been assumed that this was a sterile, if not dangerous, exercise undertaken by naive idealistic persons merely to placate Asian opinion.' In fact, he said, 'the resolution to establish the cease-fire committee secured the support of all members of the United Nations with the exception of the Soviet bloc,' and the 'United States in particular actively assisted and encouraged the members of

36 Canada, House of Commons, *Debates*, 2 Feb. 1951, p. 57
37 Lie, *In the Cause of Peace*, 354-5. Mr Pearson later recalled that the general left most of the talking to two of his assistants, and that in any case the Chinese would deal only with Nasrollah Entezam, whom they accepted in his official capacity as President of the General Assembly. They would have nothing to do with the other two members of the UN group, and at one stage Pearson and Rau could follow the negotiations only by sitting in a room across the hall and listening to the proceedings through two open doors (comments to seminar on Canadian external relations, Carleton University, 16 Oct. 1972).
38 Holmes, interview, 5 March 1968. Mr Holmes had been replaced as acting permanent representative of Canada at the United Nations by R.G. Riddell in August. He had then returned to his regular assignment as head of the United Nations Division of the Department of External Affairs, but he was now back in New York as a member of the Canadian delegation to the General Assembly. Freeman M. Tovell, who was assigned at the time to Mr Pearson's office, confirms that Wu's activities 'put a real damper on everything.' Interview, 5 May 1970
39 Pearson, letter to the author, 13 Nov. 1968

our committee in their work.'[40] But he realized from his conversations with the British and from other sources that American support for the cease-fire initiative was largely a matter of form and designed to mollify UN opinion. Indeed, when President Truman met with the American National Security Council on 11 December to discuss the Arab-Asian proposals then being formulated, this was precisely the argument that was used to defend American acquiescence in the attempt. General Marshall, the secretary of defense, after noting the disadvantages of a cease-fire from the military point of view, commented that on the other hand 'if we opposed a cease-fire our friends would think that we were objecting to a peaceful solution,' and Vice-President Barkley was similarly 'of the opinion that we should not be manoeuvered into a position where we might be accused of opposing a cease-fire.' Truman himself shared the view of those of his advisers who thought the effort 'a futile gesture because the Chinese Communists would undoubtedly refuse to talk unless they first got a price – which we could not pay.' Nevertheless, 'world opinion seemed to be strongly in favor of trying to get a cease-fire.'[41]

In spite of these adverse conditions, however, Mr Pearson 'did not give up hope that the Chinese Government might respond to reasonable proposals.'[42] On 15 December he and the other members of the group secured from the Unified Command cease-fire conditions which they felt constituted a 'reasonable basis for discussion,' and which included the cessation of hostilities, the establishment of 'a demilitarised area across Korea of approximately twenty miles in depth with the southern limit following generally the line of the 38th Parallel,' supervision of the cease-fire by a UN Commission with 'free and unlimited access to the whole of Korea,' a prohibition on the reinforcement or replacement of personnel and equipment in the theatre, a one-for-one POW exchange, and confirmation of the agreement by the UN General Assembly.[43] On the following day, 16 December, Mr Entezam sent a message to General Wu, repeated in a cable directly to Peking, notifying him that the committee had already met with representatives of the Unified Command to discuss, 'in an exploratory manner, possible conditions upon which a cease-fire might be established.' He therefore requested a meeting with the Chinese government or its representatives for the same purpose.[44]

This initiative happened to follow upon a declaration of national emergency issued by President Truman in Washington the previous night. In it the

40 Canada, House of Commons, *Debates*, 2 Feb. 1951, 57
41 Truman, *Years of Trial and Hope*, 473-4; see also Acheson, *Present at the Creation*, 512-13
42 Pearson, letter to the author, 13 Nov. 1968
43 Department of External Affairs, *Documents on the Korean Crisis*, 20-1
44 Ibid., 21-2

president had announced a major programme for rearmament and had instituted a total embargo on trade with mainland China. He had also frozen Chinese assets in the United States. According to Panikkar, however, these manoeuvres aroused more amusement than concern in Peking,[45] and it is most unlikely that they had any effect, for better or worse, on Chinese policy. In any case, on the evening of 16 December General Wu told Trygve Lie that he had received instructions to leave New York within three days and that he had informed Sir Benegal Rau that he could not negotiate with the Cease-Fire Committee.[46] The secretary-general's attempts to change his mind were to no avail. The Cease-Fire Group then transmitted a message to the Chinese authorities through the Swedish embassy in Peking requesting that they instruct Ambassador Wu to stay in New York to discuss the possibility of arranging a cease-fire. 'The fact,' as Mr Pearson later recalled, 'that the Chinese Delegation in New York refused to negotiate did not necessarily imply that the Government in Peking would be equally obdurate.'[47] Nonetheless, General Wu departed on schedule, and on 21 December Mr Entezam received a message from Peking *via* the Swedish government in which the Chinese argued that they could not negotiate with the Cease-Fire Group because the People's Republic of China had not participated in its creation, a fact which meant that the group in their view was illegally constituted.[48]

A more elaborate statement of Peking's position, confirming the substance of comments made by General Wu before his departure, was issued to the Chinese press on 22 December and conveyed to the president of the General Assembly on the following day. In it, the Chinese government reiterated its view that resolutions passed by the General Assembly in its absence were illegal, and that it therefore could have nothing to do with the Cease-Fire Committee. China had held from the beginning that the hostilities 'should be speedily brought to an end.' This could have been achieved had the United States not invaded Korea and rejected Sino-Soviet proposals for the withdrawal of all foreign troops from the peninsula. All that was required was that the Koreans be allowed to settle their internal problems by themselves. When the United States crossed the 38th parallel early in October it had 'obliterated forever this demarcation line of political geography,' and the Americans were now supporting cease-fire proposals only because their troops were suffering defeat. Since they insisted that the cease-fire be concluded on a purely military

45 Panikkar, *In Two Chinas*, 118
46 Lie, *In the Cause of Peace*, 355-6
47 Pearson, letter to the author, 13 Nov. 1968
48 Department of External Affairs, *Documents on the Korean Crisis*, 22

basis, with political negotiations following after, it was clear that all they wanted was a breathing space so that they could 'fight again when they are prepared.' In any case the Korean problem could not be divorced from the issue of American aggression against Taiwan nor from the question of China's representation at the United Nations. The thirteen Arab and Asian nations who supported the establishment of the Cease-Fire Committee genuinely desired peace, but they had 'failed to see through the whole intrigue of the United States Government in supporting the proposal for a cease-fire first and negotiations afterwards.' The fact that the thirteen-nation cease-fire resolution had been separated from the twelve-nation resolution on political negotiations, and had been given priority in the General Assembly, was an indication of the need of the Arab-Asian states to free themselves from American pressure. Similarly, the fact that the Philippines delegate, 'who always follows in the footsteps of the United States,' had supported only the first resolution was proof of the extent of American influence. If they wished 'to gain genuine peace,' therefore, the Arab-Asian nations should abandon 'the idea of cease-fire first and negotiations afterwards.' The Chinese government firmly insisted 'that, as a basis for negotiating for a peaceful settlement of the Korean problem, all foreign troops must be withdrawn from Korea, and Korea's domestic affairs must be settled by the Korean people themselves. The American aggression forces must be withdrawn from Taiwan. And the Representatives of the People's Republic of China must obtain a legitimate status in the United Nations ... To put aside these points would make it impossible to settle peacefully the Korean problem and the important problems of Asia.'[49]

Here was a classic illustration of the futility of attempting to negotiate incompatible purposes when neither side is prepared, or can be compelled, to make substantive concessions on the points at issue. The preconditions for a cease-fire laid down by the Chinese were precisely the questions upon which the Cease-Fire Group was unable to yield. The group accordingly reported to the General Assembly's Political Committee on 3 January that 'in spite of its best efforts,' it had been 'unable to pursue discussion of a satisfactory cease-fire arrangement.' It therefore felt 'that no recommendation in regard to a cease-fire can usefully be made by it at this time.'[50]

The committee's report coincided with news from the front that on New Year's Eve the Chinese had launched another major offensive. It had carried them across the 38th parallel and had again forced United Nations and South Korean troops into full retreat. By 4 January Seoul was once more in Commu-

49 Ibid., 24-8
50 Ibid., 24

nist hands. It was not surprising, therefore, that Warren Austin should now argue in the committee that 'the Chinese communist regime, by rejecting any cease-fire proposal, had closed a channel for peaceful settlement' and had 'indicated its attitude toward the efforts of the United Nations by a large-scale offensive across the 38th Parallel.' While the United Nations should continue to hold 'open the door to the negotiation of an honourable solution,' it should also 'demonstrate to the communist aggressors that the free world was united in its opinion that they were aggressors and would be resisted.' He suggested an adjournment so that the members of the Political Committee might consult with their governments in the light of changes in the military situation.[51]

The Norwegian delegate, in paying tribute to the work of the Cease-Fire Committee, wondered in spite of Mr Austin's remarks whether the group 'had given any consideration to the problem of what principles would have to be laid down as a basis for possible negotiations subsequent to the envisaged establishment of a cease-fire.'[52] To this Mr Pearson replied that the group had indeed done so, and would probably make a statement on the matter later, although 'it was quite clear that the cease-fire was an essential step to any further discussion regarding the peaceful settlement of the question.'[53] The British delegate, Sir Gladwyn Jebb, immediately suggested that 'the Group prepare a statement on the principles which would serve as a basis for further action to be taken by the First Committee,' and that in the meantime the committee should adjourn.[54] The suggestion was accepted over the opposition of the Soviet bloc, and Mr Pearson and his colleagues therefore returned once more to their discouraging diplomatic task.

Mr Pearson later told the House of Commons that the statement was drawn up only '[a]fter considerable difficulty,' noting with an obvious sense of accomplishment that it eventually 'secured the approval of fifty of the sixty member nations, including the United States and India.'[55] That the group encountered such obstacles seems in retrospect somewhat surprising since the new statement did not differ very substantially from the old. The minister's special reference to the United States and India is significant, however, because it is clear that these were the two countries which gave the Group the most trouble – the United States because it was beginning to lose patience with the entire

51 United Nations, GAOR (First Committee), A/C.1/SR.419, 461. A moving eye-witness account of the evacuation of Seoul is contained in Cutforth's *Korean Reporter.*
52 United Nations, GAOR, ibid.
53 Ibid.
54 Ibid.
55 Canada, House of Commons, *Debates*, 2 Feb. 1951, 58

cease-fire attempt and wished the assembly to authorize severe moral and economic sanctions against Peking, and India because it was becoming increasingly fearful of the consequences of isolating and alienating the Chinese and wanted accordingly to accommodate more of their demands. The Americans had already waited several weeks and could be persuaded under pressure to wait a little longer, but the group's task was complicated by the fact that the Commonwealth prime ministers were meeting in London where they were discussing a variety of proposals of their own, and Prime Minister Nehru's absence from New Delhi made it more difficult for Rau to co-ordinate his consultations with his superiors. The result was that the original draft of the statement, drawn up by the Indians, was revised several times before it was finally tabled in the Political Committee by Mr Pearson on 11 January.[56]

The Cease-Fire Group's 'Supplementary Report' briefly enumerated five general principles upon which a cease-fire and political settlement might be based, and these are worth repeating here:

1 In order to prevent needless destruction of life and property, and while other steps are being taken to restore peace, a cease-fire should be immediately arranged. Such an arrangement should contain adequate safeguards for ensuring that it will not be used as a screen for mounting a new offensive.

2 If and when a cease-fire occurs in Korea, either as a result of a formal arrangement or, indeed, as a result of a lull in hostilities pending some such arrangement, advantage should be taken of it to pursue consideration of further steps to be taken for the restoration of peace.

3 To permit the carrying out of the General Assembly resolution that Korea should be a unified, independent, democratic, sovereign state with a constitution and a government based on free popular elections, all non-Korean armed forces will be withdrawn, by appropriate stages, from Korea, and appropriate arrangements, in accordance with United Nations principles, will be made for the Korean people to express their own free will in respect of their future government.

4 Pending the completion of the steps referred to in the preceding paragraph, appropriate interim arrangements, in accordance with United Nations principles, will be made for the administration of Korea and the maintenance of peace and security there.

---

56 Pearson, letter to the author, 13 Nov. 1968. Prime Minister St Laurent was partly responsible for obtaining in London the approval of Mr Nehru, a feature of the discussions which later drew from Mr Pearson warm praise both for the Commonwealth and for the prime minister. See Canada, House of Commons, *Debates*, 2 Feb. 1951, 58

5 As soon as agreement has been reached on a cease-fire, the General Assembly shall set up an appropriate body which shall include representatives of the Governments of the United Kingdom, the United States of America, the Union of Soviet Socialist Republics, and the People's Republic of China with a view to the achievement of a settlement, in conformity with existing international obligations and the provisions of the United Nations Charter, of Far Eastern problems, including, among others, those of Formosa (Taiwan) and of representation of China in the United Nations.[57]

Mr Pearson argued in the Political Committee two weeks after presenting this document that it met 'every legitimate point that had been made by the Peking Government.'[58] But in fact it did little to meet the Chinese on substantive issues, and in the light of their continuing battlefield successes it could hardly be expected to have had much impact upon them. It is true that paragraphs one and two acknowledged in effect that peace negotiations might begin before a cease-fire had actually been concluded, whereas in earlier versions the cease-fire had to be completed first. It is true also that paragraph three provided for the staged withdrawal of all foreign troops from Korea. But the third and fourth paragraphs made it clear in addition that some form of interim arrangement for the administration of Korea and for the maintenance of its peace and security, 'in accordance with United Nations principles,' would be required pending the establishment of a unified and independent Korean government 'based on free popular elections.' Mr Pearson later told the committee that this implied 'United Nations supervision of some kind,' since this 'would be essential if the decisions were to be free and not the kind that we have seen imposed on certain Eastern European countries behind the Iron Curtain.'[59] Since these were probably the sorts of decisions for Korea which the Chinese had in mind, and since their forces were still doing well on the field of battle, it would have been surprising had Peking been prepared to accept such an arrangement. Finally, paragraph five, 'by far the most controversial section of the statement,'[60] implied that the substance, if not the details, of a cease-fire agreement had to be concluded before any discussion of more general Far Eastern issues – including that of China's representation in the United Nations – could begin. This also had been unacceptable to the Chinese, and would remain so while their prospects for military victory seemed good.

57 Department of External Affairs, *Documents on the Korean Crisis*, 29-30
58 Department of External Affairs, *Statements and Speeches*, no 51/2
59 Ibid.
60 Ibid.

For the Americans, as Dean Acheson has since recalled, 'The choice whether to support or oppose this plan was a murderous one, threatening, on one side, the loss of the Koreans and the fury of Congress and press and, on the other, the loss of our majority and support in the United Nations.' After 'painful deliberation' they chose to support it, doing so 'in the fervent hope and belief that the Chinese would reject it (as they did) and that our allies would then return (as they did) to comparative sanity and follow us in censuring the Chinese as aggressors.'[61]

In all, as Mr Pearson had told the Political Committee, the Cease-Fire Group had encountered in its deliberations not two, but four main sectors of opinion. The first – obviously including the United States – consisted of those who felt that further attemps at negotiation were weakening and humiliating the United Nations and that China should be condemned forthwith as an aggressor. The second – presumably the Indians and their supporters – comprised those who subordinated everything to the need to end the fighting and who were anxious to discuss the Korean and other Far East political issues immediately with the Chinese. The fourth included only the Soviet bloc, which advocated in effect a unilateral withdrawal of the United Nations 'aggressors.' The third was the group with which Mr Pearson himself seemed to identify, although he did not explicitly say so. This group 'agreed that, whatever might be the rights or wrongs of the matter, we should further prove our good will and our unswerving desire and, indeed, determination to bring about a peaceful solution by making one further effort at peaceful settlement before proceeding to any condemnatory resolution; that without such further effort it would be difficult to preserve the unity of the free world in the United Nations in regard to action in Korea. Some of the members of the Committee, while taking this view, were frankly pessimistic about the result.'[62]

Their pessimism was justified. After lengthy discussions in the Political Committee in which all four of these basic positions were implied or expressed, the statement of principles was approved on 13 January by a vote of 50-7-1, and the secretary-general was then authorized to transmit it to Peking. The Chinese reply, dated 17 January, was read out to the Political Committee on the 18th. In effect it rejected the five principles on the ground that they were still based on 'the arrangement of a cease-fire in Korea first, and the conducting of negotiations among the various countries concerned afterwards.' The purpose of this proposal was 'merely to give the United States troops a breathing space,' and if put into practice it 'would only help the United States to maintain

61 Acheson, *Present at the Creation*, 513. See also Gaddis Smith, *Dean Acheson*, 264-6
62 Department of External Affairs, *Statements and Speeches*, no 51/2

and extend its aggression, and could never lead to genuine peace.' The Chinese government therefore submitted four counter-proposals, as follows:

A Negotiations should be held among the countries concerned on the basis of agreement to the withdrawal of all foreign troops from Korea and the settlement of Korean domestic affairs by the Korean people themselves, in order to put an end to the hostilities in Korea at an early date.

B The subject-matter of the negotiations must include the withdrawal of United States armed forces from Taiwan and the Taiwan Straits and Far Eastern related problems.

C The countries to participate in the negotiations should be the following seven countries: The People's Republic of China, the Soviet Union, the United Kingdom, the United States of America, France, India and Egypt. The rightful place of the Central People's Government of the People's Republic of China in the United Nations should be established as from the beginning of the seven-nation conference.

D The seven-nation conference should be held in China, at a place to be selected.[63]

These proposals were badly received in the United States. Even before the Political Committee convened, Secretary of State Dean Acheson issued a statement accusing Peking of a 'contemptuous disregard of a world-wide demand for peace' and arguing that now 'we must squarely and soberly face the fact that the Chinese Communists have no intention of ceasing their defiance of the United Nations.'[64] On 19 January the American House of Representatives was to pass a resolution calling upon the United Nations to declare China an aggressor, and the performance was to be repeated in the Senate four days later. In the Political Committee itself, Warren Austin claimed that the Chinese counter-proposals constituted the reply, not of China, but 'of its masters, the Soviet ruling circles.' It was clear, he said, that 'the Peking regime had committed aggression and that the General Assembly should say so.' Peking should be called upon to remove its troops from Korea, and the United Nations, in reaffirming its determination to resist the aggression, should ask the Collective Measures Committee to consider what steps might be taken in the future and to make recommendations accordingly to the General Assembly.[65]

The United States was supported in these views by many of its allies, particularly Greece, Turkey, the Philippines, and the Latin American repub-

63 Department of External Affairs, *Documents on the Korean Crisis*, pp. 31-2
64 Quoted in Rees, *Korea*, 202
65 United Nations, GAOR (First Committee), A/C.1/SR.426, 501-3

lics. With equal predictability it was opposed by the representatives of the Soviet bloc, who claimed to regard the Chinese response as 'the first real peace plan embodying practically every issue which must be discussed in order to settle the Far Eastern situation.'[66] The Arab-Asian states, however, together with Britain, Canada, and France, were still not ready to give up the attempt to reconcile the incompatible American and Chinese positions.

On 20 January the Americans introduced at last a resolution which declared that the Chinese People's Republic had 'itself engaged in aggression in Korea.' It called upon the Peking government to withdraw its forces, and requested that members of the United Nations 'continue to lend every assistance to the United Nations action in Korea.'[67] A number of Arab-Asian delegates immediately advocated a less hasty response. The most important of them was Sir Benegal Rau, who said his government 'viewed the latest Chinese reply, not as an outright rejection of the principles approved by the Committee, but as partly acceptance, partly non-acceptance, partly a request for elucidation and partly a set of counter-proposals.' A detailed comparison of the UN statement of principles and the Chinese reply showed there was still room for discussion. Certainly it would serve no useful purpose to brand China an aggressor, for

it would hardly increase the prestige of the United Nations unless it was intended to be followed by other steps. Since the feasibility of those further steps had not yet been examined, the only result of such a resolution would be not only to leave all Far Eastern problems unsolved, but also to make them insoluble since, once such a resolution had been adopted, negotiation, even for the purpose of removing misunderstandings, would have to be abandoned. Moreover, the atmosphere for successful negotiation would disappear and the present tension in the Far East would be perpetuated and would continue unabated. For the present, the Government of India was opposed to so disastrous a course.[68]

This dispute between the powers represented by the United States on the one hand and by India on the other was due at least partly to ambiguities in the Chinese counter-proposals. Both Britain and Canada therefore attempted at this point to secure a clarification from the Chinese government. In the Canadian case this took the form of a message to Prime Minister Nehru on 18 January containing three questions drawn up in the Department of External

66 Ibid., A/C.1/SR.427, 513. The spokesman was Mr Katz-Suchy of Poland.
67 Department of External Affairs, *Documents on the Korean Crisis*, 33
68 United Nations, GAOR (First Committee), A/C.1/SR.428, 523-24

Affairs, together with a request that they be put to the Chinese through the Indian embassy in Peking. The questions, appearing over St Laurent's own signature, were as follows:

1 Do foreign troops referred to in paragraph 1 of the Chinese reply include Chinese volunteers?

2 Timing of negotiations. Do the Chinese insist that negotiations on broad political issues should precede cease-fire?

3 Representation in the United Nations. Is formal recognition of Chinese Communist Government as spokesman of China in the United Nations a precondition to agreement to a conference?[69]

Mr St Laurent's inquiry crossed in transmission with a communication to him from Prime Minister Nehru. The Indian leader did not believe that the Chinese reply was intended as an outright rejection of the UN initiative, and he urged the Canadian prime minister to intercede with the Americans not to react with undue haste.[70] St Laurent needed no special invitation. By now the Canadians in New York and Washington were already pressing the Americans to delay their condemnatory resolution until the Chinese position had become absolutely clear.[71]

The prime minister had hoped to have the Chinese reply by the afternoon of Monday, 22 January, but the difference in time zones made it impossible for Panikkar to use 'the normal channels,' and he therefore sent it directly to Sir Benegal Rau at Lake Success 'with a request to hand it over to Lester Pearson.'[72] The Political Committee met at 3:00 PM and Sir Benegal was able to open the proceedings by reading the contents of the Chinese clarification:

1 If the principle that all foreign troops should be withdrawn from Korea has been accepted and is being put into practice, the Central People's Government of the People's Republic of China will assume the responsibility to advise the Chinese volunteers to return to China.

2 Regarding the conclusion of the war in Korea and the peaceful settlement of the Korean problem, we think that we can proceed in two steps. First step: A cease-fire for a limited time-period can be agreed upon in the first meeting of the seven-nation conference and put into effect so that the negotiations may proceed further. Second

69 Department of External Affairs, 'The Korean Crisis,' *External Affairs*, III, 2, Feb. 1951, 52
70 Pearson, interview, 18 Oct. 1968
71 Ibid.; and Holmes, interview, 5 March 1968
72 Panikkar, *In Two Chinas*, 123

step: In order that the war in Korea may be concluded completely and peace in East Asia may be ensured, all the conditions for the conclusion of the war must be discussed in connection with the political problems in order to reach agreement upon the following: The steps and measures for the withdrawal of all foreign troops from Korea; the proposals to the Korean people on the steps and measures to effect the settlement of the internal affairs of Korea by the Korean people themselves; the withdrawal of the United States armed forces from Taiwan and the Taiwan Straits in accordance with Cairo Declaration and Potsdam Declaration; and other problems concerning the Far East.

   3 The definite affirmation of the legitimate status of the People's Republic of China in the United Nations must be ensured.[73]

Rau then announced that the twelve Asian nations which had sponsored the draft resolution of 12 December had already met to consider the Chinese answer and that they wished more time to engage in consultations and to obtain instructions from their respective governments. This was probably true of other delegations also, and he therefore suggested a forty-eight hour adjournment.

   Panikkar later boasted that his message 'created a sensation' in the Political Committee,[74] and there is every indication that most of the delegates were caught completely by surprise and were unsure how to react, although a number of them, including Warren Austin, suggested that the committee continue its consideration of the American resolution, which had been about to come to a vote. After some confused exchanges, the Indian motion was adopted by 27-23-6, leaving the Americans infuriated by what they regarded as an unnecessary obstruction and delay. They complained bitterly that the Canadians had been negotiating with the Chinese behind their backs, and that Washington should at least have been consulted before Mr St Laurent's message had been dispatched. To this Mr Pearson gave a cool response: such consultation would have been pointless since the Americans were already convinced of the accuracy of their assessment of China's intentions, and in any case Canada was not obliged to inform the United States on every occasion in which her government consulted with another Commonwealth power. The minister later remarked that the incident had been one of the most serious disputes in the history of Canada's relations with the United States.[75]

The Canadian delegation made no attempt to address the Political Committee on the 22nd, but as Mr Pearson later revealed to the House of Commons, the

73 Department of External Affairs, *Documents on the Korean Crisis*, 34
74 Panikkar, *In Two Chinas*, 124

government was convinced that the Chinese clarification 'seemed more hopeful, since it stated for the first time in fairly clear language that a cease-fire could be agreed upon in the first meeting of the conference called to discuss Far Eastern issues and that this discussion of political issues would not take place until after the cease-fire had been agreed on.' In view of the 'encouraging' nature of the Chinese reply, to pass the American resolution 'would be both premature and unwise. If it were not followed by some action against China, it would throw into high relief the sharp limitations of United Nations resolutions.' If, on the other hand, it were followed by 'sanctions, however modest against China, the risk of the west becoming involved in a war with China would be increased.' Not only would the passage of the resolution endanger the possibilities of negotiation, it would also 'unnecessarily highlight and exaggerate differences of view between the Asians and the western numbers of the free world and indeed bring about a formal division between the members of the western world in the United Nations.' On the other hand, the Chinese *had* engaged in aggression and *had* attacked UN forces, and therefore 'in the last resort, we could not refuse, as I saw it, to recognize the situation in a resolution of condemnation if that resolution were pressed to a vote, if it stated the actual position fairly, if it were not couched in unnecessarily provocative terms, and if it included within it provision for negotiation.'[76]

When the Political Committee reconvened on 24 January, the American position was supported by Ecuador, Venezuela, Paraguay, and Nationalist China. With minor qualifications it was supported also by Mr Shann of Australia, but was denounced by Mr Nosek of Czechoslovakia. By 25 January, however, the sponsors of the original twelve-power draft resolution had introduced a revised version of their proposal as an alternative to that of the United States. It recommended a conference of the seven states mentioned by the Chinese 'for the purpose of securing all necessary elucidations and amplifications of the [Chinese reply of 17 January] and of making any incidental or consequential arrangements towards a peaceful settlement of the Korean and other Far Eastern problems.'[77] In defending this suggestion before the committee, Sir Benegal Rau argued that it should have priority in the voting because it constituted a revision of the resolution of 12 December, which was on the agenda long before the motion of the United States.[78] He was supported

75 Confidential source
76 Canada, House of Commons, *Debates*, 2 Feb. 1951, 58-9. The view that the Chinese reply had been 'encouraging' was shared in the Department of External Affairs by Escott Reid, among others. Interview, 9 June 1969
77 Department of External Affairs, *Documents on the Korean Crisis*, 34-5
78 United Nations, GAOR (First Committee), A/C.1/SR.431, 544

on this point by Sir Gladwyn Jebb, who observed also that the Peking government had not entirely rejected the principle of a cease-fire before negotiations, that it had made it reasonably clear that the withdrawal of foreign troops would include the Chinese 'Volunteers,' and that it had now stipulated that the internal affairs of Korea would be discussed at a general political conference and not relegated, as they had originally insisted, for settlement by the Koreans themselves. The United Kingdom did not regard the seating of mainland China in the United Nations as a problem; it was not a question of admitting a new country but of deciding which government had the right to represent an existing member, and this was 'not a question of morals or behaviour but a question of facts.' The United Kingdom was 'broadly in agreement with the first five paragraphs of the United States draft resolution, although the actual wording might well require further study. But when the question arose of considering further measures before the intentions of the Peking Government had been fully and exhaustively explored, the United Kingdom delegation entertained the gravest doubt on the wisdom of any such action.'[79]

On Friday, 26 January, the proceedings were opened by Mr Pearson, who reviewed the Canadian position at length. Like the British, he thought the January communications from Peking left room for further negotiation, particularly since the Chinese were now prepared 'to enter into and conclude cease-fire arrangements before the discussion of any other subject is begun.' Their counter-proposals seemed to offer no great difficulty. Even their demand that their 'rightful place' in the United Nations be 'established as from the beginning of the seven-nation conference' was not an insurmountable problem unless they insisted upon this being settled in advance of negotiations. Since they asked only for an affirmation of their right to UN membership by the seven nations at their first meeting, this seemed not to be the case. In any event there had already been a move in the direction of admitting the mainland regime, and it had failed to reach fruition only because the outbreak of the Korean War had 'made any such action, for the time being, quite impossible.' Now, of course, the issue could not be settled until the fighting in Korea had ended and the Chinese had abandoned their 'assistance to those who have been adjudged aggressors by the United Nations.' Not prepared to go as far as the British and the Arab-Asian states in accepting the Chinese demand for admission while the fighting actually continued, the Canadian government thus seemed willing to promise support for admission contingent upon agreement to conclude the hostilities in the theatre.

79 Ibid., 545-7

Mr Pearson went on to suggest that a conference, consisting perhaps of the seven states proposed by the Chinese, be convened at Lake Success or New Delhi within a week or ten days of the decision to hold it. The first order of business would be to establish a cease-fire committee composed of representatives of the United States, mainland China, and the United Nations Commission for the Unification and Rehabilitation of Korea, together with any others upon which these three would agree. This committee would then be responsible for arranging an immediate cease-fire on the basis of the Cease-Fire Group's report of 11 January, and its work would have to be completed 'before any other items on its agenda were even considered.' Once this had been done, the conference would go on to 'consider a peaceful solution of Korean problems in accordance with the principles laid down in paragraph 2 and 3 of the statement of principles of 11 January,' covering arrangements for the withdrawal of all non-Korean armed forces, including the Chinese. After that the conference could discuss other Far East problems. It could not decide upon the admission of the Peking regime to the United Nations, since that would have to be determined at Lake Success, but it could express a viewpoint on the subject. Mr Pearson suggested also that the Peking authorities be given a specific time-period – perhaps forty-eight hours – in which to accept or reject the convening of such a conference. It might have helped, he said, had this procedure been adopted before, since it would have avoided the prolonged discussions that had taken place, and the assembly 'could then have proceeded to condemnatory action, with a far greater chance for a united front than seems to be the case at present.'[80]

The Canadian government could not support the Arab-Asian proposals because they were too broad, lacked 'the conception of an orderly sequence of events, beginning with a cease-fire and proceeding logically, through a Korean settlement, to a more general discussion of other Far Eastern questions,' and would probably lead in consequence to discussion of general issues 'before any progress whatever had been made towards arranging a cease-fire.'

The American resolution was more difficult. With an irony designed to discomfit the Latin Americans, Mr Pearson observed that if it were pressed immediately to a vote, 'delegations will have to take a decision in regard to it, and that decision is not as easy or as simple for my delegation as it seems to be for some other delegations around this table.' Was it really the duty of the United Nations to pass moral judgment on an aggressor? It had been argued that the old League of Nations had failed precisely because it had defaulted in this respect on the Ethiopian issue. But in fact the League had

80 Department of External Affairs, *Statements and Speeches*, no 51/2

collapsed not because it refused to call fascist Italy an aggressor – it had done so in 'eloquent and ringing terms' – but because it had not followed its declaration with effective action. In the present case the Canadian government still wished to hold open the door for further negotiations with Peking, even if the Chinese response thus far had 'certainly been enough to try the patience of us all.' On the other hand, the American resolution did make provision for 'a cessation of hostilities and the achievement of our objectives by peaceful means,' and its passage would not necessarily preclude further discussions if Peking wanted them. In the meantime Canada would have to support the resolution 'because it states one vital truth that is self-evident. The armed forces of the People's Government of China continue their invasion of Korea. By opposing or abstaining on this draft resolution, no matter how unwise we might think its introduction at this particular moment, we would be denying that fact of armed aggression of Korea by Chinese aggressors, and we will not do this.' The resolution was not a 'declaration of war – limited or unlimited – against China.' It was 'in the first place, a firm call to the Peking Government to desist from participation in aggression and, in the second place, a promise of peaceful settlement if it does.' As Sir Benegal Rau had said, the passage of the resolution might create an atmosphere inimical to further negotiation, but what, in the light of all the initiatives already taken, could the Peking government expect?

If the resolution were passed, however, the question of what concrete measures were to follow would still remain, and the committee charged with the task of formulating them would have 'serious responsibilities indeed.' Transgressing with ease the distinction between collective security and 'free world' defence, Mr Pearson observed that it

will have to take into account the realities of the world situation. It will have to accept the fact that while the resources of the free world, which is the only part of the world willing to support collective action, are growing stronger, they are at the moment limited. It will have to realize also, as I see it, that the free world as a whole is now under a menace far greater than anything offered by the Chinese regime in Peking, a menace which even that regime will, we hope, one day come to recognize and to resist, and that our main objective must be to hold ourselves prepared to meet that threat. We have certainly not accepted anything like the prospect of inevitable war with the Soviet Union, and we are still ready to accept genuine conciliation with members of the Soviet bloc. We cannot, however, close our eyes to the complicity of the Soviet Union in the aggression action of the North Koreans and the Chinese Communists, their subjugation of neighbouring countries, their world-wide sabotage of peace, and the continuous instigation of a new war by their propaganda machines, disguised these days as propaganda for peace. It is for these reasons, for purely defensive reasons, that I feel we must remain on guard and not allow ourselves to be deliberately distracted into weakening skirmishes or open war with a country with which we have no basic grounds to quarrel.

In the light of this analysis Mr Pearson hoped that any Committee on Collective Measures established by the assembly would 'keep before it our major objective of reaching a peaceful settlement with the Chinese on issues which we believe can be settled.'[81]

This appears in retrospect an amazing performance, and it reflects the casual facility with which western statesmen in the early 1950s could take for granted the support of the United Nations in the politics of the cold war. Having explicitly identified the UN purpose in Korea with the interests of the free world, 'the only part of the world willing to support collective action,' Mr Pearson had proceeded to apply to the United Nations the principles of western military strategy – including in particular the principle that major entanglements in the Far East should be avoided so that the defence of the European theatre might have priority. The United Nations should work for peace in Korea not merely because making peace was its business, but also because its members had to be prepared to meet elsewhere a far greater threat posed by the Soviet Union. The United Nations, in short, was the foreign policy instrument of the western alliance.

Mr Pearson's remarks were doubtless directed in this instance less to the United Nations as a whole than to the United States as an individual member. In an obvious reference to General MacArthur's anxiety to take more aggressive measures against the Chinese, he noted at the end of his address that it was the Canadian view – and Canada would welcome confirmation of it – that 'this resolution does not give the Unified Command or its commanders in Korea any authority to take action which it and they do not already possess.' Even so, there were 'one or two features' of the resolution which did 'not carry the considered judgment of the Canadian delegation,' and Canada thought that to pass it before the possibility of negotiation with Peking had been exhausted would be 'premature and unwise.' Canada would support it, however, because China was 'morally wrong' in participating in the Korean aggression and was therefore 'to be condemned.'[82]

In the light of these and similar comments by the Israeli delegate, the Arab-Asian nations later agreed to alter their resolution in order to provide

81 Ibid.
82 Ibid.

for cease-fire arrangements as the first order of business at the proposed seven-nation conference. But this was to have little effect upon what had become an inexorable progress toward the moral condemnation of the Peking regime. The Canadian attempt to postpone the voting on the American resolution pending a last approach to the Chinese ended in failure. Under pressure from Britain, France, Canada, and several other countries, the Americans did agree to accept two amendments submitted by Mr Malik of the Lebanon.[83] The first of these softened slightly the wording of a paragraph which had noted that China had 'rejected all United Nations proposals'; in the amended version China was said merely to have 'not accepted United Nations proposals.' The second added a clause which provided that the activities of the Collective Measures Committee which were put forward in the resolution would be deferred if the Good Offices Committee, also established by the resolution, reported 'satisfactory progress in its efforts.' In spite of Mr Pearson's later defence of these amendments in the Canadian House of Commons,[84] however, it is clear that they did not very substantially alter either the character of the resolution or its effect upon Peking. In its final form, the resolution found that the Chinese government, 'by giving direct aid and assistance to those who were already committing aggression in Korea and by engaging in hostilities against United Nations forces there, has itself engaged in aggression in Korea.' It called upon the Chinese regime to withdraw its forces and nationals from the theatre, affirmed the determination of the United Nations 'to continue its action in Korea to meet the aggression,' and requested 'all states and authorities' to continue to provide assistance to the UN action and to refrain from assisting the aggressors. Its final two paragraphs read as follows:

[*The General Assembly*] *Requests* a committee composed of the members of the Collective Measures Committee as a matter of urgency to consider additional measures to be employed to meet this aggression and to report thereon to the General Assembly, it being understood that the committee is authorized to defer its report if the Good Offices Committee, referred to in the following paragraph, reports satisfactory progress in its efforts;

Affirms that it continues to be the policy of the United Nations to bring about a cessation of hostilities in Korea and the achievement of United Nations objectives in Korea by peaceful means, and requests the President of the General Assembly to

---

83 United Nations, GAOR (First Committee), A/C.1/SR.435, 577
84 Canada, House of Commons, *Debates*, 2 Feb. 1951, 59-60

designate forthwith two persons who would meet with him at any suitable opportunity to use their good offices to this end.[85]

The decision was finally taken in the Political Committee on 30 January, and confirmed in the General Assembly on 1 February. The Arab-Asian resolution was first rejected in a clause-by-clause voting procedure, Canada and Britain both abstaining. The amended American resolution was then adopted by a final vote of 44 (including Britain and Canada) to 7 (Soviet bloc, Burma, and India), with 8 abstentions (Afghanistan, Egypt, Indonesia, Pakistan, Sweden, Syria, Yemen, and Yugoslavia).

In a last effort to explain the Canadian position to the Political Committee before the votes were called, Mr Pearson explained that his government could not support the twelve-power resolution because it was imprecise, 'gave too much room for further lengthy and inconclusive discussions,' and failed to give recognition to previous UN resolutions and actions on the Korean issue. This meant that it 'might be interpreted as placing the Peking Government and the United Nations itself almost on the same moral and political footing.' Moreover, whereas the US resolution included 'reasonably satisfactory machinery for cease-fire and political negotiations,' he did not think the seven-power conference, which included the USSR, would be 'satisfactory for bringing about a cease-fire in Korea.' Canada would not vote against the resolution, however, 'because it emphasized the necessity of discussion and peaceful settlement, and embodied the principle that a cease-fire must precede discussion.'

The Canadian delegation would support the American resolution partly because the Lebanese amendments had 'removed its doubts about the wisdom of certain provisions of the unamended draft.' partly because it stated in moderate terms the fact of Chinese participation in aggressive action in Korea, and partly because it 'did not close the door to peaceful negotiations, but rightly emphasized that even the report on collective measures was to be subordinated to the work of the good offices group.' Moreover, Mr Austin had been 'frank and unequivocal in agreeing that the United States proposal gave no one any authority in Korea or the Far East not already possessed under United Nations resolutions.' Hence, Canada would vote in favour of what it regarded as 'a very mild condemnation' which did not slam the door on subsequent negotiations, even though the Canadian delegation still felt the

85 Department of External Affairs, 'The Korean Crisis,' *External Affairs*, III, 2, Feb. 1951, 55. The unamended version is in Department of External Affairs, *Documents on the Korean Crisis*, 55. The 'Collective Measures Committee' to which the resolution referred had been established under the Uniting for Peace resolution, and was charged with studying and reporting on ways and means of maintaining and strengthening international security.

manoeuvre was 'premature and unwise,' since 'the methods of peaceful negotiations ... had not yet been completely exhausted.'[86]

Such was the reasoning which led the Canadians, together with the British and other allies of the United States, to support a resolution of which they disapproved. K.M. Panikkar claimed later with some bitterness that 'the people who voted for [the US] resolution knew that they were only saving America's face.'[87] But the resolution's reluctant supporters had more vital interests at heart. Among them was a concern to maintain at least a semblance of allied unity in the management of the crisis.[88] The public display of a divided front, they believed, would not only diminish even further the 'collective' ingredient in the conduct of the war – an eventuality which the Canadians among others were very anxious to avoid – but would undermine also what little capacity remained to the allied states to impose restraints upon American decision-makers. The advantage to the United States of pursuing the conflict in the name of the United Nations was that it gave the exercise the flavour of international approval and moral legitimacy; the advantage to the allies was that it provided them with some capacity for influencing – and limiting – the American effort. An irreparable split between the views of the majority of the United Nations and those of the United States government would therefore serve the objectives of neither. This was particularly the case for powers like Britain, France, and Canada, which were members of the NATO alliance, since their primary preoccupation was the Soviet threat in Europe, and their most incessant nightmare the prospect of an America diverted and weakened by an Asian war. In the final analysis the advantage in the resulting diplomatic contest had been held by the United States, since most other members of the organization stood to lose more by a rupture between Washington and Lake Success than did Washington itself.

It is sometimes very difficult in politics to decide whether the need to maintain undisturbed the health of established political connections is more, or less, important than the substance of particular issues which happen to be in dispute. The problem is due in part to the fact that the consequences of alternative courses of action often cannot be calculated with certainty in advance. Honest and well-intentioned men may therefore evaluate the options differently, and hence reach conflicting policy conclusions. Mr Pearson's decision to vote in favour of the American resolution in the United Nations raised just such difficulties. Escott Reid, for example, disagreed with the decision at

86 Department of External Affairs, 'The Korean Crisis,' *External Affairs*, III, 2, Feb. 1951, 56-7; and United Nations, GAOR (First Committee), A/C.1/SR.437, 591
87 Panikkar, *In Two Chinas*, 124
88 Holmes, interview, 5 March 1968

the time, and still thinks that it was a mistake. An abstention by Canada (and the other NATO governments, if they could be so persuaded) would have helped to avoid the alienation of Asian powers – notably India – and in his view would have produced no more than temporary resentment in the United States.[89] John W. Holmes, the head of the department's United Nations Division, had similar reservations, which he held very strongly.[90]

During the course of the discussions at Lake Success, the CCF National Executive in Canada had passed a resolution expressing the party's opposition 'to any step at the UN or elsewhere which will place further obstacles in the way of a negotiated settlement in Korea and Asia generally.' The resolution urged the government

to oppose the US resolution now before the United Nations which would brand the Chinese people's government as an aggressor. The CCF believe that if the UN passed this resolution it would be in danger of sacrificing the friendship of a large proportion of the people of Asia, and of disrupting the unity of the free world.

The CCF does not doubt that the invasion of Korea by the Chinese armies was unjustifiable and contrary to UN policy. But at this moment every effort must be made to prevent a general war. We must not give way to resentment or hysteria, or assume that war is inevitable.[91]

Citing this as an expression of the party's judgment in the House of Commons on 1 February, Mr Coldwell quoted from Mr Pearson's United Nations speech of 26 January to the minister's own disadvantage, pointing out in effect that the reservations suggested therein were inconsistent with the decision to support the condemnation of the Chinese. The CCF leader during the previous autumn had attended the sessions of the General Assembly as an observer, and he had been surprised to learn of the Canadian vote.[92] He now moved to amend the official opposition's amendment to the address by adding to it the following words: 'We further regret that while Your Excellency's advisers have generally followed a constructive course in relation to the Korean dispute, they have in relation to the resolution branding China as an aggressor supported

89 Reid, interview, 9 June 1969
90 Holmes, letter to the author, 1 Dec. 1972. Mr Holmes saw the issue as a question of tactics rather than principle, however, and in later years sometimes used the incident to illustrate the sort of situation in which a public servant might seriously disagree with his political superiors, yet feel that the differences involved were not sufficiently fundamental to warrant or justify his resignation.
91 Quoted by M.J. Coldwell in Canada, House of Commons, *Debates*, 1 Feb. 1951, 31
92 Coldwell, interview, 10 July 1970

a course which is premature and unwise at this particular moment, and which should not have been pursued until the methods of peaceful negotiation had been completely exhausted.'[93]

These views were not shared by the Progressive Conservatives, however, who complained only of the government's lack of leadership in the crisis and of the paucity of its defence preparations.[94] Nor was it shared either by the editorialists of the daily press. The predictable French-Canadian exceptions aside, editorial writers across the country recorded with accelerating emphasis through January their belief that the condemnatory resolution ought to be passed as a clear statement of opposition to aggression.[95] The CCF sub-amendment was defeated in the house without a division on 6 February. Thereafter the decision to support the American resolution was a topic only for the *post mortem* discourse of officials in the Department of External Affairs.

When President Entezam began working on the composition of the Good Offices Committee provided for in the American resolution, he turned first to his colleagues on the luckless Cease-Fire Group. At first Mr Pearson considered the possibility of accepting his invitation, but Sir Benegal Rau, who was similarly approached, was ordered by New Delhi to decline in view of India's opposition to the American proposal. Mr Pearson thereupon declined also, believing 'that if the previous membership of the cease-fire committee could not be reconstituted, a new committee was preferable.'[96] He thought in addition that his usefulness might have been impaired by his public, although qualified, support for the condemnatory resolution.[97]

In the event, the fresh approach was not enough, and the Good Offices Committee, now consisting of Mr Entezam of Iran, Sven Graftstrom of Sweden, and Dr Luis Padillo Nervo of Mexico, made no progress with the Chinese.

---

93 Canada, House of Commons, *Debates*, 1 Feb. 1951, 33

94 The Progressive Conservative amendment to the address read as follows: 'We regret that Your Excellency's advisers have failed (1) to give this nation leadership in the face of the present grave danger; and (2) to bring into being forces necessary to enable Canada to defend itself and discharge its international obligations; and (3) to take effective measures to combat inflation and the rapidly rising cost of living.' Canada, House of Commons, *Debates*, 1 Feb. 1951, 24

95 See, for example, *Victoria Daily Colonist*, 6 Jan. 1951; Montreal *Gazette*, 8 Jan. 1951; *Globe and Mail*, 13 Jan. 1951; *Montreal Star*, 9 Jan. 1951; and *Saskatoon Star Phoenix*, 11 Jan. 1951, among others

96 Pearson, letter to the author, 13 Nov. 1968

97 Walter O'Hearn, 'The "Cease-Fire" Group: "Who'll Serve?" Is Query,' *Montreal Star*, 2 Feb. 1951. See also his 'Canada Stands Up,' *Behind the Headlines*, XI, 1, Feb. 1951, 8

In the light of its failure, the Americans on 7 May presented to the Additional Measures Committee proposals for the application of a selective embargo against mainland China. After discussion and amendments, it was approved by the committee on 14 May, and three days later was adopted by the Political Committee of the General Assembly. On 18 May it passed the General Assembly itself by a vote of 47 (including Canada) to 0, with 8 abstentions (the Soviet bloc refusing to take part). The key provision of the resolution recommended that all the United Nations members apply 'an embargo on the shipment to areas under the control of [mainland China] and of the North Korean authorities of arms, ammunition and implements of war, atomic energy materials, petroleum, transportation materials of strategic importance, and items useful in the production of arms, ammunition and implements of war.' Members were to report to the Additional Measures Committee 'within 30 days' on their implementation of the recommendation.[98]

No change in Canadian policy resulted from the passage of the resolution. John Holmes, in explaining his government's supporting vote, indicated that Canada had already placed an embargo on strategic exports to China. In the Canadian view, the real advantage of an official United Nations authorization was that it would 'generalize restrictions and require some equality in the sacrifices involved.' He added that 'if any further action should be required we believe that this could be taken by extending or revising this embargo.'[99]

When Mr Pearson was asked about Canada's embargo policy in the External Affairs Committee of the House of Commons on 22 May, he gave the following reply:

On December 6, 1950, the United States government announced a complete ban on all exports to China and to Hong Kong presumably to prevent transshipment from Hong Kong to China.

While the Canadian government has not made such an announcement or applied so complete an embargo, it has effectively prohibited the shipment of strategic materials to China. The resolution which we voted for at the United Nations the other day was merely a confirmation in the form of a United Nations resolution of a policy which, in so far as Canada was concerned, had been in effect for some time.

The Canadian government would be willing to allow goods that were neither strategic nor in short supply here to go to Hong Kong. From Hong Kong they could go to China in present circumstances.

98 Department of External Affairs, 'The Korean Crisis,' *External Affairs*, III, 6, June 1951, 186
99 Ibid., 186-7

In other words, we have not put a complete embargo on all goods of any kind to China, but we have put an embargo on all goods that will assist China in any way in the prosecution of aggression in Korea.[100]

Canada's report on the implementation of the 18 May resolution was submitted to the United Nations by Mr Holmes on 16 June, and it provided additional details of Canadian policy. The export restrictions required by the UN provision were, according to the report, 'less stringent than those which had already been imposed by the Canadian Government' and therefore no changes in the Canadian regulations had been necessary: 'From the beginning of the aggression in Korea there have been no shipments of arms, ammunition or implements of war from Canada to North Korea or China. On December 9, 1950, following the intervention of Chinese Communist forces in the Korean war, the Canadian Government broadened the scope of its export controls in such a manner that individual export permits were made a requirement for the export of all commodities without exception to China, Hong Kong, Macao and North Korea.' In practice, permits were denied for the export not only of all the commodities listed under the Additional Measures resolution, but also of 'a very wide range of other goods which may be considered to be strategic.' The Canadian government would 'prevent by all means within its power the circumvention of controls on shipments applied by other states under the resolution' and would 'co-operate fully with other states in carrying out the purpose of the embargo.'[101]

It seems to be impossible now to obtain precise information with respect either to the specifications of commodities which were considered to have strategic significance, or to the number and value of the export applications which were actually rejected by the Canadian government as a result of the embargo.[102] It is clear even from the inadequate figures which are available, however, that the cost of the embargo to Canadian trade was minimal, if visible at all. Table I indicates the value of exports of Canadian produce to Hong Kong, China, Taiwan, Korea, and Portuguese Asia for the years from 1946 to 1955, and it shows that in the case of Hong Kong, Canadian exports if anything were stimulated in 1951, and that in the case of Portuguese Asia the fluctuations (and indeed the total trade) were insignificant. Exports to Korea

100 Canada, House of Commons, Standing Committee on External Affairs, *Minutes and Proceedings of Evidence*, 22 May 1951, 25
101 Department of External Affairs, 'The Korean Crisis,' *External Affairs*, III, 7, July 1951, 232-3
102 An attempt to do so produced an acknowledgement from the Department of Trade and Commerce and a promise that the Department of External Affairs would consider the matter, but no information materialized.

TABLE I[1]
Exports of Canadian Produce, 1946-55[2] (Canadian dollars)

Year	Hong Kong	China	Taiwan	Korea	Port. Asia[3]
1946	4,361,830	42,915,143		125,813	75,809
1947	6,397,502	34,984,364		30,021	146,860
1948	8,256,303	29,128,478		22,965	103,707
1949	10,099,197	13,801,203		233,220	162,373
1950	8,004,177	2,056,569		1,142,919	103,035
1951	12,032,778	367,062		213,124	107,271
1952	9,581,937	1,155,524		335,298	282,381
1953	8,999,606		1,481,698	14,991,383	189,685
1954	8,252,458	69,977	3,186,039	3,197,181	42,948
1955	7,253,406	1,016,320	1,227,136	7,514,455	174,479

1 Compiled from Canada, Dominion Bureau of Statistics for the Department of Trade and Commerce, *Trade of Canada*. II: *Exports* (Ottawa, appropriate years)
2 'Canadian Produce' is defined as including not only articles of purely Canadian origin but also imported articles of foreign origin which have been changed in form or enhanced in value by further manufacture in Canada, such as sugar refined from imported raw sugar, and rubber goods made from imported unmanufactured rubber.
3 In addition to Macao, Portuguese Asia included Goa, Damao, and Diu in India, and Portuguese Timor in the Malay Archipelago. Figures for Macao only were unavailable.

dropped very substantially in 1951 and 1952, doubtless in consequence of the wartime disruption of the Korean economy. But the decline in export trade was most perceptible in the case of China, dropping off substantially in 1950. It was ultimately to recover only under the impact of wheat sales agreements concluded by the government of John G. Diefenbaker. The decrease had actually begun to assume major proportions as early as 1949, however, and the fact that the bulk of the decline had occurred before the embargo had been applied suggests that it was the result of general political conditions and commercial policies on the mainland rather than of Canada's mild imposition of economic sanctions.

In spite of American pressure to broaden still further the scope of the restrictions, the Canadian authorities were reluctant to sever commercial ties with China entirely, a reluctance which was due more to political caution than to commercial greed. On 5 June Mr Pearson had addressed the Canadian International Trade Fair in Toronto on the subject of 'Foreign Trade in a Time of Partial Peace,' and he told his audience that international trade had 'always been a major avenue for establishing relations with other countries.' To cut off commercial transactions entirely was generally regarded as 'an indication of open hostility' and 'a final diplomatic step.' But finality in diplomacy 'is unwise unless it is forced on you.' In the case of Communist China, it was 'easy and natural to point to the United Nations casualty lists and, without further consideration, conclude that here at least the policies of partial peace are no longer applicable; that here, at least, we should adjust our thinking to a new and realistic situation and cut off all intercourse with the source of the military power we are now fighting.' But it would be unwise to induce such a permanent breach in the relations between China and the 'free world,' and to risk thereby an extension and escalation of the conflict. It was essential to prohibit the export to China of commodities of 'strategic importance,' but this did not mean that *all* forms of trade should be severed. It was his view 'that we should not allow our commercial policy toward China at this time to become more stringent than our overall foreign policy toward her, and that we should not seek to put a complete embargo on all trade with her, unless the policy of the Peking Government gives us no alternative in the matter.'[103]

With their economic sanctions thus limited by the dictates of prudence, and their peace-making diplomacy brought to an end by the 1 February resolution of the United States, Canadian decision-makers could now direct their attention to the exploits of the Canadian Army Special Force. It is necessary, therefore, to examine the politics of this military enterprise.

103 Department of External Affairs, *Statements and Speeches*, no 51/24

6

Warriors and politics

The tortuosities of diplomacy and war in the months from September to February not surprisingly placed their stamp upon the fortunes of the Canadian Army Special Force. The CASF was beset in any case with tribulations of its own, and these had begun almost immediately after the 7 August order authorizing the recruitment of personnel. For so numerous were the enlistment applications that followed upon Mr St Laurent's radio appeal, and so unprepared were army recruiting officers for the subsequent deluge, that it took over two weeks to restore a modicum of order to the management of their duties and several months to remedy the errors to which their confusion had led them. Lt-Col. Wood reports in the official history that among the blunders was the enlistment of one man with an artificial leg, and of another who was seventy-two years old.[1] According to the Defence Research Board, which subsequently undertook a study of the recruiting process, 'the precipitate manner in which this special mobilization was initiated, the mandate that all who applied should be forthwith processed, the speedy clearing of applicants which was demanded ... were regrettable features to be avoided in any similar programme hereafter. Many men were enlisted who should not have been, others were given insufficient opportunity to put business and domestic affairs in order, contractual misunderstandings, mistakes and omissions occurred ... out of which a later harvest of administrative and training grief might be expected.'[2]

1 Wood, *Strange Battleground*, 29
2 Quoted ibid., 30

The most serious of the initial processing delays took place in Toronto. The resulting complaints were so numerous that the minister of national defence, who had himself composed the full-page recruiting advertisements which were then appearing in the daily press, used the occasion of his first flight on a CF -100 jet aircraft to visit the city for a personal inspection of recruiting stations. At the Chorley Park depot he discovered 'about 500 young and likely-looking fellows waiting their turn to go through the machine' and 'press-men on the scene taking photographs of the queues.' Reflecting grimly that it 'would only take some unfortunate incident to lose the whole lot and even spoil recruiting for the whole force right across the country,' he returned to Ottawa livid with anger, and after calling General Foulkes, had a stormy meeting with the adjutant general, Major-General W.H.S. Macklin. The minister's army advisers were reluctant to relax the recruiting procedures because they knew there would be a large number of undesirables among the applicants, and these would be a later source of trouble if they were not effectively screened at the time of enlistment. The problem was complicated by the fact that some of the applicants were medically unfit, and if recruited might subsequently burden the Department of Veterans Affairs with the responsibility for treating their ailments. After considerable argument, however, the process was streamlined in such a way as to permit much of the interviewing and counselling to take place after, rather than before, the formal acceptance of applications.[3]

The ultimate result was smooth recruiting and trouble-ridden training. By 18 August General Foulkes was able to report to the Cabinet that the Special Force had already been recruited to strength, originally set at 4960 all ranks, plus a reinforcement group of 2105 (7065 in all). He now recommended that the enlistments be continued until there were sufficient reinforcements to last twelve months. The Cabinet agreed, and authorized a total recruitment of 9976. But as the consequences of the early haste became evident, even these figures 'soon ceased to have any relevance':

As of 31 March, 1951, the last month of recruiting into the Special Force, 10,208 men had been enlisted, 2,230 had been discharged or were awaiting discharge, and 1,521 cases of desertion had been handled. Of that figure, 1,020 had been apprehended, while

3 Quotations from Claxton notes, 1147; other details from Foulkes, interview, 7 March 1968. A fictional portrayal of Mr Claxton's visit to one ot the Toronto recruiting stations is contained in Wood, *The Private War of Jacket Coates*, 3-5. At the time of the interview, General Foulkes could still recall vividly the spectacle of General Macklin nursing his wounds. Claxton reports only that he telephoned the two men to advise them of the need to speed up the proceedings: 'The CGS agreed emphatically with this. General Macklin made no objection.' Claxton notes, 1148. For Mr Claxton's recruiting advertisement, see the *Globe and Mail*, 9 Aug. 1950, 7

501 were still at large. As of 28 March, there were 141 soldiers, both Special and Active Force, under sentence in Military Detention Barracks, compared with a total of 25 for the Navy and Air Force combined. The figure for discharges and unapprehended deserters, which is more than 25 percent of the total numbers enlisted, compares with 7 percent for the first seven months of the First World War and 12 percent for the same period in the Second World War.[4]

The striking feature of these tribulations, however, is not that they resulted from administrative failure, but that they reflected the success of the recruiting campaign. In circumstances like those of 1950, the motivations of army volunteers are doubtless mixed, and range from the political through the economic to the escapist and adventurist. In the absence of detailed information from the recruits themselves it is difficult to determine which of these was dominant. Intuition would certainly suggest that political motivations were comparatively unimportant, if only because the war was far away and its significance for Canada's immediate security not very readily apparent. A quick glance at the condition of the economy at the time indicates that the economic factor was probably insignificant also, and that it may even have exerted an inhibiting effect. When General Foulkes first suggested the possibility of recruiting a special force, Mr Claxton had doubted that such a unit 'could be raised soon enough, in view of the existing high employment rate as compared with 1939,'[5] a point which was raised again by other members of the government in a Cabinet meeting on 26 July.[6] It was true that there had been a minor recession during the period from late 1948 through early 1950, but by mid-August, when enlistment applications were at their peak, employment was very full. The unemployed then comprised only 1.93 per cent of the labour force.[7]

An attempt to correlate enlistment applications with unemployment figures on a regional basis yields equally negative results. If the economic factor had been particularly important, one would expect to find a higher proportion of recruits coming from areas of heavy unemployment than from areas where jobs were more readily available. In fact, however, the correlation is not only low, but in some regions breaks down entirely (see Table II).

4 Wood, *Strange Battleground*, 30-2
5 Ibid., 20
6 Claxton notes, 1143. One press report suggested at the time that the prime minister was among the doubters. See 'Ottawa View,' *Saturday Night*, LXV, 45, 15 Aug. 1950, 2
7 Figures compiled from Table 7, 'The Canadian Labour Force,' *Canadian Statistical Review*, 19

TABLE II

Data on employment and army recruitment in Canada, summer 1950

Region	No of applications, CAAF and CASF, 23 June 1 Sept. 1950	Unemployment on 19 Aug. by per cent	No of unemployed in region per application	No in total labour force per application
Nfld	395	7.02	20	288
NS, PEI, and NB	2572	4.06	7	172
Quebec	3653	2.58	10	405
Ontario	6207	1.24	4	299
Prairies	1748	0.61	3	569
BC	612	2.26	16	722

Figures on the size of the labour force and the numbers of unemployed were calculated from Table 7, 'The Canadian Labour Force,' *Canadian Statistical Review,* Jan. 1951, p. 19. 'Unemployed' are defined as 'persons without jobs and seeking work.'

The figures on enlistment applications were compiled from data provided by J.A. Blanchette, parliamentary assistant to the minister of national defence, in House of Commons, *Debates,* 7 Sept. 1950, pp. 379-80. They cover only the period from 23 June to 1 September, but this should not unduly distort the results since the bulk of the enlistments were completed by the end of August.

In the final column the concept of the 'total labour force' was employed rather than overall population because it more accurately embraces that section of the populace from which military recruits are derived, eliminating, for example, housewives, students, the retired, and the 'voluntarily idle,' as well as the permanently handicapped and the like. Nevertheless, it still includes some categories of persons – for example, working women, youths of 14-18, and men over 45 – who are, and were, ineligible for military service.

Unemployment was heavy in Newfoundland and the three Maritime provinces (7.02 per cent and 4.06 per cent respectively), medium-low in Quebec and British Columbia (2.58 per cent and 2.26 per cent), and very low in Ontario and the Prairie provinces (1.24 per cent and 0.61 per cent). One would therefore expect to find a proportionately high volume of applications in Newfoundland and the Maritimes,[8] a low volume in Ontario and the Prairie provinces, and an intermediate volume in Quebec and British Columbia. In approximate terms these expectations are fulfilled in the case of Newfoundland and the Maritimes (one application for every 288 and 172 persons in the labour force respectively), Quebec (one for every 405), and the Prairies (one for every 569),

8 Military salaries would also be more competitive with those of private industry in these areas. See Table 10, 'Employment and Earnings: By Provinces,' ibid., 28-30

although the correlation would be more complete if the positions of Newfoundland and the Maritimes were reversed.[9] On the other hand, British Columbia, with a much higher rate of unemployment than either Ontario or the three Prairie provinces, provided by far the fewest number of applicants (only one for every 722 in the labour force), while Ontario, with very low unemployment, produced applications at the relatively high rate of one for every 299 – almost equal to that of Newfoundland.

The apparent anomalies become even more pronounced if the volume of applications in each area is related to the numbers of unemployed, rather than to the rate of unemployment as a proportion of the total labour force. As the fourth column in Table II indicates, the figures fluctuate wildly from one region to the next. For example, in Newfoundland, where the number of applications as a proportion of the total work force was relatively high (one in 288), as a proportion of the unemployed it was the lowest in the country (one in 20); conversely, in the Prairie provinces the number of applications as a proportion of the total work force was relatively low (one in 569), while as a proportion of the unemployed it was extremely high (one in three). Such variations to some extent may be explained by differences in the relative suitability for military service of the unemployed in the various regions. For example, a much higher proportion of applicants in Newfoundland and the Maritimes were refused enlistment than in the Prairie provinces, a fact which suggests that many of the unemployed in the former areas may have been deterred from applying because they knew their illiteracy or some other factor would lead to an ignominious rejection.[10] It seems improbable, however, that all the variations indicated on Table II can be so simply explained.

All this evidence is obviously circumstantial, but it suggests at the very least that the economic factor was not uniformly important across the country as an incentive for enlistment, and that other influences were therefore at work. There is further evidence, moreover, to indicate that the most significant of these other influences were adventurist in character. It will be recalled that when Prime Minister St Laurent began the campaign for recruits in his radio broadcast on 7 August, he announced that in addition to the newly-formed

---

9 The Newfoundland figures may have been a reflection in part of the fact that the province only recently had entered Confederation.

10 The percentages of rejections in each area were as follows: Newfoundland, 47.1% of applicants; NS, PEI, and NB, 43.7%; Quebec, 39.4%; Ontario, 37.4%; Manitoba, Saskatchewan, and Alberta, 30.0%; British Columbia, 22.9%. Compiled from data provided by Mr J.A. Blanchette, parliamentary assistant to the minister of national defence, in Canada, House of Commons, *Debates*, 7 Sept. 1950, 379-80

TABLE III

Applications for Enlistment in the CAAF and the CASF, 23 June - 1 September 1950

	CAAF	CASF
Newfoundland	30	365
NS, PEI, NB	521	2051
Quebec	472	3181
Ontario	810	5397
Prairie provinces	245	1503
British Columbia	126	486
Total	2204	12,983

Special Force, the regular services would also be expanded.[11] Indeed, Mr Claxton and Mr Lapointe (the solicitor-general) had issued an appeal for new recruits for the regular forces as early as 20 July. Yet in the period from 23 June to 1 September, applications for enlistment in the Special Force outnumbered by almost six-to-one those for recruitment into the regular army. In the country as a whole, there were 12,983 applications (and 8389 actual enlistments) for the CASF, but only 2204 (1164 actual enlistments) for the Active Force.[12] This was probably due in part to the decision not to require for admission to the CASF the high school matriculation certificate that was demanded of recruits to the regular army.[13] Nevertheless, there was obviously much greater interest in serving on a short-term (eighteen-month) basis in an army that would be stationed in a theatre overseas, than in a force whose primary purpose and probable fate was to guard the front at home. As Table III suggests, this order of preference was consistent throughout the country, although it is true that the actual ratio of Special Force volunteers to regular recruits varied widely, from about twelve to one in Newfoundland, to four to one in the Maritimes and British Columbia. Quebec, Ontario, and the Prairie provinces, on the other hand, showed patterns very close to the national average of six to one.

The impression that the recruits were motivated more by adventurism than by economic hardship is reinforced by the fact that as many as 45 per cent of those volunteering for the Special Force were veterans of World War II, and 20 per cent were former NCOs.[14] These presumably comprised individuals who

11 See above, 89-90
12 Canada, House of Commons, *Debates*, 7 Sept. 1950, 379-80
13 Foulkes, interview, 7 March 1968
14 Wood, *Strange Battleground*, 32

had little interest in pursuing a military career in peacetime, but who could be enticed to return to the army by the prospect of service overseas. This interpretation is strengthened even further by the failure of the attempt after the spring of 1951 to convert the members of the Special Force into soldiers with Active Force status. This endeavour was the consequence of a decision to undertake a general expansion of the armed forces to meet new commitments within the framework of NATO as well as under the United Nations. But a report prepared by the army on 24 August 1953 showed that of the 10,308 men who had enlisted as Special Force volunteers on an eighteen-month basis, only 2823 subsequently joined the Active Force.[15] As Brooke Claxton later observed, ' ... The call to go and fight in Korea appealed to those who were particularly adventurous, who wanted to travel and see far-off places. It appealed to those who wanted to fight. It appealed to many who after service in the Second World War had never completely adjusted themselves to life on civvy street. It appealed to some who frankly wanted to escape from responsibility or obligations at home. While there were some misfits who had to be weeded out, generally speaking they were a good lot and they became magnificent fighting soldiers. None were murderers, none were enlisted from gaols.'[16]

And none, apparently, was seized by the character of the cause. The nature of the war, and the manner in which the issue was presented, doubtless made it possible for the recruits to see the Canadian role in positive moral and political terms, but individual decisions to enlist appear on the basis of the available evidence to have been due primarily to personal rather than to political factors. Certainly this was the view of the army itself, and when for a time in October 1950 it appeared that the force might not be required in the theatre at all, Canadian officers became concerned about the effect this could have upon the morale of the troops.[17] The later dispatches of journalists reporting on the attitudes of Canadian soldiers in the field similarly confirm the view that political motivations were not very deeply ingrained.[18] As Jacket Coates, the hero of the official army historian's novel of the Korean War, is made to observe of the men lined up in a Toronto recruiting centre, 'These guys looked hungry for something and it was probably either money or legal separation from their loved ones.'[19]

15 Ibid., 88
16 Claxton notes, 1149
17 Wood, *Strange Battleground*, 44
18 See, for example, Berton, 'Corporal Dunphy's War,' 7
19 Wood, *The Private War of Jacket Coates*, 2. Such realities did not, of course, mean that the army could afford to be indifferent about its public image. In the task of polishing its reputa-

All of this suggests, of course, that the composition of the CASF cannot by itself be taken as a very reliable indicator of political attitudes toward the war in various parts of the country. In particular it has sometimes been argued that the success of the recruiting drive in French Canada was a reflection of a revolution in French-Canadian views on defence and foreign policy, and that the identification of communism as the principal threat to western security had eroded the traditional isolationism of the Province of Quebec.[20] If there is truth in this claim, it cannot be established by reference to enlistment figures if individual decisions to enlist were based on non-political considerations.

Many of the officers were also recruited from civilian life, but in the end most of the commissioned ranks had to be filled by transfers from the regular army. The overall command of the force was assumed by Brigadier J.M. Rockingham, a brigade commander in World War II who had left the service in 1945. Rockingham was selected partly because Mr Claxton wanted a civilian veteran who would be 'on the same footing as the men to whom the Government was appealing to return to the Colours.'[21] General Foulkes had also advised him that the brigadier was an outstanding officer and that he would get along well with the American military authorities.[22] Officers of other ranks were selected on the basis of their experience and record in World War II, and since outside volunteers with the appropriate qualifications were not plentiful, the final roster showed a considerable representation from the permanent army. For example, of a total of 111 officers occupying command, staff, or technical positions, 77 came from the Active Force, as did all the

tion, however, it received in the summer of 1950 assistance from an unexpected quarter. During the recruiting drive the Nova Scotia Board of Censors ordered that a reissue of the classic 'anti-war' film, *All Quiet On The Western Front*, be withdrawn from all the theatres under its jurisdiction for a period of two months. See Robertson, 'Movie Censorship,' 11, 40
20 Mr Claxton used similar figures for this purpose in the House of Commons on 8 May 1951. On that occasion he pointed out that 3134 of 10,587 Special Force recruits came from the Province of Quebec, that is, 30 per cent of the total – almost the same as the proportion of Quebec residents in the population as a whole (29 per cent). 'I have had a special survey carried out,' he went on. 'It meant looking at every file, but I thought in the interests of national unity and justice we should do it. It was found that the proportion of Canadians in all parts of the country who joined the Special Force and whose mother tongue was reported to be French corresponded almost exactly to the Canadians of French origin in the total population.' See Canada, House of Commons, *Debates*, 8 May 1951, 2801. See also Eayrs, 'The Foreign Policy of Canada,' 679, and the same author, 'Canadian Defence Policies Since 1967,' in Canada, House of Commons, *Special Studies Prepared for the Special Committee of the House of Commons on Matters Relating to Defence*, 17. Professor Eayrs's argument is accepted also by McLin, *Canada's Changing Defense Policy*, 20
21 Wood, *Strange Battleground*, 33
22 Ibid. Confirmed by Foulkes, interview, 7 March 1968

officers in the Ordnance Corps. The proportion among officers in the infantry was considerably less (27 of 113), but still not insignificant.[23]

The problem of training and administering the hastily recruited brigade has been discussed in detail by the official historian, and need not be further examined here. A number of other issues, however, were related more directly to matters of diplomacy. Among them was the question of whether or not the CASF would be sent to the theatre at all, and if so, in what strength.

It will be recalled that early in the conflict considerable pressure had been exerted on the government, both at home and abroad, to contribute substantial ground support to the UNC's military operations. Once the decision to do so had been taken, Canadian military officials became anxious to expedite the CASF's training, so that the troops might be shipped as soon as possible to the front. Early estimates – later proven to be optimistic – placed the time required for preparation at about five months, although eventually the matter was left to Brigadier Rockingham's own discretion.[24] This meant that the force would not be ready for battle before the onset of the Canadian winter, and attention was therefore directed to the problem of finding a less inclement training location than could be found in Canada. As early as mid-August, therefore, General Foulkes had suggested that arrangements be made to transfer the force overseas to Japan to complete its training, provided only that guarantees were obtained that its proximity to the theatre of operations would not lead to its being committed to action before it was ready. On 21 August, after selecting 1 November as an appropriate date of departure, the CGS wrote to the American army chief of staff, General Collins, to inquire whether such an arrangement would be feasible. Collins replied that General MacArthur thought it would be politically unwise to attempt to train UN forces in Japan, particularly if they originated in countries not among the occupying powers. He therefore suggested Okinawa as an alternative, beginning in late November. General Foulkes agreed to this counter-proposal.[25]

On 22 August, however, the Cabinet had decided to establish a liaison staff in Tokyo under the designation Canadian Military Mission, Far East, and its commander, Brigadier F.J. Fleury, arrived in the Japanese capital with his staff on 24 September. Four days later he flew to Okinawa to inspect the proposed training area, and on 3 October reported to General Foulkes that the island

---

23 Figures compiled from data, ibid., 34
24 Ibid., 39 and 41
25 Ibid., 41. General MacArthur's reaction has been confirmed by Lt-Gen. F.J. Fleury, interview, 8 March 1968

was unsuitable for training purposes.[26] In previous years it had been occupied by a regimental combat team, but by June 1950 the American force had dwindled to little more than a battalion. By the time Fleury arrived, the only personnel remaining were engineers and administrative staff, the rest having been transferred to Pusan. The facilities, which were primitive in any case, had seriously deteriorated. More importantly, the island was composed essentially of a coral reef, and its terrain and vegetation were in no way similar to those of Korea. It was therefore almost useless as a training site for combat in the Korean theatre.[27]

By now the Okinawa plan had begun in any event to appear obsolete. The brigadier's report was filed eighteen days after the landings of the American 10th Corps at Inchon, and a full week after these forces had linked up with General Walker's Eighth Army, which had simultaneously broken out of the Pusan perimeter. On 7 October the UN General Assembly had passed its resolution authorizing MacArthur to cross the 38th parallel, and shortly thereafter the UN forces had launched a rapid advance up the peninsula.

These developments seemed to reduce the urgency of the plan to contribute Canadian troops. As early as 26 September there were reports in the press suggesting that the Canadian contingent would probably arrive too late to do more than assist in the tasks of occupation. There was speculation that the government would not be entirely pleased to see a force which it had recruited at great cost for emergency combat purposes consigned to such pedestrian duties.[28] A dispatch from the Ottawa bureau of the Canadian Press news agency on 29 September reported 'a high government source' as saying that the Cabinet would probably not support the use of the force in an occupational role, although this attitude might change if occupation troops were badly needed. In the meantime the government was contemplating the possibility of sending the force to Europe instead.[29] By 11 October the same agency was reporting that the 'feeling' in Ottawa was 'that the UN will want at least a token Canadian force in the occupation for political reasons. Informed quarters say key Cabinet ministers now feel the whole force won't be going to Korea but that Canada would probably comply with a request for a small occupation force.'[30]

Canadian military authorities were already discussing the matter with the United Nations Command. On 4 October, the day after filing his report on the

26 Wood, *Strange Battleground*, 41
27 Fleury, interview, 8 March 1968
28 Ed Hadley, 'Canadians Urged in Policy Role,' *Montreal Star*, 26 Sept. 1950
29 Canadian Press, 'Canada Not Keen on Job of Occupation,' *Montreal Star*, 29 Sept. 1950
30 Canadian Press, 'Plans Not Yet Clear,' *Montreal Star*, 11 Oct. 1950

Okinawa training site, Brigadier Fleury had his first lengthy meeting with General MacArthur. The general at this point was fully confident, according to Fleury, that operations in Korea would 'for all practical purposes, be successfully completed in one month.' This meant that the Canadian brigade would 'not arrive in time to fight in Korea,' but MacArthur still thought it should be dispatched, presumably to help in the short-term occupation which he envisaged would follow a cease-fire.[31]

Fleury's account of this meeting reached General Foulkes on 16 October. On the following day, the brigadier wired another report, this time in connection with a second meeting with the UN commander. 'General MacArthur,' he said, 'indicated Canadian Brigade would be of no repeat no significance from view small current operation. He suggests Canada might prefer to send immediately small token force to show flag.' When Fleury had protested that the Canadian brigade consisted of men who had volunteered specifically for action in Korea, MacArthur had appeared indifferent, and the brigadier concluded that he probably would not react unfavourably if the decision to send a Canadian contingent were revoked.[32]

MacArthur's suggestion of a 'token force to show flag' was not entirely in conflict with the view then being taken by some members of the Canadian Cabinet, but the final decision probably would have been postponed for a few more weeks pending the outcome of the fighting in North Korea had it not been for still another wire from Brigadier Fleury. Following closely upon that of 17 October, it advised the CGS that the American military authorities in Okinawa had already begun to build concrete floors for the proposed Canadian training camp, and that if their work were completed it would cost the government of Canada $1,300,000. With this sobering prospect before them, Canadian officials hastily initiated discussions in the United States, and on 20 October Brigadier H.E. Taber, the head of the Canadian Army Staff in Washington, advised the quartermaster general in Ottawa that General Foulkes and the Americans had agreed that some or all of the CASF would go directly to Korea. The Okinawa plan was therefore cancelled.[33]

The substance of these new arrangements was not, however, immediately transmitted to subordinate levels of command, and on the following day, 21 October, an 'Advance Water Party' of 31 officers and 317 other ranks sailed for Okinawa from Seattle to prepare for the arrival of the entire Canadian

31 See 'Brigadier Fleury's Report on His First Interview with General MacArthur, 4 October 1950,' Wood, *Strange Battleground*, 261-2
32 Ibid., 42
33 Ibid., 42-3

brigade.[34] Two days later Mr Claxton and his deputy, C.M. Drury, arrived in Washington with the Canadian chiefs of staff to discuss plans for a forthcoming meeting of the NATO Council. During the course of these conversations General Foulkes was informed that the American Joint Chiefs had recommended to the State Department that the Canadian contingent be reduced to one battalion. Foulkes so informed the vice chief of the General Staff in Ottawa, Major-General H.A. Sparling, on 26 October.[35]

The CGS in the meantime continued his discussions with General Collins in the hope of obtaining from the Americans a base suitable for training the Canadian brigade. Collins was more than helpful. General Foulkes was briefed by American staff officers on every army installation in the United States, and was told to pick whichever one he wanted. Ultimately he decided upon the infantry base at Fort Lewis in the state of Washington. It was well equipped, sufficiently close to the Canadian border to minimize the problems of operating on foreign soil, and only a short distance from Seattle, the port of embarkation.[36] As Jacket Coates is made to describe it by the official army historian,

Fort Lewis in Washington was the biggest damn Army camp I had ever seen. It had a parade square nearly a mile long and for the first few days after we arrived, you could see Canadian sergeant-majors wandering around on it with a look of awe on their faces as if they had arrived in heaven ...

[It was] a great sprawling, bustling military community with mile after mile of barracks, married quarters and training areas. The section turned over to the Canadian Army Special Force was called North Post ... [37]

General Collins' eagerness to help had been impressive. 'If Fort Lewis suits you,' he had told the Canadian CGS, 'I'll move out and you can take over.' He would also make good any deficiencies in the CASF's equipment and would provide any instruction for its use which the Canadians might require.[38]

The decision to use Fort Lewis as the training site and staging camp for most of the brigade was made on 4 November. It was agreed, however, that the 2nd Battalion of the Princess Patricia's Canadian Light Infantry would be dispatched directly to Korea late in November, there to undergo a final two months of training before assuming what were now expected to be the routine

34 Ibid., 53
35 Ibid., 43
36 Foulkes, interview, 7 March 1968
37 Wood, *The Private War of Jacket Coates*, 51
38 Foulkes, interview, 7 March 1968. The quotation is the general's approximate reconstruction of Collins' remark.

tasks of peaceful occupation. The ship carrying the Advance Water Party meanwhile was instructed to alter its course from Okinawa to Pusan, Korea. Most of the Special Force arrived in Fort Lewis before the end of November,[39] and it was there given the new designation, 25th Canadian Infantry Brigade. The 2nd Battalion, PPCLI, with a total strength of 927 men, left Seattle for Korea on the American troopship *Private Joe P. Martinez* on 25 November and arrived in Pusan on 18 December.

By now the battalion's prospects for a quiet tour of occupation duty had disintegrated at the hands of the Chinese, who had succeeded in driving General MacArthur's forces back to the vicinity of the 38th parallel. With the battalion's proposed campsite now being occupied by dislocated American units, the new Canadian arrivals were compelled to take over accommodation hitherto utilized by the Advance Water Party, whose members for the most part were shortly to be shipped back to Fort Lewis pending a final decision regarding the future of the brigade. The 2nd PPCLI, resisting with considerable difficulty pressures from the American Eighth Army to commit itself immediately to combat operations,[40] meanwhile began the completion of its training. On 13 January it suffered its first casualties under the fire of enemy snipers, and by 17 February it was taking part in its first operational manoeuvre at the front.

The remainder of the 25th Brigade, its future still uncertain, continued in training at Fort Lewis. Long after the Chinese intervention, the Canadian government and its senior military advisers clung to the hope that the brigade might be dispatched to Europe as a contribution to NATO rather than to the Far East. In a telephone conversation on 8 January, General Foulkes told Rockingham that while an assignment to Korea could not be ruled out, he would be sent to Europe in April if this proved unnecessary.[41]

Ultimately the decision depended upon the outcome of the attempt to open cease-fire negotiations with the Chinese. But even after the fate of this initiative had been sealed, the government still seemed reluctant to admit the implications of its failure. The Canadian Parliament assembled in Ottawa on 30 January, the same day the American resolution condemning mainland China as an aggressor was passed in the Political Committee of the UN General Assembly. Yet in the Speech from the Throne the government still refrained from committing itself on the future of the 25th Brigade. 'The increased menace in the Far East,' it argued, 'reinforces the mounting evidence that Communist imperialism is determined to dominate the world by force or the

39 Some were held up as the result of a train accident. See Wood, *Strange Battleground*, 47
40 See below, 206
41 Wood, *Strange Battleground*, 88

fear of force, and that the only hope of maintaining peace with freedom lies in the rapid increase of combined strength of the free nations.' The government of Canada was doing its part. One battalion of the CASF was already in Korea and the remaining units were in training at Fort Lewis, where they were 'available for service in Korea or for other employment in discharge of our international obligations.' During the session Parliament would 'be asked to approve substantially increased expenditures for defence,' including 'Canadian participation' in a newly-organized integrated force under NATO in Europe.[42] But the character of this participation was left undefined, and the future of the brigade unsettled.

Three days later, on 2 February, Mr Claxton telephoned Rockingham to inform him that 'while there was now little likelihood of the brigade going to Korea, it was possible it might go to Europe in March.'[43] The quartermaster general was still making plans to cover this contingency as late as 12 February, and in retrospect it seems clear that the government hoped simply that a request for more Canadian assistance on the ground in Korea would not be forthcoming. It could then give priority to the European theatre. As Mr Claxton told the Commons on 5 February, the brigade had been recruited 'for the special purpose of carrying out any undertaking by Canada under the charter of the United Nations and the North Atlantic Treaty,' and except for the battalion already in Korea, it would soon 'be available for service where required.' 'Without minimizing the significance of the character of the fighting in Korea,' [he added], 'it is the view of this and the other allied governments that the vital centre of our global defence is in Western Europe. It was in recognition of this strategic necessity that the North Atlantic Treaty was entered into by twelve nations less than two years ago.'[44]

But not all the allied governments agreed that the importance of European defence precluded Canada from making a larger contribution to the effort in Korea, and the inevitable request for a Canadian ground force contingent was eventually conveyed to Ottawa through General Foulkes on 20 February. After a hasty meeting of the Cabinet Defence Committee and then of the Cabinet as a whole, the minister of national defence delivered a succinct announcement to the House of Commons on the following day:

Yesterday inquiry was received from the unified command of the United Nations forces in Korea as to whether training of the balance of the 25th Canadian Infantry brigade

---

42 Canada, *Debates of the Senate*, 30 Jan. 1951, 1
43 Wood, *Strange Battleground*, 89
44 Canada, House of Commons, *Debates*, 5 Feb. 1951, 92

was complete, and if so, could it be sent to form part of the United Nations forces in Korea

This training is almost complete, and the government agreed today that the other elements in the brigade group should shortly proceed to Korea and join the second battalion of the Princess Patricia's Canadian Light Infantry there.[45]

There was virtually no comment from the House, and after the appropriate preparations and ceremonies, the 25th Brigade sailed for Korea in three American troopships on 19, 20, and 21 April. Training, auxiliary, and reinforcement units not assigned to the operational theatre left Fort Lewis and returned to the Canadian base at Wainwright, Alberta, in the following month. By 20 May elements of the new Canadian force in Korea were engaged in operations at the front.

In Ottawa, meanwhile, the government now had to confront the financial and other implications of its decision. On 4 May Mr Claxton reminded the House that Canada had agreed in December to participate in an integrated defence force under the NATO pact, and that he had signified on 5 February the government's intention of providing for this purpose a brigade group, or regimental combat team, whose precise time of arrival in western Europe would 'depend on events in Korea.' Since then, these events had 'resulted in the decision to send the 25th Canadian infantry brigade group to Korea.' The situation there did 'not warrant any assumption that that formation could be released to form part of the integrated force within a reasonable period.' Given these circumstances, the army's first priority would be to keep the Korean force up to strength, but the service would be expanded to meet other tasks as well. Among them was 'the provision of a force for western Europe.' This expansion would involve 'the formation of an additional Canadian army brigade group with supporting units ... to be known as 27th Canadian infantry brigade group.'[46]

The 'cold war' had become an expensive and demanding contest.

But expense was not the government's only concern. When states ally in battle, the conjunction of their armies creates a politics of its own, and to this not even the United Nations forces in Korea were entirely immune. The fact that the operation was being conducted ostensibly under UN auspices, when in fact it was almost completely dominated by the United States, compounded the difficulties. In the Canadian case the problem of the status of the 25th Brigade

45 Ibid., 21 Feb. 1951, 563
46 Ibid., 4 May 1951, 2703

was at first particularly acute because the politicians and permanent officials in Ottawa were themselves of divided opinion.

It will be recalled that when Mr Claxton first met with the chiefs of staff on 18 July to receive their reports of Canada's capacity to assist the United Nations in Korea, General Foulkes had suggested as the least of four possible evils the contribution of a specially recruited infantry brigade. This force ideally would operate within the context of a Commonwealth division, and would therefore require minimal supporting services.[47] Later in the month the possibility of organizing a Commonwealth divisional unit for action in Korea was raised also by the government of Australia, although Canberra did not formally request Canadian participation.[48] The British were similarly interested in a joint Commonwealth arrangement, and on 24 August Mr Pearson felt obliged to clarify the government's position to the Canadian high commissioner in London: 'Operations in Korea should have the aspect of United Nations operations ... It is in discharge of obligations under the Charter that our troops will be serving and not in any sense as members of the Commonwealth.'[49] He therefore suggested that all the contributors to the United Nations force which were using equipment of British manufacture and design, including such non-Commonwealth contingents as that of Turkey, be grouped together for logistical convenience under the title 'United Nations First Division.'

The high commissioner replied four days later that the Turks would be using American, not British, equipment, and that authorities in Whitehall were unwilling in any event to abandon the idea of a Commonwealth division. The dispute fattened the diplomatic mails for some time, the British suggesting in late November a compromise solution in the form of the title, 'The First (Commonwealth) Division, United Nations Forces.' The exchange subsided with the decision to send only one Canadian battalion, and did not re-emerge until the commitment much later of the entire 25th Brigade.

Mr Pearson deployed similar arguments in parrying the indignant jibes of the Progressive Conservative opposition in the House. Howard C. Green, a future Conservative secretary of state for external affairs, was particularly prominent among the parliamentary advocates of a Commonwealth division. On 4 September, for example, he complained that Mr Claxton seemed to be hoping that the Canadian brigade would serve either with American forces, 'or with a United Nations division in which our men would have as associates

47 See above, 75-6
48 Unidentified press report, quoted by Howard Green in Canada, House of Commons, *Debates,* 4 Sept. 1950, 217. See also T.B. Millar, *The Commonwealth and the United Nations* (Sydney 1967), 58
49 Quoted in Wood, *Strange Battleground,* 44

troops from other nations such as Turkey, Thailand – and I mean no discredit to them – and other nations which have volunteered to send troops to the Korean fight.' Reminding the members of the battlefield exploits of Commonwealth forces in the two world wars, he accused the government of 'completely ignoring tradition and history,' and argued that since 1945 it had had a tragic impact upon the balance of world affairs:

> One of the greatest tragedies of our time is that the British Commonwealth is not today a third great world power standing on an equal footing with the United States and Russia. That might have been the case. That was the case when the fighting stopped in 1945. But this Canadian government has been primarily responsible for preventing the Commonwealth from being in that position today because, right from 1944, when the late Mr. Mackenzie King said that there would be no Commonwealth bloc if he could prevent it, this government has been playing down the British Commonwealth. By the actions of the ministry, one would think that they are trying to ease Canada out of the British Commonwealth by the back door.[50]

Mr Pearson observed in reply that the brigade had been earmarked to carry out Canada's United Nations obligations, 'wherever those obligations may arise.' In adopting this policy, the government had 'started something very important, the importance of which is much broader than Korea,' for by setting this precedent it had 'begun the establishment of United Nations forces for use not only in Korea but elsewhere.' This, he conceded, did not remove the problem of how the brigade was to be used if it actually were sent to Korea, but he could not accept the view that it should necessarily be mobilized as part of a British Commonwealth division. That would depend entirely upon the unified command.

Mr Green described these observations as 'pussyfooting,' to which Mr Pearson replied that if Mr Green 'had had his way we would have made this brigade available not to the United Nations but to the United Kingdom.' The government had done otherwise, and indeed if the 'brigade should be armed with United States-type equipment, then it might be more efficient to use it in some other way.' The Unified Command would decide, and Canada would be happy to comply with whatever decision it made.[51]

In resting his final argument on the criterion of efficiency as affected by the character of the brigade's equipment, Mr Pearson had identified what his military advisers regarded as the nub of the problem. The army's equipment

50 Canada, House of Commons, *Debates*, 4 Sept. 1950, 217-18
51 Ibid., 224

policy at the time the war broke out was still unsettled, and in the Korea case the obstacles were compounded by the fact that the Canadian contribution was so small. As the official historian has observed, 'the problems faced by Canada in putting a comparatively small force into a distant Pacific theatre in combination with the United States and Britain were difficult to solve economically. Canadians had no nearby bases of their own like Hong Kong or Japan; their equipment was a mixture of British, Canadian and American; their ration scale was somewhat different and their method of re-supply and reinforcement was complicated by geography.'[52]

The Korean hostilities had begun just as the government was in the process of standardizing its equipment on the basis of American specifications. General Foulkes had been anxious from the spring of 1948 to ensure that Canada would have an armaments production capability of her own, and he had encouraged the government to sell existing war surplus stocks to friendly nations abroad or to domestic consumers. Currently warehoused inventories, he had argued, were subject to obsolescence, whereas the proceeds derived from their sale could be used to support and maintain a healthy domestic armaments industry. By September 1950 he was pointing out that Canadian armaments sales then being arranged with purchasers in NATO would involve the replacement of the army's entire existing stocks with equipment and munitions of American manufacture. This conversion would progress much too slowly, however, to be of any immediate use to the CASF and in any case he believed that a changeover at this particular juncture would lengthen the force's training period by nullifying the experience of those volunteers who had been accustomed to using the older equipment during World War II. The upshot was a decision on 16 August to equip the CASF with materiel of the older type, for the most part British in design.[53] On 21 August, therefore, three days before Mr Pearson's communication to London in support of a 'United Nations First Division,' General Foulkes sent the following message to the American army chief of staff:

This force is being equipped with UK type of equipment except for vehicles which will be either Canadian or US pattern and we hope to secure your 3.5 rocket launcher before the force goes into action. I have already approached the UK to suggest that they should maintain us in the theatre as far as equipment and ammunition replacements are concerned. It is my hope that they will organize a division composed of the various nations armed with UK type of equipment as this would certainly ease our problem and

52 Wood, *Strange Battleground*, 35
53 Ibid., 36-7; and Foulkes, interview, 7 March 1968

make General MacArthur's problem a little easier. In any event, whether the UK agrees to maintain our equipment or not we will still need your assistance in the case of rations, petrol, lubricants, etcetera.[54]

Subsequent conversations with the appropriate American authorities produced an agreement along these lines, and it received the formal approval of the Canadian Cabinet on 25 September. Ultimately, when the Commonwealth division was actually formed, the arrangement worked very well. The Canadians were alone among the Commonwealth units in making regular use of American food rations,[55] but in the end this appeared to cause the UN commander little difficulty. According to MacArthur's successor, General Matthew B. Ridgway,

The UN forces ... counted troops from many nations – from the Netherlands, from Turkey, from Greece, from the Philippines, from Norway, from Sweden, from Colombia, from France, from India, even from Thailand, in addition to the many we had long had with us from Australia and other areas of the British Commonwealth. Catering to all the peculiar preferences, in food, in clothing, in religious observances – gave our service and supply forces a thousand petty headaches. The Dutch wanted milk where the French wanted wine. The Moslems wanted no pork and the Hindus, no beef. The Orientals wanted more rice and the Europeans wanted more bread. Shoes had to be extra wide to fit the Turks. They had to be extra narrow and short to fit the men from Thailand and the Philippines. American clothing was far too big for the small men from the East. Only the Canadians and the Scandinavians adjusted easily to United States rations and clothes.[56]

The eventual effect of these logistics arrangements was to encourage the establishment of very much the sort of formation which had been espoused so vigorously by Mr Green in the House, although not for the reasons which he had had in mind. Brigadier Fleury, after making provisions for the maintenance of the PPCLIs before their arrival in Korea in mid-December, was able to report to the quartermaster general in Ottawa that servicing would be provided for the most part by the British Commonwealth Korean Base, the United States army supplying parts only for such Canadian equipment of American design as vehicles, mortars, and rocket launchers. When the battalion received its first operational orders on 15 February, it was assigned to the 27th British Commonwealth Infantry Brigade under the command of Briga-

54 Quoted in Wood, ibid., 37
55 See Preston, 'The Military Structure of the Old Commonwealth,' 118
56 Ridgway, *The Korean War*, 221

dier B.A. Coad of the British army. The arrival of the Canadians at the brigade's position on 18 February expanded its roster to include the following: an Australian battalion, a Canadian battalion, an English battalion, a Scottish battalion, a New Zealand field regiment, and an Indian field ambulance. According to an admiring British military historian, 'There is no record of any other brigade – or force of similar size – composed of so many contingents of different Commonwealth countries. It seems unlikely that there is a parallel in the history of any army.'[57]

The subsequent rotation of a number of the British components, and the replacement of the headquarters' staff by fresh personnel from Hong Kong, led on 25 April to the brigade being renamed the '28th British Commonwealth Brigade,' but its intra-Commonwealth character was retained.

With the arrival of the 25th Canadian Infantry Brigade at the front late in May, the 2nd Battalion was withdrawn from the 28th Brigade and reassigned to Brigadier Rockingham's command. Except for occasional short-term operations with the British,[58] it and other Canadian units remained thereafter under Canadian brigade-level control.

Meanwhile, at the divisional level efforts were begun almost immediately upon the arrival of the CASF to prepare for the establishment of a separate and distinct Commonwealth division. There were by this time three Commonwealth brigades in the theatre – the 25th Canadian, the 28th British Commonwealth, and the 29th Independent Infantry, which was purely British in composition. Until June these units operated for the most part independently of one another as components of American ground formations. The addition of the Canadian brigade, however, made possible the creation of a Commonwealth unit of division strength, which in the words of the division's British historian would provide a 'consequent elevation in prestige and increased participation in the planning and conduct of major operations.'[59]

Canadian motivations were more modest. Any 'consequent elevation in prestige' was bound almost certainly to accrue to the British, not to the Canadians, and since the division would be commanded by Britishers, the

---

57 Barclay, *The First Commonwealth Division*, 53
58 For example, the 2nd PPCLI was reassigned to the 28th Brigade on 2 June to establish a front-line salient; it was relieved nine days later by the Royal 22nd. Wood, *Strange Battleground*, 107-8
59 Barclay, *The First Commonwealth Division*, 83. In April 1951, following speculation in the British press on the possible emergence of a Commonwealth divisional formation, an MP observed in the British House of Commons that having a British commander in the field at the rank of a general officer (and not merely a brigadier) would be useful in dealing with the Americans. See Millar, *The Commonwealth and the United Nations*, 58

resulting 'increased participation in the planning and conduct of major operations' was unlikely to affect very substantially the fortunes and responsibilities of Brigadier Rockingham. The Department of External Affairs was in any case much more interested in describing the troops of the Special Force as soldiers of the United Nations than as soldiers of the British Commonwealth. General Foulkes' early support for the idea of a joint Commonwealth enterprise had been motivated as much by the prosaic demands of logistical necessity as by affection for the British connection. But in December the Cabinet had accepted in principle the British compromise concept of a '1st (Commonwealth) Division, United Nations Forces,' provided 'the Unified Command considered it desirable.'[60] In March 1951, therefore, when the British raised the question again following the Canadian decision to field the 25th Brigade, the new CGS, Lieutenant-General G.G. Simonds, wired London that 'Canadian Government agreeable to grouping Commonwealth troops together but adamantly opposed to any increase in Canadian Army Forces in Korea over and above ... 25 Cdn Inf Bde Group ... which already includes increment of Div troops.'[61]

To discuss the problem in detail, a meeting of officers from the liaison missions of Australia, New Zealand, South Africa, India, and Canada was held at the British War Office in London on 26 March. Predictably the resulting disagreements concerned not so much the idea of a Commonwealth division in principle as the precise contributions that were to be made respectively by each of the participating governments. War Office officials in particular were at this point anxious to withdraw from the theatre the British elements in the 27th (later the 28th) Brigade and return them to Hong Kong, where they could double as support troops for the proposed division while at the same time serving garrison duty in the colony. They were willing to provide the bulk of any additional units that would be required to round out the division, but they clearly hoped that the other Commonwealth participants would increase their respective contributions, and they argued with the Canadian representative, Brigadier R.W. Moncel, that the proposed formation would provide an excellent opportunity for training Canadian staff officers at the divisional level. None of the other countries was at first prepared to offer a significant increase in commitment, and it therefore appeared that a two-brigade division would result. But within a few days General MacArthur indicated that he was unwilling to accept the departure of the 27th Brigade, and the British therefore

60 C.M. Drury to CGS, quoted in Wood, *Strange Battleground*, 117
61 Quoted ibid. Simonds succeeded Foulkes on 1 February when the latter assumed the newly created post of chairman, Canadian chiefs of staff.

decided after all to continue to maintain the equivalent of their current contribution and to plan for a three-brigade Commonwealth contingent.

Among the consequent War Office requests was an appeal to the Canadians to provide eight officers and fourteen other ranks – about half the British contribution – for the proposed integrated divisional headquarters, together with some additional personnel for the divisional signals regiment (which was to be primarily British in composition) and for the enlargement of the hospital at the new British base in Kure, Japan. These proposals were approved by the Canadian Cabinet early in April, and Brigadiers Fleury and Rockingham were wired to that effect by the vice chief of the general staff, Major-General H.A. Sparling, on 12 April. British efforts later in the year to obtain a number of Canadians for the integrated Commonwealth staff in Kure were resisted, however, and the CGS informed Fleury on 16 July that Canada had 'reached the limit of manpower which can be allotted to the Korean theatre.'[62]

As a result of these discussions, preparations were launched for the formation of the Commonwealth division as soon as the 25th Brigade arrived at the front. During the period from 28 May to 3 June, the three Commonwealth brigades – the Canadian 25th, the Commonwealth 28th, and the Independent 29th – were concentrated in one area as a prelude to the establishment of a divisional command. The growth and organization of the divisional headquarters in Kure continued throughout the months of June and July, and by 28 July it included seven Canadian officers, shortly to be designated the 'Canadian Section, Headquarters First (Commonwealth) Division.' On the same day a ceremony was held near Tokchong, Korea, formally marking the division's inauguration. General James A. Van Fleet, the commander of the American Eighth Army, and Lieutenant-General Sir Horace Robertson, commander-in-chief of British Commonwealth forces in Japan, were among those in attendance.[63]

The formation of the Commonwealth Division produced a chain of command organized roughly as follows. The supreme commander of all UN forces operating in Korea, as of July 1951, was Lieutenant-General Matthew B. Ridgway of the US army, who had succeeded MacArthur in April, and whose headquarters were in Japan. His immediate subordinate, in control of all UN ground operations in the theatre, was the commander of the Eighth Army, Lieutenant-General James A. Van Fleet, who had assumed the post after Ridgway's April promotion. The 1st Commonwealth Division was in turn part of the American I Corps, then commanded by Lieutenant-General J.W. O'Daniel, and was itself under the command of a British officer, Major-

62 Quoted ibid., 118
63 Barclay, *The First Commonwealth Division*, 83-4

General A.J.H. Cassels, with headquarters in Kure, Japan. The 25th Canadian Brigade was commanded in turn by Brigadier Rockingham.[64] In addition, Lieutenant-General Sir Horace Robertson, an Australian whose headquarters were also in Japan, acted as commander-in-chief, Commonwealth forces in Korea. His real role as a commander was a nominal one, however, and his principal responsibility, upon which he reported to the Australian chiefs of staff in Canberra, was 'for the administration and domestic arrangements of Commonwealth troops in Korea and for the administrative units and installations – in Korea and Japan – which succoured the Commonwealth Division, but were not part of it.'[65]

The formation of the Commonwealth Division had the effect of diminishing the responsibilities of the Canadian commander in the field. So long as the Canadian Brigade was an independent force, albeit functioning under American operational command, 'the Brigadier had exercised direct operational and administrative control over all Canadian units forward of Headquarters Eighth US Army, while the troops along the Line of Communication, in rear of Army Headquarters, were controlled by his appropriate service advisers from the Canadian brigade headquarters.' By contrast, after the amalgamation he commanded the operations only of the three infantry battalions and the armoured squadron, all of the group's remaining units coming under the direct control of Divisional Headquarters. It became the general practice, however, for the latter to be used in support of Canadian operations.[66]

These changes in military organization produced little serious friction within the Commonwealth Division. There were occasional difficulties between commanding officers, but those to which Canadians were party almost always involved the Americans. This was the inevitable consequence of the fact that the Americans were ultimately in charge of the conduct of the war. As Brooke Claxton later recalled, 'the American Command sometimes found it difficult to consider the Commonwealth division and other units coming from other nations as other than American forces.'[67]

The initial disputes with American senior officers developed immediately upon the arrival of the first Canadians in the theatre. When the 2nd Battalion,

---

64 Rockingham remained commander of the 25th Brigade until 27 April 1952. Subsequent commanders were Brigadier M.P. Bogert, 28 April 1952 to 20 April 1953; Brigadier J.V. Allard, 21 April, 1953 to 14 June 1954; and Brigadier F.A. Clift, 15 June 1954 to 7 December 1954.
65 Barclay, *The First Commonwealth Division*, 87
66 Wood, *Strange Battleground*, 119
67 Claxton notes, 1150

PPCLI sailed from Seattle on 25 November it was expected that its duties would be those of military occupation, and that it would not complete its training until the middle of March. But by 18 December, when the battalion began to disembark in Pusan, the military situation had been reversed by the intervention of the Chinese, and the Americans were badly in need of help. Upon being assigned by Eighth Army Headquarters to a training area near Suwon, only twenty miles south of Seoul, therefore, Canadian officers began to fear that the Americans were hoping to use the unit in front-line action before it had been fully trained.

In anticipation of such difficulties, the Canadian authorities in Ottawa had armed Lieutenant-Colonel J.R. Stone, the battalion commander, with the following succinct directive: 'In the event that operations are in progress when you arrive in Korea you are not to engage in such operations except in self-defence until you have completed the training of your command and are satisfied that your unit is fit for operations. This restriction in your employment has been communicated to the Commander, United Nations Forces, Korea.'[68]

It developed nonetheless that the colonel's instructions had not been communicated to the commander of the Eighth Army, and when Stone flew to Seoul on 20 December to protest the forward location of the Suwon training base, his complaints were received without sympathy. General Walker had already withdrawn his forces to positions on the Imjin River and for the time being the front was quiet, but he expected a renewal of the Chinese offensive very shortly. He therefore wanted the Canadian battalion assigned immediately to the 29th British Independent Brigade, then occupying a reserve position not far from the battleline. The general's chief of staff not inaccurately argued that the battalion's training compared favourably with that of many American troops already in combat, and Lieutenant-Colonel Stone ultimately found the pressure so acute that it became necessary to produce his orders to substantiate his negotiating position. General Walker was thereby compelled to accede to his request for an additional eight-week training period. Three days later, on 23 December, the general was killed in a road accident, and his successor, General Ridgway, made no further mention of an immediate Canadian contribution. The PPCLI's were reassigned for training purposes to an area just fifty miles north of Pusan, and they departed for the front only after Colonel Stone had reported them ready for action.[69]

68 Quoted in Wood, *Strange Battleground*, 54
69 Ibid., 55-60. The arrival of the first Canadian ground forces in December 1950 nevertheless gave Captain Brock the opportunity for a sally at American expense. Arriving in Tokyo for

Difficulties of a different sort arose with the arrival in May of the 25th Brigade itself. The unit's administrative staff, including the deputy assistant adjutant and quartermaster general, Major C.J.A. Hamilton, had flown to Korea on 1 April to make advance preparations. Since there had been no decision thus far to form a Commonwealth division, it was assumed that the brigade would come under American command. Major Hamilton accordingly obtained from the Americans an empty prisoner-of-war camp and prefabricated warehouse about nine miles from Pusan in order to billet the brigade and its equipment. He recalled later, however, that he had had some difficulty in making his arrangements directly with the American authorities because of British opposition in Pusan, the British having assumed from the beginning that the Canadians would naturally come under their control.[70]

A more serious problem developed when the brigade moved to the front. Brigadier Rockingham was ordered to transport his men by road vehicles and rail to a concentration area near the battleline. The unit was to be divided into groups, and the move was to take four days, from 15 to 18 May. The arrival of the brigade, however, coincided with a UN counterattack against a major Chinese offensive, with the result that the Canadian units quickly became involved in unexpected and highly fluid operational manoeuvres. Rockingham had attended an advance briefing session on 17 May, at which he had been advised by Lieutenant-General Van Fleet that the 25th Brigade would be asked to relieve the American 65th Regiment, then in position on the south bank of the Han River. He had asked when the Canadians would be ready for action, and Rockingham had replied that they were still in transit but could be deployed at the front by the evening of Sunday, 20 May. The general agreed, but Rockingham was subsequently ordered to place his men on the line by 9:00 AM on 19 May. Most of his units at this stage were still on their way to the front, and were not scheduled to arrive in the concentration area until much later in the day. A large portion of their munitions and other supplies was expected to take even longer in reaching front line depots, and Rockingham

consultations with Admiral C. Turner Joy, the captain was directed to contact him in the briefing room at MacArthur's headquarters. As he entered, he found the briefing already in progress. The lights were turned down, and an American colonel was describing the unhappy turn of events in Korea with the help of a pointer and slides. Everything was moving down the peninsula. MacArthur, in gloomy temper, was hunched in a chair at the front of the room. As the colonel concluded his survey, he turned to his commander and said, 'I think that's all, General.' And then, as an afterthought, he pointed to Pusan: 'Oh, yes! There are some Canadians arriving here.' From the back of the darkened room came Brock's roar: 'That's right, and they're the only goddamn troops moving in the right direction.' The general took it in good form (Brock, interview, 23 July 1969).

70 Wood, *Strange Battleground*, 93

therefore questioned the order on the ground that it deprived his men of the time they required to prepare adequately for combat. The order was nonetheless repeated by the senior American authorities, among whom was Van Fleet's own chief of staff. At one point in these exchanges the brigadier became sufficiently desperate to threaten that he would resign his command rather than commit his forces before they were ready.[71]

Rockingham's 'Command Instructions' included the provision that 'No limitation is placed on your direct channel of communication on any matter with the Chief of the General Staff,' and he had been given for this purpose a special code whose only other copy was held by Lieutenant-General Simonds himself.[72] Simonds had taken this precaution largely because of the experience of Canadian commanders in the two World Wars, who had had some difficulty in working simultaneously under both foreign and Canadian chains of command. The CGS had concluded that 'it was quite wrong to place another structure between Ottawa and its field commander,' and that it was important in consequence to provide Rockingham with a channel for appealing directly to his Canadian superiors.[73] Rockingham later told the official army historian that on this occasion he very nearly resorted to using it, and that the matter had failed to come to a head only because Eighth Army Headquarters cancelled its plans for relieving the 65th Regiment. Instead it placed the Canadian brigade under an alternative American command so that it might take part in an offensive planned for the morning of 21 May. As it happened, the brigade was not ordered from its reserve position into the front line until 25 May.[74] The issue nonetheless had been potentially divisive, and not dissimilar to the one which had earlier confronted Colonel Stone. The Canadian government's professed concern for converting the United Nations action in Korea into a truly internationalist endeavour, and Mr Pearson's consequent desire to place Canada's contribution entirely at the disposal of the United Nations Command, thus did not extend without qualification to operations in the field.

After the 25th Brigade was absorbed into the Commonwealth Division such incidents no longer arose, partly because by then the Canadians had settled into the routine of the war, but more because they operated more effectively with Commonwealth than with American personnel. According to the PPCLI historian:

71 Ibid., 98
72 Rockingham's 'Command Instructions' are reproduced ibid., 263-4. See also ibid., 90
73 Simonds, interview, 9 June 1970. Another ingredient of Simonds' remedy was to maintain close personal contact with Rockingham's American commander in Korea. It was largely for this reason that he sometimes paid personal visits to the theatre.
74 Wood, *Strange Battleground*, 98-100

Every army develops its own cliches and phrases, perfectly understood by its own but strange to other ears. Working under United States command meant getting used to different terms and a new system. There were occasions when some confusion arose. When 25th Canadian Infantry Brigade arrived Second Battalion difficulties in this regard diminished; when 1st Commonwealth Division was formed our Canadian brigade was integrated into it. Its headquarters stood between US Corps Headquarters and our forces. From this time on, at the battalion level especially, the direct effects of serving under US command were fairly well filtered out at Divisional Headquarters and again by our own Brigade Headquarters. As a battalion commander I saw very few signs that our higher command was foreign ...

It was only later when I went to Commonwealth Division Headquarters as a staff officer that I realized how this happy state in the battalions was achieved. Our division worked directly under I US Corps Headquarters and was treated generally, at least on the staff side, as a United States division. We received our orders and directions in the same way as other divisions and we were required to submit our information and returns according to American procedures. Our divisional headquarters, however, always dealt with its brigades in British terms and in techniques familiar to all. Commonwealth Divisional Headquarters was not a 'post office!' It soon developed a staff which could accept American directives and convert them to understandable orders.[75]

Hence the practical effect of the Commonwealth amalgamation from the Canadian point of view was that it shifted the problem of working with the United Nations Command to the shoulders of the British, whose Major-General A.J.H. Cassels was divisional commander. Cassels was later described by Brooke Claxton as 'a quiet spoken and serious Scot ... a first class soldier ... [and] more than that ... a remarkably intelligent, resourceful and tactful diplomat,' and, moreover, 'he and Rocky had hit it off from the start.'[76] His troubles with the Americans, like those of Stone and Rockingham, arose for the most part in the initial stages. For example, when the Commonwealth Division was first being formed he encountered considerable difficulty in obtaining control of the Canadian Brigade from the Headquarters of the I US Corps. As he later reported:

My major worry during this time was to persuade I US Corps to assemble the three brigades in such locations as to make them controllable as a division. 28 and 29 Brigades were very conveniently sited side by side on the KANSAS line. 25 Canadian

75 Stevens, *Princess Patricia's Canadian Light Infantry, 1919-1957*, III, 333-4
76 Claxton notes, 1181
77 Quoted in Wood, *Strange Battleground*, 119

Bde was miles away in the Chorwon area. I was assured that by the time I took over they would be brought back into a reserve area behind 28 and 29 Brigades. I went forward on 21 July and found that 25 Brigade had been moved, but instead of being put in reserve had been lent to 25 US Inf Div (later relieved by I US Cav Div) to protect their left flank, and that I was expected to take over in that location. As this put all my brigades in the front line, and as the Canadians were separated from the others by two rivers, both of which were in flood, I protested strongly. After three days of argument and discussion it was agreed that 25 Brigade should move to a reserve area behind 28 and 29 Brigades.[77]

The Americans eventually agreed that the Canadian Brigade should be moved to the Commonwealth concentration area, but they insisted upon controlling it for a few days more as a 'mobile reserve.' It was 'to be prepared to operate offensively anywhere in Corps zone, with first priority in zone of 28th and 29th Infantry Brigades.'[78] This meant in effect that the Commonwealth Division Headquarters could not manoeuvre the Canadian Brigade without the permission of the Americans who were in charge of the corps as a whole, and it also meant that Cassels could not count on obtaining assistance from the Commonwealth reserves should he require them. The difficulty was only temporary but Cassels found it necessary in the end to demand that his relations with the American Corps Headquarters be made more explicit and his independence more clearly defined:

My main trouble during this period [he wrote later in the Division's Periodic Report] was to convince 1 Corps that, though we were more than ready to do anything that was required we did like to know the reason behind it. On many occasions I was ordered, without any warning, to do things which I considered militarily unsound and for which there was no apparent reason. Eventually I asked the Corps Commander for an interview where I put all my cards on the table. I pointed out that we worked quite differently to [sic] them, and it was impossible to expect that we could suddenly change our ways to conform with American procedure. I then asked that, in the future, we should be given our task, the reasons for that task and that we should then be left alone to do it our way without interference from the Corps Staff. The Corps Commander could not have been more helpful and, since then, things have been much better and both sides are happier. Nevertheless I regret that I cannot state that everything is now completely right. There is no doubt that they look at military problems in a very different light to us and I never know for certain what the future plan is likely to be. There have been at least five occasions when I considered invoking my directive ... I

78 Quoted ibid.

am glad to say that, so far, this has been unnecessary, but I cannot help feeling that the day may come when I really shall have to do so. I can assure you that I shall avoid it if possible.[79]

Hence, after a forthright declaration on the part of Major-General Cassels, relations between Commonwealth Divisional Headquarters and the American Command improved, just as they had done at a lower level after similar confrontations by Colonel Stone and Brigadier Rockingham. There were occasional subsequent disagreements over the efficacy of specific local operations, particularly after the front had stabilized and the cost of patrolling expeditions began to weigh more heavily upon Commonwealth officers than their return in captured enemy territory and personnel. On at least one occasion Major-General Cassels reported friction with the I US Corps on this issue,[80] and the matter gave the Canadian minister of national defence cause for considerable alarm during a visit to Korea in the winter of 1951-2.[81] By comparison with other compaigns in other wars, however, the operations in Korea were relatively free from serious strife among the various national contingents. On the whole, the soldiers quarrelled less than the diplomats.

In Tokyo, the relations between the Canadian Military Mission and United Nations Command Headquarters were even more amicable than was the co-operation at the front. This was as true under General MacArthur as it was under his less politically troublesome successors. Lieutenant-General F.J. Fleury, then a brigadier and the commander of the mission from September 1950 to August 1951, recalls now that General MacArthur and his staff were both hospitable and informative.[82] At no time during his stay did he encounter a situation in which he was unable to obtain a full, advance briefing, even with respect to plans which were highly classified. MacArthur saw him readily upon request, and usually with considerable dispatch, and the brigadier's relations with other American officers were greatly facilitated by the fact that he had known personally about fifty of them before his arrival in Tokyo.[83] The remainder he met very rapidly during the course of his duties.

79 Quoted ibid., 120
80 Ibid.
81 Claxton notes, 1179-85, 1211-12
82 Fleury, interview, 8 March 1968
83 The fact that Canadian and American officers were so often personally acquainted facilitated co-operation at all levels. General Simonds found this particularly helpful in maintaining liaison with American field commanders during the course of his attempts to protect Rockingham from being subjected to pressure by senior United States military staff. On one occasion

As commander of the Canadian Military Mission he was invited to attend the regular 8:00 AM daily briefings of the American staff, which were conducted in substantial detail by a variety of middle-ranking United States officers.[84] The American communications network was made available to Canadian liaison officers even for messages transmitted in Canadian code, and Lieutenant-General Fleury cannot now remember a single instance in which a request for support or assistance of any kind was refused. On one occasion he filed a plea for twenty-four tanks, worth seven or eight million dollars, to be made available as soon as possible, and to his amazement they were released for Canadian use at considerable cost to the strength of American units within as little as fourteen days.[85] According to General Simonds, 'The Americans bent over backwards to meet every requirement.'[86]

Simonds' maintenance of personal contact helped him to secure the removal of an unsatisfactory intermediate American commander. Interview, 9 June 1970

84 American briefing practices, however, were sometimes a source of amusement – and occasionally of despair – for Canadian officials. Commenting later on the briefings he had received during his visit to Korea, Brooke Claxton noted that he and his colleagues gradually 'came to have less and less confidence in the appreciations and figures we were given ... Briefs would begin: 'Sir: During the last twenty-four hours operations our air force made 300 sorties, destroyed eight locomotives, five bridges, 263½ motor vehicles,' and so on. We suspected and found that our suspicions were right, that there was hardly a substratum of truth in these assertions. It looked as if the Americans used a series of multiplying factors. If the plane sortied for two hours, and in such and such a latitude dropped so many bombs, then it must have killed and wounded so many Chinamen for each hour or bomb. Later that day Rockingham was to tell us that the same kind of computation would apply to battle casualties. In a certain minor engagement the number of Chinese known to be killed or wounded could be counted on one's fingers. No sooner had his return arrived at headquarters than an irate staff officer was on the phone complaining about the inaccuracy of his report. He was asked how many rounds of what types of ammunition had been fired and told the casualties he had caused were – and then he was given a set of figures twenty times larger than what in fact he knew to be the case.' Claxton notes, 1178-9.

The diplomats disliked the style as well as the substance. Escott Reid can recall being briefed with Mr Pearson by a senior American intelligence officer during their visit to Tokyo early in 1950. The argument was conveyed by various generals referring to a series of placards which were placed on a stand and rotated on command by an army major. An initial placard would suggest, for example, that the United States had occupied Japan with 'n' number of objectives. The objectives would be printed in a vertical list. Subsequent placards would deal respectively with each objective, showing how it had been achieved. As Mr Reid has since observed, 'It was most unconvincing, since real decisions are not made this way at all. It was the first time I had been subjected to an American military briefing. I remember wondering whether they hadn't something better with which to keep their majors occupied than rotating placards when a general tapped the lecturn with his pointer.' Reid, interview, 9 June 1969, and letter to the author, 21 Nov. 1972

85 Fleury, interview, 8 March 1968

86 Simonds, interview, 9 June 1970

Brigadier Fleury received his orders from General Foulkes (later General Simonds) in Ottawa, and most of his activity was devoted to military rather than political affairs. Once a week or more, however, he was briefed on political issues in a meeting with Arthur R. Menzies, the head of the Canadian diplomatic mission to Japan, who in turn was kept informed by the brigadier on military developments.

Brigadier A.B. Connelly, who commanded the Military Mission from November 1951 to August 1952, shares Fleury's view that conditions were equally good under MacArthur's successor, General Matthew B. Ridgway, and the co-operative atmosphere was sustained in turn under General Mark Clark.[87] Connelly, like Fleury, was briefed daily in American staff meetings and received what he still regards as excellent treatment. Like Fleury, too, he found his job easier by virtue of the fact that he was already acquainted personally with many of the American staff officers, including the G-2. Both officers are agreed that such friction as was in evidence occurred not in Japan but in the theatre itself, and that it tended to dissipate once the American commander in each case had been adequately informed of what the Canadians regarded as the prerequisites of effective co-operation.

The armies quarrelled seldom, the navies even less. This was due partly, in the Canadian case, to the modesty of the naval contribution. It reflected also the relative invulnerability of naval forces in Korea to enemy attack and the consequently diminished level of risk involved in most naval operations. Ultimately, however, it derived from the fact that ships at sea enjoy greater self-sufficiency than comparable military formations on the ground, and hence in the Korean context were less dependent on allied forces for the pursuit of day-to-day operations. The official history recounts the details of the Canadian naval experience in Korea in uncritical terms, but even taking this into account the evidence suggests that there was very little internavy conflict.

The first three Canadian destroyers to operate in Korea were ordered to leave for Pearl Harbor on 5 July 1950, and like the army they confronted problems of maintenance and supply which reflected the modest size of their contingent. Because they had no fleet train to service their needs, they were forced 'to depend upon the USN and Royal Navy for fuel, ammunition, much of their supplies and of course base facilities.'[88] The details of these arrangements, and indeed the composition of the command to which the destroyers were to report, had not been settled at the time of their departure, which was

87 Fleury, interview, 8 March 1968; Connelly, interview, 7 March 1968; and Foulkes, interview, 7 March 1968
88 Thorgrimsson and Russell, *Canadian Naval Operations in Korean Waters*, 4

two days ahead of the Security Council resolution confirming that the United States would be responsible for designating the supreme commander. Their assignment orders were not received until 12 July, two hours after their arrival in Pearl Harbor. They were then informed that they would come under General MacArthur's operational, although not administrative, command, and that they should report directly to him for further instructions. Arrangements were to be made 'on repayment basis' for the destroyers 'to draw supplies from US sources.' Items peculiar to the RCN would be shipped 'via US transport on demand.'[89] General MacArthur shortly thereafter advised the Canadian commander, Captain J.V. Brock, that he would receive further instructions upon his arrival at the American naval base in Guam. At Guam the three destroyers were ordered to proceed to Sasebo harbour in Kyushu, Japan, where they arrived on 30 July.[90]

By now the organization of the UN's naval command had been completed, and its basic structure was to last for the duration of the war. Its main feature was a division of responsibility which assigned to the British the control of naval operations along the west coast of the peninsula, and to the Americans the responsibility for those in the east. Admiral C. Turner Joy reported later that this decision, reached on 6 July, was based on 'purely tactical' considerations: ' ... the east coast with its longer coastline and more numerous accessible targets required more ships for blockade, as well as bombardment and interdiction missions, than the British could muster. Furthermore, since our fast carriers would be operating most of the time in the Sea of Japan it was thought best from the standpoint of coordination to have US ships rather than British operating in the same area as the carriers.' The arrangement also involved less risk of incidents at sea between American and Communist Chinese vessels, an eventuality which most American and allied officials were anxious to avoid.[91]

Rear Admiral Brock has since reflected in wry amusement upon the fact that while the east coast of Korea is certainly longer than the west coast as the crow flies, it is also much less heavily indented and hazardous to navigation. In his view, therefore, the units under British command were not let off so lightly as Turner Joy's account implies. In any event, Brock regretted the

---

89 Quoted ibid., 5
90 The arrival in Korean waters of the Canadian flotilla did not go entirely unnoticed in capitals abroad. Radio Moscow's English-language newscaster announced to his overseas listeners shortly thereafter that the 'imperialist American Navy in Korea [has] been joined by the rice-fed louts from Canada who are paid 50 cents a week.' Quoted in Plosz, 'The Navy's Unorthodox War,' 29
91 Thorgrimsson and Russell, *Canadian Naval Operations in Korean Waters*, 11, 27, 2

decision to separate so clearly the British and American spheres of operation, since otherwise 'the navies could have learned a great deal from one another under conditions in which there was no great hazard to naval vessels.'[92] He had, however, to accept this loss of opportunity, and his three destroyers were allotted to various elements in the British Command. Thereafter, in the words of the official history,

the Canadian Destroyer Division Pacific virtually ceased to exist as a single unit for operational purposes and, for the duration of the Korean campaign, it was only occasionally that three Canadian destroyers served together on the same operation under Canadian command. Such an arrangement was necessary under the circumstances. Had the Canadian contribution consisted of, shall we say, a carrier and a division of screening destroyers supported by a fleet train, it would have been logical to operate it as a separate group. Since the force consisted of three destroyers only, it was inevitable that to use the ships to best advantage it was often necessary to operate them as individual units. Thus it came about that, though Captain Brock would have preferred to keep his division together for operational purposes, and though Admiral Andrewes did his best to comply with his wishes, it was not often that the three Canadian destroyers served side by side against the enemy in Korea.[93]

Even on those occasions when the Canadian ships were working together in the same fleet and performing the same general task – participating, for example, in the enforcement of the coastal blockade – they tended to function 'as individual units within British formations rather than as a division.'[94] There were occasional exceptions. During the Inchon landings, for example, the small Canadian force was engaged as a cohesive unit under Captain Brock's command in conducting escort and blockading operations, albeit without serious threat of enemy opposition.[95] Early in December 1950, after the Chinese intervention, the Canadian Destroyer Division operated again as a distinct naval element in supporting the withdrawal of a portion of the Eighth Army from the North Korean port of Chinnampo on the west coast. The official naval historian later described this as 'without doubt the most important mission performed by the Canadian Destroyer Division as a group during

---

92 Brock, interview, 23 July 1969. Admiral Brock's point about the navigational complexity of west coast operations is conceded by the official American historians. See Cagle and Manson, *The Sea War in Korea*, 295
93 Thorgrimsson and Russell, *Canadian Naval Operations in Korean Waters*, 12
94 Ibid., 13
95 Ibid., 17. On this occasion, Brock's command included not merely the Canadian destroyers, but ships from the American, Dutch, and Australian fleets as well. Interview, 23 July 1969

the entire Korean conflict.'[96] But by and large the three original destroyers and their successors operated as separate and independent units under foreign command, usually British. Very occasionally one of the Canadian ships was assigned for specific operations to American control. For example, after the passage of the General Assembly resolution of 7 October, the *Athabaskan* was ordered into east coast waters in order to assist in the support of a UN amphibious landing at Wonsan. The reasons were political rather than military. The proposed landing site was located far above the 38th parallel, and it had therefore been decided that token forces should be provided by as many of the contributing navies as possible in order to give the action a genuine 'United Nations' flavour. Ships were accordingly supplied by Australia, Britain, Canada, France, New Zealand, and South Korea, although the Americans naturally comprised the bulk of the naval forces involved.[97]

But these were the exceptions, not the rule, and the rule itself was reinforced when Captain Brock and the *Cayuga* were relieved in March 1951 by Commander A.B.F. Fraser-Harris and the *Nootka*. An Englishman who had transferred from the Royal Navy to the RCN after World War II, Fraser-Harris now became the new commander, Canadian Destroyers Far East, and unlike Brock he saw little point in attempting to keep the Canadian ships together. In April he informed his immediate British superior, Rear-Admiral A.K. Scott-Montcrieff, 'that the three Canadian destroyers operating in this theatre are for operational purposes three individual units subject only to ... [the Admiral's] operational requirements.'[98] As the official historian has observed, this 'change in policy, coupled with an increase in naval activity on both coasts, was to mean that henceforth the three Canadian ships were to operate together at sea, and find themselves together in harbour, even less frequently than before.'[99]

The arrangements seem nevertheless to have worked well, although there were occasional communications difficulties. Rear-Admiral Brock can recall having to direct his staff to 'boil down' the excessively detailed and elaborate orders he received from the American command in advance of the operations at Inchon (they provided even for the delivery ashore of barber's chairs). Again, at Chinnampo, the hyperbole evident in communications from American army officers led him to overestimate the gravity of their military predica-

---

96 Thorgrimsson and Russell, *Canadian Naval Operations in Korean Waters*, 31-6. Quotation is from 35
97 Ibid., 21, 28, n45
98 Quoted ibid., 46. Scott-Montcrieff succeeded Admiral Andrewes on 10 April.
99 Ibid. Fraser-Harrison was in turn succeeded by Commander J. Plomer of the *Cayuga* in July 1951, but no change in policy appears to have resulted. The *Cayuga* was then in the theatre for the second time.

ment, and hence to take navigational risks in achieving their rescue which he would otherwise have avoided.[100] But in most instances such problems were neither serious nor intractable. When two of the Canadian destroyers, the *Athabaskan* and the *Huron*, joined British, Australian, and American carriers and destroyers in the spring of 1951 for attacks on east-coast shore communications near Wonsan, the *Athabaskan*'s commander reported: 'This international force, involving ships of four countries, worked together from 8th April to the 15th April in near perfect harmony ... There were no inter-service difficulties that affected the efficiency of the operations. Communications were good, manoeuvring was rapid and correct. Fuelling and storing was carried out from both British and US logistic ships. Command relationships were excellent.'[101] Thereafter it became the general practice to keep one of the Canadian vessels on the east coast as much as possible, and subsequent Canadian naval operations were highly decentralized.

On administrative, as opposed to operational, matters, there was initially some disagreement between Captain Brock and his British superior, Rear-Admiral W.G. Andrewes. In their first interview Andrewes took the position that since the Commonwealth vessels would be operating together in the same theatre, the provisions of the Visiting Forces (British Commonwealth) Act automatically applied. This would have meant that Andrewes, as the senior Commonwealth officer, would have been in command not merely of the combat operations of the Canadian destroyers, but also of the administration of pay and allowances, internal discipline, and the like. Brock recalls that in ordinary circumstances he would not have challenged this arrangement, especially since it would have relieved him of irritating administrative responsibilities. Given, however, that the overall campaign was under United Nations rather than Commonwealth auspices, he felt it would be appropriate to reserve as much administrative autonomy as possible. It was politically more useful to be able to report the presence of 'many' Commonwealth contributions rather than of one, not least because emphasis on the number and diversity of the national contingents involved would strengthen the moral legitimacy of the United Nations cause.

Admiral Andrewes at first offered stiff resistance, arguing that the Act was automatically in force whenever Commonwealth units were operating together. Brock's recollection, however, was that it had to be invoked by an explicit directive of the Governor-in-Council. He won his point, and the substance of

100 Brock, interview, 23 July 1969
101 Quoted in Thorgrimsson and Russell, *Canadian Naval Operations in Korean Waters*, 50

the dispute, when one of Andrewes' aides was detailed to check the text of the Act.[102]

With respect to logistics, the *ad hoc* arrangements for servicing the Canadian fleet through the appropriate American and British units functioned well.[103] By 20 July 1950, ten days before the arrival of the Canadian naval contingent in Sasebo, Japan, the naval member of the Canadian Joint Staff in Washington had concluded an agreement with the American authorities providing that the United States would supply logistic support in the case of all items common to both navies, with payment being made directly to Washington by Ottawa. Ammunition posed a more difficult problem, since the Canadian ships were armed in many cases with British weapons, and separate arrangements therefore had to be made with the Royal Navy for the supply of these and other items peculiar to the British naval tradition, for example, wearing apparel and rum. Items unique to the RCN were supplied from Canada by sea and air.[104]

The decentralized character of Canadian naval operations was accentuated by the fact that ultimate administrative responsibility for individual vessels rested not with a single Canadian authority but with their respective home bases. This offered no particular problem so long as the ships involved all came from the Canadian Pacific coast, but with the arrival of the *Nootka* in January 1951, Halifax was represented as well as Esquimalt. Thereafter the senior Canadian naval officer in Korea had to forward separate reports for the ships under his command to their respective flag officers on the Atlantic and Pacific coasts.[105]

But in general the system ran smoothly. Canadian ships, like those of other navies in the theatre, used Sasebo as their main operating base. While the Sasebo harbour was located within the American zone of Japanese occupation, both the American and British navies used its facilities for their support vessels during the Korean hostilities, and this meant that the Canadians were able to milk their two main sources of supply at the same time. Some items were obtained indifferently from either American or British sources as dictated by convenience. Fuel, for example, was acquired from the Americans in Sasebo, from British oilers in Korean west coast waters, and from American oilers in east coast waters. Ammunition was requisitioned from either source, depending upon the specifications of the weapons involved. The fact that a Canadian

---

102 Brock, interview, 29 July 1969. The statute involved was the Visiting Forces (British Commonwealth) Act, 1932-3
103 Ibid.
104 Thorgrimsson and Russel, *Canadian Naval Operations in Korean Waters*, 135
105 Ibid., 136

naval liaison officer was not stationed in Sasebo until February 1952 testifies to the relative ease and informality of the logistic arrangements.[106]

The naval facilities at the Commonwealth base in Kure were used much less frequently, partly because they were farther removed from the theatre of operations, partly because they did not carry American supplies, and partly because their stocks were less complete than those at Sasebo. On the other hand, the Kure repair facilities were efficient, cheap, and readily available, the medical and hospital services extensive, and the entertainment ashore attractive, and the port was therefore occasionally utilized as an alternative Canadian base.[107]

But the amicable co-operation of the allied navies in Korea was not always duplicated by allied policy-makers, and to their long and tedious progress towards ending the war it is necessary now to turn.

---

106 Ibid., 136-8
107 Ibid., 137. The favourite shore leave port, however, was Hong Kong.

7
The long wait

On 1 February the United Nations had condemned the Chinese as aggressors. Now they had to continue the war. The Canadians, like the others, could only hope that from the ensuing carnage there would emerge the conditions of a successful peace. The objectives remained as before – to end the fighting as quickly as possible on the basis of the restoration of the *status quo ante bellum,* and to do so without extending the hostilities beyond their current territorial and military limits.

But there was a tension between the two halves of this programme. If the Chinese and North Koreans were to be brought to the negotiating table in circumstances which would encourage them to accept even the minimum requirements of the United Nations Command, they had to be convinced that their failure to comply would lead to the infliction of unacceptable damage upon themselves. Yet to convey such an understanding might well require an escalation of military effort, which would carry with it in turn the risk of war on a larger scale. The result was a division among western policy-makers. Some advocated the acceleration of military pressure in order to convince the Chinese of the efficacy of a hasty peace; others supported a stabilization of the front in combination with an overall posture of restraint, hoping that such a strategy would both soften the Chinese and diminish the prospect of a general war in the Far East.

The first of these positions was represented most notably by General MacArthur and right-wing Republicans in the United States,[1] the second by

1 And of course by the South Koreans themselves.

the Truman administration and, with even greater conviction, by many of America's allies, Canada included. Since General MacArthur was the United Nations commander, and since right-wing Republicans were not without influence in American politics, it was natural for Canadian and allied policy-makers to fear their power, and to encourage the president and his staff not to authorize unduly belligerent military initiatives. Ottawa's preoccupation with this enterprise was to continue with fluctuating intensity throughout the remainder of the war.

But it was some time before these anxieties were again expressed by Canadian officials in public. In the interval, the government appeared content to leave the peacemaking to the Good Offices Committee, and to confine its own efforts to monitoring the progress of the war. By 20 January the UN forces had managed to stablize the front, and thereafter began slowly to advance once more up the peninsula. When asked in the House of Commons whether the United Nations would re-cross the 38th parallel, Mr Pearson replied evasively that the matter had been discussed by 'representatives of governments with forces participating in Korean operations,' and that he could state in consequence 'that the political significance of any new move across the parallel deep into North Korean territory is fully appreciated.' The decision, he thought, 'should be a collective one,'[2] but he offered no further details. A similar question posed on 13 March, precisely one month later, elicited an equally circumspect response.[3]

In the meantime a dispute had been brewing between American authorities in Washington and their theatre commander, and it was shortly to arouse Mr Pearson to the point of public protest. MacArthur's relations with Washington had been difficult even in the early weeks of the war,[4] but the latest and terminal phase had begun not long after the Chinese intervention. With the ignominious, although apparently not deflating, spectacle of defeat before him, the general in the last week of December once more reiterated to the Joint Chiefs of Staff his view that he should be permitted to order attacks on Manchurian airfields, that a blockade should be imposed against the China coast, and that the Chinese forces in Formosa should be brought to bear both in Korea and for diversionary purposes against China itself. Hitherto such measures had been rejected 'for fear of provoking China into a major effort, but we must now realistically recognize that China's commitment thereto has

2 Canada, House of Commons, *Debates,* 13 Feb. 1951, 306
3 Ibid., 13 March 1951, 1185
4 See above, 96 ff

already been fully and unequivocally made and nothing we can do would further aggravate the situation as far as China is concerned.[5]

With the president's approval, the Joint Chiefs replied to the effect that these proposals had been rejected after 'careful consideration.' A naval blockade would have to wait upon either a stabilization of the front or a complete evacuation, and would require in any case negotiations with the British because of their trade with China through Hong Kong. Naval and air attacks on China itself would not be authorized unless the Chinese attacked American forces outside Korea, and the troops in Formosa were more useful where they were. The general was therefore ordered to 'defend in successive positions ... inflicting maximum damage to hostile forces in Korea, subject to primary consideration of the safety of your troops and your basic mission of protecting Japan. Should it become evident in your judgment that evacuation is essential to avoid severe losses of men and materiel you will at that time withdraw from Korea to Japan.'[6]

MacArthur replied in protest, and further exchanges ensued until finally, on 13 January, President Truman dispatched a personal message to convey 'something of what is in our minds regarding the political factors.' The message in retrospect reveals not merely that American policy-makers were in some degree constrained by the anxieties of their allies, but demonstrates also that Truman was already deploying allied views as an instrument for bargaining with his unruly commander. The substance of the cable began with a far-reaching list of American policy objectives in the Korean campaign, most of them bearing on the need to display firm resolve before the 'world-wide threat' of the Soviet Union. This inventory of purposes was succeeded by the following paragraph:

Our course of action at this time should be such as to consolidate the great majority of the United Nations. This majority is not merely part of the organization but is also the nations whom we would desperately need to count on as allies in the event the Soviet Union moves against us. Further, pending the build-up of our national strength, we must act with great prudence in so far as extending the area of hostilities is concerned. Steps which might in themselves be fully justified and which might lend some assistance to the campaign in Korea would not be beneficial if they thereby involved Japan or Western Europe in large-scale hostilities.[7]

5 MacArthur, *Reminiscences,* 431
6 Quoted ibid., 432-3
7 Quoted in Truman, *Years of Trial and Hope,* 494. For an uninhibited account of Washington's relations with MacArthur in this period, see Acheson, *Present at the Creation,* 513-17

For the time being MacArthur was silenced. According to his own account, he wired the president that his forces would do their best, and told his staff that Truman's message 'finally settles the question of whether or not we evacuate Korea. There will be no evacuation.'[8] There followed the gradual recovery of the UN military position and the long, gruelling weeks in which the general's forces battled to regain the 38th parallel. By mid-March Seoul itself had been retaken, the border had been reached, and the question of whether the United Nations would attempt once more to cross the parallell into North Korea could no longer be postponed.

At this stage the Departments of State and Defense were both in support of a renewed attempt to negotiate a cease-fire. 'The reasoning,' as the president later recalled, 'was that, in the first place, since we had been able to inflict heavy casualties on the Chinese and were pushing them back to the 38th parallel, it would now be in their interest at least as much as ours to halt the fighting, and secondly, the invaders stood substantially ejected from the territory of the Republic of Korea.'[9] The State Department therefore composed a presidential announcement which was discussed by Secretary Acheson, General Marshall, and the Joint Chiefs of Staff on 19 March. It was agreed that General MacArthur should be informed of their intention and his recommendations requested. The general was therefore cabled on 20 March as follows:

State Department planning a Presidential announcement shortly that, with clearing of bulk South Korea of aggressors, United Nations now preparing to discuss conditions of settlement in Korea. United Nations feeling exists that further diplomatic efforts toward settlement should be made before any advance with major forces north of 38th parallel. Time will be required to determine diplomatic reactions and permit new negotiations that may develop. Recognizing that parallel has no military significance, State has asked Joint Chiefs of Staff what authority you should have to permit sufficient freedom of action for next few weeks to provide security for United Nations and maintain contact with enemy. Your recommendation desired.[10]

The second sentence of this communication suggests that the State Department had been in consultation with members of the United Nations during the course of planning its diplomatic initiative, and this is confirmed by a statement by Mr Pearson in the House of Commons on the same day. Asked once again whether UN forces would cross the 38th parallel, he commented that

---

8 MacArthur, *Reminiscences,* 435
9 Truman, *Years of Trial and Hope,* 497
10 Quoted ibid.

'There is a real difficulty from my point of view in dealing with this matter because at this moment, even this afternoon, informal discussions are going on in Washington with the other countries participating in the Korean campaign on the subject of what would be a proper political directive, if a directive should be issued, for the United Nations Command in Korea on this matter.' Because the question was still under discussion, he did not think it 'desirable' at that time to express a Canadian position. In any case it 'would be unwise and unfair to the commander and to the men in the field to tell the enemy exactly what we were going to do in a military way when we reached that particular line.' Both military and political issues were involved, and it was possible that there would be tactical crossings of the parallel for military purposes. But the political considerations were equally important, if not more so. General Ridgway had already announced that a military stalemate was developing in the theatre. If the UN forces did 'reach the position of a sort of de facto cease-fire roughly along the line of the 38th parallel,' the minister thought 'we should take advantage of that position, that military stabilization, to reopen negotiations with the people on the other side,' although he knew this might be difficult.[11]

The official Canadian view was thus not very different from that of the Truman administration, and for a brief interval it appeared to be acceptable also to General MacArthur. The general replied to the JCS cable on 21 March, indicating that he lacked sufficient forces in any case to seize control of North Korea, and that accordingly no additional directives were necessary.

On the same day officials in Washington completed the final details of the planned presidential initiative, and consulted 'with the Washington representatives of the other nations that had troops in Korea in order to obtain their approval to [sic] the proposed draft.'[12] The draft observed briefly that the United Nations forces in Korea had driven the aggressors back with heavy losses 'to the general vicinity from which the unlawful attack was first launched last June,' that there remained the problem of restoring 'peace and security in the area in accordance with the terms of the Security Council resolution of June 27, 1950,' and that the Unified Command was 'prepared to enter into arrangements which would conclude the fighting and ensure against its resumption.' This, the draft noted, would 'open the way for a broader settlement for Korea, including the withdrawal of foreign forces from Korea.' On the other hand, until 'satisfactory arrangements for concluding the fighting have been reached, United Nations military action must be continued.'[13]

11 Canada, House of Commons, Debates, 19 March 1951, 1442-3
12 Truman, Years of Trial and Hope, 498
13 Quoted ibid, 498-9

The draft, although supported by the allies, was never delivered. While it was still being discussed General MacArthur on 24 March issued what he later described as a 'routine communique,' and which he claimed to have prepared before his having received the JCS cable of 21 March.[14] In it he gave a confident summary of battlefield conditions and argued that the successful operations of United Nations forces in the theatre had demonstrated the serious 'military weaknesses' of mainland China and 'its complete inability to accomplish by force of arms the conquest of Korea.' The enemy, he said, 'must by now be painfully aware that a decision of the United Nations to depart from its tolerant effort to contain the war in the area of Korea, through an expansion of our military operations to his coastal areas and interior bases, would doom Red China to the risk of imminent military collapse. These basic facts being established, there should be no insuperable difficulty in arriving at decisions on the Korean problem if the issues are resolved on their own merits, without being burdened by extraneous matters such as Formosa or China's seat in the United Nations.' The 'fundamental questions' were of course political, not military, and required a diplomatic solution, but 'Within the area of my authority as the military commander ... it should be needless to say that I stand ready at any time to confer in the field with the Commander-in-Chief of the enemy forces in the earnest effort to find any military means whereby realization of the political objectives of the United Nations in Korea, to which no nation may justly take exception, might be accomplished without further bloodshed.'[15]

MacArthur's motivations in issuing this public declaration are controversial and have been the subject of extensive speculation and debate in the literature of the Korean War and of civil-military relations, and they need not be further discussed here.[16] Their practical effect, however, was to undermine the conditions that had given the proposed cease-fire initiative some possibility of success. The general had announced publicly that the Chinese had been defeated in the field and that their continued intransigence would expose their country to 'imminent military collapse.' Since in reality the Chinese had *not* been defeated on the field, such an ultimatum could leave them no choice but to demonstrate their prowess by perpetuating the hostilities. Moreover, as the

14 MacArthur, *Reminiscences,* 440
15 Quoted ibid., 441-2, and in Truman, *Years of Trial and Hope,* 449-501
16 There are many works dealing with General MacArthur and with his political activities during the Korean War. See, for instance, Spanier, *Truman-MacArthur Controversy*; Higgins, *Korea and the Fall of MacArthur*; Whitney, *MacArthur*; Willoughby and Chamberlain, *MacArthur, 1941-1951*; Gunther, *The Riddle of MacArthur*; Rovere and Schlesinger, jr, *The General and the President*

Department of External Affairs later observed, the 'statement contradicted the decision taken by the Political Committee of the United Nations on January 13, 1951, when it adopted, with the concurring vote of the United States, a statement of principles in which the Korean problem was linked to Formosa and Chinese representation in the United Nations.'[17]

President Truman regarded this as an act 'in open defiance of my orders as President and as Commander in Chief.' It was 'a challenge to the authority of the President under the Constitution' and it 'also flouted the policy of the United Nations.' He therefore 'could no longer tolerate his [MacArthur's] insubordination,' and resolved that he should be dismissed. The State Department, meanwhile, was beseiged with 'rush inquiries' from capitals around the world wanting to know whether the declaration had been indicative of a shift in American policy.[18]

On 24 March the JCS cabled the general to remind him of a presidential directive issued on 6 December ordering him to clear his public statements through Washington. On the same day the State Department attempted to retrieve the situation by offering a public clarification: 'General MacArthur is conducting United Nations military operations in Korea under military directives issued through the United States Joint Chiefs of Staff which ... are fully adequate to cover the present military situation in Korea. The political issues, which General MacArthur has stated are beyond his responsibility as a field commander, are being dealt with in the United Nations and by intergovernmental consultations.'[19]

For the next several days the question of MacArthur's position was under intensive review in Washington, and was the subject of considerable diplomatic traffic. Canadian representatives in the American capital expressed their 'horror' in discussions with officials in the State Department, only to find they were preaching to the converted.[20] On 31 March, in an address which he had drafted personally to the Canadian Bar Association,[21] Mr Pearson brought Canada publicly into the lists and tilted a lance directly at the UN commander. He was not, he observed, one of those who thought the Peking Government 'would soon collapse' in the event that the conflict in the Far East spread to mainland China. The sole beneficiary of such a development would be the USSR. Hence no action should be taken in the Far East 'which would weaken

17 Department of External Affairs, 'The Korean Crisis,' *External Affairs,* III, 4, April 1951, 119
18 Truman, *Years of Trial and Hope,* 501
19 Quoted in Department of External Affairs, 'The Korean Crisis,' *External Affairs,* III, 4, April 1951, 119
20 Campbell, interview, 20 Oct. 1968
21 LePan, interview, 5 March 1968

what is still the main front of the Free World – Western Europe.' The war in Korea ought therefore to be contained, and attempts should be made to negotiate an honourable peace. The United Nations should refuse 'to be stampeded into action, such as a massive attack towards the Manchurian border, if such action were possible militarily but felt to be unwise politically.' In any case, the chances for a Korean settlement were 'not increased by the kind of talk which weakens the unity of action of those who are participating in that operation.'

There were, he went on, 'two main threats to this unity of action.' The first arose from the fact that the United States was carrying the brunt of the responsibility for waging the war, and sometimes felt that it was receiving insufficient support from its friends in the United Nations. This irritation should be recognized and understood. But to give the Americans support did 'not mean an automatic response of "Ready, aye Ready" to everything that Washington proposes.'

It may mean constructive criticism of, and even opposition to, courses or proposals which we in Canada may think are unwise and concerning which it is our duty to express our views. I know that such criticism and opposition will be exploited by our Communist enemies for their own nefarious purposes. Because of this we should put forward our point of view, whenever we can, in private and try to persuade our friends as to its reasonableness. If we succeed, well and good. If we do not, we will have to decide whether to maintain our position in public or whether to abandon it because the acceptance of our viewpoint may not be so important as the maintenance of the united front.

Evidently this was an occasion for which the proclamation of one's position in public was appropriate, for the minister went on bluntly to remark that

The other danger to our free world unity arises when those who have been charged by the United Nations with military responsibility make controversial pronouncements which go far beyond that responsibility, and create confusion, disquiet and even discord. It seems to me to be as unwise, indeed as dangerous, for the generals to intervene in international policy matters as it would be for the diplomats to try to lay down military strategy. This is a case, I think, where the specialist should stick to his specialty. Otherwise, unnecessary difficulties are created, and that wholehearted cooperation between friends which is so essential is hindered.[22]

22 Department of External Affairs, *Statements and Speeches,* no 51/13

The man who was soon to become renowned in Canada for his support of quiet diplomacy was deploying here the most raucous techniques of the craft. However, he does not now recall having intended his address as political nourishment for President Truman (of whose plans for dismissing MacArthur he was still in ignorance), nor indeed as anything other than an expression of his own official and personal reaction.[23] On the other hand, there is no doubt that the speech attracted considerable attention in Washington, and the Canadian position was raised more than once during the Senate investigations of the following May and June into the conditions surrounding the general's recall. On 10 May, for example, Senator Wayne Morse of Oregon asked the secretary of defence if he knew 'whether or not some of our United Nations allies, and particularly Canada, filed rather strong protests with our Government' as a result of the general's 24 March statement. General Marshall gave no specific reply and referred the Senate to Mr Acheson for details, although he conceded that MacArthur's pronouncements had created uncertainty among the allies about the substance of American policy.[24] On 4 June Senator Morse raised the matter again with the secretary of state:

Senator Morse ... Is it not ... true, or do you recollect reading about it in the public press, that Mr. Pearson of Canada went so far as to make some public statements about his Government's concern over the extension of the war in Korea, and he included in his public statements, at least as reported in the press, a direct reference to MacArthur himself?

Secretary Acheson. I remember that speech by Mr. Pearson. I didn't remember that particular reference in it. Mr. Pearson was a member of the Good Offices Committee, which was set up, and he and the President of the Assembly, and I believe the Swedish representative, were the three members.

He was very much concerned with the dangers which would come from an extension of the military operation, and I think was taking a very leading part in exploring every possibility of having a negotiated settlement.

Senator Morse. Is it not true that Mr. Pearson, in some of his statements that at least got into American newspapers and periodical references, implied that Canada had to face the fact as to whether or not it could be a participant in an Asiatic program that involved commitments on the mainland of China.

Secretary Acheson. I don't recall that part of his speech, but I can well believe that that question would produce very serious problems for the Canadian Government.[25]

23 Pearson, interview, 18 Oct. 1968
24 United States, Senate, *Military Situation in the Far East,* 10 May 1951, 483
25 Ibid., 4 June 1951, pp. 1880-1. Secretary Acheson's recollection that Mr Pearson was a member of the Good Offices Committee was of course inaccurate.

Representatives of the Truman administration have always insisted that allied views were not the significant factor in the dismissal decision. The president's memoirs describe the essence of the conflict in terms of civil-military relations and the need to maintain the supremacy of the civil arm.[26] When asked in the Senate whether the British or any other ally of the United States in Korea 'had a voice in removing MacArthur,' General Marshall replied firmly, 'They did not. They were not advised, there was no suggestion that I know of, there was nothing of that sort whatever that I know of.'[27] Secretary of State Dean Acheson, when asked about charges that 'General MacArthur's recall might have been influenced by pressure from some of our allies on this Government,' answered with equal brevity: 'That is not correct, sir. There was no pressure, representation, or request of any sort by any of our allies.'[28]

This last remark seems less than candid in view of the publicly available evidence of allied protestations and Truman's own admission that MacArthur's statement raised a 'diplomatic furor,'[29] but there is little doubt that the general would have been fired regardless of allied views. The final insubordination took the form of a letter written to Representative Joseph W. Martin as early as 20 March, but not made public until Martin read it out in the House on 5 April. In it MacArthur reiterated his view that Washington should follow in Korea 'the conventional pattern of meeting force with maximum counter-force,' and expressed agreement with Martin's belief that Chinese troops on Formosa ought to be used to open a second front in the war. 'It seems strangely difficult [the letter continued] for some to realize that here in Asia is where the Communist conspirators have elected to make their play for global conquest, and that we have joined the issue thus raised on the battlefield; that here we fight Europe's war with arms while the diplomats there still fight it with words; that if we lose this war to Communism in Asia, the fall of Europe is inevitable, win it and Europe most probably would avoid war and yet preserve freedom. As you point out, we must win. There is no substitute for victory.'[30]

Truman had already decided on MacArthur's recall, but this latest development gave new urgency to his task. After securing the unanimous agreement

26 See Truman, *Years of Trial and Hope,* especially 502-4
27 *Military Situation in the Far East,* 9 May 1951, 427. Canadian representatives in Washington were informed of the pending dismissal decision, but only shortly before it was publicly announced. Campbell, interview, 20 Oct. 1968
28 *Military Situation in the Far East,* 1 June 1951, 1733
29 Truman, *Years of Trial and Hope,* 501

of his senior advisers, the president on 10 April deprived him of all his commands and appointed General Ridgway in his place.

This is not the place to discuss the far-reaching political consequences of this decision within the United States, but as the Canadian Press reported on 11 April, 'There were no tears shed in the Canadian capital ... While External Affairs Minister Pearson declined to comment, the official attitude here is one of approval and coincides with representations Canada has made privately in Washington.'[31] The government's official silence continued through subsequent months, and as Mr Pearson indicated at the time, he had 'had no knowledge whatever of General MacArthur's dismissal before that dismissal was announced in the newspapers.'[32] Members of the Canadian foreign and military policy communities were nevertheless intensely relieved by the president's decision, and by the selection of General Ridgway as the new United Nations Commander.[33]

A considerable measure of anxiety remained, however, not least of all because of the tumultuous welcome with which MacArthur was received on his return to American soil.[34] By now Mr Pearson and his senior advisers had become genuinely disturbed not only by the crusading flavour of much of American policy vis-à-vis the Soviet bloc, but also by the erratic and emotional atmosphere within which the policy appeared to originate. The minister therefore began to think that a more public display of his reservations had become necessary, even at some cost to the outward appearance of allied unity.[35] On 10 April, therefore, he delivered an address on 'Canadian Foreign Policy in a Two-Power World' to a combined meeting of the Empire and Canadian Clubs in Toronto, in which he argued that while Canada's relations with the United States were growing 'steadily closer' on a basis of 'mutual understanding and a fundamental friendliness ... we need not try to deceive ourselves that because our close relations with our great neighbour are so close, they will always be smooth and easy.' Canadians were anxious to support the

30 Quoted ibid., 505, and in MacArthur, *Reminiscences*, 439-40
31 Canadian Press, 'Ottawa Approves MacArthur Firing,' *Toronto Star*, 11 April 1951
32 Canada, House of Commons, *Debates*, 16 April 1951, 2043. Confirmed by Mr Pearson in interview, 18 Oct. 1968
33 Brock, interview, 23 July 1969; Holmes, interview, 5 March 1968; LePan, interview, 5 March 1968; Pearson, interview, 18 Oct. 1968; Reid, interview, 9 June 1969; Simonds, interview, 9 June 1970. Some, like Brock, felt, however, that the manner in which the general was advised of his recall was unsatisfactory. For an explanation, see Acheson, *Present at the Creation*, 522-4
34 Spanier, *Truman-MacArthur Controversy*, 211-20
35 Confidential source. That this loss of confidence in American policy-makers was known in Washington to be widespread among allied governments is evident from Acheson's memoirs. See *Present at the Creation*, 527-8

United States in the execution of its responsibility for world leadership, but they were 'not willing to be merely an echo of somebody else's voice.' The government certainly had to pull its weight, 'But this does not mean that we should be told that until we do one-twelfth or one-sixteenth, or some other fraction as much as they are doing in any particular enterprise, we are defaulting. It would also help if the United States took more notice of what we *do* do, and, indeed occasionally of what we say. It is disconcerting, for instance, that about the only time the American people seem to be aware of our existence, in contrast say to the existence of a Latin American republic, is when we do something that they do not like, or do not do something which they would like.' It was part of the responsibility of the Department of External Affairs to ensure that minor disagreements with the United States did not turn into major divisions.

Nevertheless, the days of relatively easy and automatic political relations with our neighbour are, I think, over. They are over because, on our side, we are more important in the continental and international scheme of things, and we loom more largely now as an important element in United States and in free world plans for defence and development. They are over also because the United States is now the dominating world power on the side of freedom. Our preoccupation is no longer whether the United States will discharge her international responsibilities, but how she will do it and how the rest of us will be involved.[36]

No more succinct description of Canada's strategic position throughout the diplomacy of the Korean War could be devised than that contained in the last sentence of this paragraph, and no comment more effective in winning American attention than that embodied in the first. Many years later Mr Pearson described his remarks as 'balanced,' 'objective,' and 'obvious,'[37] but so prominent and plentiful were the reports in American newspapers at the time, and so indignant the response, that Hume Wrong felt obliged to attend the next meeting of the Committee of Sixteen in support of his second secretary, knowing very well that the issue would raised.[38] He was not disappointed. The assistant secretary for United Nations affairs, John D. Hickerson, launched immediately into a vigorous and colourful attack, and demanded an explanation. Because Canadian-American relations were so close, he said, the two governments could talk very frankly, but to do so in public had a bad effect

36 Department of External Affairs, *Statements and Speeches,* no 51/14
37 Pearson, *Words and Occasions,* 101
38 Campbell, interview, 20 Oct. 1968

upon other powers. Wrong cooly replied that he thought Mr Pearson had made a very good statement, and delivered a telling exhortation in its defence. By the time he had finished, the atmosphere had returned more or less to normal.[39]

A few days later General MacArthur returned to the United States, there to receive the adulation of a national hero. On 19 April, before a joint meeting of both houses of Congress, he delivered an oration so powerful in its defence of his view of the issues in Korea that it raised in the minds of some a Bonapartist spectre.[40] But the climax of the speech was personal:

I am closing my fifty-two years of military service. When I joined the Army even before the turn of the century, it was the fulfillment of all my boyish hopes and dreams. The world has turned over many times since I took the oath on the Plain at West Point, and the hopes and dreams have long since vanished. But I still remember the refrain of one of the most popular barrack ballads of that day which proclaimed most proudly that – 'Old soldiers never die, they just fade away.'

And like the old soldier of that ballad, I now close my military career and just fade away – an old soldier who tried to do his duty as God gave him light to see that duty. Good-by.[41]

Of the attendant Congressmen, many were reduced to tears. But in Ottawa, where Mr Pearson, Mary Macdonald, the minister's executive assistant (Freeman Tovell), and a handful of others had gathered round a portable radio to hear the performance, the reception was more detached. In the recollection of Mr Tovell, the minister's comment was to the effect, 'Oh, gee! What a ham!'[42]

On the following day the City of New York honoured the General with its traditional ticker tape parade. An estimated seven and a half million people crowded the sidewalks. Among the 3249 tons of streamers and debris later cleaned from the streets were the shredded remains of copies of the speech in which Mr Pearson had publicly advised MacArthur to stick to his speciality. Softly shimmering in the eddies of air, they had floated down upon the general's cavalcade as it passed beneath the windows in the New York office of Canada's permanent delegation to the United Nations.[43]

39 Ibid. The committee in subsequent sessions continued to play an important role as a vehicle for the expression of disagreements with American policy.
40 See Rees, *Korea*, 227. For the complete text of MacArthur's address, see his *Reminiscences*, 454-60
41 MacArthur, *Reminiscences*, 460
42 Tovell, interview, 5 May 1970
43 Holmes, interview, 5 March 1968

There was some satisfaction, then, that the efforts of the peacemakers could be resumed without fear of sabotage by the military commander. New opportunities were not long in coming. Communist Chinese offensives in April and May were successfully resisted by the United Nations forces, and western diplomats began to hope that these costly failures would convince the Peking regime that control of South Korea was not worth the price. The conflict had become a war of attrition. In a survey of world affairs delivered in the House of Commons on 14 May, Mr Pearson argued that the only viable UN policy was 'to continue inflicting heavy losses on the aggressors ... and at the same time to avoid any measures which are not absolutely necessary from a military point of view, and which might lead to the spreading of the conflict.' This, he hoped, would make the Chinese 'realize that it is not China but Russia which is being served by the aggression in Korea,' and would encourage them to enter into negotiations for a settlement. But he was not immediately optimistic. The pacific inquiries of the Good Offices Committee and of individual countries had all been rebuffed by the Chinese regime. Canada, moreover, had 'kept in constant touch with the Indian Government on this question,' and Mr Pearson knew that the approaches of the Indian ambassador in Peking had 'not given any grounds for believing that the Chinese communists are yet ready to negotiate on any terms that could conceivably be acceptable to the United Nations.' Until there was some indication of a change in Chinese policy, therefore, diplomacy would have to 'take a second place to arms.'[44]

But the steady improvement of the UN position at the front during the next few days began to raise the minister's hopes. He told the Commons External Affairs Committee on 22 May that so long as the battle continued to rage there was little the United Nations or its agencies could do 'to start the wheels of negotiation going again.' Nevertheless, the UN's military successes made him more optimistic that negotiations might soon be initiated by the authorities in Moscow and Peking. The UN bargaining position was now stronger than it had been during the defeats of December, and it was possible that the Chinese were having second thoughts. There had recently been 'a good deal of rumour' that the Soviets and Chinese were actually 'throwing out feelers for a negotiated settlement,' although this had not been confirmed by any information available to his department.[45]

If the Soviets and Chinese had taken no initiatives, if was not for want of invitations. On 17 May, for example, Edwin Johnson tabled a resolution in the American Senate urging that a Korean armistice be arranged along the 38th

44 Canada, House of Commons, *Debates,* 14 May 1951, 3012-13
45 Canada, House of Commons, Standing Committee on External Affairs, *Minutes of Proceedings and Evidence,* 22 May 1951, 9

parallel by 25 June, the first anniversary of the war, and his proposal received wide coverage in the news media of the USSR.[46] On 26 May Mr Pearson himself tried to lay some groundwork. In a United Nations broadcast entitled 'The Price of Peace' – part of a series arranged by the Secretariat's Department of Public Information – he surveyed the purposes of the United Nations in Korea and elsewhere, remarked upon the heavy costs that were being inflicted upon the participants in the war, drew attention to the dangers of military escalation, and observed that 'We can prevent all this by banding together our strength to defeat aggression, as we are now doing in Korea; by being ready to seize any opportunity for an honourable settlement by negotiation which may present itself, and by strengthening the social, economic and moral fabric of the world.' The 'fighting men' in the theatre naturally wished 'a clear-cut and victorious result,' but 'victory in this type of limited United Nations war' might not involve the 'complete capitulation of the enemy.' It consisted rather of 'the achievement of our objectives,' which remained 'the defeat of aggression against the Republic of Korea.'[47] Continuing the war would cost a great deal; ending it would cost very little. Such was the essence of Mr Pearson's message to Peking.

The secretary-general, Trygve Lie, offered a similar calculus in an address delivered in Ottawa on 1 June. It was time, he said, 'for a new effort to end the fighting in Korea.' The aggressor had been thrown back across the 38th parallel, and if a cease-fire could be arranged there, followed by a restoration of peace and security in the area, then 'the main purpose of the Security Council resolutions of June 25 and 27 and July 7, 1950,' would be fulfilled.'[48] The General Assembly resolution of 7 October, which had established the unification and democratization of all Korea as objectives of the United Nations in the war, was thus tactfully omitted from Mr Lie's catalogue, and on the same day Dean Acheson publicly advised the American Senate that he did not understand Korean unification 'to be a war aim.' Next day he reiterated explicitly the Truman administration's view, developed in National Security Council meetings on 2 and 16 May, that a cease-fire arranged near the parallel 'would accomplish the military purposes in Korea.'[49]

46 Rees, *Korea,* 261
47 Department of External Affairs, *Statements and Speeches,* no 51/23
48 Quoted in Lie, *In the Cause of Peace,* 362
49 Quoted in Rees, *Korea,* 262. The formulation of this policy in meetings of the National Security Council is mentioned in Truman, *Years of Trial and Hope,* 516. Acheson's own account blames the confusion between the UN's long term political objectives in Korea on the one hand, and the immediate military objectives of the war on the other, on General MacArthur. See *Present at the Creation,* 531

A little later in the month Mr Lie circulated a memorandum entitled 'Ideas Concerning Attainment of a Cease-Fire in Korea,' in which he suggested that it might be possible to arrange cease-fire negotiations between the military commanders in the field. The negotiators would discuss only the cease-fire and would have no authority to raise wider political issues. As the secretary-general pointed out later in his memoirs, 'this assumed that Peking was prepared to abandon its stand for discussion of political matters like Chinese representation and Formosa until a cease-fire was effected,' but 'the fresh United Nations military success made it an assumption worth testing.'[50]

The prospect of initiatives being taken by the United Nations, or by any of its individual members, was not, however, entirely welcome in Washington. As Dean Acheson later recorded, there were recollections in the American capital of 'the anguish caused by the UN First Committee's Five Principles for Discussion which we in the State Department thought it best to accept and which our fellow citizens rejected in no uncertain manner. Not being eager for further UN initiatives, it was incumbent upon us to devise our own,' especially since American policy-makers were unanimous in concluding 'that exploration through the public procedures of the United Nations or through leaky foreign offices like the Indian would be fatal.'[51] A number of informal inquiries resulted, culminating in a 31 May meeting between George Kennan – then at Princeton University on leave of absence from the Department of State – and Yakov Malik, the Soviet ambassador to the UN. Malik lacked instructions, but at a second meeting on 5 June he was able to report 'that the Soviet Government wanted peace and a peaceful solution in Korea and as rapidly as possible.' The Soviets could not themselves appropriately participate in cease-fire discussions, but the Americans should approach the North Koreans and Chinese.[52]

The first Canadian official to hear of this development was Peter Campbell, who in the absence from Washington of Hume Wrong was called to the telephone by Dean Rusk at 2:30 in the morning and asked to come immediately to the State Department. When he arrived he found Rusk and Hickerson, who informed him that they had received indications that the North Koreans were prepared to begin negotiations.[53]

---

50 Lie, *In the Cause of Peace,* 362-3
51 Acheson, *Present at the Creation,* 531. The 'Five Principles' were those devised by the Cease-Fire Group and approved by the Political Committee of the General Assembly on 13 January. See above, 162-3
52 Acheson, *Present at the Creation,* 532-3
53 Campbell, interview, 20 Oct. 1968

Campbell was taken completely by surprise, but it was not long before the possibilities became public. On 23 June Malik delivered a UN radio address in the same series on 'The Price of Peace' to which Mr Pearson had contributed on 26 May. In it he remarked that

The Soviet peoples ... believe that the most acute problem of the present day – the problem of the armed conflict in Korea – could be settled.

This would require the readiness of the parties to enter on the path of a peaceful settlement of the Korean question. The Soviet peoples further believe that as a first step discussions should be started between the belligerents for a cease-fire and an armistice providing for the mutual withdrawal of forces from the 38th Parallel.

Can such a step be taken? I think it can, provided there is a sincere desire to put an end to the bloody fighting in Korea.

I think that, surely, is not too great a price to pay in order to achieve peace in Korea.[54]

This appeared to confirm that the Soviets were now willing to consider, in advance of a political settlement, negotiations for a cease-fire in the area of the 38th parallel, and that they were prepared to distinguish the armistice problem from wider Far Eastern issues relating to the status of Formosa, China's representation in the United Nations, and the political future of Korea itself. Hence, while the American ambassador in Moscow was obtaining further confirmation directly from the Soviet foreign minister, the interest of the other UN actors involved was immediately aroused. Trygve Lie was on holiday in Norway when informed of Mr Malik's comments, and after issuing a statement urging that 'negotiations for a military cease-fire now be entered into at the earliest possible date,' made plans to return to New York.[55] At London airport during a stopover, he discussed the new development with Kenneth Younger, the British minister of state, and Mr Pearson, who was visiting Britain for talks with Herbert Morrison, the minister of foreign affairs. During the interval the secretary-general told newsmen that the Soviet suggestion looked like 'a sincere statement which has to be taken seriously,'[56] and Mr Pearson was reported by the Canadian Press, and later in *External Affairs*, as saying that if 'Malik's statement should be a satisfactory basis for a proposal from Moscow, then we should make the most of it. If the USSR is anxious to end the conflict

54 Quoted in Rees, *Korea,* 263
55 Lie, *In the Cause of Peace,* 363. Mr Lie's statement was read in the Canadian House of Commons by Mr St Laurent. See Canada, House of Commons, *Debates,* 25 June, 1951, 4617
56 Lie, *In the Cause of Peace,* 364

in Korea on terms we can accept, then we should certainly follow it up,'
although there were clearly some ambiguities that had to be tested and resolved.[57] On 25 June one year to the day after the outbreak of the war, Radio Peking
quoted an editorial from the *People's Daily* saying that the Chinese people fully
supported Mr Malik's cease-fire proposal, and with this signal that the Peking
regime approved of the Soviet initiative, the excitement began to mount. So
feverish was the activity of Canadian diplomatists that in reply to a question
in the Commons regarding their efforts, Prime Minister St Laurent prefaced
his account of their movements with the complaint that it was 'difficult to give
a categorical answer, because there are talks going on in many different
places.'[58] For the most part, however, this diplomatic industry was designed
less to peddle policy than to acquire information. Although during the long
months of negotiation which lay ahead the Canadians in Washington would
convey a steady stream of protests and representations to the American authorities,[59] in the end the making of the peace was left largely to the generals.
This was a reflection of the limitations placed upon the scope of the armistice
talks. Mr Lie's memorandum of mid-June had suggested that the negotiations
be concerned with cease-fire problems only, and that they be undertaken by
the military commanders rather than by diplomats. When the American ambassador in Moscow inquired on 27 June into the meaning of Mr Malik's radio
address, he was told that the USSR similarly conceived of the proposed discussions in military terms, involving only the commanders in the field; political
issues would not be considered.[60] On 28 June the secretary-general declared
that in his view the United States possessed the authority to conclude a
cease-fire agreement without further recourse to the Security Council or to the
General Assembly. Political negotiations, on the other hand, would require
additional UN authorization.[61] The practical result was that the armistice talks
were conducted by the UN Command on American instructions. Other governments with armed forces in the theatre were kept informed of their progress,
and in varying degrees they were sometimes even consulted, but the United
Nations itself played no active role.[62]

57 Canadian Press, 'Pearson Favors Parley,' *Montreal Star,* 25 June 1951. See also Department
   of External Affairs, 'The Korean Crisis,' *External Affairs,* III, 7, July 1951, 232
58 Canada, House of Commons, *Debates,* 29 June 1951, 4890-1
59 Campbell, interview, 20 Oct. 1968
60 Rees, *Korea,* 284. See also Acheson, *Present at the Creation,* 533
61 Rees, *Korea,* 284
62 See Goodrich, 'Korea: Collective Measures Against Aggression,' 178-9

The Americans, very shortly after Malik's radio address, approached the members of the Committee of Sixteen to obtain their approval of the proposal that the initiative should be taken through the offices of the field commander. They based their case on several arguments: first, that it would be difficult for them to conduct the negotiations at a political level, given that the United States recognized neither the North Korean nor the Chinese regime; second, that negotiating through field commanders would help 'to exclude from the talks political questions such as Formosa, the recognition of Communist China and its membership in the United Nations, and Indochina'; third, that the United Nations itself was clearly not a viable alternative, as the experience of General Wu's visit to New York had demonstrated; fourth, that the prospect of there being negotiations at all was itself 'dictated by the relation of forces on the battlefield'; and fifth, that in any case neither the Chinese nor the Soviets had accepted official responsibility for the operations of Chinese forces in Korea, since these were supposed to be 'volunteers' acting on their own initiative.[63]

The Committee of Sixteen accepted the field commander arrangement, and in the early stages of the talks the Canadian government was reasonably content with this procedure. Parliament had prorogued on 30 June, before the negotiations had begun, but when it reassembled in October Mr Pearson told the Commons that in the Canadian view the discussions 'have been very well conducted and well handled by General Ridgway. We also have reason to know that General Ridgway, in the conduct of these negotiations, has taken great pains to let the governments which have forces in Korea know what he is doing, and why he is doing it. There are meetings in Washington every two or three days, sometimes more often than that, where reports come back from Korea and where discussions take place with the representatives of all the governments contributing forces to the Korean operation.'[64]

By the following March his enthusiasm had dampened, but still he displayed no great disillusionment with the American effort. It was, he told the House, 'exceedingly difficult to detect much progress' in the talks. They took 'the form of offensives and counter-offensives, attacks and counter-attacks,' and it was 'impossible to be either optimistic or pessimistic about an eventual satisfactory conclusion.' Everyone would agree, however, that they were 'being conducted by the United States negotiators on behalf of the United Nations with persistence and with patience.'[65]

63 Acheson, *Present at the Creation*, 533
64 Canada, House of Commons, *Debates*, 23 Oct. 1951, 317
65 Ibid., 21 March 1952, 664

But by June 1952, as the negotiations were about to enter their second year, there were signs that his own patience was beginning to wear a little thin. He noted that in accordance with the Cease-Fire Group's five principles of January 1951, 'political discussions as such are not to be held until an armistice has been arranged and the fighting has ceased.' The 'political content' of the talks had 'now become significant.' But whether this meant that 'the machinery on the United Nations side for conducting them should be modified, or whether, indeed, an effort should be made to move the discussions from Korea itself,' was a matter on which he did 'not wish to express any opinion at this time.'[66]

By the autumn of that year the minister was ready to inflict public pressure upon the Americans to treat more flexibly the issues still in dispute, and in concert with the leaders of other powers he was to resort once more to the United Nations as a vehicle for amplifying Canada's influence over American policy.

But this was a year and a half after the talks had begun. In the interval the government's diplomacy was discreet, and its public declarations were devoted mainly to the reiteration of established opinions. The negotiations themselves comprised a depressing spectacle, for from the beginning they were marked by a propensity for prolonged and unproductive disputation that was without precedent in the history of diplomatic affairs. The talks began not long after President Truman authorized General Ridgway on 29 June to broadcast a message to the Communist commander-in-chief indicating that he was informed that the latter might wish to have a meeting to discuss an armistice, and that he would be willing to name a representative to such a meeting should the Communists show a desire to hold one. The reply was favourable, and after initial discussions by liaison officers from both sides, the talks began on 10 July in the village of Kaesong, located between the opposing battlelines about three miles south of the 38th parallel.

The Committee of Sixteen in Washington meanwhile had agreed upon a list of seven armistice provisions to be presented by the UN Command:

1 Enforcement of a cease-fire throughout Korea under conditions that would guarantee the security of both commands for the period of the armistice.

2 Establishment of an appropriate twenty-mile buffer zone, with the southern extremity of the zone running from just south of the 38th Parallel on the west coast of the peninsula to a point about fifteen miles north of the Parallel on the east coast.

66 Ibid., 23 June 1952, 3194

3 Both sides to stay on their side of the demilitarized zone and to go no nearer than three miles offshore of the other's territory.

4 A halt of shipments of war material, troops and replacements to Korea or increases in the number of troops in Korea.

5 Establishment of an international commission – not necessarily under the United Nations – with unrestricted access to all Korea to supervise the truce.

6 Exchange of prisoners.

7 Provision of security of troops and refugees and other problems.[67]

President Truman's personal instructions to General Ridgway noted that the UN Command's 'principal military interest in this armistice lies in a cessation of hostilities in Korea, an assurance against the resumption of fighting and the protection of the security of United Nations forces.' There was no certainty that the Communists were 'prepared to agree to an acceptable permanent settlement of the Korean problem,' and it was therefore important that any armistice agreement concluded by the two sides 'be acceptable to us over an extended period of time.' The talks 'should be severely restricted to military questions,' and in particular the General 'should specifically not enter into discussion of a final settlement in Korea or consideration of issues unrelated to Korea, such as Formosa and the Chinese seat in the United Nations.' He was 'authorized to adopt, for negotiating purposes, initial positions more favourable to us than the minimum conditions' elaborated in his instructions, but in so doing he was to take great care 'not to allow talks to break down except in case of failure to accept our minimum terms; not to appear to overreach to an extent to cause world opinion to question our good faith; and not so to engage US prestige in a negotiating position as to make retreat to our minimum terms impossible.' The UN minimum position was essential, 'but we must recognize that it will not be easy for opponents to accept.'[68]

According to David Rees, the Joint Chiefs in Washington at this point expected the negotiations to last about three weeks, possibly six if they went very badly.[69] In fact they survived for two years and seventeen days, occupied 575 regular meetings, and absorbed eighteen million words.[70] Except for occasional profferings of advice in the Committee of Sixteen, however, Canada played no perceptible role in them until late 1952, and there is little need here

67 Vatcher, *Panmunjom,* 27-8
68 Quoted in Truman, *Years of Trial and Hope,* 519-20
69 Rees, *Korea,* 285
70 Vatcher, *Panmunjom,* 1

to describe their dreary course during the interval.[71] From the start there were attempts on the Communist side to conduct the discussions as if they comprised a battlefield for propaganda war, and when the UN Command retaliated in kind the inevitable result was slow progress. It took the disputants sixteen days to agree even on the agenda, which by the time it was settled on 26 July included five items:

1 Adoption of agenda.

2 Fixing of military demarcation line between both sides so as to establish a demilitarized zone as a basic condition for the cessation of hostilities in Korea.

3 Concrete arrangements for the realization of cease-fire and armistice in Korea, including the composition, authority, and functions of a supervisory organ for carrying out the terms of cease-fire and armistice.

4 Arrangements relating to prisoners of war.

5 Recommendations to the governments of countries concerned on both sides.[72]

Following the adoption of the agenda, the negotiators considered Item 2. The Communists argued that the military demarcation line should be established at the 38th parallel, which was a recognized boundary whose violation by the South Koreans and their allies had precipitated the war in the first place. For the United Nations, Vice-Admiral Turner Joy insisted by contrast that the line should be located along the military front, thereby reflecting the true military realities. The UN Command's policy on this issue was due partly to the fact that it regarded the 38th parallel as an indefensible position that would be difficult to secure should there be delays in achieving a political settlement in Korea following the armistice. It was due also to the Command's realization that acceptance at this early stage in the talks of the parallel as the final demarcation boundary would reduce the UN's capacity to exert pressure on the opposing side by threatening a military advance. In any case, if positions were established along the 38th parallel, they would require a doubling of the length of the UN's military lines.[73]

So intense was the acrimony that developed over this issue that on 10 August – following a five-day recess – the two delegations confronted one another across the conference table in complete silence for a full two hours and eleven minutes. The only communication between them took the form of a note

71 For full accounts of the armistice negotiations, see ibid., and Turner Joy, *How Communists Negotiate*

72 Quoted in Vatcher, *Panmunjom,* 43

73 Ibid., 47

passed by one of the Communist representatives to the chief North Korean delegate, General Nam Il, in such a manner as to be clearly visible to their opponents. 'The Imperialist errand boys,' it read, 'are lower than dogs in a morgue.'[74] Later in the month the Communists agreed to a suggestion by Admiral Joy that the matter be delegated to a subcommittee which could then attempt to make recommendations to the plenary session, but the subcommittee's proceedings were terminated after six meetings when the Communist delegation alleged that allied aircraft had been bombing the neutral zone around Kaesong. The UN Command in the meantime had complained of similar violations of the zone's neutrality by conspicuously armed Communist troops. The charges and countercharges became increasingly elaborate with each successive round of allegations, and the talks were recessed on 23 August. The suspension lasted sixty-three days, and the negotiations were not resumed in plenary session until 25 October, this time in the nearby village of Panmunjom.

Throughout this period there was little comment from the Canadian government. In his report on foreign affairs to the re-assembled House of Commons on 22 October, Mr Pearson devoted only two short paragraphs from his sixteen legal-size pages to the cease-fire negotiations. The first expressed the hope that 'the period of delaying tactics by the communists' was over and that an armistice could be arranged. The second complimented General Ridgway on his management of the negotiations, and offered a motto for the guidance of western policy-makers: 'Trust in Kaesong but keep your powder dry.'[75]

There is evidence that the dry powder was having the greater effect, for during the two-month suspension the United Nations forces made significant advances at the front, and when the Chinese and North Koreans returned to the bargaining table, they gave up their insistence upon establishing the 38th parallel as the line of demarcation.[76] After a month of additional discussion, formal agreement was reached on Item 2. The terms provided for a demilitarized zone four kilometres wide centered on the line of military contact, with the qualification that the line already established could not be changed if agreement were reached on the other items on the agenda within thirty days. This had the effect of rendering concerted attempts by the UN Command to

74 Quoted ibid., 54
75 Department of External Affairs, *Statements and Speeches,* no. 51/42
76 Vatcher, *Panmunjom,* 79-80. The military action is described in Rees, *Korea,* 299-300. Rees accepts this view of the reasons for the Communist concession (297 and 301-9). The point that successful negotiation in such cases requires a strong military position from which to bargain is forcefully argued also by Turner Joy. See *How Communists Negotiate,* Chapter XIV, *passim.*

improve its military position pointless for the duration of the thirty-day period, and in the interval the Communist forces worked feverishly to strengthen their defences.[77]

Agreement on the agenda had taken the negotiators just over two weeks; agreement on the line of demarcation absorbed an additional four months; and agreement on Item 3 (concrete arrangements for the realization of a cease-fire) was to require five months more. Throughout this period, and indeed for the duration of the hostilities, the military situation was virtually stabilized, with each side now relatively impregnable to large-scale enemy assault. The result was that the military confrontation took the form largely of skirmishes for possession of tactically advantageous positions, usually located atop the rugged ridges and hills so characteristic of Korean topography. Such engagements took an enormous toll in human casualities – so enormous, in fact, that the Commonwealth Division on occasion refused to initiate them.[78] But they had little effect upon the overall military balance, except that they increased its rigidity by adjusting and strengthening the defensive capabilities of the opposing forces. This in turn meant that neither of the negotiating teams at Panmunjom was able to impose a settlement upon its opponent, with the result that in the absence of other incentives to reach agreement the discussions could drag on interminably.

The negotiators turned to Item 3 on 27 November, immediately after settling the line of demarcation. The initial UNC position was that there should be no further enlargement of forces after the armistice was implemented, and that a commission should be appointed, together with an appropriate supervisory staff, to oversee the cease-fire. This inspectorate was to have 'free access to all parts of Korea.' In addition, the UN Command demanded a post-armistice prohibition on the construction and improvement of airfields throughout the peninsula. General Nam Il rejected this last suggestion, presumably because it would have the effect of perpetuating the UNC's superiority in the air. He refused also to accept the provision for granting 'free access' rights to the armistice commission, arguing that this would constitute 'a brazen interference in the internal affairs' of North Korea. His counterproposals included the withdrawal of all foreign troops from Korea as a whole, and of all armed forces without qualification from Korean coastal islands, which were then held mostly by the United Nations Command. He thereby rejected the UNC argument that while the opposing forces should not be increased after

77 Vatcher, *Panmunjom,* 86
78 See above, 211

the conclusion of the armistice, rotation and replacement should be permitted within the established limits.[79]

There followed several weeks of haggling both in subcommittees and in plenary sessions as the opposing teams argued the details of their respective proposals, and of various alternatives. Meanwhile, the talks were complicated further on 11 December when another subcommittee began working on Item 4, relating to prisoners of war. This was to be the most intractable issue of the entire two years of discussion, a circumstance which was to become increasingly evident as the winter wore on. The only cheering note in this phase was the agreement reached on 19 February regarding Item 5, 'Recommendations to governments of countries concerned on both sides.' After only two weeks of debate, the negotiators agreed on the following formula: 'In order to ensure the peaceful settlement of the Korean question, the military Commanders of both sides hereby recommend to the Governments of the countries concerned on both sides that, within three (3) months after the Armistice Agreement is signed and becomes effective, a political conference of a higher level of both sides be held by representatives appointed respectively to settle through negotiation the questions of the withdrawal of all foreign forces from Korea, the peaceful settlement of the Korean question &c.'[80]

It is hardly surprising that the two delegations should find it an easy matter to decide that their superiors should meet sometime in the future to discuss an undefined number of political problems to which the question of the cease-fire was not immediately related. The speed with which agreement was reached on this issue was thus a reflection more of its short-term insignificance than of any new atmosphere in the armistice proceedings. In any case, by the end of April three vexing and important issues remained. The first concerned the UNC's demand for a prohibition on airfield construction after the conclusion of the armistice, a provision which the Communists adamantly refused to accept. The second involved the composition of the Neutral Nations Supervisory Commission (NNSC) which was to be established for the purpose of inspecting and supervising the execution of the cease-fire and armistice: the Communist delegation insisted that in addition to Poland, Czechoslovakia, Norway, Sweden, and Switzerland, the USSR should also be included among the commission's members; the UN Command, on the other hand, refused to accept the Soviet Union on the ground that it was not only an interested party but a primary instigator of the war. The third issue concerned the dispute over the principle of non-forcible repatriation of prisoners of war, and requires elaboration.

79 Rees, *Korea,* 311-12
80 Paragraph 60 of the final armistice agreement. Quoted ibid, 482

The POW question materialized late in 1951 when it became clear that a large number of the prisoners held in United Nations camps were unwilling to return to their homelands. The matter was complicated in the early weeks of discussion by disagreements over the POW statistics deployed respectively by the two sides. But the core issue was the UN Command's insistence that POW repatriation be voluntary. The Command's motivations were partly humanitarian and partly political. They were humanitarian to the extent that the UNC felt unable to return anti-Communist prisoners to societies which were almost certain to exact grievous penalties in retribution for their disloyalty. They were political in that the Command knew that the refusal of many of their prisoners to return to North Korea, and in some cases to China, provided an opportunity for an enormous propaganda victory. In any case, if the prisoners were denied sanctuary, future dissidents within the Soviet bloc would be deterred from running the risk of defection. The Communist delegation, doubtless after making similar calculations of its own, insisted upon total repatriation.

By April 1952 little progress had been made either on this or on the other two issues still in dispute. On 28 April, therefore, Admiral Joy presented a package offer in which the UNC abandoned its insistence upon the prohibition of airfield construction in the post-armistice period and indicated that it was prepared to drop Norway from membership on the NNSC provided that in return the Communists would abandon their demand for Soviet participation on the commission and accept the principle of non-forcible repatriation of prisoners of war. After several days of discussion it was announced on 7 May that the Communist delegation had accepted all these provisions except the last. Only the issue of POW repatriation therefore stood in the way of a successful armistice.

In announcing these results to the House of Commons on the same day, Mr Pearson argued that the provisions of the UN Command proposal were 'scrupulously fair to the communists' and that they provided 'a convincing demonstration of ... good faith.' So far as the repatriation issue was concerned, it was unthinkable that the United Nations forces in Korea should undertake the invidious task of forcing these men to return to communist rule. The United Nations command can obviously make no concession on this point other than to allow the communists to have the 62,000 men interviewed either by a neutral body or by joint Red Cross teams from both sides in order to satisfy themselves that these individuals have made their decisions of their own free will and not under compulsion. This the United Nations command has offered to allow.' All the members of the House, he went on, would 'regret profoundly the communist refusal of this offer that could have brought an end to the fighting in Korea on terms that would have been fair and would not have betrayed the principles of the United Nations charter which governed the original intervention.' Perhaps they would reconsider their position. In any event he hoped that there would 'be no need for a resumption of full-scale hostilities.'[81]

The minister was pleased, then, with the conduct, if not with the progress, of the negotiations. The UN Command had been reasonable and flexible in its approach to the talks, and had shown itself prepared to make concessions on all but the most fundamental issues. There was now only one outstanding dispute upon which it was not prepared to give way, and in this it was clearly on the side of the angels. There would be no compromise on a matter involving so profound a moral principle. Only the absence of a sense of justice and compassion among the Communist delegates stood in the way of an armistice agreement.

This was a spiritually comforting assessment. Yet Canadian disenchantment with the UNC's POW policy was at this point only hours away, for shortly after Mr Pearson's statement to the House there began a revolt among prisoners in United Nations compounds on Koje Island which was not only to undermine the UN's moral advantage at Panmunjom, but was to generate one of the most volatile of the conflicts arising from the Korean War between Canada and the United States.

Koje Island protrudes from the sea in the shape of a rough cross about thirty miles southeast of Pusan. At its nearest point it comes within five miles of the Korean mainland. Its overall dimensions are about twelve by twenty miles, and it consists for the most part of barren and rocky hills. Traditionally a base of operations for Korean fishermen, at the outbreak of the war it had been used as a reception centre for refugees displaced by the advancing North Korean army. In the spring of 1951, however, it had been selected also as a site for the maintenance of enemy prisoners of war, most of whom had been captured after they were cut off from their lines of retreat by the landings at Inchon. By the autumn of that year there were more than 160,000 prisoners on the island, in addition to the constantly increasing number of civilian refugees.

Almost from the beginning there had been violent incidents, not only between the prisoners and their guards, but also among the prisoners themselves. It soon developed that more than 60,000 of the men interned were 'anti-communist,' or for various other reasons were unwilling to return to their homelands. The balance, however, were firmly loyal to their leadership, and believed it their duty to continue the prosecution of the war to the extent that

81 Canada, House of Commons, *Debates,* 7 May 1952, 1953-4

their currently restricted environment allowed. They were encouraged, if not commanded, in this undertaking by their superiors at home, with whom they were in constant communication by radio and through agents among the refugees and fishermen. Their task was made easier by the comparative lack of control imposed upon their activities by the UN Command. In order to reduce the cost of their maintenance, they had been placed in huge compounds housing in some cases more than 6000 men. The UN guards, numbering not more than 7000, had been ordered for propaganda reasons not to utilize force or other disciplinary action in the conduct of their duties. As a result 'there was no bed check, no roll call, no inspection of quarters. The guards, in the main raw recruits and misfit officers – the discard of the line outfits – were jittery and terrified by tales of Oriental cruelty. And so, when a prisoner walked into one of the Koje compounds he actually passed out of control of his captors.'[82] Robert Leckie's description of one of the many incidents on the island illustrates the degree to which the prisoners had become a law unto themselves: 'Once, as the guard was being changed at Compound 78, a mob of prisoners dragged one of their terrified captives into view and shouted: "Yankees, see and beware. This is what we do to the traitors who oppose us." Whereupon they cut off the man's tongue, allowed him to stumble about for a few moments, uttering terrible muted cries of pain, and then beat him to death – jeering at the Americans who were sickened at the sight.'[83]

This demonstration late in 1951 was followed by others, and by early 1952 the prisoners were openly being given military training in the compounds, while POW buildings were decked with red flags. In February there were riots and disorders which resulted in the death of one American guard and 75 prisoners, and the wounding of 39 Americans and 139 POWs. Other riots followed and on 29 April, at the request of the senior POW officer, Colonel Lee Hak Koo, Lt-Col. Wilbur Raven, the assistant to the camp commander, entered Compound 76 for a conference, there to be forcibly confined and mistreated for three hours before being released.

The climax followed shortly thereafter, when Colonel Lee demanded an interview with Brigadier-General Francis Dodd, the American commander of the camp. In spite of Colonel Raven's experience, the Brigadier-General and

---

82 Leckie, *Conflict*, 33. POW statistics in this period were unreliable, since the UN Command had been unable to conduct a prisoner census. As General Mark W. Clark, Ridgway's successor, put it later in his memoirs, 'We didn't know exactly how many prisoners were on the island, for the fanatical Communists hadn't permitted our authorities inside some compounds for many months. Therefore our camp officials had been unable to count their prisoners.' Clark, *From the Danube to the Yalu*, 39

83 Leckie, *Conflict*, 338-9

his assistant acquiesced. The meeting took place at the gate of Compound 76 on 8 May (7 May in North America), the same day the Communist delegation at Panmunjom turned down Admiral Joy's package proposal for concluding an armistice agreement. After an hour of unproductive discussion, the two officers turned to leave. They were then seized by a detail of prisoners returning from latrine duties, and General Dodd was dragged inside the compound. Colonel Raven saved himself from capture, with the help of a guard, by clinging to a gatepost.[84]

General Dodd was promptly relieved by Brigadier-General Charles T. Colson, an unfortunate choice since Colson and Dodd were close friends. At the demand of the prisoners and through the intermediary services of the entrapped General Dodd, Colson began several days of negotiations on the conditions for Dodd's release. The result on 11 May was that General Colson signed a letter satisfactory to the prisoners, and Dodd was allowed to leave the compound. Two days later the contents of the letter were made public, and they included the following:

I do admit that there have been instances of bloodshed where many prisoners of war have been killed and wounded by UN forces. I can assure you that in the future the prisoners of war can expect humane treatment in this camp according to the principles of international law. I will do all within my power to eliminate further violence and bloodshed. If such incidents happen in the future, I will be responsible.
... I can inform you that after General Dodd's release, unharmed, there will be no more forcible screening or any rearming of prisoners of war in this camp, nor will any attempt be made at nominal screening.[85]

With this document at their disposal the Communists possessed ammunition with which to reverse the propaganda war at Panmunjom. General Mark W. Clark, who was due to replace General Ridgway as UN commander on 12 May, reported later that Admiral Joy was 'absolutely flabbergasted by the Dodd incident,' complaining ruefully that he was 'certainly going to take a beating over this at the conference table.'[86] And so he did. His opponents had argued for some time that their refusal to accept the principle of non-forcible repatriation was due to the fact that the UNC had coerced and intimidated the

---

84 Rees, *Korea,* 323; Leckie, *Conflict,* 342-3. See also the editorial entitled, 'Koje Prisoners,' *New York Times,* 18 May 1952
85 'Koje Prisoners,' *New York Times,* 18 May 1952
86 Clark, *From the Danube to the Yalu,* 39

prisoners who were refusing to return home. The Colson letter was now 'triumphantly quoted ... as proof of their accusations.'[87]

But it was less the situation in Panmunjom than the measures taken to remedy the trouble on Koje-do that brought Ottawa into the fray. On assuming his command, General Clark had immediately repudiated the Colson letter as the product of extortion and ordered that its author be replaced as Koje commander by Brigadier-General Hayden L. Boatner. Colson and Dodd on General Clark's recommendation were subsequently demoted to colonel,[88] while Boatner, a field commander, undertook to restore a modicum of order among the prisoners. On the afternoon of 22 May, while Boatner was still labouring industriously at his task, the Canadian chief of the general staff received a telegram from Brigadier Bogert, the new commander of the 25th Brigade, reporting that on orders from Commonwealth Division Headquarters, and at the request of the UN Command, he had disptached 'B' Company of the 1st Royal Canadian Regiment for guard duty on Koje Island. He indicated that a British company would be going also, and that the journey to the island would be undertaken the next day.[89]

The process through which the American request arrived at Brigadier Bogert's headquarters with the status of an 'order' is now somewhat obscure, but its original source is clear. After Dodd had been released by his captors, General Mark Clark had visited Koje-do to inspect the situation for himself. By now the United States, which had provided all the guards, was receiving the entire blame for conditions on the island, and after examining the problem at first hand the UN commander decided that it would be advisable to call in a company of Canadians, together with similar units from other UN contingents, in order to give the POW operation a United Nations (as opposed to a purely American) flavour.[90]

The American liaison officer, Colonel Farnsworth, therefore intercepted the commander of the Canadian Military Mission in Tokyo, Brigadier A.B. Connelly, on his way to his daily intelligence briefing and advised him of General Clark's proposal. The brigadier said he would have to refer the matter to Ottawa. Farnborough then indicated that the general wished if possible to avoid such a time-consuming procedure, and asked Connelly for his own opinion. Connelly replied that it seemed to him a purely military operation and therefore acceptable, but that the decision fell within the responsibility of

87 'Koje Prisoners,' *New York Times*, 18 May 1952
88 For the report of the secretary of the army, Frank Pace, jr, see 'Text of the Pace Letter on Generals,' *New York Times*, 24 May 1952. See also Collins, *War in Peacetime*, 348
89 Wood, *Strange Battleground*, 193. Bogert had replaced Rockingham on 28 April.
90 Connelly, interview, 7 March 1968

Brigadier Bogert, who was the commander in the field. He heard no more of the matter until he went to the regular morning briefing on the following day and there learned to his surprise that the Canadian company had already been dispatched to the island.[91]

In the meantime, after receiving Bogert's report General Simonds had immediately advised General Foulkes, who in turn had informed the minister of defence. Mr Claxton and his colleagues were not pleased. They had not been consulted on the matter by the American authorities, and while in one sense the supervision of prisoners of war constituted a purely military function coming within the jurisdiction of the field commander, at the same time the conduct of operations on Koje-do had received heavy criticism around the world, and had developed accordingly into a political issue. Not unnaturally the Americans wished to mitigate their humiliation by identifying the problem with the United Nations as a whole. Aware of this intent, the Canadians sought with equal determination to protect their own reputation from similar damage.[92] The prime minister believed in particular that the use of Canadian guards on the island would have a bad effect on Canadian public opinion.[93] More generally, there was some fear that the POW problem would be a continuing one, with which Canada should have as little as possible to do. If Canadian troops became embroiled in it now, they might still be embroiled in it long after the war had come to an end.[94] The Canadian ambassador in Washington was therefore asked on 22 May to contact the American secretary of state in what was to be a vain attempt to have the order revoked.[95]

Lieutenant-General Simonds in the meantime dispatched a message to Connelly demanding to know why he had not informed Ottawa of the decision to reinforce Boatner with Commonwealth troops. The Brigadier had in fact composed a message to Ottawa on the evening of the same day that he had been approached by Colonel Farnsworth, but thinking it was a routine military matter, and not wishing to send it *via* the American communications system, he had resorted instead to the diplomatic bag. The arrival of his report on the appropriate desks in Ottawa was therefore long delayed.[96] He now gave the following reply to Simonds: 'My first knowledge of proposal to move UN troops other than US to Koje-do 22 May when UN Liaison Officer told me

91 Ibid.
92 Campbell, interview, 20 Oct. 1968; Foulkes, interview, 7 March 1968; Holmes, interview, 5 March 1968; LePan, interview, 5 March 1968; MacKay, interview, 7 March 1968
93 Wood, *Strange Battleground*, 193
94 Foulkes, interview, 7 March 1968
95 Wood, *Strange Battleground*, 193
96 Connelly, interview, 7 March 1968

matter under consideration and asked if any objections. Replied would refer to Ottawa but was told C.-in-C. UN Command hoped it would not be necessary to consult governments at this time.'[97]

This appeared to indicate that the Americans might have been planning to present the governments involved with a *fait accompli* (and also that Brigadier Connelly might have been their unsuspecting accomplice). The brigadier added that Lieutenant-General Bridgeford, General Robertson's successor as commander-in-chief, Commonwealth Forces in Korea, had apparently decided to comply with General Clark's request on 21 May, without informing the Canadian Military Mission. That Bridgeford had indeed issued the order was confirmed in a separate telegram from the commander of the Commonwealth Division, Major-General A.J.H. Cassels, and Bridgeford himself reported to London that his directive had resulted from General Clark's decision 'that guards at Koje-do PW Camp shall be UN commitment rather than purely American.'[98]

Since the authorities in Ottawa disapproved of the substance of this decision, it was natural for them to object also to its being made without their consent. In requesting the views of the chief of the Imperial General Staff in London, General Simonds made his own views very clear: 'I consider Cassels' and Bogert's action correct ... but take exception to action of Bridgeford and Connelly in accepting assignment which has political implications without reference to and consultation with Commonwealth governments concerned. Latter requirement is clearly stipulated in Bridgeford's directive and situation was not of an emergent operational nature precluding delay for consultation.'[99]

The British were reluctant to take the matter further. They conceded that General Bridgeford would have been 'wiser' to delay his decision pending consultations with the home governments, but they did not regard his action as improper and preferred not to disturb without good reason the amicable course of allied relations in the theatre.[100]

The government in Ottawa was in a less generous mood. Its members were firm advocates of collective United Nations action, perhaps, but they remained jealous nationalists and cautious politicians nonetheless. Since their private inquiries in Washington had come too late to affect the decision, they now planned the delivery of an indignant public protest. It was not, however, an easy task, for the substance of the Canadian complaint was that the Americans

97 Quoted in Wood, *Strange Battleground,* 193
98 Quoted ibid.
99 Quoted ibid., 194, from wire dated 28 May 1952
100 Ibid.

had handled the situation on Koje-do very badly and were attempting to distribute the responsibility for present and future difficulties among the other contributors to UN operations in Korea. Yet if such a complaint were publicly conveyed, it would have the side-effect of reinforcing the Communist propaganda barrage at Panmunjom.[101] It was therefore decided to lodge the protest on old and familiar grounds – that is, the principle of the unity of Canadian armed forces in action. If nothing else, this would at least satisfy the Canadian public that the government would not accept lightly the casual assignment of Canadian combat troops to menial and ignominious duties. In any case, the unity principle had been a part of Brigadier Rockingham's original Command instructions, which had provided that

The principle of the separate entity of the Canadian Force ... shall at all times be maintained. While the grouping of forces is a matter for the operational command to decide, it is anticipated that in the normal course of operations or other activities of the United Nations Forces, your tasks and undertakings will be so allotted or arranged, having regard to the size of the Canadian Force, that its Canadian entity will readily be preserved.

While the extent and degree of integration between the Canadian and United Nations Forces, or elements thereof, will be determined by local conditions and circumstances, it is the intention that, notwithstanding the separate nationalities of the Forces, they should be able to participate and associate together in the joint effort with flexibility and with minimum adjustment.[102]

The Americans were confronted accordingly with the following blunt communication, later read out to the House of Commons by Mr Pearson on 26 May:[103]

---

101 Two senior diplomatists of the day have pointed out that a blunt statement of the main reason for the Canadian reaction would have been impolitic. Holmes, interview, 5 March 1968; and LePan, interview, 5 March 1968. General Foulkes agreed that the question of the unity of the Canadian contingent was not the real issue. Interview, 7 March 1968

102 Wood, *Strange Battleground*, 263

103 There appears to have been some difficulty over the timing of the diplomatic communication and the public announcement of its delivery. In answer to a question by George Hees in the Commons about press speculation on this issue, Mr Pearson described the sequence of events as follows: 'Before the statement which I gave to the house upon the Koje matter was made on May 26 our ambassador in Washington had left a copy of that statement with the State Department. In diplomatic parlance, I suppose it would have been called an oral note – a note of the statement that I was to make that afternoon in the House of Commons in Ottawa. A copy of that statement was handed also to a representative of the United States embassy in

The Canadian government recognizes the importance of re-establishing and maintaining effective control over communist prisoners of war captured in Korean operations. The Canadian government also recognizes that custody of prisoners of war is a military responsibility which should be performed in accordance with military requirements.

It has, however, been a long established policy of the Canadian government that Canadian forces dispatched abroad for military operations should remain under Canadian command and control and that, except in the event of a military emergency which does not permit of time for consultation, no part of these forces should be detached therefrom except after consultation and with the agreement of the Canadian government.

The Canadian government therefore views with concern the dispatch of a company of the 25th Infantry brigade to Koje island without prior consultation with the Canadian government, and hopes that it may be possible to re-unite this company with the rest of the Canadian brigade as soon as possible. Meanwhile, the Canadian forces concerned will, of course, carry out loyally the orders of the unified command with respect to participation in guarding prisoners of war on Koje island. The Canadian government also wishes to be reassured that, if it is proposed in the future to detach any Canadian forces from Canadian command and control for military or other duties, this will be done only after consultation and with the consent of the Canadian government, except in the event of a military emergency which does not permit of time for such consultation.[104]

The public appearance of this document was not received with pleasure in Washington. American officials in the State Department were furious, including the secretary, Dean Acheson. John Holmes has recently commented that there "is good reason to believe that it was exasperation over Canadian policy on Korean prisoners of war that drove Dean Acheson into the Canada-phobia

Ottawa. It is, therefore, strictly accurate to say – no matter what press reports may have stated to the contrary – that the statement which was made in the House of Commons in Ottawa was made after its contents had been conveyed to the United States government through the state department and through the United States embassy in Ottawa.

'When the state department received this oral note from the ambassador they said that if a formal reply were desired it would be preferable to resubmit the oral note in the form of a formal diplomatic note. That was done the next day, and a formal reply was received the day before yesterday [June 18]. The actual terms of the statement, in the form of an oral note delivered by the ambassador to the state department and by this department to the United States embassy here, were in the possession of the United States government before the statement was made.' Canada, House of Commons, *Debates*, 20 June 1952, 3495

104 Ibid., 26 May 1952, 2552-3

that has affected him since that time.'[105] General Omar Bradley complained to General Foulkes that Canadian politicians were always taking advantage of American troubles and mistakes, and that whenever Washington was in difficulty, they took a different line for purposes of political propaganda. He and General Collins both indicated that if requested to do so they would have been pleased to exempt the Canadian units from Koje service, but they were irritated by the publicity.[106] An unidentified American official is reported by the Canadian army historian to have remarked that if unity was the only Canadian concern, the UN Command could easily arrange to assign the entire brigade to the island.[107] The *Washington Post* thought the note 'more than a trifle silly.'[108] General Clark himself later wrote that he was 'surprised at the criticism from Canada, 'and thought it 'essential that each of the United Nations share as fully as possible not only in the contributions of men and weapons, but also in the varied responsibilities, many of which were onerous.' The JCS had 'suggested that for political as well as military reasons it might be well to have a showing of UN troops on Koje,' and with this Clark himself agreed. Foreign liaison officers had 'agreed with the plan' and 'none had raised any objection to the movement of their troops to Koje.' It was, after all, 'a United Nations command and one of its important responsibilities was to control and guard the recalcitrant POWs, all of whom were UN POWs, and many of whom had been captured by the Canadians themselves.' It was only later that he had discovered the reason for the Canadian reaction: 'The local Canadian commander on the spot agreed to the movement of Canadian troops to Koje, but apparently his government did not adequately understand our plan. Therefore the assignment of Canadians to Koje hit Canada with a surprise impact.'[109]

The Canadian government had certainly been surprised, but it was not in this instance lacking in understanding, as Washington well knew. In any case, the State Department's reply was designed to soothe. As Mr Pearson para-

---

105 John W. Holmes, 'Canada made easy for Yankees,' *The Globe Magazine,* 17 Feb. 1968. The fury of American officials is confirmed by Campbell, interview, 20 Oct. 1968. Some External Affairs officials believe, however, that Acheson's sense of irritation with Canadian policy may have preceded the incident at Koje-do. Robinson, interview, 5 May 1970. Disagreements arising, of course, from the Chinese intervention and other issues had been fuelling the Secretary's temper for some time.

106 Foulkes, interview, 7 March 1968

107 Wood, *Strange Battleground,* 195

108 Quoted from the 11 June edition by Keirstead, *Canada in World Affairs: September 1951 to October 1953,* 168, n51

109 Clark, *From the Danube to the Yalu,* 226-7

phrased it in the Commons two days later, ' ... the United States government states its appreciation of the importance attached by the government of Canada to the maintenance of Canadian forces as a unit, and the feeling underlying Canada's traditional position in this matter, and therefore, the United States government desires to meet the wishes of the Canadian government in so far as is practicable without endangering the United Nations military effort in Korea.' 'This friendly assurance,' Mr Pearson went on, 'is welcomed and the qualification is understood and quite acceptable, as it was, of course, never our intention that the natural desire to keep Canadian forces together under Canadian command should be permitted to endanger the United Nations military effort in Korea.'[110]

Whatever the attitude in Washington, the reaction in Moscow was a display of ill-concealed delight. In the view of Moscow Radio, the Canadian government had 'made it clear that it did not wish to share responsibility for the brutalities to which the Korean and Chinese war prisoners are subjected on Koje. At the same time it is evident from the protest of the Canadian Government that the latter fully admits the flagrant violations of international agreements by the United States command in Korea ... '[111]

Neither the substance of the Canadian protest nor the manner in which it had been conveyed had earned, however, the approval of the Conservative opposition, and they now brought their guns to bear. George Hees, their chief spokesman on the issue in the House, complained on 20 June that the Americans had been given no choice but to accept the Canadian protest because Mr Pearson had issued it in public. He argued, indeed, on grounds which in subsequent years were to become almost Mr Pearson's private preserve. 'If a government,' he said, 'which has reached adult stature in the handling of external affairs wishes to send a protest to an allied government with regard to some matter, I believe that it does so in a quiet, restrained and unpublicized manner.' In this case, the government's 'unfortunate outburst' had received a great deal of headline publicity, and because it concerned a matter of such minor importance, it made 'us look rather ridiculous in the eyes of our allies.' The government should understand 'the need of a field commander to feel free to assign troops under his command to normal duties, of a temporary nature, and within the theatre of operations.'[112]

Since the government had indeed rested its case on the principle of the separate entity of the Canadian armed forces, and not on its real complaint that

110 Canada, House of Commons, *Debtates,* 19 June 1952, 3416
111 Keirstead, *Canada in World Affairs,* 168, n51
112 Canada, House of Commons, *Debates,* 20 June 1952, 3481

the Americans were attempting to distribute abroad the responsibility for their incompetence on Koje Island and for future difficulties which were bound to ensue, Mr Pearson had no choice in defending himself but to invoke the same argument again.[113] When Mr Drew pursued him further with critical quotations from the *Washington Post,*[114] the minister was still unable to muster an alternative rationale. Ultimately he agreed 'that in any difference of opinion with a friendly government we must always weigh two factors, namely the protection of our own national interests and the effect that any public discussion and division of opinion would have on the unity and the solidarity of the coalition.' But in this case 'an important matter of principle' was involved, and 'to emphasize this Canadian interest' the government had 'decided it would be well to make our statement publicly in the House of Commons.'[115]

On the island itself there was little further difficulty. The Canadian and British detachments were welcomed by Brigadier-General Boatner on 26 May in an address in which he said that he was pleased to have Commonwealth troops under his command and that he thought their 'formal' discipline would have a good effect. On 5 June the two companies together assumed control over some 3200 prisoners in Compound 66.[116] In the meantime Boatner had been constructing smaller compounds in order to divide the POWs into groups of more manageable size, and on 10 June his troops began the break-up of Compound 76, which had been the centre of most of the earlier outbreaks. With the help of tanks, tear gas, and concussion grenades, the prisoners were successfully redistributed to their new quarters. In the process one American and 41 prisoners were killed, and 13 Americans and 274 prisoners wounded. A search of the remains of the compound later revealed a weapons stockpile which included 3000 tent-pole spears, 1000 Molotov cocktails, 4500 knives, and a large assortment of clubs, hatchets, hammers, and flails.[117]

The remaining compounds were broken up without serious incident, and the prisoners in Compound 66 were transferred 'in an orderly fashion' under Anglo-Canadian care on 12 June. Thereafter the Commonwealth contingents assumed miscellaneous guard duties until their relief by American units on 8 July. By 14 July the Canadians had rejoined their parent brigade.[118]

The files now were closed on the Koje affair, but it had a melancholy sequel. It had been the misfortune of Brigadier A.B. Connelly, the commander of the

---

113 Ibid., 3482
114 Ibid., 3488-9
115 Ibid., 3496-7
116 Wood, *Strange Battleground,* 195-6
117 Leckie, *Conflict,* 347
118 Wood, *Strange Battleground,* 196

Canadian Military Mission in Japan, to neglect to report with sufficient speed to his seniors in Ottawa the assignment of Canadian troops to duty on Koje-do. On 25 August 1952, he was replaced by Brigadier R.E.A. Morton and recalled to Canada, ostensibly to take a course at the National Defence College in Kingston.[119] When he arrived, however, he was directed to apply for retirement and then dispatched without public announcement on a four-month terminal leave. The brigadier was forty-four; the normal age of retirement for his rank, fifty-five.

The matter would never have become public had the story not been published, on 7 October, by the *Chicago Tribune.* Connelly's tale of woe had been unearthed initially by Victor Mackie, the Ottawa correspondent of the *Winnipeg Free Press,* who had been informed that the brigadier was hunting for a civilian job.[120] Either because the brigadier had indicated that he would prefer to keep the story quiet,[121] or because of decisions made at the editorial level,[122] the *Free Press* failed to publish a report. Three days later it was scooped by the *Tribune,* whose sources were in Tokyo.

The Public Relations director of the Department of National Defence, W.H. Dumsday, then issued the following uninformative announcement: 'Brigadier Connelly is on retirement leave which will extend over a period of some months. The department does not normally give reason for retirements, except that senior officers are retired when there is no further suitable employment for them. With regard to the report that he was retired for his failure to immediately notify the Canadian government of the intention to use Canadian troops on Koje island, the department has no comment.'[123]

Neither had Mr Claxton, and Mr Pearson was quoted in the *Regina Leader-Post* on 7 October as saying only, 'I know nothing about it.'[124] There was something of an outcry in the press, and finally on 1 December General G.R. Pearkes raised the matter in the House of Commons, pointing out that Connelly had an excellent military record, and that his early retirement was going to cost the government about $50,000 for which it would receive no services in return. The government, he suggested, had been embarrassed by its own

119 Date obtained ibid., 277. See also 'The Services: Fired or Retired?' *Time,* Canada Edition, IX, 16, 20 Oct. 1952. Confirmed by Connelly, interview, 7 March 1968
120 *Time,* IX, 16, 20 Oct. 1952. Confirmed by Connelly, interview, 7 March 1968
121 Connelly, interview, 7 March 1968
122 *Time* magazine reported that the *Free Press* decision not to run the Connelly story was made at the request of Liberal government officials. See 'The Services: Fired or Retired?' *Time,* Canada Edition, IX, 16, 20 Oct. 1952
123 Quoted by G.R. Pearkes in Canada, House of Commons, *Debates,* 1 Dec. 1952, 209
124 Ibid.

handling of the Koje affair, and 'a whipping boy had to be found. Of course the darling of the government [Mr Pearson] could not be chastised. Somebody had to take the beating for him.' This, he implied, was hardly fair to the Brigadier: 'It may have been an error in judgment on the part of Brigadier Connelly when he did not send back by wire the fact that the matter of sending a company of Canadian troops to Koje Island was being considered and merely reported it in a written statement, but it would hardly seem that one such error in judgment would be full and sufficient justification for cutting short the career of an officer who had already rendered such distinguished service and from whom the people of Canada might well expect to have additional valuable service rendered.'[125]

General Pearkes also read an extract from a letter to Brigadier Connelly from the UN commander thanking him for his 'outstanding service' to the United Nations during his tour of duty in Japan, and another to Mr Claxton from Major-General Riley F. Ennis, the American G-2 in Tokyo, in which Ennis expressed regret that the brigadier had been recalled and attributed to him a long list of excellent qualities.[126]

Except to inquire vainly into the manner in which General Pearkes had obtained these documents, Mr Claxton refused to be drawn. Mr Pearson was not in the House, but on 8 December he made it bluntly clear that neither he nor his department had 'made any representations, oral or written, formal or informal, to the Department of National Defence about Brigadier Connelly and the Koje incident at any time.' Neither he nor his department had 'had anything whatever to do with this retirement.'[127] It is clear now that External Affairs officials sympathized with the brigadier's plight and thought him to be an innocent political scapegoat. The decision had in fact been made by the minister of national defence on the insistent advice of the military.[128] In any case Mr Pearson's statement was the last official word on what had become a volatile, if short-lived, quarrel in Canadian-American relations.

In the meantime the long and dreary sessions at Panmunjom continued without progress. On 8 May Admiral Joy had requested that he be relieved as senior UNC negotiator in the event that the Communists rejected his package proposal of 28 April, and on Joy's own recommendation he was replaced on 22 May by Major-General William K. Harrison, jr, of the US army. Like his

---

125 Ibid., 211-12
126 Ibid., 212
127 Ibid., 8 Dec. 1952, 418
128 Confidential sources

predecessor, General Harrison faced in subsequent months a bewildering variety of propaganda allegations and looked on helplessly as the discussions were transformed into little more than competitions in the delivery of invective. The UN Command was accused of waging bacteriological warfare against the people of Korea and mainland China, of making use of prisoners of war to test the destructive capabilities of atomic weapons, of applying gruesome tortures to its captives on Koje Island and elsewhere, of conducting repeated violations of the neutral zone in the conference area, and so on.

These charges were not entirely without effect elsewhere in the world. The bacteriological warfare allegations were especially credible to some audiences, not least because of the presence of genuine epidemics of disease in North Korea.[129] But although the accusations were repeated with regularity in the Soviet press after January 1952, they did not directly arouse the public interest of Canadian authorities until late in the spring of the same year. Their concern at that time was due almost entirely to the activities of Dr James G. Endicott, a fifty-four-year-old former United Church minister who was then full-time national chairman of the Canadian Peace Congress, widely regarded as a Communist 'front' organization.[130] The first indication that Dr Endicott was involved in the germ warfare controversy appeared on 24 March, when he wired the secretary of state for external affairs from China that his 'personal investigations' had produced evidence of large-scale bacteriological attacks on the mainland Chinese.[131] Shortly thereafter, on 10 April, he held a press conference in Mukden which was subsequently broadcast over Peking Radio. In it he was reported to have claimed that infected insects were being bred for

129 Vatcher, *Panmunjom,* 156-7. The charges were supported also by germ warfare 'confessions' obtained by the North Korean and Chinese authorities from captured American pilots.

130 Dr Endicott qualified in many respects as an 'old China hand.' He had graduated with an MA from Victoria College in Toronto in 1925, and after being ordained went to China as a missionary for a period that was to last twenty-one years. From 1938 to 1941 he had acted as an adviser to Chiang Kai-shek, but had changed his political views during the remaining years of World War II. He had been well regarded by the Canadian ambassador in Chungking, Major-General Victor Odlum, who had made it a practice to forward Endicott's correspondence to Ottawa as representative of an independent point of view. In 1946 Dr Endicott resigned from the church when his superiors protested his participation in student political demonstrations against the Chiang Kai-shek regime, and after returning to Canada he began publishing, early in 1948, a four-page left-wing periodical entitled the *Canadian Far Eastern Newsletter.* He became chairman of the Peace Congress in 1949. See Fraser, 'How Dr Endicott Fronts for the Reds,' 7-9, 49

131 Wood, *Strange Battleground,* 199. Colonel Wood cites as his source, *External Affairs Records,* 'Chronological History, Bacteriological Campaign.' There seems to be some doubt, however, about the 24 March date, since a later Endicott communication quoted by Mr Pearson in the House suggests that Endicott's first cable was sent on 1 April. See Canada, House of Commons,

American military use at the Suffield Experimental Station in Alberta. Later he publicly repudiated these reports, but nevertheless continued to arouse the attention of the press after his return to Canada by accusing the Americans of bacteriological atrocities.

On 21 April Mr Diefenbaker raised the matter in the House of Commons, asking in particular whether the government had investigated Dr Endicott's 'dastardly statement' about Canadian participation in the production of germ warfare materials. Mr Stuart S. Garson, the minister of justice, requested time to investigate.[132] After further inquiries in the House, Mr Pearson on 12 May issued a 'statement on behalf of the government.' He began by saying that the government accepted entirely the official denials of the charges by the American secretary of state and the UN Secretary-General. So far as the Canadian position was concerned, it was 'a slanderous falsehood to say that Canada has participated in any way in any form of germ warfare' It was 'equally false and equally slanderous, but more cowardly and despicable, to imply without stating it in so many words that Canada is making any preparations in this field except for defence against such warfare.' The fact that the Communists had refused to accept proposals put forward by the UN countries with forces in Korea that the germ warfare charges be made the subject of an investigation by the International Red Cross or the World Health Organization was proof of their bad faith. Members of the Communist party and their fellow travellers would 'condemn in unmeasured terms the policies of their own and other free countries,' while propagating 'any lie, however vicious, which is uttered against their own country and its friends on behalf of soviet communist imperialism.' 'Some of these persons,' Mr Pearson went on, 'have a passion for publicity, and I do not wish to minister to that passion by referring to them by name. As long as they are Canadians they have the rights, of course, of Canadian citizenship, but within the law. If they break the law they can be punished. However, we should, I suggest, be careful not to make martyrs of them in a way which would only make them more dangerous to us and more useful to the communists. It is, I think, a small price to pay for freedom and for the preservation of human rights to permit such persons to condemn and discredit themselves by their own malicious and false statements as long as they stay within the law.'[133]

Debates, 12 May 1952, 2102. Dr. Endicott's decision to appeal directly to Mr Pearson may have reflected the fact that the Pearson and Endicott families had been acquainted through their common interest in the United Church, and the two men had at one time corresponded on a first name basis. See Fraser, 'How Dr. Endicott Fronts for the Reds,' 48

132 Canada, House of Commons, Debates, 21 April 1952, 1427

133 Ibid., 12 May 1952, 2101-2

Pressed by Mr Drew specifically on the Endicott case, Mr Pearson acknowledged that he had received a telegram in which Dr Endicott had asked for an opportunity to make a personal report to the minister before issuing a public statement. On Mr Pearson's authorization, the acting under-secretary had replied as follows: 'I have been instructed by the Secretary of State for External Affairs to forward to you the attached summaries of statements which you are reported to have made during your recent visit to Europe and to China. This is the most accurate report of these statements which we have been able to secure and I am directed to ask you whether you confirm or deny or wish to amend the statements contained in them which you are reported to have made.'[134]

Dr Endicott then announced to the press that he had been sent a 'questionnaire' by the department, which he did not intend to answer. Instead he planned to seek a personal discussion with Mr Pearson himself. He thereupon dispatched a letter to the minister in which he indicated that he would shortly be giving public addresses on 'the use of germ warfare by the United States' forces against the Chinese people' to audiences in Massey Hall and in Maple Leaf Gardens in Toronto. 'I would welcome,' he wrote, 'a chance to present the facts to which I was a witness both to you and to the external affairs Committee, as well as to the Canadian people.' As regards the questionnaire, he had 'been unable to trace any authority possessed by your department which gives the right to question Canadian citizens in such a way.' The purpose of the questions was unclear, and until the situation was clarified he 'must decline to submit to cross-examination from your officials.'[135] Mr Pearson refused to grant the interview.

This report seemed generally to satisfy the opposition, but Mr Drew wanted to know whether Dr Endicott could not be prosecuted under recently revised sections of the Criminal Code, in view of the fact that his statements might have been accepted by some Canadians and could therefore be having 'a damaging effect upon the state of mind of many of our people.' Mr Garson, the minister of justice, replied that the matter was still under 'very serious consideration' by a committee in his department, but he would have an opinion 'shortly.'[136]

---

134 Quoted ibid., 2102
135 Ibid.
136 Ibid., 2103. Changes had been introduced in the Criminal Code in 1951 in order to adapt certain of its provisions to a situation in which Canadian forces were engaged in combat without being officially at war with a legally defined enemy. The revision to which Mr Drew referred was the addition of the following subsection to the section in the code which defines the crime of treason: 'Treason is ... (i) assisting, while in or out of Canada, any enemy at war

In practice Mr Drew's fears appear to have been misplaced. On 20 September the Canadian Institute of Public Opinion was to issue the results of a poll in which respondents had been asked whether they thought that reports that the United States was using germ warfare in Korea were true. Only 3 per cent answered that they were 'definitely true' and only 10 per cent that they 'may be true.' A further 19 per cent thought they were 'probably false' and 52 per cent believed they were 'absolutely false.' The balance had no opinion.[137]

But if Dr Endicott's charges were lacking in credibility, they were not thereby deprived of publicity, and his speeches in Maple Leaf Gardens and elsewhere were given wide coverage in the press during May and June. This led to further inquiries in the House of Commons – on 18, 20, and 23 June – on the question of whether or not he would be prosecuted. Finally Mr Garson reported on 25 June that his department had decided to take no action. This was partly because it was 'probable that the ringleaders of the Communist conspiracy would like us to prosecute their dupes and tools such as Dr Endicott,' since prosecution 'would give them more publicity and might give them the appearance of martyrs.' So far as Dr Endicott himself was concerned, 'a prosecution and conviction could add little to the discredit he has already brought upon himself by allying himself with the forces of oppression, terror and atheism.' Furthermore, the government was anxious not to do anything to damage the principles of free speech and free press, in spite of the fact that Dr Endicott had consistently subjected these principles to abuse.[138]

Two days later Mr Garson tabled in the Commons a joint statement by three independent Canadian entomologists which demolished the evidence presented by the Chinese and by Dr Endicott in support of the germ warfare allegation.[139] The Conservatives raised briefly the possibility of prosecution once again on 3 July, but Parliament went into summer recess on the following day and there was no further debate. Elsewhere, public interest declined as it became clear that the Chinese were unwilling to expose their charges to the test of neutral investigation.

While the government thus dealt with the repercussions in Canada of the Communist propaganda effort, the armistice negotiations continued to flound-

with Canada, or any armed forces against whom Canadian forces are engaged in hostilities whether or not a state of war exists between Canada and the country whose forces they are, or ... ' Quoted in Mr Garson's reply to Mr Drew, ibid., 2104
137 Canadian Institute of Public Opinion, 'Three Per Cent of Canadians Think "Germ War" Charges True,' release, 20 Sept. 1952
138 Canada, House of Commons, *Debates,* 25 June 1952, 3673-4
139 Ibid., 27 June 1952, 3864

er. On 7 June General Harrison on Mark Clark's orders informed his opponents that the UN delegation would not return to the conference table until 11
June.[140] As the summer wore on, recesses of this kind increased both in
number and in length, until on 8 October the talks were suspended for an
indefinite period. As Harrison put it to his opposite number: 'The United
Nations Command has no further proposals to make. The proposals we have
made remain open. The UNC delegation will not come here merely to listen
to abuse and false propaganda. The UNC is therefore calling a recess. We are
not terminating these armistice negotiations, we are merely recessing them. We
are willing to meet with you again at any time that you are ready to accept
one of our proposals or to make a constructive proposal of your own, in
writing, which could lead to an honourable armistice ... I have nothing more
to say. Since you have nothing constructive we stand in recess.'[141]

Six days later, on 14 October, the General Assembly began its Seventh
Session in New York, the first in its new and permanent headquarters. Its
president was the Canadian secretary of state for external affairs. Confronted
by the virtual collapse of the negotiations at Panmunjom, it resumed consideration of the problem of a cease-fire in Korea for the first time since the passage
of the resolution of 1 February 1951. The ensuing discussions were not entirely
welcomed by American policy-makers, who were in pursuit of continued
support for their armistice terms. Unhappily for them, as their secretary of
state later observed, this was an objective which 'required holding the British
steadily on course with us, keeping the support of the Latin American and
European states, a group that could defeat any harmful proposal and was
essential to any useful one, and, finally, guarding against proposals of two
adroit operators, Krishna Menon of India, leader of the Arab-Asian states, and
Lester B. Pearson of Canada, President of the Assembly.'[142]

The first public hint of official Canadian disapproval of the decision to
suspend the negotiations came on 17 October in a general address to the
Plenary Session by Paul Martin, the leader of the Canadian delegation. While
commiserating with the UN Command negotiators, 'whose patience has been
so sorely tried in these past months,' and while expressing the 'hope that we
at this Assembly will not complicate' their task, he noted also that his delegation would 'take it as a fundamental premise that present hostilities must be
limited to the Korean peninsula and that the search for an orderly settlement
of those hostilities by negotiation must be continued.' The sole purpose of the

140 Clark, *From the Danube to the Yalu,* 107-8. See Vatcher, *Panmunjom,* 162-3, for the texts
of the exchange.
141 Quoted in Vatcher, *Panmunjom,* 166-7
142 Acheson, *Present at the Creation,* 696

UN intervention – 'resisting and defeating aggression' – had been achieved, or would be if a truce could be 'negotiated on the basis of the present battle lines.'[143]

The first of several resolutions on the POW repatriation issue was prepared by the Americans. It was introduced in the Political Committee on 24 October under the co-sponsorship of the United States and twenty other countries, Canada and Britain among them. After noting 'with approval' the tentative agreements already concluded, and the efforts taken by the UNC to 'achieve a just and honourable armistice,' the resolution called upon the Chinese and North Korean regimes 'to avert further bloodshed by having their negotiators agree to an armistice which recognizes the rights of all prisoners of war to an unrestricted opportunity to be repatriated and avoids the use of force in their repatriation.'[144] This amounted to little more than an attempt to re-emphasize the principle of non-forcible repatriation, and to give the UN negotiators the moral support of the organization upon whose behalf they were at work. To that extent it was of limited significance. As Mr Martin told the committee on 3 November, it had one specific objective, 'to impress upon the enemy the determination of Member States of the United Nations to protect the interests of the individual in a situation of peril as they resolved in 1950 to protect an infant State against the peril of aggression.' Within the limits set by the resolution's basic principle, however, it did not preclude concrete new proposals 'which might lead to an armistice.' Mexico had already 'submitted a draft resolution which ... was inspired by the highest motives of statesmanship and humanity,' and it 'might profitably be studied further.' The Assembly should be receptive to other possibilities.[145]

This amiably flexible posture was the consequence of several days of private diplomatic conversations. Mr Pearson early in the session had discussed with the Canadian delegation the possibility of introducing a resolution dealing explicitly with POW repatriation, incorporating within it the principles of the twenty-one power draft. He had also suggested this possibility to the British and the Americans. But before the idea had been more precisely defined, Krishna Menon of India had initiated an inquiry of his own with Pearson, Martin, and Padillo Nervo of Mexico. From this conversation there emerged agreement that, while the principle of non-forcible repatriation should be

---

143 Department of External Affairs, *Statements and Speeches,* no 52/39
144 For the text of the resolution, see United Nations, GAOR (Annexes Seventh Session, Agenda 16), Document A/C.1/725, 29
145 Department of External Affairs, 'Statement on Korea,' *External Affairs,* IV, 11, Nov. 1952, 389

adhered to, the right of repatriation should also be recognized, and that the entire repatriation process might best be supervised by a neutral agency.[146]

While this proposal was being more fully developed, a Soviet resolution introduced on 29 October and providing in effect for the postponement of any settlement of the repatriation question until after the conclusion of 'an immediate and complete cease-fire,' was defeated in the Political Committee by a vote of 41 to 5, with 12 abstentions.[147] The Mexican resolution mentioned by Mr Martin was introduced on 2 November, and a Peruvian proposal was presented two days later, but neither of these played a significant role in subsequent debate. The diplomatic contest was thus reduced to a competition between the American twenty-one power draft on the one hand, and the Indian alternative on the other.[148]

Dean Acheson was first alerted to the 'plan Krishna Menon was hatching' by Selwyn Lloyd, the British minister of state, on 28 October. He took a dim view of it. The idea, as he later described it, 'was to turn the prisoners over to a commission under vague instructions looking toward repatriation.' This, Menon had argued, 'would produce an armistice and any arguments about its administration would be between the Communists and the 'protecting powers' – that is, the commission – rather than with the United Nations Command.' Acheson 'strongly opposed this nebulous idea, which had every vice, since the Eighth Army would have to control the prisoners and bear all the risks of a breakdown in the armistice without any control over the administration of the vital prisoner-release part of it.' In a conversation with Pearson on 31 October he discovered that the Canadian 'had joined the cabal too.'[149]

The reconciliation of the opposing positions now became a principal preoccupation of Anglo-Canadian diplomacy. There ensued a series of discussions which involved, among others, Acheson, Menon, Pearson, Martin, and Lloyd, together for a time with Anthony Eden and Robert Schuman, the foreign ministers respectively of Britain and France. From his exchanges with Pearson, Menon, and Lloyd, Acheson concluded 'that Menon, using his fuzziness

---

146 Pearson, letter to the author, 13 Nov. 1968
147 United Nations, GAOR (First Committee), A/C.1/SR.536, 184. The text of the resolution is available ibid. (Annexes Seventh Session, Agenda 16), Document A/C.1/729, 30
148 There were a number of other draft resolutions – notably one initiated by the Indonesians – in private circulation, but these were never brought into open discussion.
149 Acheson, *Present at the Creation,* 700. By this time the Menon proposal had been widely discussed among Commonwealth delegations, and Mr Pearson can still recall Mr Acheson's resulting displeasure. Letter to the author, 13 Nov. 1968. Krishna Menon reports that the Americans 'were very angry' because he had outflanked the twenty-one power resolution of which they were the primary advocates. See Brecher, *India and World Politics,* 37

of expression and unwillingness to furnish any written text as handmaidens of deception, had enmeshed the other two in a proposal that was an about-face ... Though none of the three would be candid, the result of their proposal seemed to be that those prisoners who agreed would be repatriated, and those who did not would be held prisoners until they did agree. In this way the principle of repatriation and of the negation of force both appeared to be observed.' The secretary was 'now almost ready for a showdown, first with the conspirators, and then in the General Assembly.' The twenty-one power draft 'was intended to get Assembly support for the terms submitted at Panmunjom on September 28 and rejected, thus leaving our position with strong international support for our successors in office [that is, the Republican administration of General Eisenhower] when they took over on January 20, 1953. Menon's attempt was to transfer the writing of the armistice terms from Panmunjom and the United Nations Command to New York and the General Assembly under the leadership of India and the Arab-Asian bloc with British and Canadian support. We were determined to prevent this.' He therefore asked President Truman for instructions, and was rewarded with a presidential stipulation 'that the United States Government will strongly oppose any resolution which does not clearly affirm and support the principle of non-forcible repatriation.'[150]

Confronted by so determined a resistance, Mr Pearson and Mr Martin suggested a number of changes in the Indian draft, which had at last appeared in writing, in an attempt to make it more palatable to the American delegation.[151] In explaining Canada's role in helping to reconcile the Indian and American positions, Mr Menon subsequently remarked that the

matter was handled by Paul Martin. The main role he played was to push me rather than push the other side. I had to amend my own resolution two or three times in some details under his pressure. I brought the period of explanation down to three months, for instance, which created difficulties for me but did not affect the basic principles. In fact, they told me from Delhi, after I had got agreement, that it need not have been done. We added two clauses – by that time I had come to the conclusion that the thing was to get an agreement – and one or two amendments which were quite unnecessary were agreed to by me. I believe myself that Canada feared that the thing might break down altogether. It was probably Paul Martin's first entry into this business. Mr Pearson was not handling it.[152]

150 Acheson, *Present at the Creation,* pp. 700-1
151 Pearson, letter to the author, 13 Nov. 1968. See also Ronning, 'Canada and the United Nations,' in Gordon, *Canada's Role as a Middle Power,* 40
152 Brecher, *India and World Politics,* 38

The Indian resolution was finally presented to the Political Committee on 17 November, but it was then still unacceptable to the Americans. At a meeting of the sponsors of the twenty-one power draft, Acheson spoke against it, 'but offered to amend ours to incorporate a repatriation commission, provided it had a neutral chairman with powers of effective executive action.' However, 'Eden and Pearson argued for taking Menon's resolution as a basis and carried a majority with them.' Acheson had to be content with an agreement that the United States should draft a revision of the Menon proposal for a small group which had been established to revise its wording.[153]

Hoping to strengthen his bargaining position, the American secretary of state within forty-eight hours managed to secure a statement from a spokesman for the incoming Republican administration committing General Eisenhower to the principle of non-forcible repatriation.[154] In the meantime the 'struggle with the British and Canadians went on in and out of the group of twenty-one, and took the form of a debate not only as to how far amendments should go but also whether the Menon resolution should be given priority and whether this should be done before or after amendment.' Both 'Eden and Pearson feared that Menon might withdraw his resolution – which had become the accepted vehicle of action – if it was treated severely.' Acheson was by now 'unwilling to trust anyone.'[155] Mr Pearson's perception, on the other hand, was that the Canadian and British delegations were merely performing mediatory roles, acting as a 'go-between' with 'India on the one side and the Americans on the other.'[156]

At the height of these heated discussions, Acheson paid a previously scheduled state visit to Ottawa. Pearson had planned originally to go with him, 'but at the last moment sent word that his duties as President of the Assembly precluded it.' As Acheson later observed, 'By separating, each left his rear exposed to hostile action, but I left an energetic and able lieutenant, Ambassador Ernest Gross, in charge in New York, while both Pearson and his aide [Paul Martin] were there, leaving Ottawa exposed.'[157] The Secretary tried to make the most of his opportunity. Invited to a meeting of the Canadian Cabinet on the morning of Saturday, 22 November, he chose to offer some comments on 'the problems that the new mass diplomacy posed in conducting international discussion through assemblies and public debate.' The legislative procedures of democratic countries were 'very ill adapted to ... international

153 Acheson, *Present at the Creation*, 702
154 Ibid.
155 Ibid., 703
156 Pearson, letter to the author, 13 Nov. 1968
157 Acheson, *Present at the Creation*, 703

meetings,' and he had been struck in particular by 'the vast separation that existed between the few with the responsibility and capability for taking whatever action might be necessary and the many not only willing but eager to prescribe what that action should be and how it should be managed.' A case in point was the prisoner-of-war issue then being discussed in New York, where opinion ran counter to the American military view that there were 'dangers' in 'an armistice unaccompanied by a prompt and complete disposition of the prisoners, of whom tens of thousands would fight repatriation or indefinite captivity.'

Brooke Claxton interrupted to observe that he and many others thought the American generals were wrong, to which Acheson replied that this merely proved his point. 'Our generals were on the spot and in command – at the request of the United Nations – of six American divisions and twelve Korean divisions, equipped, trained, and supported by us, who with welcome but token assistance from others were fighting this war.' In his view, 'the military opinion that should be listened to was that which bore the responsibility of command.' According to Acheson's account, Prime Minister St Laurent agreed, and the discussion went on to other things. 'The point,' Acheson wrote later, in an apparent over-estimation of the prime minister's personal involvement, 'had been made where it counted, and no more talk seemed necessary.'

Early on Sunday, 23 November, the secretary returned to New York, where 'high agitation reigned.'[158] That morning, largely as a result of comments made during a press conference by Ernest Gross, a report of serious differences between the United States and Great Britain on the issue of the Indian resolution appeared on the front page of the Sunday edition of the *New York Times,* a discomfiting development which Acheson perceived as having a moderating effect upon Mr Pearson.[159] Later that afternoon the group of twenty-one met in the offices of the American delegation on Park Avenue to discuss Menon's most recent draft. The latter went part of the way towards meeting Acheson's objections by stipulating that in the event that the post-armistice political conference was unable to agree on the disposition of prisoners who did not wish to be repatriated, the United Nations would itself assume responsibility for their care and maintenance 'until the end of their detention.' But the American secretary of state felt that still further changes were required in order to ensure that the prisoners would not be incarcerated indefinitely. He also believed that the necessary alterations could be made immediately. Selwyn

158 Ibid., 704
159 See 'US and Britain Split Openly in UN on Indian Truce Plan; Eden Rejects Amendments,' *New York Times,* 23 Nov. 1952; and Acheson, *Present at the Creation,* 705

Lloyd, on the other hand, took the view that Menon ought to be given another chance to produce an acceptable compromise draft, and Acheson was forced with reluctance to agree.[160] On the following day, 24 November, the Soviet ambassador to the United Nations, Andrei Y. Vishinsky, altered the entire picture by vigorously denouncing the Indian initiative, thereby persuading the bulk of the UN membership that the enterprise would ultimately bear little fruit. With the stakes thus reduced to inconsequence, the disputants could afford to be flexible.[161] When the twenty-one co-sponsors of the American resolution met again on 25 November, they were able to agree that although their own draft had appeared first, the Indian resolution should receive priority in the voting. The Americans still insisted upon having a cut-off date for the final release of all non-repatriated POWs, and for a time this continued to delay a settlement. On the following day, however, agreement was reached when Menon produced a draft deleting the reference to the 'detention' of unrepatriated POWs, and providing that in the event the political conference had not settled the matter within sixty days of its meeting, the disposition of the prisoners would be assumed by the United Nations itself. Subsequently, on the suggestion of the Danes, the waiting period was reduced to thirty days.

In its final form, the resolution thus requested the president of the General Assembly to forward a series of proposals to the Chinese and North Korean regimes which included the following important features: first, that a Repatriation Commission be established consisting of representatives of Czechoslovakia, Poland, Sweden, and Switzerland, or alternatively of representatives of four states not participating in the hostilities, two to be nominated by each side, excluding the permanent members of the Security Council; secondly, that this commission assume custody, in demilitarized zones, of all prisoners of war held by both sides; thirdly, that the Commission arrange for the speedy return to their homelands of all those prisoners wishing it, but that fourthly, the commission be entrusted also with the duty of ensuring that force 'shall not be used against the prisoners of war to prevent or effect their return to their homelands'; fifthly, that each party to the conflict have an opportunity 'to explain to the prisoners of war ... their rights and to inform the prisoners of war on any matter relating to their return to their homelands and particularly their full freedom to return'; sixthly, that the prisoners themselves were simi-

160 See '21 Lands Ask India For Clarification of New Korea Plan,' *New York Times,* 24 Nov. 1952; and Acheson, *Present at the Creation,* 705
161 Acheson's view was that Vishinsky's speech had united the allies in part by undercutting Menon. Acheson, *Present at the Creation,* 705. See also 'Vishinsky Rejects India's Truce Plan, Insists on His Own,' *New York Times,* 25 Nov. 1952

larly to 'have freedom and facilities to make representations and communications to the Repatriation Commission and to bodies and agencies working under the Repatriation Commission, and to inform any or all such bodies of their desires on any matter concerning themselves, in accordance with arrangements made for the purpose by the Commission.' Finally, the resolution provided for the POWs who refused to return home:

> At the end of ninety days after the Armistice Agreement has been signed the disposition of any prisoners of war whose return to their homelands may not have been effected in accordance with the procedure set out in these proposals, or as otherwise agreed, shall be referred with recommendations for their disposition, including a target date for termination of their detention to the political conference to be called as provided under article 60 of the draft armistice agreement. If at the end of a further thirty days there are any prisoners of war whose return to their homelands has not been effected under the above procedures or whose future has not been provided for by the political conference, the responsibility for their care and maintenance and for their subsequent disposition shall be transferred to the United Nations, which in all matters relating to them shall act strictly in accordance with international law. [162]

Such was the formula by which the quarrel had been resolved. But Mr Martin's defence of it before the Political Committee on 27 November revealed his awareness that, for the time being at least, it was an empty victory. The Canadian delegation, he said, had viewed the Indian initiative 'with real enthusiasm and renewed hope' as a means of bridging the gap which had developed in Panmunjom with respect to prisoners of war. 'We believed when the Indian draft resolution was first introduced, as we still believe today, that it was a practical and positive effort to implement' the more important ideas which have been brought before this Committee' with respect to the POW problem. Indeed, his delegation still regarded 'the Indian proposals as the possible bridge which may provide for communication between the opposing views and which may lead to an understanding upon which real agreement can be based,' but it was obvious from the flavour of his remarks that he was not optimistic. [163] As Mr Pearson later explained to the House of Commons, the process of overcoming the differences which had developed between the United States and other members of the United Nations had been 'made less difficult ... by the Soviet attitude toward the resolution, which was one of complete,

162 See United Nations, GAOR (Annexes Seventh Session, Agenda 16), Document A/2278, especially 40-2
163 Department of External Affairs, *Statements and Speeches,* no 52/53

unalterable and violent opposition.'[164] But the Soviet reaction meant also that the initiative had little chance of success.

The Americans had thus discovered once again that United Nations support for their enterprises abroad did not come entirely free of charge, and that Canada was prominent among those in the habit of collecting the fee. Confronted by so determined a band of creditors, they had given way, although not without exacting compromises in return. On 3 December the Indian resolution was passed in the General Assembly by a vote of 54 to 5 (Soviet bloc), with one abstention (Nationalist China). Yet in the short run they had lost very little, for the Soviet attitude turned out to be an accurate measure of the Chinese response. Mr Pearson in his capacity as president of the General Assembly forwarded the resolution to the Chinese and North Korean authorities on 5 December with his 'personal appeal' that they give it their 'most thoughtful and sympathetic consideration.'[165] In a cable dated 14 December, Chou En-lai replied that the General Assembly had 'adopted a resolution supporting the United States Government's position of forcibly retaining in captivity prisoners of war in contravention of international conventions, and facilitating the continuation and expansion of the war now raging in Korea.' Such an action was 'clearly illegal and void and [was] firmly opposed by the Chinese people.' Following these observations was a stream of propaganda invective directed against the United States, the General Assembly, and the UN Command's treatment of prisoners of war. The message was followed three days later by a similar response from North Korea.[166]

From the beginning, Mr Pearson had not expected very much. His own objectives were merely to derive a formula which incorporated the principle that no POW should be compelled either to defect or to return home, to outline a mechanism through which this principle could be implemented in practice, to win for a resolution embodying these ingredients the support of all the non-Communist members of the United Nations, and especially of those from Asia, and in consequence also to make it clear where the responsibility for the continuation of the hostilities actually lay. The proposed solution would then be available for implementation at such time as the Communists became genuinely motivated to reach a settlement.[167] It was obvious now that the time had not yet come.

---

164 Department of External Affairs, *Statements and Speeches,* no 52/54
165 United Nations, GAOR (Annexes Seventh Session, Agenda 16), Document A/2354, especially 45-6
166 The Chinese and North Korean replies are reproduced ibid., 47-52
167 Pearson, letter to the author, 13 Nov. 1968. See also his statement in Canada, House of Commons, *Debates,* 11 Feb. 1953, 1848

With the arrival of the Chinese and North Korean replies the United Nations resumed its customary passive role in the conduct of the armistice negotiations, and the responsibility for undertaking new cease-fire initiatives came to rest once again with the UN Command. For Washington this responsibility had now become a heavy burden, for the horror of a war that maimed and killed but did not bring results had produced in the United States an angry public clamour which could no longer be ignored. During the presidential election campaign of the autumn of 1952, the Republicans had regarded the unsettled war in Korea – 'Truman's War,' as some of them termed it – as one of their strongest political weapons,[168] and they made the most of it. The climax of their efforts was contained in a speech delivered by Eisenhower on 24 October in which the general promised that the 'first task of a new Administration will be to review and re-examine every course of action open to us with one goal in view: to bring the Korean War to an early and honourable end,' and in which he pledged to advance this purpose, should he be elected, by taking a personal trip to Korea.[169] In the polling on 5 November he received 33 million votes to Stevenson's 27 million, not least because of his promise to make peace in the Far East. The president-elect visited the theatre during the first week of December, and assumed the formal responsibility for making good his campaign promise upon his inauguration in the following month.

In pursuing an armistice, the Republican administration enjoyed a number of advantages which had not been available to its Democratic predecessor. Not least among them was the fact that the Republicans had acquired their power at about the same time as the stalemate in the theatre was losing its profitability for the other side. The Communist negotiators by the winter of 1952-3 had obtained about as much in the way of propaganda benefits from the armistice talks as they could hope to achieve, and thereafter their returns were bound to diminish. They had successfully demonstrated their capacity to hold a sophisticated western army at bay – at least in the context of a limited war – and they had obviously achieved their objective of preventing the unification of Korea under American or United Nations auspices. The perpetuation of the deadlock was unlikely to produce still further gains, but it would inevitably involve a continuing drain on Chinese manpower and economic resources at a time when the Peking government was anxious to stabilize its internal position. The changes in Sino-Soviet policy which were encouraged by these conditions were accelerated, moreover, by the death of Stalin on 5 March 1953.

168 'One of our strongest weapons,' Sherman Adams later wrote of the Republican campaign, 'was the unsettled Korean War, which some Republican orators had been calling "Truman's War." ' See his *Firsthand Report*, 42

169 For an account of how this speech was developed, see the reminiscences of its principal author, E.J. Hughes, in his *The Ordeal of Power*, 32-5. See also Adams, *Firsthand Report*, 42-4

The changes may have been accelerated also by the expectation that the new government in Washington would be more intractably belligerent than its predecessor in conducting the cold war in general, and the Korean War in particular. This expectation had been cultivated assiduously both during and after the election campaign by the new secretary of state, John Foster Dulles, who had the support not only of right-wing elements in the Republican camp but also of General Eisenhower himself. An attempt to intensify the psychological effect of this situation upon the enemy was initiated in the president's first State of the Union message on 2 February, thirteen days after his inauguration. During the course of his address Eisenhower observed that the American Seventh Fleet had been instructed in June 1950 to prevent attacks upon the island of Formosa, and also to insure that Formosa would not be used as a base for attacking mainland China. Since the time of that order the Chinese had invaded Korea and recently had rejected the UN armistice proposals sponsored by India. Consequently there was 'no longer any logic or sense in a condition that required the United States Navy to assume defensive responsibilities on behalf of the Chinese Communists, thus permitting those Communists, with greater impunity, to kill our soldiers and those of our United Nations allies in Korea.' The president would therefore issue 'instructions that the Seventh Fleet no longer be employed to shield Communist China.' The order did not imply an 'aggressive intent,' but the United States had 'no obligation to protect a nation fighting in Korea.'[170]

This announcement had considerable impact in the United States, where it was widely assumed that the Republicans had 'unleashed' the Chiang Kai-shek regime against the mainland Chinese. It did not go unnoticed, either, by some of America's allies. In Britain Anthony Eden told the House of Commons on 3 February that the Foreign Office had protested the decision and had warned that it might 'have very unfortunate political repercussions without compensating military advantages.'[171] Prime Minister Nehru of India complained that it intensified 'the fear psychosis of the world.'[172] In Ottawa, Mr Pearson at first confined himself in the House of Commons to a relatively mild public reproof in the form of a reiteration of the Canadian view that the defence of Formosa should not be 'confused' with the defence of Korea, and that the island 'should be neutralized, so far as that is possible, while hostilities continue.'[173] So unexcited was the official Canadian response that the *Washington Post* was moved to point out in admiration that the deneutralization

170 Quoted in Donovan, *Eisenhower,* 28
171 Quoted ibid., 29
172 Quoted ibid.
173 Canada House of Commons, *Debates,* 5 Feb. 1953, 1639

announcement had aroused in Canada little of the uneasiness reported from parts of Europe. This was particularly significant because the United States could 'usually rely on Canada for realism in foreign affairs as well as plain speaking when the occasion demands it.'[174] Mr Pearson later conceded, however, that Canada had taken 'steps at once through our ambassador in Washington to make immediate inquiries as to what it [the announcement] involved, what the implications were, if any, and to discuss the matter with the state department.' The government regretted that the Americans had 'found it necessary to take this action.' He was 'not condemning them for it,' but he regretted that they thought it necessary, given that 'the military advantages ... might be neutralized by the political disadvantages.'[175]

This was Anthony Eden's echo, but the alarm it signified was less, for Mr Pearson went on to suggest that the situation in 1953 was very different from that in June 1950, not least because the Chinese had intervened in the war. He had had conversations with Mr Dulles the day before (15 February) and had acquainted him with the Canadian viewpoint on Far East affairs. Dulles had advised him of the background of the American decision, and Mr Pearson thought 'we should do our best to understand the United States position ... and to appreciate their anxiety over the stalemate which has developed.' In return, the Americans should appreciate, as he believed they did, the Canadian desire to avoid an extension of the hostilities.[176] Privately, Mr Pearson thought the deneutralization order might be intended as a tactical manoeuvre to reduce domestic political pressure for tougher action in the war.[177]

Whatever its motives, it is possible that the president's decision did have a salutary effect on the negotiations. On 22 February General Clark dispatched to his opposite number a letter in which he suggested that the two sides arrange to 'repatriate those seriously sick and wounded captured personnel who are fit to travel, in accordance with provisions of Article 109 of the Geneva Convention.'[178] Three weeks after Stalin's death, on 28 March, the general received a reply in which the Communists agreed to his proposal and suggested that 'the reasonable settlement of the question of exchanging sick and injured prisoners of war of both sides during the period of hostilities should be made to lead to the smooth settlement of the entire question of prisoners of war,

174 The *Post*'s editorial was reported by the Reuters news agency and the item was run in the *Ottawa Citizen*, 11 Feb. 1953. It was quoted by H.R. Argue in Canada, House of Commons, *Debates*, 16 Feb. 1953, 1982
175 Canada, House of Commons, *Debates*, 16 Feb. 1953, 1994
176 Ibid.
177 Pearson, letter to the author, 13 Nov. 1968
178 Quoted in Vatcher, *Panmunjom*, 180

thereby achieving an armistice in Korea for which people throughout the world are longing.' They proposed, therefore, that the armistice negotiations be resumed, and that liaison officers from both sides meet in order to arrange an appropriate date.[179] On 2 April the Communists enclosed with correspondence confirming detailed arrangements for the meeting as proposed by General Clark a copy of a statement made by Chou En-lai on 30 March following his return from Stalin's funeral in Moscow. In this statement the Chinese foreign minister noted that the only issue standing in the way of a successful armistice agreement was the question of the release and repatriation of prisoners of war. The Chinese and North Korean governments were 'prepared to take steps to eliminate the differences on this question so as to bring about an armistice.' They therefore proposed 'that both parties to the negotiations should undertake to repatriate immediately after the cessation of hostilities all those prisoners of war in their custody who insist upon repatriation and to hand over the remaining prisoners of war to a neutral state so as to ensure a just solution to the question of their repatriation.'[180]

This was to concede the substance, if not the details, of the Indian resolution, and it led to the fruitful resumption of the armistice negotiations. Liaison officers from the two sides met on 6 April and by 11 April had concluded an agreement for the exchange of sick and wounded prisoners. The exchange – know as 'Operation Little Switch' – began on 20 April and was completed on 26 April. In the meantime, after a further exchange of preliminary correspondence, the negotiations were resumed in plenary session.

At these meetings, the first since 8 October, General Nam Il produced a proposal for resolving the POW issue. It included the following principal features: first, an exchange within two months of the conclusion of the Armistice Agreement of all prisoners wishing repatriation; secondly, the transfer of all remaining prisoners to a neutral state, acceptable to both parties, where for a period of six months the countries involved would have the freedom and facilities to send personnel to discuss with them the question of their return to their homelands; and thirdly, the repatriation within this period of all those POWs who changed their minds after discussion, the remainder to be assigned to the continuing custody of the neutral state pending the settlement of their future at the post-armistice political conference.[181]

The UN Command found two principal faults with this proposal. The first was the requirement that those prisoners who were not repatriated directly be transferred physically to the territory of a neutral state; it was General Harri-

179 Ibid., 180-1
180 Ibid., 181-2
181 The text of the proposal is reproduced ibid., 186-7

son's view that neutral supervision could more conveniently be arranged on Korean soil. The second was the provision that the destiny of those POWs who refused repatriation would ultimately be left to the political conference for decision; since this conference was no more likely to agree than were the armistice negotiators themselves, the prisoners would be left with the choice of returning home or of facing indefinite incarceration. Disagreement developed also on two minor issues: first, on the question of what neutral state or states would be acceptable to both sides; and secondly, on the length of time allowed for 'explanations,' the UN Command taking the view that this should be considerably reduced.

On 7 May the Communists introduced revised proposals which provided for the establishment of a Neutral Nations Repatriation Commission (NNRC) comprised of the four states already named in the Neutral Nations Supervisory Commission, with the addition of India. This commission would take custody of the prisoners in Korea, and its decisions would be reached by majority vote. The explanation time was reduced from six months to four. The fate of those POWs who refused repatriation was still, however, to be decided by the post-armistice political conference.[182]

On 13 May the UN Command countered with still other proposals reducing even further the explanation time and providing that only Indian forces would take actual custody in Korea of the non-repatriates, who would be freed with civilian status after sixty days. The counter-proposals provided also that the Indian representative would act as chairman and executive agent of the NNRC. More importantly, as a palliative to Syngman Rhee, they also provided for the immediate release of all Korean (as opposed to Chinese) non-repatriates upon the conclusion of the armistice.[183]

This last provision was unacceptable not only to the Communists, but also to those members of the United Nations who had been most enthusiastic in their support of the Indian resolution of the previous December. According to Norman Altstedter, 'Canada asked for clarification of what appeared to be differences between the UN Command stand at Panmunjom and the plan backed by the UN Assembly,'[184] and in fact discussions in the Committee of Sixteen in Washington were both vigorous and prolonged.[185] The Americans argued that the Indian proposal had no formal status in Panmunjom because it had been rejected by the Communists at birth. This apparently resulted in criticism that the UN Command negotiators were 'giving the Communists

182 Ibid., 190, and Rees, *Korea,* 416
183 Ibid.
184 Altstedter, 'Problems of Coalition Diplomacy,' 262
185 Campbell, interview, 20 Oct. 1968

ammunition for their propaganda charge that the UN Command did not want a truce.'[186] More generally, it resurrected the belief – always latent among America's allies in the war – that the UNC was acting in defiance of the wishes of its ostensible parent body. When asked about the new proposals in the House of Commons on 14 May, Mr Pearson would concede only that they were 'under discussion' and that until the discussions were completed he 'would prefer to say nothing about them.'[187] This was the last day of the session and the matter therefore did not come up again, but Chester Ronning has confirmed Altstedter's thesis that the State Department was at this time under heavy allied pressure to modify its position. Noting that the Chinese armistice terms were 'almost identical with those outlined in the resolution adopted by the UN.,' and that the United States, 'without taking the time to consult its UN partners in the Korean military action,' had rejected these proposals and put forward a plan of its own which was 'not in line with the UN terms,' Mr Ronning wrote later that

Canada feared that continuation of the war in Korea could have most dangerous consequences. A request which was also supported by the United Kingdom and France, was then made to the USA to offer the terms as given up by the UN. The State Department agreed to modify a few of the American counterproposals but the Communists rejected them. Canada then took the very strong stand that we could not share the responsibility of turning down the possibility of an armistice on our own terms, when the alternative was the continuation of hostilities which were so potentially dangerous to world peace.

To make short the story of the discussions, particularly between Canada and the United States, the President of the United States finally accepted the Canadian view and ordered the American representatives at Panmunjom to offer armistice terms as endorsed by the UN. The armistice in Korea was signed in July, 1953.

Mr Ronning goes on to argue that this Canadian contribution to the Korean armistice 'was fully as important as the Suez success to which greater importance was attached because Korea was away off in Asia.'[188]

If this was really the case, then the quiet of their diplomacy has deprived Canada's public servants of a just round of applause. Certainly their efforts go unrecorded in the literature of the Eisenhower administration and the Korean

186 Altstedter, 'Problems of Coalition Diplomacy,' 263
187 Canada, House of Commons, *Debates,* 14 May 1953, 5352
188 Ronning, 'Canada and the United Nations,' 41-2

War.[189] Indeed, these tough-minded sources attribute the final conclusion of the armistice more to the blunt nuclear posturings of John Foster Dulles than to restraints imposed upon the United States by well-meaning friends.[190] In any case, after high level talks among the allies had taken place in Washington, General Clark was authorized on 23 May to suggest new proposals which provided for the transfer of *all* prisoners to the NNRC in the custody of Indian forces and under an Indian chairman. Those wishing to return home would be repatriated within sixty days, and a further period of ninety to 120 days would be devoted to 'explaining' their position to the non-repatriates. Thereafter they would either be released with civilian status or their future would be otherwise determined by the UN General Assembly. The day before, Mr Dulles had indicated to Prime Minister Nehru in New Delhi that the United States would broaden the war if the proposals were turned down, and his warning was subsequently conveyed by the Indians to Peking.[191]

These proposals were delivered to the Communist negotiators in Panmunjom on 25 May, and with minor modifications they were accepted on 4 June. After changes in detail, the Senior Delegates signed the final 'Terms of Reference' on 8 June. Delays in the proceedings subsequently developed when Syngman Rhee, seeing in the agreement the end of his hopes for a unified and independent Korea, released on 18 June some 27,000 'anti-Communist' North Korean prisoners of war, doubtless in the belief that this might foil the settlement. There was indeed an outcry from the Communist negotiators, but it was no louder than that emanating from capitals in the West,[192] and after the

189 They are not mentioned, for example, in Rees, *Korea*; Vatcher, *Panmunjom*; Turner Joy, *How Communists Negotiate*; Hughes, *The Ordeal of Power*; Adams, *Firsthand Report*; or Donovan, *Eisenhower*. Nor are they referred to in books on John Foster Dulles' conduct of American foreign policy, such as Goold-Adams' *The Time of Power*. John Holmes believes that Mr Ronning's account may to some extent exaggerate the significance of the Canadian role. Communication with the author, August 1969

190 For an account of Dulles' nuclear threats in this context, see Rees, *Korea*, 416-20. Mr Pearson was not aware that the threats were being made, but thought later that the Chinese agreed to an armistice merely because they had no more to gain from the war. Interview, 18 Oct. 1968

191 Rees, *Korea*, 417. Eisenhower believed that this was the decisive factor in bringing about an agreement. Dale Thomson, letter to the author, 3 Dec. 1967

192 The Canadian reaction was as vigorous as any. In a speech at an Ontario political meeting, and in discussions afterwards with reporters, Mr Pearson announced bluntly that Canada was 'under no obligation to support or participate in any operation brought on by the government of the Republic of South Korea and not by decision of the United Nations.' The United Nations was about to discharge its commitment by signing a truce which 'was to have constituted an honorable ending of the fighting.' Now the South Korean government after two years of armistice talks had decided 'to take this disconcerting, distressing and dangerous intervention in Korea.' Its action must be condemned. After all, if the armistice failed through

Americans had disciplined the South Korean president with appropriate inducements,[193] the final armistice agreement was signed on 27 July.

So ended the 'limited war.' Altogether it had cost its protagonists, east and west, more than four million military and civilian casualties – the dead, the wounded, and the missing.[194] Of the nearly 22,000 personnel in the Canadian army, and the more than 3600 in the navy, who saw service in Korea,[195] the final toll was as follows: 11 army officers and 298 other ranks killed in action, died of wounds, or officially presumed dead; 59 officers and 1143 other ranks wounded or injured in action;[196] 91 soldiers killed from non-battle causes; three sailors killed in action; three sailors lost overboard; two army officers and 30 other ranks, together with one RCAF pilot, captured.[197] On 26 November 1953, the minister of national defence, Brooke Claxton, estimated that the *direct* cost of the war to Canada was approximately $200 millions, although if 'you take into account the indirect costs and add in a fair and proper proportion of the overhead for administration and training ... you might easily arrive at a cost to Canada of the Korean War, three, four or five times as great.'[198]

Korea was thus not Canada's most expensive battle, but it showed well enough that even modest roles in world affairs can exact a heavy price.

lack of South Korean co-operation with the UN Command, as Mr Pearson later pointed out in a message to Rhee himself, 'it would be the Korean people who would suffer first and suffer most.' See Ralph Hyman, 'Won't Use Canadians In Civil War: Pearson,' *Globe and Mail*, 19 June 1953; and Walter O'Hearn, 'A Message to Rhee; Pearson's Words Will Echo Far,' *Montreal Star*, 24 June 1953. Government representatives in Washington protested strongly to the American State Department. Campbell, interview, 20 Oct. 1968

193 For a general review of this episode, see Rees, *Korea*, 421-9
194 Ibid., 434
195 Wood, *Strange Battleground*, 257; and Thorgrimsson and Russell, *Canadian Naval Operations in Korean Waters*, 133
196 Wood, *Strange Battleground*, 257-8
197 Masters, *Canada in World Affairs, 1953 to 1955*, 78
198 Canada, House of Commons, *Debates*, 26 Nov. 1953, 360

8

Geneva epilogue

In publicizing his government's 'deep satisfaction' with the armistice in Korea, Prime Minister St Laurent on 26 July also expressed the hope that it would 'lead to a political settlement in that ravaged peninsula, and eventually to a general settlement of outstanding issues in the whole of the Far East.'[1] If the soldiers could rest, the diplomats thus had yet another battle to wage. It was to be even less decisive than the last.

The prime minister's sentiments were shared by Mr Pearson. On the very same day, he announced that he would reconvene the General Assembly on 17 August to prepare the way for a political conference and to deal in addition with the problems of Korean restoration and reconstruction.[2] In the event, however, it was to be a futile exercise. The United Nations was to have as little control over the post-armistice political negotiations as it had had over the original decision to countervail the North Korean attack.

The discussions in the Assembly's Political Committee dealt mainly with the composition of the proposed conference. The play of alternative proposals served merely to divide the Americans once again from their allies. The American representatives took the view in particular that the conference should be attended only by states which had contributed armed forces to the

1 Department of External Affairs press release, 'Statement by the Prime Minister, Mr St Laurent, on the announcement of the signing of an armistice in Korea,' 26 July 1953
2 Department of External Affairs press release, 'Statement by the President of the United Nations General Assembly, Mr. L.B. Pearson, on the announcement of the signing of an armistice in Korea,' 26 July 1953

conduct of the hostilities, and that each participant should be bound only by those decisions or agreements to which it adhered. This, they argued, was in line with the relevant section of the Armistice Agreement (Paragraph 60), which had provided for 'a political conference of a higher level *of both sides.*' The addition of other delegations would only make agreement more difficult to obtain. Moreover, it would broaden the scope of the discussions to the point where settlement even of the Korean question might become impossible. The conference should deal with the Korean issue first; other problems could be considered later or by another meeting.[3] The Americans therefore supported a draft resolution which embodied these principles, and which was introduced by fifteen powers which had contributed armed forces to the UN Command.[4]

The United States position was not shared without qualification, however, by all of the remaining fourteen co-sponsors. In particular, four of the Commonwealth countries objected to the absence of India from the roster of proposed delegations. Australia, Canada, New Zealand, and the United Kingdom accordingly co-sponsored an additional resolution recommending that India, too, participate in the political discussions.[5] The case which was mobilized in support of this proposal by Paul Martin, the leader of the Canadian delegation, was representative of the Commonwealth view. As he told the committee on 19 August, he agreed with the position taken by France, which was that Paragraph 60 of the Armistice Agreement ought not to be taken too literally. It was 'a recommendation of the military commanders,' nothing more. In any case, the UNC 'side' in the conflict was the United Nations itself, and the organization's objective, surely, was to 'get to the Conference those countries who should be there if the Conference is to have its best chance of achieving successful results in terms of the future peace and security of the area.' The Canadian delegation did not 'much care whether you call it a round table or a cross table conference or a polygonal conference'; the important thing was 'to get those who must be there *around* a table.' This was all the more important because the conference would be 'a unique opportunity not only for settling an issue which for the past three years has threatened at any moment to touch off a general conflagration, but for reducing, as a direct consequence of any success in Korea, dangerous tensions in Asia and other parts of the world.' The Canadian government believed 'that the great and growing impor-

3 United Nations, GAOR (First Committee), A/C.1/SR.613, 701 (Mr Lodge)
4 For the text of this resolution see ibid. (Annexes Seventh Session, Agenda 16 continued), Document A/L.151/Rev.1, 3-4. The sixteenth contributing power was South Africa, whose government did not co-sponsor the resolution.
5 Ibid., Document A/L.153, 4

tance of India in Asian affairs and the leading role which she has played in and out of this Assembly in efforts of conciliation, which have greatly facilitated the achievement of the armistice we are now celebrating, entitle her to participate in the Political Conference.' Canada would therefore vote for Indian participation: 'Without belabouring the point,' Mr Martin went on, with reference to the United States, 'I would earnestly appeal to, as the saying goes "absent friends" not to block the participation of any state whose presence is essential for the holding of an effective Conference. It is the responsibility of everyone of us to consider and urge the interests of our own government and people, but no one leader or nation today can, in this interdependent world, legitimately frustrate the will of most of its friends on an issue of not merely local but world-wide importance.'[6]

But the Americans stood firm. The presence of the Indians would incorporate extraneous issues in an already sensitive agenda, and might jeopardize the conference by antagonizing the South Koreans. In any case, New Delhi's relations with Peking were too sympathetic for American taste. In the blunt recollection of a senior Canadian diplomat who at the time was high commissioner to India, 'the Americans were at their most bloody-minded vis-à-vis the Indians in this period.'[7] The result was that the Commonwealth proposal was adopted in the Political Committee on 27 August, but only by an ordinary majority of 27 to 21, with 11 abstentions.[8] This was sufficient to allow the resolution to go before the General Assembly in Plenary Session, but it was clear that it would not there receive the requisite majority of two-thirds, and the Indian delegation therefore requested that it not be put to a vote.[9]

The United States did agree, however, that the conference might include the USSR, although with belligerent rather than with neutral status. Soviet participation had been suggested in an additional draft resolution co-sponsored by Australia, Denmark, New Zealand, and Norway which recommended 'that the Union of Soviet Socialist Republics participate in the Korean political conference provided the other side desires it.'[10] Canada voted in favour of this proposal on the ground that 'it would be quite unrealistic to hold a conference such as we have in mind without the Soviet Union which should take her full

6 Department of External Affairs, *Statements and Speeches*, no 53/34
7 Reid, interview, 9 June 1969
8 See United Nations, GAOR (First Committee), A/C.1/SR.613, especially Mr Lloyd for the United Kingdom, 702-3; Sir Percy Spender for Australia, 704-5; and Mr Munro for New Zealand, 705-6.
9 United Nations, GAOR (Plenary Meetings), A/PV.429, 724-5 (Mr Menon)
10 For the full text of this resolution see ibid. (Annexes Seventh Session, Agenda 16 continued), Document A/L.152/ Rev. 2, 4

share of responsibility not only for peace-making but for peace-keeping.'[11] The resolution was adopted in the Assembly by a vote of 55-1-1 on 28 August, and on the same day the fifteen-nation resolution was passed by 43 to 5, with 10 abstentions.[12]

In the end it was shown to be a wasted effort. The key fifteen-nation resolution had delegated to the United States the task of arranging 'with the other side for the political conference to be held as soon as possible, but not later than 28 October 1953 [that is, within the three-month period specified in Paragraph 60 of the Armistice Agreement], at a place and on a date satisfactory to both sides.'[13] After a prolonged initial exchange of messages through the Swedish government, a series of meetings began at Panmunjom on 26 October. Immediately there were disputes over the agenda, the North Korean and Chinese representatives demanding that the composition of the conference be agreed upon first, and the American delegate, Arthur Dean, insisting that the settlement of a time and place should be given priority. Eventually it was agreed that both these issues would be discussed simultaneously by sub-committees, but this procedural device served merely to transfer the conflict to subordinate levels of debate. In particular, the Communists insisted that the Soviet Union attend the conference as a neutral and not as a member of the Communist side, while Mr Dean argued that in practice the USSR could not be a neutral and would vote automatically on substantive issues with the Chinese and North Koreans. There was disagreement also over the question of the participation of neutral states generally: the Communists suggested that the conference should include delegations from India and three other neutral powers (Indonesia, Pakistan, and Burma were specifically mentioned), while the Americans would agree only to the presence of representatives from governments with practical experience in Korea (for example, the members of the NNRC), and these merely as non-voting observers. In addition, the Communists favoured holding the conference in New Delhi, while Mr Dean insisted upon Geneva, and there were other differences over the time of meeting.[14]

There was no progress, and when on 12 December the Communists accused the United States of having colluded with Syngman Rhee in releasing the

11 Department of External Affairs, *Statements and Speeches,* no 53/34
12 Department of External Affairs, 'Canada and the United Nations,' *External Affairs,* V, 10, Oct. 1953, 296
13 United Nations, GAOR (Annexes Seventh Session, Agenda 16 continued), Document A/L.151/Rev. 1, 4
14 See Rees, *Korea,* 437; and Department of External Affairs, 'Canada and the United Nations,' *External Affairs,* VI, 1, Jan. 1954, 17-18

27,000 North Korean prisoners in June, Mr Dean broke off the discussions and returned to Washington. With that, all efforts under United Nations auspices to arrange a political conference collapsed.

Notwithstanding such distressing manifestations of political reality, the Canadian government continued throughout the autumn officially to regard the Korean affair as a triumph for the United Nations and the principle of collective security. In an address in Toronto on 23 October, three days before the discussions in Panmunjom were to begin, Mr Martin argued that the

United Nations met its responsibility promptly and squarely when the North Korean aggression occurred. In determining to take collective action against the aggressor, the nations concerned accepted the fact that aggression in one part of the world constitutes a threat to every other part. Failure to face up to this issue would have made a mockery of the whole collective security principle and would have been an open invitation to international lawlessness. While it may be necessary at times to balance our collective security obligations against the limited resources at our disposal, no act of aggression can be allowed to go unnoticed.

The prolongation of the fighting which had resulted from the Chinese intervention had had a 'depressing effect on a war-weary world,' and had demonstrated that the costs of collective security might be high. Nevertheless, the 'response of the sixteen member nations who sent troops to Korea to fight together under the United Nations banner demonstrated for the first time that collective military action could be mounted by an alliance whose members sought only to preserve the peace. Surely this is a lesson that will by now have been well learned by those Communist countries which seek to impose their will by force of arms.'[15]

Alas, the 'alliance ... to preserve the peace' had a highly selective membership, and its capacity for engineering a secure and happy international order was therefore somewhat narrowly confined. In the case of Korea, there is evidence that even Mr Pearson had long since begun to despair of the effort. As early as 23 September, in his farewell address as president of the General Assembly, he had observed that a Korean peace settlement 'should be possible' if there were 'good faith and good will on both sides,' but he had noted with emphasis underlined that this was a 'big "if." '[16] By early 1954, with the Panmunjom failure still a fresh memory, he had fallen victim to an even deeper

15 Department of External Affairs, *Statements and Speeches,* no 53/40
16 Ibid., no 53/27. The Eighth Session of the General Assembly opened on 15 September.
17 Ibid., no 54/2

gloom. Speculating before an audience in Montreal on 5 January on the prospects of the New Year, he warned his listeners not to 'expect too much from any particular meeting, at Berlin or Bermuda or Panmunjom; or read too much into plausible answers from the Kremlin to selected questions.' A note of caution was in order: 'It would be a mistake to pitch our hopes too high for a speedy and satisfactory solution at these conferences of all the cold-war problems which plague us. Many of these problems arise not so much from particular situations, as from the very nature of the relationship between Communism and the free world; a relationship which is likely to be with us as long as we live.'[17]

Shortly thereafter, on 1 February, the NNRC's administration of the POW problem in Korea came to an end,[18] and the foreign ministers of the United States, Britain, France, and the Soviet Union subsequently agreed in a meeting in Berlin to hold a conference on Far East questions at Geneva, beginning on 26 April. In addition to the 'Big Four,' all the countries that had participated in the Korean hostilities, including the two Koreas and mainland China, were to be invited to attend. With the exception of South Africa, all of them did so. But Mr Pearson left for the discussions with little hope. In an interview on the CBC immediately before his departure, he conceded that he personally did not 'feel too optimistic about the prospects of dramatic or quick successes in Geneva at this time,' although it would be foolish and wrong to have no hope at all.[19]

The meetings in Geneva in the spring of 1954 comprised not one conference, but two, and they had different memberships. The first, which the Canadians did not attend, was concerned with the problem of Indo-China. Since it began with the French garrison at Dien Bien Phu under heavy siege, and continued after its fall, it captured not only the bulk of newspaper headlines, but most of the available diplomatic energy as well. In so volatile a context, the second conference – devoted to the half-quiescent issue of Korea – seemed to the representatives of the great powers in particular little more than a time-consuming intrusion upon larger matters. Anthony Eden, for example, reports

18 The final tally of prisoners who refused repatriation included 21,809 Communists, 14,227 of them Chinese and 7582 Korean; and 347 on the allied side, of whom 21 were Americans and one was British. None of the 33 Canadian POWs refused repatriation. See Rees, *Korea,* 438-9
19 Department of External Affairs, 'Views on the Geneva Conference,' *External Affairs,* VI, 5, May 1954, 162. The pessimism of the Canadian delegation has been confirmed by Mr Pearson, interview, 18 Oct. 1968, and by John W. Holmes, interview, 5 March 1968. See also Holmes, 'Geneva: 1954,' 462

that he stressed in conversations with the Soviet delegate the importance of getting 'on with the Indo-China talks.' Korea was much less urgent, for 'there was no fighting there and matters could be allowed to remain for the time being in their present state.' He records in addition his complaint that during much of the period when the Indo-China discussions were in progress, 'the Korean Conference was also in session, and Molotov and I had often to act as chairman there. We made no real progress over Korea, but these meetings and their preparation made heavy demands upon our strength and time.'[20] Few of the negotiators felt in any case that the political future of Korea was a matter upon which much progress could be made. Given the incompatibility of the objectives of the two 'sides' and the absence of a decisive military outcome, the possibility of their reaching an acceptable agreement was slight. As one of the Canadian participants has since observed, the 'Canadians suffered no illusions about the willingness of the Communist side to accept a suitable arrangement for reunification because we realized that the pressures on them to do so were not strong enough.' Assuming a settlement might not be reached, therefore, the secondary Canadian objectives were to ensure the continuation of the armistice in the theatre, and to make provision – within the framework of the United Nations and the appropriate resolutions of the General Assembly – for the resumption of political negotiations at a more propitious time in the future.[21]

But if the negotiations on Korea were ritualistic, they were not routine. On the contrary, they generated considerable acrimony among the representatives of the United Nations powers, and in the ensuing quarrels the Canadians were once again arrayed in diplomatic combination against their American counterparts. Little of this was evident in the plenary proceedings of the conference, where for the benefit of their opponents and the press the allied governments displayed a united front. But in the informal meetings of the United Nations group, where attempts were made to hammer out an agreed policy, the differences were wide and the arguments vigorous. Their intensity was compounded by personal irritations which had resulted from disagreements between the British and the Americans on the question of Indo-China,[22] and which had

---

20 Eden, *Full Circle,* 117-8. See also Holmes, 'Geneva: 1954,' 458, for a comment on the difficulties of negotiating in an 'atmosphere at a meeting when world order totters, and battling armies and fleeing refugees are lighting flames which could spread anywhere.'
21 Holmes, 'Geneva: 1954,' 462; and interview, 5 March 1968. Much of the following account of diplomatic exchanges on the Korean issue at Geneva is based on discussions and correspondence with Mr Holmes.
22 The fullest available account of the Indo-China talks at Geneva is Randle's *Geneva 1954.*

accentuated the animosity latent in the relations of Anthony Eden and John Foster Dulles. The Eden-Dulles conflict was particularly distressing to Mr Pearson, partly because of the importance of Anglo-American amity in the conduct of Canadian external affairs generally, but more immediately because it meant that the British, who tended to share the Canadian view of the Korean problem, were reluctant to endanger further their relations with the United States by pressing hard on what was for London a secondary issue. In regular meetings of the Commonwealth representatives, which were held at the British villa, the Australians made it clear that while they, too, sympathized to some extent with Canadian views, their government did not think the matter worth a major row with Washington. Only the New Zealanders were prepared to back the Canadians fully in pushing the matter home.

The essence of the difference between the Canadian and American views was a matter less of substance than of attitude, tactics, and style. The American position, both supported and rationalized by that of the South Koreans, was that no compromise was acceptable in negotiating with the Communist powers. Proposals satisfactory to both the Republic of Korea and the United Nations should be developed for the unification and democratization of the peninsula, and presented to the Communists on a take-it-or-leave-it basis. The Canadian and New Zealand view, shared, but not vigorously supported, by Great Britain and to a lesser extent by Australia, was that the United Nations lacked the means of imposing any solution upon the Communist representatives which they were unwilling to accept voluntarily, and that a rigid posture was therefore strategically inappropriate. It followed that within the general principles laid down by previous General Assembly resolutions the UN group should approach the problem as flexibly as possible, aiming not so much for an immediate compromise solution as for the maintenance of room for manoeuvre in the event that negotiations were subsequently resumed under more auspicious conditions.

These differences in attitude found their substantive expression not long after the beginning of formal exchanges with the Communist representatives on 27 April. The North Koreans, with the support of mainland China and the Soviet Union, then proposed that there should be elections throughout the peninsula to establish a National Assembly as a basis for a unified Korean government. The elections would be supervised by a commission consisting of representatives elected from undefined 'Democratic social organizations' by the legislatures of the two Koreas, and governed by a unanimity rule. In the meantime steps would be taken to withdraw all foreign forces from the peninsula within a period of six months. The proposals were accompanied by attacks upon American policy and by allegations that the United States had been responsible for the outbreak of the war.[23]

The representatives of the United Nations powers not unnaturally offered a somewhat different interpretation of the causes of the war, and in any case refused to agree that a joint Korean commission would be capable of supervising genuinely free elections throughout the country. The North Korean government, although representing a minority of the Korean people and comprising in the UN view the guilty party in instigating the war, would have equal representation on the commission and the capacity to veto its proceedings. More seriously, its delegates would almost certainly subvert the electoral process. The proposal for the withdrawal of all foreign forces would mean that the United Nations units would have to be removed to parent bases across the seas, while the Chinese would be able to influence the course of Korean politics from their vantage point on the Manchurian border. As expressed on the same day by Eduardo Zuleto Angel of Colombia, therefore, the initial 'western' position was that free elections should be held throughout Korea 'under the supervision and with the assistance and advice of the United Nations Commission for the Unification and Rehabilitation of Korea,' which had been established by the General Assembly resolution of 7 October 1950. In this way the Geneva conference would fulfil its 'primary endeavour,' which 'should be to find a formula that will reconcile the desire to unify Korea and give it its independence through free and democratic elections supervised by the United Nations, with the General Assembly's reiterated declaration that the Government of the Republic of Korea is a legitimate Government founded on elections which truly expressed the free will of the electorate of the part of Korea in which the United Nations Commission was able to observe and advise, and that this Government is the sole such Government in Korea.' An alternative formula would be acceptable only if it met 'three essential conditions':

1) if it established a democratic and representative régime – which means that the number of electors belonging to each political party must be proportionate to the number of their representatives;
2) if it involved no violation of United Nations resolutions;

23 Department of External Affairs, 'The Korean Phase of the Geneva Conference,' *External Affairs,* VI, 8, Aug. 1954, especially 239-40. The full text of the North Korean proposal is in Great Britain, Secretary of State for Foreign Affairs, *Documents relating to the Discussion of Korea and Indo-China at the Geneva Conference,* 4-5.

3) if it provided that the elections should be held under United Nations supervision so as to ensure the electors' independence and freedom.[24]

Given the Communists' perception of the United Nations as the instrument of their enemies, rather than as the impartial executor of the principle of collective security, and given also the organization's incapacity to impose such an arrangement by force, the Canadian view – not publicly revealed – was that these terms were excessively rigid. The Americans – in particular, John Foster Dulles, the secretary of state, and Walter Robertson, the assistant secretary of state for Far Eastern affairs – were taking in the Canadian view a moralistic position which under the prevailing circumstances was both unrealistic and counterproductive. Dulles' attitude, as he himself summarized it in the plenary session on 28 April, was that 'When we negotiate with the Soviet Communists and their satellites, we are confronted with something far more formidable than individual or national lust for glory. We are confronted with a vast monolithic system which, despite its power, believes that it cannot survive except as it succeeds in progressively destroying human freedom.' Since in his view 'Communist doctrine authorizes accommodation when the opposition is strong,' it followed that it was 'our task here [that is, the task of the United Nations powers at the conference] to show such strength – strength of honorable and non-aggressive purpose – that the communists will find it acceptable to grant unity and freedom to Korea.'[25] But to display determination of this intensity before an opponent who is under no pressure to reach agreement is to encourage, not accommodation, but stalemate, and for this reason the Canadians, in combination with the New Zealanders, began in meetings with the other United Nations powers to press, against severe American and South Korean opposition, for the adoption of a somewhat more relaxed posture.

In the interest of preserving the appearance of allied unity, however, their anxieties were concealed in the plenary sessions. Mr Pearson's first formal address to the conference was delivered on 4 May and consisted for the most part in a rebuttal of the North Korean allegations and a criticism of their proposals. In particular, the insistence of the North Korean delegate, General Nam Il, that the all-Korean commission function by agreement on 'both sides' meant that it 'would operate as the Communist members wished, or not at all.' This would make it 'completely unworkable, unfair and inacceptable.' The members of the commission, moreover, would be representatives of what were

24 Secretary of State for Foreign Affairs, *Documents*, 7-8
25 Ibid., 12

called 'democratic social organizations,' but these were not well defined and might exclude non-communist groups. In any case the commission could never be an effective guarantee of freedom 'in districts where bitter animosities and fears and local tyrannies would make impartial Korean supervision quite impossible.'[26]

The rest, and indeed the bulk, of Mr Pearson's speech consisted of denials of Sino-Soviet and North Korean charges that the Americans had been the aggressors in Korea, a performance which he believed necessary because of the wide publicity given to the conference proceedings. As he later explained to the House of Commons, 'To reply to the slanderous attacks and abusive propaganda which form such a depressing proportion of the communist speeches at meetings of this kind is a time-consuming and unpleasant task, but when the eyes of the world are focused on a conference it is a task which I think we cannot afford to forego lest it should be supposed in any part of the world, especially in this case in the Asian part of the world, that silence may indicate some kind of consent.'[27]

In general substance the speeches of the other western delegates were very similar, and the negotiations therefore made no progress. On 22 May the Chinese foreign minister, Chou En-lai, conceded that co-operation between North and South Korea might be difficult and therefore proposed that a neutral nations supervisory commission should be established under other than United Nations auspices to assist the joint Korean commission.[28] This failed to change the substance of the communist proposal, however, and the suggestion was not favourably received by the 'western' powers, Canada included.[29]

On the same day the delegate from South Korea presented an alternative proposal which called for free elections within six months in North and South Korea, under United Nations supervision as laid down in earlier resolutions of the General Assembly. Representatives were to be elected on a basis which would reflect the distribution of population throughout the peninsula as determined by a census also conducted under UN supervision. Chinese Communist forces would complete their withdrawal from Korea one month before the

26 Ibid., 34. See also Department of External Affairs, 'The Geneva Conference,' *External Affairs,* VI, 6, June 1954, 170, and *Statements and Speeches,* no 54/28
27 Canada, House of Commons, *Debates,* 28 May 1954, 5186
28 Department of External Affairs, 'The Korean Phase of the Geneva Conference,' *External Affairs,* VI, 8, Aug. 1954, 243. For the full text of Chou's speech, see Secretary of State for Foreign Affairs, *Documents,* 54-8
29 Canada, House of Commons, *Debates,* 28 May 1954, 5196-7

elections were held, while UN forces would not do so until the unified government was in control of all Korea.[30]

The South Koreans were unwilling to modify their position, and they were
supported by the Americans, who thought they had a strong moral case. To
some extent the proposals represented a minor victory for the Commonwealth
powers, because initially the South Korean representatives, with American
agreement, had held that United Nations supervision of elections would be
necessary only in the North, given that South Korean electoral practices had
long ago received the stamp of UN approval. The principle of supervision
throughout the peninsula had been accepted only at the request of the Commonwealth delegations.[31] Nevertheless, the South Korean proposals perpetuated the disunity on the allied side, for other 'western' delegations,
Canada's and New Zealand's most prominent among them, considered them
unrealistic and one-sided. The Canadian representatives 'recognized the moral
case for such a position,' but knew also that 'the Korean War had ended in
a truce, not in the imposition of unconditional surrender.' Together with the
New Zealanders, therefore, they 'kept up resistance to the position imposed
by the Americans and the South Koreans.' The other 'western' delegations
tended to sympathize with their position, but 'were not prepared to differ with
the Americans over what seemed to be, and undoubtedly was, the less important issue at Geneva.' The two Commonwealth powers were therefore unsuccessful in bringing about a change in allied policy.[32]

Mr Pearson in the meantime had returned to Ottawa, leaving John Holmes
and Chester Ronning to represent the Canadian case. On 28 May he provided
the House of Commons with a seven-point summary of the Canadian position.
It stipulated (1) that 'a unified Korea should preserve the state structure for
Korea which has been endorsed by the United Nations [that is, that it should
be independent and democratic], with such constitutional changes as might be
necessary to establish an all-Korean government'; (2) that 'free and fair elections' for a constituent national assembly and 'possibly also for a president'
should be held 'with a minimum of delay'; (3) that these elections should be
based on 'equitable representation by population over the whole of Korea'; (4)
that 'such elections ... should be supervised by an international agency agreed

---

30 Department of External Affairs, 'The Korean Phase of the Geneva Conference,' *External
Affairs,* VI, 8, Aug. 1954, 242-3. For the full text of the ROK proposal, see Secretary of State
for Foreign Affairs, *Documents,* 53-4
31 Randle, *Geneva 1954,* 165
32 Holmes, 'Geneva: 1954,' 462-3. See also Department of External Affairs, 'The Korean Phase
of the Geneva Conference,' *External Affairs,* VI, 8, Aug. 1954, 243

on, if possible, by the Geneva conference but acceptable to the United Nations,' and probably consisting of 'nations which do not belong to the communist bloc and which did not participate in military operations in Korea'; (5) that 'arrangements should be made for the withdrawal of all foreign forces from Korea by stages' in such a way that their departure 'would begin at once ... and be completed within a short time after the Korean government had begun to function'; (6) that there should be 'a reaffirmation of international responsibility under the United Nations to participate in the relief and rehabilitation of Korea through economic and material assistance'; and (7) that there should be 'an international guarantee under the auspices of the United Nations of the territorial integrity of unified, free and democratic Korea.'[33] Mr Pearson noted also that the Canadian delegation had hoped that a proposal of this kind could be put forward jointly by all sixteen western powers, but in spite of the fact that their views had been very similar, this had not yet been possible.

In the meantime Holmes and Ronning were continuing their battle within the meetings of the Commonwealth and United Nations groups. The main obstacle was the fourth of Mr Pearson's seven points – that is, the suggestion that electoral supervision might be conducted by an agency consisting of non-Communist and non-combatant powers, rather than by a United Nations commission. By now the Americans were fully aroused, and some of the exchanges were intense. At one stage the two Canadian officials discussed the possibility of making the disagreement public, but were instructed from Ottawa to maintain the external appearance of unity among the UN powers. In the end it was impossible to win the Americans over, and with most of the other allies reluctant to raise the matter to the level of an open diplomatic break with Washington, the Canadians and the New Zealanders lost their cause by a vote of 13 to 2. In so doing, however, the Canadian representatives made it very clear that they reserved their freedom of action in the event of a future conference, and that their government did not regard itself as being bound by the position adopted by the UN group as a whole, a reservation which angered the Americans – now under the leadership of their under secretary, Walter Bedell Smith – but left them helpless.[34]

In retrospect, it seems unlikely that allied agreement would have made much difference, even in the long term. Certainly the outcome of the Geneva conference itself would have been little affected. On 5 June the Soviet delegate, Vyacheslav Molotov, rejected the South Korean proposals on the ground that

33 Canada, House of Commons, *Debates,* 28 May 1954, 5187
34 Holmes interview, 8 June 1970

they would allow the Rhee regime to unify the country in its own way and with foreign support. He presented the view that the conference should come to an agreement instead on broad fundamental principles based on the proposals put forward by General Nam Il of North Korea.[35] The first western response to this statement came from the acting head of the Canadian delegation, Chester Ronning, who undertook on 11 June to deliver still another account of western objections to the North Korean and Sino-Soviet positions, concluding that 'in the long run it will be better if we squarely face the facts of our disagreement and acknowledge them than to delude ourselves with false hopes and lead the people of the world to believe that there is agreement when there is no agreement.'[36]

In reporting on these developments to the House of Commons on the same day, Mr Pearson observed:

This Korean conference has been going on now for more than six weeks, and if we do not get some satisfactory answers soon from the communists on the matter of free elections, and all that that term implies, and if the communists are not prepared to agree to international supervision of an election by a workable commission acceptable to the United Nations and composed of genuine neutrals, the United Nations side may shortly have to consider whether it is worth while continuing this effort at Geneva to reach agreement for the peaceful unification of Korea.[37]

No further progress was made and on 15 June the Korean conference came to a close. On the same day, the fifteen allies, together with the Republic of Korea, issued a declaration in which they announced that they had 'earnestly and patiently' tried to reach agreement on the basis of two fundamental principles:

1 The United Nations, under its Charter, is fully and rightfully empowered to take collective action to repel aggression, to restore peace and security, and to extend its good offices in seeking a peaceful settlement in Korea.
2 In order to establish a unified, independent and democratic Korea, genuinely free elections should be held under United Nations supervision, for representatives in the

---

35 Department of External Affairs, 'The Korean Phase of the Geneva Conference,' *External Affairs*, VI, 8, Aug. 1954, 243. For the full text of Molotov's speech, see Secretary of State for Foreign Affairs, *Documents*, 64-8
36 Department of External Affairs, *Statements and Speeches*, 54/32. Also in Secretary of State for Foreign Affairs, ibid., 79-84
37 Canada, House of Commons, *Debates*, 11 June 1954, 5830

National Assembly, in which representation shall be in direct proportion to the indigenous population in Korea.[38]

The sixteen powers therefore believed that it was 'better to face the fact of our disagreement than to raise false hopes and mislead the peoples of the world into believing that there is agreement where there is none.' They had 'been compelled reluctantly and regretfully to conclude that, so long as the communist delegations reject the two fundamental principles which we consider indispensable, further consideration and examination of the Korean question by the Conference would serve no useful purpose.'[39]

For the Canadians, however, there was at least one happy consequence of the Geneva encounter to relieve the prevailing gloom. In December 1952 Squadron-Leader A.R. MacKenzie, one of twenty-two RCAF fighter pilots who were serving in Korea on secondment to the Fifth US Air Force, was brought down over enemy territory and taken prisoner.[40] He had not been released in the POW exchanges after the armistice, and it was not certain that he was alive. It was therefore one of the objectives of the Canadian delegation in Geneva to take advantage of the opportunity for informal conversation with the Chinese to inquire after his condition and to discuss the possibility of his return. Chester Ronning, who knew Chou En-lai and a number of the other Chinese delegates personally, and who could speak their language, raised the matter with the Chinese foreign minister in private discussion.[41] Chou promised to

---

38 Secretary of State for Foreign Affairs, *Documents,* 100-1. The Canadians did not approve of the phrase 'under United Nations supervision,' preferring a formula more open to alternative supervisory methods. They made it clear to the United Nations group that they did not feel bound by the policy implications of the phrasing that was used.
39 Ibid., 101
40 See Historical Section, General Staff, Army Headquarters, *Canada's Army in Korea,* 88
41 Mr Ronning's habit of engaging in easy conversation with the Chinese delegates was for the Americans a constant source of annoyance and suspicion. Walter Robertson, the American assistant secretary of state for Far Eastern affairs, had instructed his own staff to avoid any such informal contact with their Chinese opposite numbers, and he viewed Mr Ronning's behaviour with considerable alarm. Arnold Heeney later recorded in his memoirs that Robertson's 'deep emotions combined with his inflexibility to the point of irrationality on Korea in particular and the Far East in general made him an exceedingly difficult person with whom to deal.' When Heeney paid him a courtesy call shortly after arriving as Canadian ambassador in Washington in the summer of 1953, the first 'mention of Korea let loose a flood of argument and emotion. Without bitterness or sarcasm but with determination and obvious sincerity, Robertson made the extreme United States case against any political conversations with 'the other side' – and at such length that it was difficult for me to get away at the end of forty minutes' (*The Things that are Caesar's,* 119).

make inquiries, and shortly thereafter Ronning was advised that MacKenzie was alive and well, and would eventually be released. There ensued a long delay lasting until November 1954, during which the Department of External Affairs had to make a considerable effort to persuade Canadian newsmen not to jeopardize the situation by intervening, as they were planning to do, with publicized inquiries of their own. It also proved necessary to restrain the United Nations Command from exploiting the issue for propaganda purposes.[42] Word of MacKenzie's release from prison finally arrived in November, and he crossed over the border at Hong Kong on 5 December.[43] Fifteen American airmen, similarly detained, were not released until the summer of 1955.

Diplomatically, the stalemate was now complete. On 27 July 1953 the sixteen members of the United Nations with troops in Korea had issued a declaration stating that they would support the armistice and do everything possible to bring about a united, independent, and democratic Korea. They also warned that if the attack were renewed, they would 'again be united and prompt to resist,' and that the 'consequences of such a breach of the armistice would be so grave that, in all probability, it would not be possible to confine hostilities within the frontiers of Korea ... '[44] After the failure of the Geneva conference the Canadians, in company still with the New Zealanders, continued their skirmishing with the Americans on the question of allied posture vis-à-vis the pursuit of a political settlement. In particular they persisted in their view that it was unnecessary and ill-advised for the fifteen UN powers to insist in their report to the General Assembly upon 'United Nations supervision' of any future all-Korean elections. Alternative supervisory arrangements might well be devised which would be more acceptable to the Communist side. In arguing their case, which they threatened to incorporate in an explicit reservation if they were not given satisfaction, they were to some extent successful. The final report, while asserting that 'appropriate supervision' was necessary to 'ensure that the elections are held under conditions of genuine freedom,' stated only that 'such supervision must be impartial and effective and

---

42 Holmes, interview, 8 June 1970
43 Wood, *Strange Battleground,* 249
44 The declaration had been drafted in negotiations among the Washington representatives of the sixteen powers in January 1952 (Rees, *Korea: The Limited War,* 436). The Canadians had not approved of parts of the original American version, which had stated in categorical terms that a renewal of the hostilities would lead to conflict beyond the borders of Korea itself. On their insistence, the wording had been altered in such a way as to convey a less belligerently threatening impression (telephone conversation with Alex I. Inglis, former resident historian, Department of External Affairs, 21 Dec. 1972).

should be under the authority and auspices of the United Nations' – a formula which allowed of somewhat greater flexibility.[45]

When the question of the unification of Korea was discussed in the General Assembly in subsequent years, the Canadian representative regularly seized the occasion to reiterate Ottawa's view that it was necessary only to ensure that the supervising agency was *acceptable* to the United Nations; it did not have to be a UN instrument *per se*. It might, for example, 'consist of nations which did not belong to the communist bloc and which did not participate in military operations in Korea.'[46] Initially these public proclamations of the Canadian view were not well received by American policy-makers, but in due course they came to be regarded as routine.[47]

By the end of 1954 two-thirds of the Canadian armed forces stationed in Korea had been withdrawn, and in the spring of 1955 all those remaining, with the exception of some 500 auxiliary troops, had also sailed for home.[48] By June 1957 the last of the auxiliary personnel had similarly departed.[49] On 14 January 1963 Howard Green announced that Canada had established a diplomatic mission in Seoul, a commentary as much upon the assumed permanence of the North-South division as upon the scope of Canadian-Korean affairs.[50]

Only in the summer of 1972, with the introduction of 'hot line' communications between Seoul and Pyongyang, did it begin to appear that the Koreans might someday be able to do for themselves what the rest of the world had failed to do for them.

45 United Nations, GAOR (Annexes Ninth Session, Agenda 17), Document A/2786, 3
46 Quoted in Department of External Affairs, *Canada and the United Nations, 1954-55*, 12
47 Holmes, interview, 8 June 1970
48 Masters, *Canada in World Affairs, 1953 to 1955*, 78
49 Wood, *Strange Battleground*, 257. Canada still maintains a small Liaison Group with the United Nations Command, the liaison officer serving also as the Canadian member of the Participating Nations' Advisory Group to the United Nations Command Military Armistice Commission. See Plourde, 'Korean Sojourn,' 20-3
50 Department of External Affairs, 'Relations between Canada and Korea,' *External Affairs*, XV, 2, Feb. 1963, 80-2

9

Analytical alternatives

By now it will be very clear to the readers of this volume that the principal organizing device for the material presented in the foregoing chapters is historical. The narrative is influenced by a perspective of place (Canada) and time (roughly twenty years after the fact), and the evidence is chronologically selected and arranged in such a way as to highlight an argument, or thesis, about the objectives and methods of Canadian policy in the Korean context. It is not, however, examined with reference to an explicit theory of foreign policy behaviour, such as might be found in the formal literature of political science, nor is it treated in the light of a carefully articulated 'conceptual framework.' There are, moreover, no proclamations of working hypotheses, operating assumptions, or explanatory tools. In some form or other all these are certainly in evidence, for no intelligible accounting of a political (or any other) phenomenon is possible without them, but their presence is implicit in the discussion rather that expressly defined.

It will be obvious in addition that, if the occasional aphorism is discounted, no systematic attempt has been made anywhere in the main body of the text to generalize beyond the limits set by the material itself. The 'events' are 'described' as if they actually were, or might very well be, unique to the Korean case, and the question of whether or not they are reflective of patterns which recur in other contexts is simply not discussed.

The result, therefore, is a highly descriptive and theoretically unadorned case-history. But it can be argued – and political scientists usually *do* argue – that investigations of this sort can have functional utility (as opposed to mere intrinsic interest) only to the extent that they can be made to teach lessons –

that is, yield inferences which, for purposes of explanation, and even of prediction, can be translated and applied in original or amended form to similar cases elsewhere. Such 'spill-over' effects can of course take place within different ranges of intellectual sophistication and self-awareness. For example, it is often remarked that repeated exposure to case histories gives one a 'feel' for the subject, and there herein lies their chief advantage. History does not in detail repeat itself, but a knowledge of historical cases gives one a sense of being 'at home' in the presence of certain types of phenomena, and provides a kind of 'understanding' or 'wisdom' which tends if nothing else to bring one's expectations more closely in line with the probable, and one's behaviour more proximately in accord with the possible. In some versions of the argument there is the additional thought that it may also bring one's purposes more nearly in train with the 'good.' On such assumptions, indeed, is founded much of the case for exposure to the liberal arts as the most appropriate vehicle for general education.

With considerable justice, however, the more sophisticated case-study theorist often complains that such concepts as 'feel,' 'understanding,' and 'wisdom' are too vague by far to account for the way in which these lessons are learned, and that more precise and self-conscious formulations of the intellectual processes involved must be devised. But this position leads in turn to embroilment in a morass of highly complex and technical questions. How far, and under what conditions, is it appropriate to derive general rules from specific instances? What kinds of rules are they likely to be? In particular, what is the minimum level of abstraction at which they may be formulated without sacrificing the capacity to apply them with advantage to other contexts? For if they are based on excessively detailed specifications of prior conditions (there are too many 'independent variables'), they may be relevant for so narrow a range of actual experiences as to be unprofitable and uninteresting. They may also become unmanageable for the researcher, who in testing them must obtain, measure, and correlate evidence (or 'data') from the 'real world,' and who therefore has a legitimate and unavoidable interest in economy. Again, what is the maximum level of abstraction which is consistent with the maintenance of explanatory or predictive utility? As official practitioners of foreign policy often have cause to point out, it is not uncommon for academic propositions of the 'if-x-then-y' variety to be expressed at so general a level that for practical purposes they are useless or trivial. Still again, how does one decide upon the 'representativeness' of a particular case? Was the Korean experience, for example, 'representative' of Canadian diplomatic practice in general, and if it was, in what respects, under what conditions, and how do we know? Is it possible to devise typologies of cases, each type within each typology having its own identifiable patterns? If so, how does one go about deciding whether one case is sufficiently 'like' another to warrant their being grouped together for analytical purposes? How explicit can the parameters of each typology be? And how can the matching of analytical 'types' to concrete evidence be achieved in studies of the 'real world,' where political phenomena appear in a highly disordered condition, implanted, as they are, in a chaos of apparently unique combinations of potentially relevant 'causes,' 'influences,' or 'variables'?[1]

No attempt to answer such questions, or to review their theoretical implications, will be undertaken here. The debate to which they have given rise in the theoretical literature, however, has served to emphasize a fundamental characteristic of political analysis which has not always received explicit attention in the past, and which has a direct bearing on the observations that are offered below. It amounts to the obvious point that where one finishes in any analysis of a given political phenomenon depends in large degree on where one starts. To put the matter more precisely, the explanations and prescriptions which an analyst derives from his examination of particular events depend for their substance not merely on the properties of the events themselves, but also on the concepts and assumptions upon which the investigation is based.[2] No accounting of an 'external' phenomenon is an exact replica of the 'real' thing. Even the most detailed and painstaking descriptions of political minutiae are in this sense skeletal. Assuming they have been carefully executed within the operational procedures defined by, or implicit in, the premises upon which they are based, the test of their 'validity' is not the degree to which they accurately 'mirror' an external 'reality,' but the extent to which they 'work' – that is, provide a functional and coherent ordering of the phenomena with which they deal.

Given the complexity of political life, it follows from all this that the 'story' of any political event can be told in many different ways, and that, depending

---

1 The elusive and perplexing intricacy of such inquiries explains why those who speak in the informal language of 'feel' seem so often to have the better of the argument. By conceding that 'lessons' are indeed learned through case histories (in much the same way as one is taught by one's own experience), they lay claim to what common observation and common sense alike show clearly to be true. By denying that the process through which these lessons are absorbed and applied can be made intellectually explicit, or by asserting that the exercise, even if successful, would not be worth the effort, they avoid the epistemological difficulties from which the tortured theorist of case-study analysis is unable to escape. One of the strengths of the 'traditionalist' is that he finds it easier to get on with the job.

2 The most thorough and painstaking attempt to date to illustrate this observation by referring to alternative 'explanations' of a specific phenomenon is in Allison, *Essence of Decision.* See also Bell, 'Ten Theories in Search of Reality,' in his *The End of Ideology,* 300-34

on the focus of inquiry, it is possible for there to be multiple 'explanations' of 'what happened.'[3] The fact that the number of analytical perspectives is, in theory if not in practice, extremely high is a reflection in part of the vast array of variables that are at work in political life, any one or more of which can be singled out for special attention. It is a reflection, too, of the fact that 'explanations' can be offered at different levels of abstraction, as well as at different degrees of remove in time and space from the events being explained. 'For the want of a nail,' as the popular ditty has it, 'the shoe was lost; for the want of a shoe, the horse was lost; for the want of a horse ... ' and so on. The net result is that the analyst is compelled, whether he likes it or not, to make a choice from a multitude of possible questions and research strategies. The act of choosing may not be obvious or self-conscious, but it is always there. If it were not, the resulting 'explanations' would be incoherent and unintelligible.

One of the most important practical implications of all this for the investigator who aspires to systematic analysis is that it imposes upon him an obligation to keep his 'conceptual framework' and focus of attention explicitly in view whenever he begins to work with his evidence, so that the kind of enterprise in which he is engaged is made absolutely clear. What follows is designed in part as a demonstration of the benefits that can be derived from accepting this obligation. It consists of an attempt to consider the Korean experience as an example of the conduct of Canadian foreign policy from the vantage point of a succession of distinct perspectives. All of them focus on the behaviour of Canadian policy-makers, and even within these narrow limits, they comprise a highly selective and incomplete sample of the analytical possibilities. It will quickly become clear, moreover, that they are not mutually exclusive categories, and have not been derived from any systematic typology

---

3 This is not intended to imply that all such explanations would be equally useful. Most will be useful for some purposes, but not for others. Many will not be useful at all. Nor is it suggested that *any* explanation will do. Within a particular frame of reference, it is obviously possible for an accounting of a given event to be patently false. To use a simple example, it might be 'explained' that 'Government A responded with action B to situation C because decider D made the decision, and decider D held belief E about situation C.' This would be 'proven' wrong if it were established (1) that D did not in fact make the decision; or (2) that D did make the decision but did not hold belief E about situation C; or (3) that D did make the decision and did hold belief E about situation C, but action B was not 'entailed' in belief E; or, more improbably, (4) that D did make the decision, and did hold belief E about situation C, and action B was entailed in belief E, but belief E was not brought to bear on the problem at the time of decision; or (5) some combination of these. If, on the other hand, the explanation were shown to be 'true,' this would not rule out the possibility of their being *other* useful explanations, focussing on different variables and/or different levels of abstraction.

of 'variable clusters.' The first two perspectives, for example, are inter-related in the sense that they both focus on individual decision-makers as the unit of analysis, although from somewhat different vantage-points. Perspectives C and F, on the other hand, differ substantially from the others in being more concerned with policy *processes* than with policy *outputs*. It follows from this somewhat arbitrary eclecticism that no attempt has been made to rank-order the various analytical orientations in terms of their respective explanatory 'potencies,' although attention is drawn from time to time to the way in which two or more of them overlap, and to the extent to which they are, or are not, mutually supportive. The discussion, in short, is reflective of a number of the strains in the literature of Canadian foreign policy studies, but is not intended to yield an ordered set of 'building blocks' for the construction of an integrated 'theory' (or 'pre-theory'). On the other hand, an effort has been made to give explicit attention to the premises of each of the various perspectives in turn, and to indicate how they lead respectively to quite different patterns of pre-scriptive advocacy (although in practice these tend to be mixed up together). These are exemplified by some of the more recurrent themes in Canadian foreign policy debates. Only in the case of the first perspective, however, can it be claimed that the present book attempts a reasonably full analysis. In all the others, a thorough investigation would have required a study of somewhat different conception and design. The brief discussions that follow should never-theless be sufficient to demonstrate the richness of the various alternatives and the degree to which they can draw attention to aspects and implications of a particular political phenomenon which might otherwise be overlooked.

'BEHAVIOUR' AS THE EXPRESSION OF 'RATIONAL CHOICE'

Almost all of the literature of diplomatic history, and the bulk of contempo-rary foreign policy analysis, is geared to the unique – that is, it proceeds by describing how identifiable individuals perceived particular problems and situations, and why they responded in the way they did. In such studies, the analyst tells 'what happened' after the fashion, 'A thought Y about (situation/problem) X, and therefore did (response/solution) Z.' The assumption throughout is that the decision-makers are 'rational' in the general sense that they act purposefully on the basis of assessments of reality and in the light of comparative evaluations of the consequences of at least some of the alternative courses of action which are open to them. The objective of the analyst is to examine what these assessments, evaluations, and actions really were. In the ideal world of theory, a fully 'rational' decision-maker would, of course, exam-ine *all* the possible courses of action, compare the full range of costs and benefits entailed in each of them, and select the one which offered the maximum return consistent with his priorities in such other areas of his responsibility as required expenditures of scarce resources. To put it in the jargon of economists, he would seek to maximize his marginal utilities. In the real world of practice, however, not every possible course of action will be taken into account; for a variety of reasons the policy-maker's attention will be directed only to a few of his options, and sometimes to no more than one or two. Even within the range of choices which he actually considers, moreover, not all the costs and benefits of the alternatives will be fully known, and in varying degrees he will usually be compelled to act in conditions of uncertainty. Under these circumstances, the 'rationality' of his behaviour will be 'partial' or 'limited,' and fall appreciably short of the ideal.[4] But within these limits he will still make his decisions purposefully – that is, with objectives in view, and with reference to at least a rough calculation of means-ends relationships. He may, of course, make 'mistakes' – the objectives may be grossly unrealistic, the choice of strategies inappropriate or counterproductive, and so on – but his behaviour is assumed at least to be intellectually 'coherent' in the sense described above. The random behaviour of the totally 'mad' would be counted as a special case – that is, the 'explanation' of the behaviour would lie in the madness itself, and not in any intelligible accounting of sequences of perception, reasoning, and response.

This is the variety of analysis that the decision-makers themselves tend to find most meaningful, for it orders their perceptions of their environment and accounts for their behaviour in terms which they recognize as being directly related to their actual experience. The approach entails a description of the conditions they confronted, a record of their calculations in response to those conditions, a more or less detailed account of what they did, and a report of the results. Assuming the details to be reasonably full and accurate, an analysis conducted at this level will seem to them both familiar and 'real.' If it includes also a qualitative evaluation of their performance, the arguments involved will seem to be very much in character with the ones which were actually considered during the course of the decision-making process, even if the decision-makers disagree with them.

This can readily be recognized as the predominant level of discussion in the present study, and it therefore should not require additional illustration here. The bulk of the preceding text is devoted, in effect, to a narrative account of

---

4 See Allison, *Essence of Decision,* 31-2. For a widely cited discussion of this problem, see Braybrooke and Lindblom, 'Types of Decision-Making,' in Rosenau, ed., *International Politics and Foreign Policy,* 207-16.

what Canadian foreign policy decision-makers thought, said, and did in response to specific events and conditions at home and abroad. Whether the book is 'good' or 'bad' depends, in part, on the degree to which the narrative is sufficiently accurate and detailed to constitute a convincing account of 'what happened,' assuming the individuals involved to have been 'rational' men pursuing definable purposes under concretely perceived conditions. The principal advantages of the approach are (1) that it is readily recognized and understood by political participants and observers alike; (2) that it directs attention to the political process at its most clearly observable and definable point – that is, the point of decision; (3) that it helps to resolve the problem of 'economizing on variables' (selecting the 'influences' which in some significant way can be said to have really 'counted'), for it allows the economizing to be done by the decision-makers themselves (the analyst takes into consideration only what the decision-makers themselves seem consciously to have perceived and to have regarded as relevant); and (4) that it facilitates the process of evaluating the policies that ensued and of assigning political responsibility for the results. The disadvantages arise from the fact that the approach elaborates the specific at the expense of the general, and hence can inhibit the identification of more broadly relevant patterns of behaviour. It may also give too much emphasis to 'explanations' of a type which are consistent with the ones that are visible to the decision-makers themselves (in effect, the responsibility for developing and testing 'theory' is abrogated to those whose behaviour is to be explained), thereby exposing other potentially useful theories – whether conflicting or complementary – to unwarranted neglect.

The approach does not, on the other hand, preclude the analyst from identifying such recurring patterns as may appear in successive sequences of perception, reasoning, and response. Indeed, the assumption that the behaviour of the decision-makers is the product of 'rational' calculation leads to the expectation that unless there are substantial changes of context or personnel, a succession of similar situations will be treated in much the same way. To specify fully the ingredients of this treatment is to provide an account of the decision-makers' calculus, or strategy. This involves *some* degree of analytical abstraction from the 'particulars' of each situation, but not very much, and the focus is still on self-conscious processes of 'rational choice.' It is this sort of analysis which yields the central theme of the preceding chapters – that is, the argument that Canadian policy-makers sought to maximize the role of the United Nations in the politics of the Korean War as a means of imposing multilateral constraints on the exercise of American power. The case is made that this strategy recurred in each phase of Canadian activity from the time of the Temporary Commission to the Geneva conference of 1954, and that it premised the minutiae of Canada's diplomatic behaviour throughout. On this accounting, each 'particular' issue in the diplomacy of the war is seen as having posed for the decision-makers a problem of tactical choice in the context of parameters set by a general strategic posture.

If one progresses from this sort of empirical analysis to the exercise of 'evaluative' judgment, the criteria which are brought to bear tend naturally to be a reflection of the ingredients of 'rational' action, and the targets of evaluation are the performances of the decision-makers themselves. The questions which are regarded as interesting therefore relate most often to the decision-makers' perceptions of their environment, to their identification of the range of options open to them, to their assessments, in the light of their overall objectives, of the probable costs and benefits of the various alternatives, and to their practical implementation of their chosen course of action. Were they, for example, 'right' or 'wrong' about the intentions and capabilities of other actors, friendly or hostile? If they were wrong, why were they wrong? Was the error 'avoidable'? That is, in terms of assigning responsibility for the results, is it possible to say that sufficient evidence was available at the time to lead them to the 'right' conclusion had they exercised their powers of judgment at a level of performance which could reasonably have been expected of them? Or has the identification of the 'error' become possible only with the advantages of hindsight? Again, whatever their analysis or 'definition' of their situation, did they consider fully and carefully all the feasible options that were at their disposal? Were there other possibilities that they should have considered? If so, was their failure in this respect 'excusable' – that is, due to circumstances which they could not reasonably be expected to have overcome? Still again, did they accurately assess the costs and benefits of the various alternatives to which they addressed themselves? That is, did they make false predictions of the consequences of alternative courses of action? If they did make such mistakes, were they 'avoidable' given the evidence available at the time? Did they in fact pursue the 'impossible,' or miscalculate the effect of their decisions on the behaviour of other actors? And in implementing their decisions, were they skilful? Did they, for example, display an effective sense of timing, and were they subtle in their conduct of diplomatic manoeuvres and negotiations?

As a rule such inquiries as these are not posed in quite so explicit a fashion, and often the answers, if any, will be little more than implicit in the analyst's treatment of specific details. The questions may be impossible in many instances to answer at all, insofar as they raise problems that cannot be resolved except by reference to hypothetical history. In complex cases, for example, it may be very difficult to ascertain with any degree of conviction that a different decision would have produced better results, for there is no way of putting the matter to an empirical test. Arguments based on 'counterfactual' propositions – that is, propositions about what would have been the case had certain prior 'facts' been different – can certainly be the object of serious, even persuasive, speculation, especially if the context is uncomplicated (the variables are few), and if the calculations of all the actors involved have subsequently become known. But they will be deployed, without reservation, only by the incautious, or by the polemically-inclined.

If the analysis falls entirely within the parameters of the evaluative criteria set by the idiosyncratic 'rational actor' approach, and if it reveals weaknesses in policy performance, the implication in practical terms is that the decision-makers were themselves deficient. They made 'mistakes' for which they stand personally condemned. They should have been more perceptive, more logical, more skilful. The decisions would have been 'better' – that is, more effective – had other men, having a greater measure of these and other qualities, been in their place. That the individuals involved may have operated under conditions of great difficulty is appreciated, and these conditions may provide adequate excuse for their 'failure.' If so, this implies that 'individual' or 'personality' variables were insignificant, and suggests the need to undertake additional lines of investigation – into domestic or 'systemic' constraints, for example (see below). But if not, the decision-makers must themselves assume full responsibility. Their 'fault' may lie with the premises upon which their behaviour was based (although to establish this, the analyst would have to go on to consider questions regarding their 'operational code,' and the like, as in Section B below). Alternatively it may rest with their technical inefficiency in securing information (Section F), or some other factor. However that may be, if the decision-makers are still in office, the suggestion is usually that they ought to be replaced (they are 'incompetent'). In other cases, they may suffer no more than dimished historical reputations. But the central point here is that the focus on indidivual actors as agents of 'rational choice' in particularistic contexts entails a primary evaluative interest in the performance of individual persons, and only a secondary interest in the conditions under which they work.[5]

5 It should be observed that the emphasis here is on the efficiency or effectiveness with which the decision-makers 'rationally choose,' assuming that their overall objectives are to be taken as 'given.' It is possible, of course, to disapprove of their goals. Many social scientists would argue that normative issues of this sort do not fall properly within their professional field of inquiry. Whether, on the other hand, a strict separation of empirical and normative questions can be so easily achieved is a matter over which there is considerable disagreement and debate. If the focus on individual actors *is* expanded to include this sort of normative evaluation, it leads ultimately to what E.H. Carr has called the 'Bad King John and Good Queen Bess' theory of history. See his *What is History?* 40

In the present case, the derivation of qualitative evaluations of the performances of individual Canadian policy-makers has not been a primary concern. The principal purpose of the analysis has been to 'explain' their behaviour rather than to assess its calibre. Evaluative comments are sprinkled through the text, and in many sections they are implicit in the material, but the objective has not been to sit in judgment over a cast of historical characters, nor has the treatment been geared to generating prescriptions for the conduct of Canada's external relations. Some may regard this as a cowardly evasion of responsibility; others may argue that the preceding chapters are more heavily polluted with value judgments than this portrayal of their contents would appear to suggest. However that may be, it is worth noting that whenever evaluative questions have, in fact, arisen explicitly in the text, the answers have come more readily when the problem posed by speculating from hypothetical history can somehow be overcome. For example, it is possible to argue in retrospect (page 17) that Mackenzie King had a much more accurate understanding of the international politics entailed in the Temporary Commission of 1947-8 than did his opponents in the Cabinet and the Department of External Affairs.[6] It follows that in this instance, and in this respect, he was more perceptive than they. It is similarly possible to conclude now that the Canadian assessment of the hazards of crossing the 38th parallel in the autumn of 1950 was more accurate than the analysis which eventually triumphed in the United States.[7] Still again, it can be demonstrated that there were conceptual confusions in the notion of 'collective security' which permeated the rhetoric of Canadian statesmen, and indeed this comprises one of the secondary themes of the analysis contained in this book. On the other hand, Escott Reid's inquiry into whether he should have tried more vigorously to change Mr Pearson's decision to vote in favour of the resolution of 7 October, which authorized the advance into North Korea, is much more problematic. This is partly because it is difficult in the absence of evidence from the official files to determine how vigorous his protests actually were. More importantly, however, it is impossible now to ascertain whether it would have been reasonable at the time to expect that a more persistent effort would have made a difference. That is, would it have been reasonable for Mr Reid in the early autumn of 1950 to assume (a) that if he tried hard enough, he might have a chance of persuading Mr Pearson to change his views, and (b) that if Mr Pearson were converted,

6 To say this does not, however, compel one to approve also of his policy recommendations.
7 Throughout the text, in fact, there is implied a judgment to the effect that the Canadians held a much more constructive assessment of east-west relations than the Americans. Whether this is a 'fair' evaluation, or is reflective merely of national bias, is a matter for others to decide.

he in turn might be in a position to affect the outcome?[8] In the absence of clear answers to these questions, neither Mr. Reid nor such independent observers as may be interested in the complexities of his dilemma can do more than offer speculative guesses on the respective probability of various 'might-have-beens.' The same is true of many of the other decisions which raised tactical issues of this sort – for example, the decision to vote in favour of the resolution of 1 February, and the decision at the 1954 Geneva conference to conceal Canada's disagreement with the Americans behind a facade of allied unity. In such cases as these, calculations of the consequences of alternative postures can lead to little more than guesstimates.

To repeat, all these questions, and others like them, are essentially concerned with the evaluation of behaviour which is assumed to be the product of 'rational choice,' and which is analyzed in terms of its having been designed to deal with concrete problems arising in particular contexts having specific properties. But other perspectives, having different premises, are possible, and they lead to other kinds of evaluative criteria.

'BEHAVIOUR' AS THE EMBODIMENT OF AN 'OPERATIONAL CODE'

By removing to a slightly higher plain of abstraction, it is sometimes feasible to devise from the evidence provided by the behaviour and utterances of individual decision-makers certain general observations about the attitudes and working assumptions which underlie their conscious responses to specific situations. That is, one may assume that the decision-makers function on the basis of fundamental premises about the nature and meaning of politics, and in the light of more or less settled evaluations of the respective merits of alternative political 'styles,' or sets of tactical procedures and rules. What the decision-makers do may in this way be affected by their political 'culture.' The ingredients of this culture may therefore become in turn an explicit subject for examination. It is still assumed that the decision-makers act 'rationally' in the sense discussed above, but the range of choices which they actually consider, and the manner in which they derive their estimates of the probable consequences of the various possible alternatives, are viewed as being limited and defined by the precepts of their political philosophy and by their preferences for particular methods of political action. The individuals involved may be self-consciously aware of these underlying ingredients of their behaviour, or

8 It is possible, of course, to argue that Mr Reid should have tried harder even if he had no chance of success – that is, that he should have placed the integrity of his personal views ahead of any calculation of their practical effectiveness. This sort of suggestion raises very complex issues, however, and it is not clear how such a disagreement might be resolved.

they may not. In the latter event, of course, the ingredients themselves can be identified only if they are consistently implied by what the decision-makers say and do. But in either case, the interest of the analyst is not so much in the details of particular decisions as in the general framework of premises within which the decisions were reached. In some cases, this preoccupation may even imply the view that the process by which one policy alternative is chosen from a range of considered possibilities is little more than trivial, since the options which the decision-maker explicitly evaluates will all be generally similar. On this view, the *significantly* different alternatives are held to be the ones that were excluded from serious consideration at the outset of the decision-making process by the impact of the decision-maker's political culture on his perceptions and goals. The tenets of this culture are then regarded as especially important because they are the determinants of the decision-maker's most fundamental 'choices.'

The search for such operating assumptions and tactical rules is sometimes conducted in a fashion so systematic that the results can be displayed as a numbered sequence of carefully grouped but simply formulated propositions. These are then occasionally referred to by specialists in this sort of analysis as the decision-makers' 'operational code.'[9] No attempt will be made here to embark on such refinements, but a few observations on the assumptions and style of Canadian diplomacy as implied by the evidence of the Korean case may warrant some attention. At this stage in the discussion, the focus will be on Mr Pearson himself,[10] although much of what follows seems to have applied in the 1950s and 60s, and probably still applies, to the Canadian policy community as a whole. Some of the implications of assuming that a key decision-maker's political culture is not uniquely his own, but is shared by a wider community of policy-makers, or an even larger group of general publics, will be considered briefly below.

Implicit in much of Mr Pearson's behaviour was the assumption that politics is concerned with the resolution of conflict. Conflict is inevitable and persistent, and therefore political activity is permanent. It can, however, be conducted with varying degrees of civility, as measured by the extent to which it is characterized by violent behaviour. 'Good' politics is politics which proceeds peacefully, and through which conflicts are resolved by negotiation and

9 For recent examples of, and references to, this sort of work, see Holsti, 'The "Operational Code" Approach to the Study of Political Leaders,' 123-57; and McLellan, 'The "Operational Code" Approach to the Study of Political Leaders,' 52-75

10 Evidence bearing on some of the observations that follow can also be found in Mr Pearson's writings, notably his *Democracy in World Politics, Diplomacy in the Nuclear Age, Words and Occasions,* and *Mike: The Memoirs of the Right Honourable Lester B. Pearson.*

compromise. 'Bad' politics takes over when the willingness of conflicting parties to search for 'acceptable' solutions to their differences comes to an end. Whenever this happens, disputants tend to engage in behaviour (for example, fighting) which is counterproductive not only in the sense that it leads to an immediate deprivation of values all around (for example, loss of life and property), but also in the sense that it increases the intransigence of both 'sides' and makes the settlement of their quarrels even more difficult to secure than before. A 'good' political system, therefore, is one which allows for the peaceful settlement of differences and for the reconciliation of conflicting parties, and 'good' political attitudes are attitudes which support the construction, maintenance, and effective operation of just such a system. It follows that 'progress' in international politics (and presumably also in domestic politics) consists in the creation of structures and processes which are conducive to 'peaceful settlement' activities, and in the cultivation of attitudes, norms, and practices which encourage these structures and processes to work.

It does not follow from all this that there should not be serious differences over political morals, or that one cannot hold and pursue strong views about the nature of the 'just' or 'good' society. It does follow, however, that if disagreements on such matters are so firmly entrenched that they cannot be resolved by persuasion, it is better to concentrate on the resolution of pragmatic conflicts of interest than to try to alter an opponent's basic political beliefs or to compel him to revise the manner in which he conducts his internal affairs. For to persist in the pursuit of his 'reform' is simply to escalate tensions in ways which are destructive of the 'good' (that is, functional, or workable) political process described above.

It also follows that it is pointless, even counterproductive, to seek the impossible or to strive for goals which are beyond one's capabilities. Most men are weak; doubtless all in some degree are sinful. One hopes that they will improve – that is, that they will become more tolerant, humane, flexible, and dispassionate in their dealings with one another. But in the meantime one must take them as they are and avoid the pointless pursuit of what in the real world cannot be achieved. This applies as much to the search for the fulfilment of exclusively national objectives as to the quest for a peaceful international order. In sum, one's aspirations should be tailored to one's power.

A corollary of this general principle of politics is that in the international community of sovereign states, institutions designed to accomplish the peaceful resolution of conflict should be structured to reflect, not merely 'the possible,' but the distribution of capabilities among those who determine what the limits of the possible really are. To put the matter more precisely, if the distribution of 'roles' or responsibilities within such institutions is too grossly at odds with the distribution of power (however defined) among the actors involved, the institutions will collapse (if not literally, then in the sense that they fail to fulfil their function). It is conceivable that this circumstance will change as the (group) norms of the international community become more fully developed. But the development of norms is a slow process, and in the meantime 'power' is the base currency of international politics. Within narrow limits its value from time to time may be inflated or diminished, and its expenditure by others is sometimes subject to the influence of persuasion, but in the end its supremacy cannot be denied.

These general propositions lead in turn to a range of special advocacies and tactical practices. On the basis of them, for example, it was almost automatic for Mr Pearson (along with Mackenzie King and other members of the Canadian foreign policy community) to attempt to influence the construction of the United Nations in a way which would correlate the assignment of responsibilities with the possession of power, and allocate the performance of specific functions in accordance with the distribution of appropriate capabilities. It was as natural to insist upon the awarding of a special place in the decision-making process to middle powers as it was to accept in vital matters of collective security the pre-eminent place of great powers.[11] Once the structure was established, moreover, it readily followed that its supporters should be encouraged to behave in ways which would strengthen its effectiveness. If they failed to do so, as in the case of the United States in the context of the Temporary Commission, or in the final phases of the Korean armistice negotiations, they had to be reminded of their obligations. If they persisted, however, in their wilful intransigence, it was better to let them have their way than to risk their permanent alienation. Progress in such matters is slow, and comes in the wake of many defeats.

By much the same reasoning, the fact that one did not approve of the way the Chinese conducted their internal affairs did not mean that one should refuse to deal with them. Nor did it mean that one should endanger the possibility of workable (that is, conflict-resolving) negotiations by indulging in moral condemnations of the sort that were embodied in the resolution of February 1951. Nor again did it mean that one should commit oneself inflexibly to rigid postures founded on high principles, as the Americans were thought to be doing at Geneva. Nor, finally, was it sensible to intensify and perpetuate the level of hostility by erecting unnecessary barriers to effective communication and exchange in other fields (for example, in non-strategic trade).

11 See Eayrs, *In Defence of Canada: Peacemaking and Deterrence,* chapter 2; Pearson, *Mike,* I, chapters 13 and 14; and Soward and McInnis, *Canada and the United Nations,* chapter 1

In dealing with allies, Mr Pearson's assumptions with regard to the significance of 'power' as an ingredient of international affairs entailed the tactical view that the possibilities for containing the behaviour of great power decision-makers are increased if they can be induced to operate within a multilateral arena. In such a context they are subject to the demands and pressures of smaller states, whose representatives can sometimes be mobilized in concert. At the same time, however, it is vital to recall that the essence of great power status in world affairs is the capacity in the final analysis to treat lesser powers as incidental. This being the case, the leverage of small power statesmen is always limited by the degree to which their views are regarded as important by the great power policy-makers whom they seek to influence. Hence, in the Korean case, Washington could be constrained, but only to a point. The location of the 'point' might be obscure, and different decision-makers in Ottawa (and elsewhere) might be prepared in approaching it to accept different degrees of risk, but to cross the line (as the Indians were often wont to do) was to accept the possibility of driving the Americans from the multilateral arena entirely, and thereby of losing everything. The calculations of the 'constrainers' must therefore be computed with care, and they must in the extremity be willing to muffle their convictions and accept political reality, entailing the ultimate authority of the powerful, for what it is. To do otherwise is to indulge in noble posturing (such as the Americans exhibited vis-à-vis the Chinese, and the neutrals vis-à-vis the Americans) at the expense of productive (that is, workable, functional, or conflict-resolving) results. 'Marginal' states had to be content with marginal influence. The 'big' decisions – to intervene in Korea in the first place, to cross the 38th parallel, to condemn the Chinese – had to be left in the last resort to the big battalions.

Students of Mr Pearson's writings, and of his diplomatic and political career as a whole, would probably have little difficulty in identifying additional illustrations of these various principles at work – for example, during the Suez crisis of 1956, or, domestically, in his subsequent handling of the federal government's relations with the province of Quebec – and obviously they could be extended and elaborated in more systematic form. Even in the informal guise in which they appear above, however, they are suggestive of how the 'operational code' perspective can generate a quite different, yet potentially illuminating 'explanation' of a phenomenon like the government's role in the diplomacy of the Korean War.

If the analysis is advanced strictly along the lines defined in the foregoing, it depends for its persuasiveness partly, of course, on the acceptance of the further assumption that the only significant Canadian decision-maker was Mr Pearson himself, or at least that Mr Pearson was the decision-maker who always had the 'final say.'[12] If it is claimed that other members of the policy community were also influential in the making of decisions, the argument from operational code analysis is insufficiently explanatory, even on its own limited terms, unless these other individuals can be shown to have been guided by the same, or very similar, philosophical and instrumental beliefs. If this can be established, the code becomes linked with the policy elite as a whole, and not merely with a single leader.[13] If not, the analysis may serve well enough as a partial explanation (in this case) of Mr Pearson's personal behaviour, but it cannot be held to account for the output of the foreign policy community in general.

It is possible, of course, to extend this sort of analytical focus into a wider context. For example, it can be held that the operational code of the responsible minister, and/or of the overall membership of the foreign policy community, is reflective more broadly of the dominant strains of the country's 'political culture' at large. Observations of this type are almost always impressionistic, and given the intangible character of the relation between government behaviour on the one hand, and the political beliefs of domestic constituents on the other, it is often difficult to assess their relevance. The argument, however, might briefly go like this: the diplomacy practised by Mr Pearson and his colleagues in the context of the Korean War was a reflection of the pragmatic, problem-solving approach to government which is the most characteristic feature of Canadian domestic politics. In its distrust of ideological argument, its preoccupation with the containment of conflict, its emphasis on pragmatic bargaining as a means of resolving differences, its suspicion of statements of grand or general purpose, its careful attention to the timing and tactics of diplomatic manoeuvre, its continuous matching of short-term objectives to immediate capabilities, its overriding concern for the preservation of the institutions and mechanisms of the political process – in all these, Canadian diplomatic practice in the Korean case exemplified the country's general political style. On this accounting, therefore, the Canadian approach to the diplomacy of the war is viewed fundamentally as a product of national political culture,

---

12 Whether it is reasonable to make this claim is a question which is considered in the next section.

13 Attempts to discuss what might be described as the 'political culture' of Canadian foreign policy can be found in two articles by Hockin: 'Federalist Style in International Politics,' in Clarkson, ed., *An Independent Foreign Policy for Canada?* 119-30; and 'The Foreign Policy Review and Decision Making in Canada,' in Hertzman, *et al, Alliances and Illusions,* 93-136. See also McNaught, 'Ottawa and Washington Look at the U.N.,' 414-38; and Newman, *The Distemper of Our Times,* 35-48

and the members of the foreign policy elite are regarded as its willing vehicles of external expression.[14]

To repeat, it is not very clear how 'explanations' of behaviour which are rooted in claims respecting the widespread acceptance of philosophical beliefs of this order of abstraction can be subjected to effective empirical tests. Even if it could be demonstrated through survey and other techniques that such beliefs were widely held, the problem of establishing clear causal linkages between the prevalence of the beliefs on the one hand, and, say, Mr Pearson's reaction to the intervention in the Korean War of the Communist Chinese on the other, is more than a little perplexing. A close examination of Mr Pearson's social, religious, political, and educational background, and that of his colleagues in the decision-making process, would appear to be an essential minimum requirement. Empirically well founded or not, however, arguments of this order of generality are commonly advanced in the literature, and they are sometimes regarded as no less illuminating for being intuitive.

It may be useful to call attention here to the degree to which the operational code style of analysis permits a measure of predictive generalization which is quite beyond the capacity of the idiosyncratic 'rational actor' model discussed in Section A. In the latter case, the assumption is that the actor will always behave in some sense 'rationally,' and if his objectives do not change, consistently, but the focus of attention is on the details of his calculations and behaviour in specific instances, and these in turn are seen to depend on the immediate conditions and properties of the particular case. The focus of the specialist in operational codes, on the other hand, is on much more general patterns of behaviour, and his mode of argument commits him to the prediction that these patterns will recur as long as the rules of the code are effectively brought to bear. If, for example, he concludes from the evidence of the Korean case that Mr Pearson's behaviour was governed by a coherent body of philosophical and instrumental beliefs, he will expect him to behave in much the same way in other contexts at other times – assuming, of course, that the minister does not experience a radical change of political faith. If Mr Pearson

---

14 See Hockin, 'Federalist Style in International Politics.' At this level of abstraction, however, the explanatory value of the analysis begins to weaken because it cannot account for deviations from the general pattern. For example, the Progressive Conservative secretary of state for external affairs in later years, Howard Green, was presumably as much a product of Canadian political culture as Mr Pearson, yet on cursory examination appears to have subscribed to a quite different set of operational rules. The only way out of this difficulty is to acknowledge the presence within Canada of more than one school of political thought, associated, perhaps, with different political parties, regions, socio-economic classes, vested interests, or whatever. But to fall back to this position amounts to a retreat from an initial over-generalization.

is replaced in office by someone whose beliefs are significantly different, changes in the conduct of foreign policy will be expected to ensue. Again, if the argument is that the operational code evident in the Canadian response to the Korean case was common to the foreign policy community as a whole, and if it is assumed in addition that policy elites in general have a habit of effectively 'socializing' their new recruits, the same behaviour patterns will be anticipated even through successive replacements of individual personnel – unless, again, there is some sort of revolutionary upheaval. And so also with the even more generalized arguments from national political culture.

Similarly, an analyst of this school who embarks on evaluative judgments will tend to focus his attention on the ingredients of the operational code rather than on the particular calculations of the moment. To refer again to one of the most interesting examples suggested by the Korean experience, if the analyst believes that the government was wrong in deciding to vote, against its own convictions, in favour of the February 1951 resolution condemning the Chinese as aggressors, his position will be based, not on the view that an abstention or negative vote would have contributed more effectively to the resolution of the conflict – such arguments are the preserve of the 'rational actor' school – but rather on the ground that the utilitarian calculus actually employed in the making of the decision was inappropriate. To put it another way, he would argue in effect that while Mr Pearson might have been right in his assessment of the short-term consequences of alternative courses of action, he was wrong in thinking that a comparison of these consequences was a sufficient basis for decision. He would have done 'better' to have acted in accordance with what he believed to be 'right in principle'[15] rather than in the light of what he believed to be 'right-because-least-damaging-now-given-the-conditions-of-the-case.' This sort of criticism would place the analyst in a position very similar to the one implied in the rhetoric and behaviour, for example, of the Indians, but it would also amount to a direct assault upon Mr Pearson's conception of good political practice.

In prescriptive terms, the implication of this style of analysis is that the 'actors' who subscribe to the offending operational doctrines should be persuaded to change their views, or replaced, if they are still in office, by persons whose views are different. As a matter of practical politics, this may be regarded as a relatively realistic aspiration if the culprit is a single decision-maker. It will obviously be much more difficult if the beliefs and practices involved are associated with an entire policy elite, whose defences are likely to be very strong. If the political culture of the country as a whole, or of major classes

15 On close examination this may mean little more than 'right in the very long run.'

and vested interests within it, is thought to be at fault, the obstacles may appear to be insurmountable.

'BEHAVIOUR' AS THE OUTCOME OF THE DISTRIBUTION OF ROLES

A decision-maker's behaviour is affected not merely by the values he holds, the practices he believes in, and the problems he confronts, but also by the office he occupies and the way in which he and other participants in the policy-making process perceive it. This being another 'variable,' it suggests in turn another analytical perspective, and it is therefore not surprising that the business of 'role analysis' can be discovered among the manifold enterprises of social science.[16] In the case of foreign policy studies, the suggestion is that a 'country's' external behaviour depends at least in part on the way in which the relevant 'foreign policy' functions are allocated among various office-holders, and on what the respective rights and responsibilities of the different offices involved are assumed by the participants to be. The idiosyncratic characteristics of the individuals who actually occupy the offices may still be regarded as important, but they are not in this perspective the primary focus of attention. Personal values and perceptual orientations are viewed here as coming into play only after the parameters of decision have been drastically reduced by a prior distribution of responsibilities, and by the limits which are imposed on the individual office-holder's freedom of action as a result of the way in which his role in the policy community is defined.

Role analysis is a highly technical activity, and the literature it generates appears in several disciplines. As the initiated will readily discover, the observations that follow are not based on extensive knowledge of this work. They are designed merely to show that the role analysis focus can draw attention to aspects of the making of foreign policy, in particular contexts, which might otherwise be overlooked.

If one confines one's attention to roles performed within the Canadian foreign policy community *per se,* one emerges in the Korean case with a list of potential role-players which includes, among the politicians, the prime minister, the secretary of state for external affairs, the minister of national defence, and members of the Cabinet not directly involved in the affairs of the

---

16 In the foreign policy field questions about the interaction of personality, role, and organization variables are given particular attention in the literature on decision-making. The most influential conceptual work has been done by Richard C. Snyder and his associates. See in particular Snyder, Bruck, and Sapin, *Foreign Policy Decision-Making.* Also relevant are Allison, *Essence of Decision,* and Rosenau, 'Pre-Theories and Theories of Foreign Policy,' in his *The Scientific Study of Foreign Policy,* 95-149.

war, and in the professional public service, certain senior military officers, together with officials from the relevant divisions and desks of the Department of External Affairs. It is not feasible here to consider all these in any detail; assuming there were the necessary space, the absence of evidence from the official files would in any case make a full analysis impossible. But even on the basis of the available material, it is clear that both the distribution of roles within the community, and the way in which the respective players perceived their own roles vis-à-vis those of others, tended on the Korean issue to amplify the involvement of the secretary of state for external affairs.[17] To take the political, or cabinet, level first, it has frequently been observed in the general literature on the Canadian foreign policy community that Prime Minister St Laurent's respect for Mr Pearson's judgment resulted in his being given a relatively free hand in the external field,[18] and the Korean experience supports this view. In stark contrast with the practice of Mackenzie King (as illustrated in the affair of the Temporary Commission), St Laurent assumed a role which was next to invisible in public, and essentially permissive behind the scenes. This was especially true after the decision to recruit the CASF had been reached. The prime minister's lead, moreover, was for the most part followed by other members of the Cabinet, partly, no doubt, because they shared Mr St Laurent's perception of Mr Pearson's credentials. In any case, it is reasonable to hypothesize that the display of prime ministerial support which Mr Pearson enjoyed was a source of inhibition to such other ministers as would have liked to quarrel with his proposals.

There were a few exceptions to this general pattern, but they were narrowly confined to two main categories – namely, cases in which the resources and expertise of another ministry were relevant, and cases in which the issues involved were potentially significant for domestic politics. The delays preceding the announcement of the plan to recruit the Special Force, for example, reflected not only the technical military concerns of the Department of National Defence and its minister, but also the anxieties of several members of the Cabinet over the possibility of political repercussions in the province of Quebec. Mr Pearson, as a foreign minister preoccupied with constituencies in the United Nations, Washington, and elsewhere, was eager to obtain an early decision, but in the end he was compelled to wait until Mr Claxton and some

17 This presumably served in turn to enhance the significance of Mr Pearson's personal values and precepts in the making and execution of Canadian policy. In this sense, the operational code perspective can be viewed as acquiring additional strength from the analysis of roles. On the other hand, the conclusion in this instance of the role analyst would not necessarily compel him to accept the operational code variable as significant.

18 See, for example, Eayrs, *The Art of the Possible,* especially 26-7; and Farrell, *The Making of Canadian Foreign Policy,* especially 29

of his other Cabinet colleagues had been satisfied with regard to their respective interests. A similar amalgamation of military, diplomatic, and political issues was involved also in the decision to object to the assignment of Canadian troops to POW guard duty on Koje-do in 1952. But for the most part, the trust in Mr Pearson's values and expertise was sufficiently pervasive at the ministerial level to lead to his being given a free hand to operate within them as he thought appropriate in the light of external conditions.

At the level of the professional public service, as in the Cabinet, the lower limits of Mr Pearson's latitude of decision were established by the simple fact that he was the minister in charge of the Department of External Affairs. Again, however, the specific circumstances of the day served to expand the importance of his role beyond the minimum which would accrue in any case to his official position. It often happens, of course, that a minister very quickly becomes the prisoner of his staff – dominated by their expertise, by their control of his daily agenda, and by their accounts of the advantages and disadvantages of alternative courses of action. But in the context of the Korean War such instruments of bureaucratic influence were blunted. As it happened, Mr Pearson was as visibly 'expert' in the conduct of world affairs as his advisers; indeed, in most cases his experience surpassed theirs. Moreover, the problems which emerged for Canadian diplomacy, while politically complex, were not technically obscure. It was therefore difficult for an adviser to lay claim to special influence by virtue of possessing superior competence. (In this respect Mr Claxton's relations with his military advisers were somewhat different.) In the areas in which it was necessary to operate under conditions of uncertainty – for example, during the attempt to anticipate the response of the Chinese to the advance into North Korea – it could be argued that one 'guesstimate' was as good as the next, and in this context the 'winning' guess might just as well be that of the most senior player. Hence, neither Escott Reid at the time of the crossing of the 38th parallel in the autumn of 1950, nor John Holmes on the occasion of the passage of the resolution of February 1951, nor Chester Ronning at Geneva in 1954, pressed their respective cases to the limit.

One can think again of exceptions, but these involved minor or tactical issues. For example, Hume Wrong's vigorous protests from Washington early in the war to the effect that in a time of crisis there was a limit to the number of missives he could carry with dignity to the Department of State reflected an interpretation of the prevailing atmosphere in the American capital which could be obtained only on the scene. His pleas were therefore bound to have weight in Ottawa. Such cases aside, however, it is clear from an examination of the respective roles assumed by senior members of the foreign policy community that the secretary of state for external affairs was by far the most significant single player. If the issues had been more technical, more numerous, or more relevant for the course of domestic politics; if the minister had been less experienced; if the bureaucracy had been larger and more complex; if the prime minister had been less trusting; if a wider range of government departments had been directly involved – if any of these conditions had pertained, the pattern might have been different. But given the circumstances as they actually were, considerable significance can be attached to Mr Pearson's personal beliefs as an ingredient in the making of Canadian policy. The student of role analysis, moreover, would be entitled to predict that this pattern of ministerial dominance would recur unless these circumstances were changed.

Having reached this sort of conclusion in the context of a specific case, the role analyst who proceeds to the level of evaluation and prescription, and finds that he disapproves of the behaviour which he has examined, may pursue arguments and proposals very similar to those of either the 'rational actor' or 'operational code' schools as defined above. In addition, however, he may be drawn into ancillary arguments bearing on the distribution of functions among various players, and on the freedom of action assigned to particular roles. For example, he might argue that on the matter of Korea the secretary of state for external affairs had been given too much latitude, and that more of the diplomatic decision ought to have been made collectively by the Cabinet as a whole. Or again he might suggest – in connection, for example, with the administration of recruitment into the CASF – that the minister of national defence had expanded his role into an area of professional military concern which, notwithstanding its potential significance for domestic politics, should have been left in the hands of his military staff. The argument here would not be simply that Mr Claxton had administered the details of the recruitment process badly, although this would certainly be implied by the criticism, but rather that they were beyond his competence in the first place. If the roles involved had been more appropriately allocated, 'better' results would have ensued.

Lest all these arguments seem elaborately trivial, it may be worth pointing out that the general conclusion that Mr Pearson dominated the formulation and execution of Canadian policy seriously affects the relevance for the Korean case of certain other commonly discussed models of foreign policy decision-making. Take, for example, what Professor Graham Allison has termed the 'government (or bureaucratic) politics' model.[19] The starting assumption here is that foreign policy behaviour results not from the 'rational' calculus of a single decision-maker, or even of a decision-making 'team,' but rather from the interactions of competing bureaucratic players. Each individual decision-mak-

19 *Essence of Decision,* 144-84

er is perceived as occupying a competitive position in a hierarchical structure. Each has his own set of interests, his own perceptions of external and internal 'reality,' and in consequence, his own policy preferences. Disagreements and conflicts inevitably ensue. They are resolved by game-like bargainings and manoeuvres. External behaviour (in the case of the analysis of foreign policy) is thus seen as consisting of the 'resultants' or 'outcomes' of these games, and not as the product of 'rational decisions.' It may be that each individual player acts 'rationally' in the context of his own bureaucratic 'position,' which inevitably differs from that of any other player, but this is not the same thing as saying that the players together act 'rationally' with reference directly to the conditions of the external environment.[20]

This model is particularly attractive to some American scholars because it accords well with many of the patterns of behaviour which are generated by the enormous size and complexity of the American policy community. Clearly, however, its explanatory value diminishes to the extent that decision-making is abrogated to a single player – in the Korean case, to Mr Pearson. Clearly, also, the proposals which arise from the model as remedies for 'deficient' performance – usually involving a simplification and/or centralization of decision-making processes – cease in such a context to have relevance.

If, on the other hand, the analysis of roles had produced different results, the bureaucratic politics model might have acquired significant explanatory utility. This is perhaps best illustrated by the case of the Temporary Commission, which arose in a context in which the role of the secretary of state for external affairs, then Mr St Laurent, was not so broadly defined as it was later to become under Mr Pearson. In this instance, the 'policy' that eventually emerged was different from what either Mr St Laurent or Mr King, on the basis of their respective reasonings, would really have preferred. It was instead a compromise 'outcome' of the bargaining which followed upon the conflict between these two principals and their various subordinates and allies. In short, the government's external behaviour can here be usefully 'explained' by reference to the bureaucratic model in a way in which, say, Mr Pearson's decision to support the aggressor resolution of 1 February cannot.

Consider, as another example, what Professor Allison has termed the 'organizational process' model of foreign policy-making. In this conceptualization, the government's behaviour in external affairs is viewed as consisting of 'outputs of large organizations functioning according to standard patterns of behaviour.'[21] Individual decision-makers are seen less as rational 'choosers' of

20 Individual players, of course, may deploy their own interpretations of these conditions as instruments of persuasion in the context of their strategic bargaining.
21 *Essence of Decision,* 67-100

specific courses of action than as triggers of standing organizational routines, or 'programmes,' over which they do not, at least in the short run, have detailed control. The result is that their latitude of decision is very much confined by the resistance of their organizations to manipulation from the 'top.' 'Analysis of formal governmental choice,' as Professor Allison puts it, then 'centers on the information provided and the options defined by organizations, the existing organizational capabilities that exhaust the effective choices open to the leaders, and the outputs of relevant organizations that fix the location of pieces on the chess board and shade the appearance of the issue. Analysis of actual government behaviour focuses on executionary outputs of individual organizations as well as on organizational capabilities and organizational positioning of the pieces on the chess board.'[22]

Clearly, however, the explanatory fertility of such a model diminishes with the size of the organization involved and the degree to which the resources necessary for the formation and implementation of decisions can be garnered and manipulated by individuals at the centre. In the case of Canada's involvement in the Korean War, for example, the fact that the Department of External Affairs was relatively small, that it possessed no resources essential to the conduct of Canadian diplomacy which could not be harnessed by the minister himself (the resources required consisted basically of political and intellectual skills), and that the centres of 'action' (principally Ottawa, New York, and Washington) were all within easy range of the minister's personal intervention, had the effect of diminishing the importance of the 'variables' which the organization model serves to emphasize. It is possible that this conclusion might be challenged by the evidence contained in the official files, and of course it can be argued that Mr Pearson's response to the outbreak of the war reflected a standing department 'programme' (comprised, for example, of directives like the following: 'Whenever possible, act with a view to bringing the management of international conflicts under the auspices of the United Nations') which anyone in his place would have been similarly 'bound' to pursue. But on the available evidence this does not appear a very useful or convincing way of looking at the matter. This being the case, it follows that an analyst who disapproved of Canadian behaviour would probably not be inclined to think of organizational reform as a particularly salient remedy.[23]

22 Ibid., 67
23 In later years, however, when the Department of External Affairs seemed to the Trudeau government to have become resistant to ministerial control, its organizational structure and position came under direct attack. The government's remedial strategy was directed in part to the renovation of its internal organization and composition, and in part to the strengthening of alternative sources of decision (for example, the Prime Minister's Office).

In the case of certain other aspects of Canada's involvement in Korea, however, an analysis from the perspective of organization theory may seem more appropriate. Consider, for example, the decisions regarding the recruitment, equipment, and deployment of the Canadian Army Special Force. Because the mobilization and management of armed forces require advance planning, standing resources, delegation of specialized functions, centralized co-ordination of decentralized effort, operational and procedural routines, and all the other ingredients of complex organizational life, organization variables might be expected in this area to have been clearly in evidence. And so they were. The decision to recruit a Special Force rather than to deploy units already in service; to equip the force largely with British-style arms; to link it with Commonwealth contingents; to delay its departure for the theatre, and after that its departure for the front; to assign Canadian naval units for the most part to operations involving Commonwealth vessels – all these decisions and others like them were obviously reflective of organizational factors. Among them, for example, were the existing priorities of Canadian security policy, the size and composition of the forces already in being, the previous experience of, and organizational linkages with, British (as opposed to American) military campaigns, the origin and design of available stores of equipment, and so on. In effect, when the war broke out and the military establishment was asked what it could do, General Foulkes delivered, not his own, but his organization's reply. In the light of his report, Mr Claxton was placed essentially in the position of having to tell the Cabinet that it could, if it wished, do less, but that without resorting to extraordinary, and therefore very costly, measures (for example, conscription), it really could not expect to do more, or to do it differently. Baldly stated, this amounts to saying that while the government's *diplomatic* role in the Korean war can be more convincingly accounted for by reference to variables deriving from the office and person of the secretary of state for external affairs than by explanations rooted in the characteristics of his departmental establishment, the reverse holds true for its *military* role.

And again if the analyst of the organization school disapproves of, say, the timing, size, composition, command structure, or whatever, of the military contingent, the implication for evaluative and prescriptive purposes is that the responsibility should be assigned to organization 'programmes' – a larger active force should have been available, standing recruitment and training procedures should have been more efficient, contingency plans should have been more fully developed, and so on. Once more, in short, the focus of prescriptive attention is determined by the perspective from which the analysis begins.

'BEHAVIOUR' AS THE DERIVATIVE OF SYSTEMIC POSITION

To consider still another possibility, the behaviour of foreign policy decision-makers can be viewed as if it is determined, not by their own beliefs or by characteristics of their policy-making process, but by their country's 'place' in the international 'system.' Within this framework, a 'country (or 'national actor,' as the jargon sometimes has it) is assumed to play a more or less clearly defined role in the international community (seen as a 'system of interactions') in somewhat the same way as individuals may be regarded as playing roles in the context of a bureaucratic structure. The 'country' responds to the challenges of the international environment in patterned and predictable ways (patterned, that is, at a certain level of analytical abstraction) according to the manner in which it relates, in terms of its capabilities, geographical location, and so forth, to other powers, and the way these other powers relate to one another. From such perspectives as this are derived theories of the 'balance of power,' bipolar, tripolar, and multipolar models of the international system, various elaborations involving the incorporation of 'subsystems,' and the like. The assumption throughout is that the structure of the international system in this broad sense is a significant and identifiable variable affecting in patterned or recurring ways the behaviour of individual 'actors.' These in turn are usually regarded as 'states' responding in a more or less comprehensively 'rational' way to the characteristics of the system, but without much reference to domestic demands and constraints or to the idiosyncratic values and beliefs of individual decision-makers or policy elites. In other words, given that the structure of the system has certain identifiable characteristics in terms of the distribution of power and other factors, the assumption is that one can predict that the various actors involved will follow certain definable categories of patterned behaviour. Within the general limits established by these patterns, there may of course be individual variations depending on the play of other, less general or 'fundamental,' variables.

Most of the work in this field[24] has centred on the systemic interactions of great powers, or of small powers which are 'great' within the confines of their own small subsystems (for example, Israel and the United Arab Republic in the subsystem of the Middle East). Hence the emphasis in the literature on the 'balance of power,' on 'bipolar' relationships, on zero-sum as opposed to variable-sum games as models of international bargaining, and so forth. Small-

24 Among the more prominent examples of the *genre* are: Kaplan, *System and Process in International Politics*; McClelland, *Theory and the International System*; and Scott, *Functioning of the International System*. For a general introduction to the use of systems analysis in political studies, see Young, *Systems of Political Science*.

er powers operating in non-bipolar contexts have not been very thoroughly examined. No attempt will be made here to remedy this deficiency – some might think in any case that the vacuum is not worth filling – but the systems focus does serve to highlight certain features of the Canadian response to the Korean War which might not otherwise receive explicit attention. These relate in particular to the identification of the international actors whose behaviour was immediately relevant for the conduct of Canadian policy, and whose relations with one another were so structured as to impose constraints upon the freedom of action of Canadian decision-makers.

Thus, given the structure of the international community of the day, and the intense hostility which had developed between 'east' and 'west' after the Second World War, the most important actor from the Canadian point of view was obviously the United States. Canada operated, in effect, as one of a group of allied powers which were ultimately dependent upon the Americans for the preservation of their security. The United States, in turn, was the principal source of policy for the western powers as a whole in their contest with the communist 'east.' As expressed in the language of the systems approach, Canada's position was structured within an American dominated subsystem, which in turn was operating at one pole of a larger system of east-west interactions. Under these circumstances it was clear that Canadian security ultimately depended on whether or not the global system proved to be stable. The government in Ottawa therefore had a vital interest in the workings of the system as a whole. Canadian influence, however, could be exerted at this global level only through the United States – that is, indirectly, by way of activity initiated within the 'subsystem' of western allies. Given the limits of Canadian power, and of Canada's 'place' in the international hierarchy, there was certainly no way in which Canadian decision-makers could hope to affect directly the objectives or expectations of the Soviet Union, China, and the other members of the eastern polar group. The attentions of the communist governments were naturally focussed on the United States, whose policy-makers ultimately controlled the general pattern of western activity in the cold war. If the Canadians were to influence the interactions which were taking place at the global level, therefore, they had to do so by moderating the behaviour of the only 'world,' or 'polar,' actor to whom they had access – that is, the United States. For this reason, the bulk of Canada's diplomacy in the context of the Korean War was concerned with the constraint of American policy, and many of the government's more subtle diplomatic calculations were devoted to identifiying the point beyond which it could not hope to engage in productive action – in effect to identifying the limits of Canada's 'systemic role.' To exceed these limits was, in fact, to endanger the effective 'maintenance' of the subsystem. Such few initiatives as were taken by Canadian officials to deal directly with the Chinese were therefore conducted under multilateral auspices and with explicit American agreement (as in the case of the Cease-Fire Group), or alternatively were designed to secure responses from the opposing subsystem which would make it easier for the Canadians and their diplomatic allies to persuade the Americans to moderate their views (as in the case of Prime Minister St Laurent's three-question inquiry of Peking in January 1951). To the extent, moreover, that they tried to force the conduct of American policy into the United Nations, they can be regarded as having attempted to restructure the channels of systemic interaction in such a way as to expand to the maximum possible degree the parameters of their own role. The evidence of the Korean case suggests, in fact, that Canadian decision-makers (and especially Mr Pearson) perceived Canada's role in the international community in precisely these systemic terms – terms which accorded well with the principles of their 'operational code.'

The evaluative and prescriptive debates which arise from this sort of analytical perspective tend, of course, to hinge on whether the decision-makers involved accurately perceived their country's 'location' in the international systemic structure, and if they did, whether they properly understood and interpreted the limits imposed by this location upon their latitude of 'effective' action. In the Korean case, were they 'right' in perceiving Canada as an inevitable member of the western subsystem, and did their exercise of their role either exceed, or fall short of, their real systemic capabilities? Did they, in effect, over- or under-estimate their 'power'?

From this vantage point, those Canadian commentators who in recent years have complained of what they perceive as a lack of 'independence' in Canadian foreign policy can be viewed as attacking the apparently unquestioned acceptance by Canadian decision-makers of precisely this sort of subsystemic role.[25] Those who advocate, for example, a policy of neutrality may be regarded as defenders of a unilateral initiative which would have the effect of removing Canada from the American-dominated 'western' subsystem to some other location (perhaps a third 'pole') in the world systemic structure, on the ground either that this would free Canadian decision-makers from what is perceived as excessive American influence, or that it would enhance their effectiveness in world affairs generally, or a combination of both. Those who support the existing patterns, on the other hand, deploy one or more of several arguments

25 See, for example, Minifie, *Peacemaker or Powder-Monkey*; the same author's *Open at the Top*; and many of the articles in Clarkson, ed., *An Independent Foreign Policy for Canada?*

in return.[26] They may, for example, claim simply that such a systemic relocation is impossible by virtue of domestic pressures within Canada. These are
said to result either from the various forms of existing American penetration
(this amounts to a claim that it is already too late), or from the importance
which Canadians themselves attach to the interests which they perceive themselves as sharing with the United States, or both. Alternatively, it may be
suggested that the unilateral adoption of a neutrality posture, given the high
visibility of 'shared' American and Canadian values and strategic and other
interests, would be impracticable because it would not be accepted as genuine
by the rest of the international community. In both these sets of arguments,
the basic point is that Canada's present location in the global system and its
subsystems are structured beyond the point of unilateral decision. In addition,
it may be claimed that if such a relocation were achieved, Canadian influence
over the maintenance of the global system would be diminished, not enhanced,
because such importance as Canada now enjoys is derived precisely from the
high degree of access to the American 'pole' which her exceptional subsystemic
position gives her. By abandoning the subsystem, she would be able to influence none of the major actors except through co-operative action within the
third 'pole' – that is, with other neutrals. Given the character of the global
system's overall patterns of interaction, the capacity of neutrals to influence
the course of world affairs is seen in turn as less continuous and less significant
than that of polarized allies within the present subsystem.[27]

For anyone who wishes to choose between such competing claims as these,
the practical problem is that of devising criteria for deciding which of them
is 'true,' and of implementing the empirical tests to which these criteria give
rise. This problem is difficult, however, because the arguments are advanced
at so broad a level of analytical abstraction as to invite conflicting interpretations of how their status is affected by the evidence of specific cases. At the
very least, they suggest the need to introduce at the outset a series of qualifications based on the identification of different categories of 'issue.' Systemic, or
subsystemic, patterns of interaction may thus be seen to vary from one type

26 The best and clearest statements for the defence are those of Peyton V. Lyon. See especially
   his *The Policy Question.*
27 From the vantage point of the 1970s, perhaps the most interesting feature of all these arguments is their growing irrelevance, for they have become on both sides increasingly difficult
   to sustain as the structure of the international system has been transformed. The development
   of *détente* in east-west relations and the related loosening of the ties of alliance within both
   of the polar subsystems have effectively served to rearrange many of the most salient features
   of the external setting of Canadian foreign policy. This, more than any other factor, lies at the
   root of Mr Trudeau's recent foreign policy review.

of issue to the next, and so on.[28] But this is to raise yet another range of analytical problems, and these cannot be considered here.

'BEHAVIOUR' AS THE RESULT OF DOMESTIC CONSTRAINTS

If it is possible to view the options of foreign policy decision-makers as significantly circumscribed by such factors as the limits of their personal roles in the foreign policy community, and the constraints imposed upon them by the structure of the international environment, it is possible also to see them as confined by the demands of their domestic constituents. To take this perspective one step further, it can be argued that 'foreign policy' amounts to efforts by policy-makers to fulfil domestic demands in the international arena. It can also be seen as a sequential mosaic of attempts to adapt the pursuit of such demands to conditions abroad – that is, to conditions which in various and constantly changing ways make it impossible to fulfil the demands without limit. Through this focus, foreign policy is viewed as having domestic roots, and the domestic sources of foreign policy become the object of explicit attention.[29]

The notion of a 'demand' in this context is a little misleading because it implies explicit articulation. That is, it seems to portray decision-makers as if they responded in concrete cases to the clearly expressed desires of identifiable domestic publics. The fact is, of course, that in an on-going political system there are vast ranges of 'demands' which are never expressed, or even discussed, but which are nonetheless implicit in the pursuit of policy. The demands, moreover, are often extremely general (for example, the 'demand' that the government preserve the 'national security'), in which case they do not provide 'recipes,' or clear guidelines from which the decision-makers can determine what they are expected to do. This is sometimes very convenient for the decision-makers, because it allows them to defend almost any policy they like in, say, 'national interest' terms without their running the risk that their

28 Whether systemic interactions in one issue-area have 'spill-over' effects in other issue-areas is, of course, one of the recurring questions in Canadian debates on Canadian-American relations. If Canada fails to co-operate with the planners of American security policy, for example, will one of the consequences be a deterioration in Ottawa's capacity to obtain concessions in, say, the field of trade or the movement of capital? Increasingly in recent years the answers to such questions have tended to be affirmative. From this perspective, one of the most striking features of Canada's diplomacy in the context of the Korean War was the fact that Mr Pearson was able, within broad limits, to press the Americans very hard without having to worry about the possiblity of direct repercussions in other areas.

29 As they do, for example, in Roseanau, *Domestic Sources of Foreign Policy.* See also his *The Adaptation of National Societies.*

constituents will be able to demonstrate the contrary by applying a visible test. On the other hand, in some situations it can cause them anxiety because they may have to take action – and hence risk political 'punishment' – without being certain of the 'public will' (however this may be defined).

In the Korean case one is struck by the relatively low significance (with one important exception) of *explicitly articulated* demands, and hence by the highly permissive character of the domestic environment within which the policy-making community was able to act (assuming that it remained within the range of broadly 'acceptable' courses of behaviour). The one exception to this was the demand for a Canadian military contribution to the United Nations cause. The evidence shows that initially the policy-makers were uncertain about the degree of domestic support that would accrue to the recruiting of a Canadian contingent, particular in French Canada. It soon became clear, however, that the attentive publics, far from merely acceding to such a contribution, would insist upon it, at least in English Canada, and the government's most serious domestic difficulty of the war was the problem in the summer of 1950 of finding ways to satisfy this demand in the absence of an existing supply of readily available and suitably trained military forces. In a sense it was compelled to confront the consequences of its own foreign policy rationale, for it had based its conduct of external affairs since 1945 on the purposes of the United Nations, and it had invoked these purposes immediately upon the outbreak of the war. Since the 'public' had been attracted to such declarations, and had found them persuasive, the policy-makers now came under considerable pressure to show that they meant what they said. The doubts about French Canada were resolved partly by the decision to rely on volunteers, and partly by the fact that it soon became evident that the opposition in Quebec was sufficiently muted to obviate any danger of serious political controversy.

For the rest, the decision-makers received little in the way of explicit public directives. But this is not to say that they were undirected. There were obvious limits beyond which they could not go. For example, in terms of domestic politics it seems clear that it would have been impossible for them to have contributed to the military campaigns of the North Koreans or the Chinese.[30] Indeed, such theoretical 'options' were never even considered, any more than was the possibility of voting on Korean resolutions in the General Assembly in support of the Soviet Union. It would have been exceedingly difficult for Canadian policy-makers to have contemplated merely an explicit posture of neutrality, and it seems probable, given the domestic response to

---

30 This is to argue from hypothetical history, with all the disadvantages that that implies. But the case seems to have weight nonetheless.

delays in their decision to participate in military operations, that even a silently passive position of non-involvement would have aroused a domestic storm. The posture advocated, for example, by *Le Devoir* almost certainly would have excited a severe reaction elsewhere in Canada had it become official policy.

In practice, of course, the members of the foreign policy community in Ottawa perceived themselves as being under very few such domestic constraints, but this was simply because their own perceptions of what constituted in the context appropriate courses of action were very closely aligned with those of the great majority of their constituents. Had the decision-makers wished to take a new and unexpected tack, the limits imposed upon their latitude of decision by their domestic publics would then have emerged as clearly defined obstacles. How far they could have gone in challenging their constituency is a question to which there are only speculative answers. Quarrels about the 'possible' in politics are always quarrels about the uncertain, which probably explains why there are so often debated with heat. But in the end it is clear that Mr Pearson and his colleagues perceived themselves to be 'free' because they had no desire to move beyond the length of their chains. Within these limits, on the other hand, they enjoyed a genuine capacity to exercise their tactical and strategic skills in whatever fashion they liked.

The fundamental compatibility of the views on Korea of the Canadian policy elite on the one hand, and of their domestic constituents on the other, tends to make this approach in the present case a rather unsatisfactory perspective from the vantage point of the foreign policy critic. In other circumstances, however, it can be suggestive of a broad range of 'remedial' activities, most of which will be directed to changing the balance of domestic forces which the decision-makers perceive to be interested and involved. All the usual methods of placing governments under domestic pressure – through the activities of interest groups, for example, or *via* the mass communications media – may appear to be relevant. In some instances the matter in dispute may even become a subject of electoral competition, in which case the assumption of the critics is that the existing political leadership is irretrievably tied to the 'wrong' domestic constituents and must therefore be replaced by a leadership which is loyal to the 'right' ones. Again, if the policy elite is seen to be linked with so powerful and pervasive a group of domestic forces that there is no hope through regular political processes of replacing its members with men who represent other, quite different sectors of society, the tendency may be to recommend irregular – even revolutionary – methods of political action. This, for example, would be the position of classical 'Marxists' and many of their contemporary derivatives. In all these cases, the 'variables' which are seen to be most immediately relevant as a source of policy, and hence also as a target for political action, are rooted in the policy-makers' domestic environment.[31]

'BEHAVIOUR' AS THE REFLECTION OF FLOWS OF INFORMATION

Still another variable which in recent years has become an explicit focus of analytical attention is the 'information' or 'communications' variable.[32] In this branch of the literature the analyst begins with the assumption – safe enough – that underlying every phase of the political process is a process of communication. Information – whether true or false, reliable or suspect, full or incomplete – is seen to be necessary for the identification of problems, the implementation of decisions, the examination of results, the distribution of punishments and rewards, the revision of policies, and so on. It follows from this that information, and the capacity to obtain and absorb it, is power. Carefully and properly interpreted, it yields optimal decision-making; mismanaged and misused, it ensures failure and ineffectuality. This is seen to be as true for policy communities as a whole, acting within their internal and external environments, as it is for individual decision-makers, performing as ambitious members of hierarchical organizations. Much of the literature on the making of foreign policy is therefore concerned with questions bearing, for example, on the causes of failures of foreign policy 'intelligence' – that is, with accounting for the fact that foreign policy communities often behave as if they were ignorant of the 'facts,' or as if they had misinterpreted the 'evidence' of external 'reality' to which they had ready access.[33] Since in many cases it is clear that some degree of 'ignorance' is unavoidable, attention has also been paid in this context to the problems and consequences of making decisions under conditions of uncertainty.[34] In cases, however, in which intelligence breakdowns can be regarded as genuine 'failures,' they are usually viewed as being rooted in an apparent inability to gather, organize, and deliver to the

31 The domestic environment can, of course, be influenced, or 'penetrated,' by governmental, or private action from abroad. It is for this purpose, indeed, that governments maintain propaganda establishments and the like as ancillary instruments of statecraft.
32 The best known general work in this field is probably Deutsch, *The Nerves of Government.* No attempt will be made here to deal, however, at this level of sophistication.
33 Some of the more interesting work in this area has its roots in psychology. See, for example, Jervis, 'Hypotheses on Misperception,' 454-79. For an analysis of the Korean case from this perspective, see DeWeerd, 'Strategic Surprise in the Korean War,' 435-52. Probably the most detailed case-study dealing with this sort of question is Wohlstetter's *Pearl Harbor.*
34 See, among others, Schelling, *The Strategy of Conflict,* and Braybrooke and Lindblom, *A Strategy of Decision.*

decision-makers sufficient pertinent information to allow them to devise 'effective,' 'workable,' or 'realistic' policies in response to the conditions with which they are confronted. The causes of such failures range all the way from lack of resources, and administrative or structural inefficiencies (organizational factors), through breakdowns in communication arising from the rivalries of individual personnel (bureaucratic politics factors), to the prevalence among the significant decision-makers and/or intelligence gatherers of inappropriate images, expectations, and theories in relation to their political environment (operational code and related factors). Each category of 'explanation' entails, moreover, it own variety of corrective action, including the reorganization of the policy machine, the reeducation of the policy elite, and so on.

If one considers even very generally the Canadian response to the Korean War through this sort of analytical lens, one is struck immediately by the fact that Canadian decision-makers, unlike their American counterparts, were not compelled within their own sphere of operations to reach decisions under conditions of ignorance. While it is true, for example, that the North Korean attack caught *all* the western allies by surprise, there is a sense in which this was significant only for the United States, since the behaviour of the other western actors (as 'subsystemic' players) was contingent upon the American response. Given the decision to intervene, the 'surprise' character of the enterprise had serious implications for American military personnel (they had to act in haste and without adequate preparation), and much of the Washington policy community's activity during the first seven days of the hostilities was devoted to the development of a more complete intelligence evaluation.[35] By contrast, while the Canadians were similarly surprised by the outbreak of the fighting, and while they were equally surprised by the American military intervention, they nevertheless had more than sufficient time to work out their response with calculated care. Moreover, whereas the main focus of American attention was on the North Koreans, the Soviets, and the Chinese – that is, on actors whose intentions were unclear and whose behaviour was unpredictable – the main focus of Canadian attention was on the Americans – that is, on actors to whose reasonings and purposes they had nearly full access. The only period in which this was not true was in the late autumn of 1950, when it seemed that the Truman administration might not be able to control the behaviour of the field commander. This in turn generated in Ottawa what Escott Reid has since described as a 'nightmarish' sense for uncertainty about the actual course of American policy. But for the Canadians this was an exceptional circumstance, whereas for the Americans it was a difficulty which persisted throughout the war. The Americans were constantly forced in making decisions to speculate upon the intentions, the will, and the resources of their opponents, and to do so in the knowledge that all such speculations were based on inadequate evidence. The Canadians confronted few such difficulties, at least in the areas of decision which directly concerned them.

The only occasions on which the wider imponderables that were at the centre of American preoccupations became directly relevant for the Canadians were those on which the successful application of Canadian pressure depended upon the capacity to persuade the Americans to accept a view of their opponents which could not be 'proved.' For example, when the question of an advance into North Korea was being considered in tha autumn of 1950, the Canadians were afraid that the Chinese might in consequence enter the war, and hence they urged a policy of restraint. Some American decision-makers harboured similar doubts, but in the end they decided that these were not sufficiently cogent to be incorporated as a major premise of American policy. The Canadians were unable to persuade them otherwise because they had no way of demonstrating the accuracy of the alternative view.

In general, however, Canadian decision-makers were not unduly hand-icapped by lack of information, nor were they troubled by mismanagement or misinterpretation of the 'data' at their disposal. Their uncertainty about Soviet intentions in Europe made them cautious in the deployment of their troops to the Far East, but on the whole their dilemmas were less dilemmas of substance than of tactics – how much pressure should be applied on Washington? through which channels? at what time? in whose company? for how long? In answering such questions, they had an enormous fund of experience upon which to draw, along with the advantage of direct day-to-day communications with their immediate diplomatic targets. This may well be a recurrent luxury in the conduct of Canadian foreign policy, and it is possible that it is a generally distinctive feature of small power diplomacy in the context of subsystems of co-operating states. If so, its implications may be worth the serious attention of specialists in the field.

'HISTORICAL' CONSEQUENCES: A BRIEF REVERSION

Those who specialize in the various analytical perspectives discussed above could obviously derive observations from the evidence of the Korean case much more systematically than has been attempted here. Given the particular requirements of their respective frameworks, there is little doubt either that they could construct research 'designs' which would generate data of much greater use to them than the material contained in the narrative of this book.

---

35 For a full discussion, see Paige, *The Korean Decision,* especially 290-5.

There are, moreover, many other possible ways of looking at foreign policy behaviour, and many other questions to be asked. The foregoing reflections have been designed merely to indicate a few of the possible lines of inquiry, and to consider on a comparative basis some of their fundamental premises and prescriptive implications.

To revert briefly to the 'historical' mould, however, it is worth recalling that political affairs have an impact on the long term as well as the short. Certainly they do not start from a clean slate, but rather develop in the context of a past which imposes controls upon the velocity and direction of their progress in the present. In other words, each historical phase establishes a set of limiting parameters for the next. The process by which the 'past' intrudes in this way upon the 'present,' and the 'present' upon the 'future,' can be viewed from various perspectives, and once again, from different levels of analytical abstraction. Without belabouring further the methodological issues, however, it should suffice here to point out that the war in Korea had a profound effect upon the conduct of Canadian security policy throughout the 1950s and 60s. The experience convinced the foreign policy community in Ottawa as much as it did the officials of other allied governments that the western world was threatened militarily as well as politically by the Soviet Union and its 'satellites.' In response to this perception the government was induced to undertake in addition to the raising of the Special Force a massive programme of rearmament in all three services. This programme determined the specifications of the Canadian armed forces for nearly two decades, and its effect upon Canadian defence policy is still very much in evidence. Since the war had a parallel impact upon the perceptions of decision-makers in other allied capitals, and led to similar responses there, the result was an external environment for Canadian policy which made subsequent changes of direction very difficult. These rigidities were almost certainly reinforced by the bureaucratic influences which must have become evident within the departments of external affairs and national defence after the 1950-1 pattern of commitments had been fully established. Insofar as the perceptions of the policy-makers were shared by, and conveyed to, the attentive sectors of the Canadian public, the rigidities were reinforced also by the support which they received from the domestic political environment (until the emergence, at least, of widespread academic and other cirticism in the 1960s).

More broadly, the identification of Canada with the American-dominated 'subsystem,' which was apparent much earlier, became as a result of the Korean experience much more firmly entrenched. The external setting of Canadian foreign policy grew more narrowly defined and more tightly bound, a consequence which began to weaken only with the development in the late

1960s of softer perceptions of the Soviet Union and China. The Korean War delayed Canada's recognition of the Peking regime by twenty-one years. It also reinforced patterns of involvement in United Nations diplomacy which were to persist into the early 1960s, and which began to decline only as the organization's membership expanded to include countries whose representatives were less amenable to Canadian influence and less preoccupied with east-west issues. The Canadian Army Special Force was conceived as a contribution to an enterprise in collective security, and thereafter portions of the Canadian armed services were kept in reserve for this purpose. To that extent the Canadian involvement in Korea was a precedent for peace-keeping operations of a somewhat different kind in subsequent years.

From the hostilities in Korea were thus derived many of the patterns – both trivial and significant – of Canadian foreign and defence policy for the ensuing two decades. The patterns have only now begun to change.

Sources

OFFICIAL PUBLICATIONS AND DOCUMENTS

CAGLE, MALCOLM W. and FRANK A. MANSON. *The Sea War in Korea.* Annapolis, United States Naval Institute, 1957

CANADA, DEPARTMENT OF DEFENCE PRODUCTION. *First Report: April 1 to December 31, 1951.* Ottawa, Queen's Printer, 1952
– *Second Report: January 1 to December 31, 1952.* Ottawa, Queen's Printer, 1953
– *Third Report: January 1 to December 31, 1953.* Ottawa, Queen's Printer, 1954
– *Fourth Report: January 1 to December 31, 1954.* Ottawa, Queen's Printer, 1955
– *Fifth Report: January 1 to December 31, 1955.* Ottawa, Queen's Printer, 1956
– *Sixth Report: January 1 to December 31, 1956.* Ottawa, Queen's Printer, 1957
– *Seventh Report: January 1 to December 31, 1957.* Ottawa, Queen's Printer, 1958
– *Eighth Report: January 1 to December 31, 1958.* Ottawa, Queen's Printer, 1959

CANADA, DEPARTMENT OF EXTERNAL AFFAIRS. *Annual Reports* (1950 to 1954). Ottawa, Queen's Printer, 1951-5
– *Canada and the Korean Crisis.* Ottawa, King's Printer, 1950
– *Canada and the United Nations* (annually, 1948 to 1954). Ottawa, King's/Queen's Printer, 1949-55

- *Documents on the Korean Crisis.* Ottawa, King's Printer, 1951
- *External Affairs* (monthly, 1949-65). Ottawa, King's/Queen's Printer, 1949-65
- Korean War: Analysis of Canadian Editorial Comment (26-30 June). Ottawa 1950
- *Statements and Speeches* (irregular series, 1950-4). Ottawa, Department of External Affairs, 1950-4
- *We the peoples ... Canada and the United Nations, 1945-1965.* Ottawa, Queen's Printer, 1966
CANADA, DEPARTMENT OF NATIONAL DEFENCE. *Canada's Defence Programme, 1949-50.* Ottawa, King's Printer, 1949
- *Canada's Defence Programme, 1951-52.* Ottawa, King's Printer, 1951
- *Canada's Defence Programme, 1952-53.* Ottawa, Queen's Printer, 1952
- *Canada's Defence Programme, 1953-54.* Ottawa, Queen's Printer, 1953
- *Canada's Defence Programme, 1955-56.* Ottawa, Queen's Printer, 1955
- *White Paper on Defence.* Ottawa, Queen's Printer, 1964
CANADA, DOMINION BUREAU OF STATISTICS. *Canadian Statistical Review: January 1951.* Ottawa, King's Printer, 1951
CANADA, DOMINION BUREAU OF STATISTICS FOR THE DEPARTMENT OF TRADE AND COMMERCE. *The Canada Year Book* (1950-3). Ottawa, King's/Queen's Printer, 1950-3
- *Trade of Canada: Volume II – Exports* (1946 to 1955). Ottawa, King's/Queen's Printer, 1947-56
CANADA, HOUSE OF COMMONS. *Debates,* 1948 to 1957
- *Special Studies for the Special Committee of the House of Commons on Matters Relating to Defence.* Ottawa, Queen's Printer, 1965
CANADA, HOUSE OF COMMONS, STANDING COMMITTEE ON EXTERNAL AFFAIRS. *Minutes of Proceedings and Evidence* (1951 to 1954). Ottawa, Queen's Printer, 1951-4
CANADA. *Proceedings of the Conference of Federal and Provincial Governments, Ottawa, December 4-7, 1950.* Ottawa, King's Printer, 1951
CANADA, SENATE. *Debates,* 1950 to 1955
DEMOCRATIC PEOPLE'S REPUBLIC OF KOREA, MINISTRY OF FOREIGN AFFAIRS. *Documents and Materials Exposing the Instigation of the Civil War in Korea.* Pyongyang 1950
DZIUBAN, COLONEL STANLEY W. *Military Relations Between the United States and Canada, 1939-45.* Washington, USGPO for the Office of the Chief of Military History, Department of the Army, 1959
GREAT BRITAIN, FOREIGN OFFICE. *Korea: A Summary of Developments in the Armistice Negotiations and the Prisoner of War Camps.* Cmd. 8596. London, HMSO, 1952

GREAT BRITAIN, SECRETARY OF STATE FOR FOREIGN AFFAIRS. *Documents relating to the discussion of Korea and Indo-China at the Geneva Conference, April 27-June 15, 1954.* London, HMSO, 1954

HISTORICAL SECTION, GENERAL STAFF, ARMY HEADQUARTERS. *Canada's Army in Korea: The United Nations Operations, 1950-53, and Their Aftermath.* Ottawa, Queen's Printer, 1956

LINKLATER, ERIC. *Our Men in Korea.* London, HMSO, 1952

PEOPLE'S REPUBLIC OF CHINA. 'Statements and Reports on the American Crime of Waging Bacteriological Warfare in China and Korea,' Supplement to *People's China,* 16 April 1952

THORGRIMSSON, THOR and E.C. RUSSELL. *Canadian Naval Operations in Korean Waters, 1950-1955.* Ottawa, Queen's Printer for the Naval Historical Section, Canadian Forces Headquarters, 1965

UNITED NATIONS, GENERAL ASSEMBLY. *Official Records,* 1947 to 1953

UNITED NATIONS, SECURITY COUNCIL. *Official Records,* 1950 to 1953

UNITED STATES, DEPARTMENT OF STATE. *Department of State Bulletin,* 1950 to 1954

UNITED STATES, SENATE. *Military Situation in the Far East: Hearings before the Committee on Armed Services and the Committee on Foreign Relations, United States Senate, Eighty-Second Congress, First Session.* Washington, USGPO, 1951

WOOD, LIEUTENANT COLONEL HERBERT FAIRLIE. *Strange Battleground: Official History of the Canadian Army in Korea.* Ottawa, Queen's Printer for the Army Historical Section, Canadian Forces Headquarters, 1966

INTERVIEWS

Rear Admiral J.V. Brock, Chester, Nova Scotia, 23 July 1969; and Halifax, 29 July 1969
Mr Peter G.R. Campbell, Halifax, 20 October 1968
Mr M.J. Coldwell, Halifax, 10 July 1970
Brigadier A.B. Connelly, Ottawa, 7 March 1968
Lieutenant General F.J. Fleury, Ottawa, 8 March 1968
General Charles Foulkes, Ottawa, 7 March 1968
Mr A.D.P. Heeney, Ottawa, 7 March 1968
Mr John W. Holmes, Toronto, 1 and 5 March 1968, and 8 June 1970
Principal Douglas V. LePan, Toronto, 5 March 1968
Professor R.A. MacKay, Ottawa, 7 March 1968
Mr Geoffrey Pearson, Ottawa, 18 October 1968
The Right Honourable Lester B. Pearson, Ottawa, 18 October 1968
The Honourable J.W. Pickersgill, Ottawa, 13 March 1968

Principal Escott Reid, 9 June 1969
Mr H. Basil Robinson, Ottawa, 5 May 1970
Lieutenant General G.G. Simonds, Toronto, 9 June 1970
Brigadier Harold E. Taber, Toronto, 7 June 1969
Mr Freeman M. Tovell, Ottawa, 5 May 1970

COLLECTIONS OF PAPERS

Most of the pertinent collections of official and private papers are still closed to academic scrutiny. The most useful collection to which the author had partial access was the Brooke Claxton collection, housed in the Public Archives of Canada. The C.D. Howe Papers, also housed in the PAC, offer very little material of direct relevance to the diplomacy of the Korean War. The T.A. Crerar Papers and the Grant Dexter Papers, both in the custody of the Douglas Library, Queen's University, contain a few items of marginal importance.

GENERAL

General and secondary materials bearing on the Korean War are voluminous. Many of the better known titles in English are included in the accompanying List of Works Cited. Specialists may wish to consult the bibliography in the doctoral dissertation from which this book is largely derived (Denis Stairs, 'The Role of Canada in the Korean War,' University of Toronto 1969, 541-61). For an extensive, if somewhat dated, bibliography on the war as a whole, see Carroll H. Blanchard, jr, *Korean War Bibliography and Maps of Korea,* Albany 1964

List of works cited

ACHESON, DEAN. *Present at the Creation: My Years in the State Department.* New York, W.W. Norton, 1969

ADAMS, SHERMAN. *Firsthand Report: The Story of the Eisenhower Administration.* New York, Harper, 1961

ALLEN, H.C. *Great Britain and the United States: A History of Anglo-American Relations (1783-1952).* London, Odhams, 1954

ALLISON, GRAHAM T. *Essence of Decision: Explaining the Cuban Missile Crisis.* Boston, Little Brown, 1971

ALTSTEDTER, NORMAN. 'Problems of Coalition Diplomacy: The Korean Experience.' *International Journal,* VIII, 4, autumn 1953

ATTLEE, C.R. *As It Happened.* London, Heinemann, 1954

BARCLAY, BRIGADIER C.N. *The First Commonwealth Division.* Aldershot, Gale and Polden, 1954

BARKWAY, MICHAEL. 'Korea: What Has It Done to Us?' *Saturday Night,* 21 Nov. 1950

BELL, DANIEL. 'Ten Theories in Search of Reality: The Prediction of Soviet Behavior,' in his *The End of Ideology.* Glencoe, Ill., Free Press, 1960

BERTON, PIERRE. 'Corporal Dunphy's War.' *Maclean's,* 1 June 1951

BLOOMFIELD, LINCOLN P. *The United Nations and U.S. Foreign Policy.* Boston, Little, Brown, 1960

BOWETT, D.W. *United Nations Forces.* New York, Praeger, 1964

BRAYBROOKE, DAVID and CHARLES E. LINDBLOM. *A Strategy of Decision: Policy Evaluation as a Social Process.* New York, Macmillan, 1963

- 'Types of Decision-Making,' in James N. Rosenau, ed. *International Politics and Foreign Policy.* Rev. ed. New York, Free Press, 1969
BRECHER, MICHAEL. *India and World Politics: Krishna Menon's View of the World.* London, Oxford University Press, 1968
CAGLE, COMMANDER MALCOLM W. 'Inchon – The Analysis of a Gamble,' *United States Naval Institute Proceedings,* LXXX, 1, Jan. 1954
CAGLE, MALCOLM W. and FRANK A. MANSON. *The Sea War in Korea.* Annapolis, United States Naval Institute, 1957
CARIDI, RONALD J. *The Korean War and American Politics: The Republican Party as a Case Study.* Philadelphia, University of Pennsylvania Press, 1968
CARR, E.H. *What Is History?* London, Macmillan, 1961
'Change Needed at Defence.' *Saturday Night,* 1 Aug. 1950
CLARK, MARK W. *From the Danube to the Yalu.* New York, Harper, 1954
CLARKSON, STEPHEN, ed. *An Independent Foreign Policy for Canada?* Toronto, McClelland and Stewart, 1968
COLLINS, J. LAWTON. *War in Peacetime: The History and Lessons of Korea.* Boston, Houghton Mifflin, 1969
COTTRELL, ALVIN J. and JAMES E. DOUGHERTY. 'The Lessons of Korea: War and the Power of Man.' *Orbis,* II, 1, spring 1958
CUMMINS, GERALDINE. *Unseen Adventures: An Autobiography covering Thirty-four Years of Work in Psychical Research.* London, Rider, 1951
CUTFORTH, RENE. *Korean Reporter.* London, Wingate, 1952
DEUTSCH, KARL W. *The Nerves of Government: Models of Political Communication and Control.* New York, Free Press, 1966
DEWEERD, H.A. 'Strategic Surprise in the Korean War.' *Orbis,* VI, 3, fall 1972
'Direct & Immediate Menace.' *Time,* Canada Edition, 2 Nov. 1962
DONOVAN, ROBERT J. *Eisenhower: The Inside Story.* New York, Harper, 1956
DZIUBAN, COLONEL STANLEY W. *Military Relations Between the United States and Canada, 1939-1945.* Washington, Office of the Chief of Military History, Department of the Army, 1959
EAYRS, JAMES. *The Art of the Possible: Government and Foreign Policy in Canada.* Toronto, University of Toronto Press, 1961
- 'The Foreign Policy of Canada,' in Joseph E. Black and Kenneth W. Thompson, eds. *Foreign Policies in a World of Change.* New York, Harper, 1963
- *In Defence of Canada.* II: *Appeasement and Rearmament.* Toronto, University of Toronto Press, 1965

- *In Defence of Canada.* III: *Peacemaking and Deterrence.* Toronto, University of Toronto Press, 1972
EDEN, SIR ANTHONY. *Full Circle.* London, Cassell, 1960
EGGLESTON, WILFRID. 'Capital Comment: A Great Address by Pearson.' *Saturday Night,* 12 Sept. 1950
FARRELL, R. BARRY. *The Making of Canadian Foreign Policy.* Scarborough, Prentice-Hall, 1969
FRASER, BLAIR. 'Backstage at Ottawa.' *MacLean's,* 15 Aug. 1950
- 'Backstage at Ottawa.' *Maclean's,* 1 Sept. 1950
- 'Backstage at Ottawa.' *Maclean's,* 15 Sept. 1950
- 'How Dr. Endicott Fronts for the Reds.' *Maclean's,* 15 July 1952
- *The Search for Identity: Canada, Postwar to Present.* Toronto, Doubleday, 1967
- 'The Secret Life of Mackenzie King, Spiritualist.' *Maclean's,* 15 Dec. 1951
- 'Win or Lose, the Russians May Get Korea.' *Maclean's,* 1 Jan. 1951
FRENCH-CANADIAN OBSERVER, 'French-Canadian Opinion on NATO and Korea.' *International Journal,* VIII, 2, spring 1953
GEORGE, ALEXANDER L. 'American Policy-Making and the North Korean Aggression.' *World Politics,* VII, 2, Jan. 1955
GOODRICH, LELAND M. *Korea: A Study of* U.S. *Policy in the United Nations.* New York, Council on Foreign Relations, 1956
- 'Korea: Collective Measures Against Aggression.' *International Conciliation,* no 494, Oct. 1953
GOOLD-ADAMS, RICHARD. *The Time of Power: A Reappraisal of John Foster Dulles' Command of American Power.* New York, Doubleday, 1960
GORDENKER, LEON. *The United Nations and the Peaceful Unification of Korea.* The Hague, Nijhoff, 1959
- 'The United Nations, the United States Occupation and the 1948 Election in Korea.' *Political Science Quarterly,* LXXIII, 3, Sept. 1958
GOW, J.I. 'Les Québécois, la guerre et la paix, 1945-60.' *Canadian Journal of Political Science,* III, 1, March 1970
GREY, ARTHUR L. jr. 'The Thirty-Eighth Parallel.' *Foreign Affairs,* XXIX, 3, April 1951
GUNTHER, JOHN. *The Riddle of MacArthur.* New York, Harper, 1951
HAMMOND, PAUL Y. 'NSC-68: Prologue to Rearmament,' in Warner R. Schilling, *et al. Strategy, Politics, and Defense Budgets.* New York, Columbia University Press, 1962

HARRISON, W.E.C. *Canada in World Affairs, 1949-1950.* Toronto, Oxford University Press for Canadian Institute of International Affairs, 1957

HEENEY, ARNOLD. *The things that are Caesar's: The memoirs of a Canadian public servant.* Toronto, University of Toronto Press, 1972

HIGGINS, TRUMBULL. *Korea and the Fall of MacArthur.* New York, Oxford University Press, 1960

HISTORICAL SECTION, GENERAL STAFF, ARMY HEADQUARTERS. *Canada's Army in Korea: The United Nations Operations, 1950-53, and Their Aftermath.* Ottawa, Queen's Printer, 1956

HOCKIN, THOMAS A. 'Federalist Style in International Politics,' in Stephen Clarkson, ed. *An Independent Foreign Policy for Canada?* Toronto, McClelland and Stewart, 1968

- 'The Foreign Policy Review and Decision-Making in Canada,' in Lewis Hertzman, *et al. Alliances and Illusions: Canada and the* NATO-NORAD *Question* (Edmonton, Hurtig, 1969)

HOLMES, JOHN W. 'Geneva: 1954.' *International Journal,* XXII, 3, summer 1967

HOLSTI, OLE. 'The "Operational Code" Approach to the Study of Political Leaders: John Foster Dulles' Philosophical and Instrumental Beliefs,' *Canadian Journal of Political Science,* III, 1, March 1970

HOYT, EDWIN C. 'The United States Reaction to the North Korean Attack: A Study of the Principles of the United Nations Charter as a Factor in American Policy-Making.' *American Journal of International Law,* LV, 1, Jan. 1961

HUGHES, E.J. *The Ordeal of Power: A Political Memoir of the Eisenhower Years.* New York, Atheneum, 1963

HUTCHISON, BRUCE. *Mackenzie King: The Incredible Canadian.* London, Longmans, Green, 1953

'International Organizations: Summary of Activities,' *International Organization,* IV, 4, Nov. 1950

JERVIS, ROBERT. 'Hypotheses on Misperception.' *World Politics,* XX, 3, April 1968

JONES, S. SHEPHARD and DENYS P. MYERS, eds. *Documents on American Foreign Relations, January 1938-June 1939.* Boston, World Peace Foundation, 1939

JOY, ADMIRAL C. TURNER. *How Communists Negotiate.* New York, Macmillan, 1955

KAPLAN, MORTON A. *System and Process in International Politics.* New York, John Wiley and Sons, 1957

KEIRSTEAD, B.S. *Canada in World Affairs: September 1951 to October 1953.* Toronto, Oxford University Press for the Canadian Institute of International Affairs, 1956

KENNAN, GEORGE F. *Memoirs: 1925-1950.* Boston, Little, Brown, 1967

KUNZ, JOSEF L. 'Legality of the Security Council Resolutions of June 25 and 27, 1950.' *American Journal of International Law,* XLV, 1, Jan. 1951

LECKIE, ROBERT. *Conflict: The History of the Korean War, 1950-53.* New York, Putnam's, 1962

LIE, TRYGVE. *In the Cause of Peace.* New York, Macmillan, 1954

LINKLATER, ERIC. *Our Men in Korea.* London, HMSO, 1952

LYON, PEYTON V. *The Policy Question: A Critical Appraisal of Canada's Role in World Affairs.* Toronto, McClelland and Stewart, 1963

LYONS, GENE M. 'American Policy and the United Nations' Program for Korean Reconstruction.' *International Organization,* XII, 2, spring 1956
– *Military Policy and Economic Aid: The Korean Case, 1950-1953.* Columbus, Ohio, State University Press, 1961

MACARTHUR, DOUGLAS. *Reminiscences.* New York, Fawcett, 1965

MAHURIN, WALKER. *Honest John.* New York, Putnam's, 1962

MASTERS, DONALD C. *Canada in World Affairs, 1953 to 1955.* Toronto, Oxford University Press for the Canadian Institute of International Affairs, 1959

MAY, ERNEST R. 'The Nature of Foreign Policy: The Calculated Versus the Axiomatic.' *Daedalus,* XCI, 4, fall 1962

MCCUNE, GEORGE M. *Korea Today.* Cambridge, Mass., Harvard University Press, 1950

MCCLELLAND, CHARLES A. *Theory and the International System.* New York, Macmillan, 1966

MCLELLAN, DAVID S. 'The "Operational Code" Approach to the Study of Political Leaders: Dean Acheson's Philosophical and Instrumental Beliefs.' *Canadian Journal of Political Science,* IV, 1, March 1971

MCLIN, JON B. *Canada's Changing Defense Policy, 1957-1963.* Baltimore, Johns Hopkins, 1967

MCNAUGHT, KENNETH. 'Ottawa and Washington Look at the U.N.' *Foreign Affairs,* XXXIII, 4, July 1955

MILLAR, T.B. *The Commonwealth and the United Nations.* Sydney, University of Sydney Press, 1967

MINIFIE, JAMES M. *Open at the Top: Reflections on U.S.-Canada Relations.* Toronto, McClelland and Stewart, 1964
– *Peacemaker or Powder-Monkey: Canada's Role in a Revolutionary World.* Toronto, McClelland and Stewart, 1960

NEUSTADT, RICHARD E. *Presidential Power: The Politics of Leadership.*
New York, John Wiley & Sons, 1962

NEWMAN, PETER C. *The Distemper of Our Times.* Toronto, McClelland
and Stewart, 1968

'North American Defense: Coordination in Canada and the USA.' *Round
Table,* XL, 160, Sept. 1950

O'HEARN, WALTER. 'Canada Stands Up.' *Behind the Headlines,* XI, 1, Feb.
1951

– 'The Allies and the War: Can We Play Our Few Cards Better?'
Saturday Night, 19 Dec. 1950

'Ottawa View.' *Saturday Night,* 1, 8 Aug. 1950

PAIGE, GLENN D. *The Korean Decision: June 24-30, 1950.* New York, Free
Press, 1968

PANIKKAR, K.M. *In Two Chinas: Memoirs of a Diplomat.* London, Allen
and Unwin, 1955

PEARSON, LESTER B. *Democracy in World Politics.* Toronto, Saunders,
1955

– *Diplomacy in the Nuclear Age.* Toronto, Saunders, 1959

– *Mike: The Memoirs of the Right Honourable Lester B. Pearson.* I:
1897-1948. Toronto, University of Toronto Press, 1972

– *Words and Occasions.* Toronto, University of Toronto Press, 1970

PICKERSGILL, J.W., ed. *The Mackenzie King Record.* I: *1939-1944.*
Toronto, University of Toronto Press, 1960

PICKERSGILL, J.W. and D.F. FORSTER, eds. *The Mackenzie King Record.*
IV: *1947-1948.* Toronto, University of Toronto Press, 1970

PLOSZ, A.J. 'The Navy's Unorthodox War.' *Public Affairs,* XIII, 4, summer
1951

PLOURDE, SERGEANT J.R. 'Korean Sojourn.' *Canadian Forces Sentinal,* III,
1, Jan. 1967

POTTER, PITMAN B. 'Legal Aspects of the Situation in Korea.' *American
Journal of International Law,* XLIV, 4, Oct. 1950

PRESTON, RICHARD A. 'The Military Structure of the Old Commonwealth.'
International Journal, XVII, 2, spring 1962

RANDLE, ROBERT F. *Geneva 1954: The Settlement of the Indochinese War.*
Princeton, Princeton University Press, 1969

REES, DAVID. *Korea: The Limited War.* London, Macmillan, 1964

REID, ESCOTT. 'The Conscience of the Diplomat: A Personal Testament.'
Queen's Quarterly, LXXIV, 4, winter 1967-8

RIDGWAY, MATTHEW B. *The Korean War.* Garden City, NY, Doubleday,
1967

ROBERTSON, GEORGE HILLYARD. 'Movie Censorship: The Scandal You Take For Granted.' *Maclean's,* 15 Jan. 1952

RONNING, CHESTER A. 'Canada and the United Nations,' in J. King Gordon. *Canada's Role as a Middle Power.* Toronto 1966

ROSENAU, JAMES N., ed. *Domestic Sources of Foreign Policy.* New York, Free Press, 1967

– 'Pre-Theories and Theories of Foreign Policy,' in his *The Scientific Study of Foreign Policy.* New York, Free Press, 1971

– *The Adaptation of National Societies: A Theory of Political System Behavior and Transformation.* New York, Caleb-Seiler, 1970

ROVERE, RICHARD H. and ARTHUR M. SCHLESINGER, jr. *The General and the President.* New York, Farrar, Straus & Young, 1951

SCHELLING, THOMAS C. *The Strategy of Conflict.* New York, Oxford University Press, 1963

SCHNABEL, LIEUTENANT-COLONEL JAMES F. 'The Inchon Landing: Perilous Gamble or Exemplary Boldness?' *Army,* IX, 10, May 1959

SCOTT, ANDREW M. *The Functioning of the International System.* New York, Macmillan, 1967

SIMMONS, ROBERT R. 'The Korean War: Containment on Trial,' paper delivered at the annual meeting of the American Political Science Association, Washington, DC, Sept. 1972

– 'The Strained Alliance: Peking, P'yongyang, Moscow and the Politics of the Korean War,' unpublished PHD dissertation, University of California, Los Angeles, 1972

SMITH, GADDIS. *Dean Acheson.* New York, Cooper Square, 1972

SNYDER, RICHARD C., H.W. BRUCK, and BURTON SAPIN. *Foreign Policy Decision-Making.* New York, Free Press, 1962

SOWARD, F.H. and EDGAR MCINNIS. *Canada and the United Nations.* New York, Manhattan Publishing for the Carnegie Endowment and the Canadian Institute of International Affairs, 1956

SPANIER, JOHN W. *The Truman-MacArthur Controversy and the Korean War.* New York, W.W. Norton, 1965

SPENCER, ROBERT A. *Canada in World Affairs.* V: From UN to NATO, *1946-1949.* Toronto, Oxford University Press for the Canadian Institute of International Affairs, 1967

STACEY, C.P. 'Canadian Military Policy, 1928-1953,' in Canadian Broadcasting Corporation. *25 Years of Canadian Foreign Policy.* Toronto, CBC Publications Branch, 1953

STANLEY, GEORGE F.G. *Canada's Soldiers: The Military History of an Unmilitary People.* Rev. ed. Toronto, Macmillan, 1960

STEVENS, G.R. *Princess Patricia's Canadian Light Infantry, 1919-1957,* III. Griesbach, Alberta, Historical Committee of the Regiment, the Hamilton Gault Barracks, 1958

'The Dominion,' *Time,* Canada Edition, 14 Aug. 1950

'The Services: Fired or Retired?' *Time,* Canada Edition, 20 Oct. 1952

THOMSON, DALE. *Louis St. Laurent: Canadian.* Toronto, Macmillan, 1967

THORGRIMSSON, THOR and E.C. RUSSELL. *Canadian Naval Operations in Korean Waters, 1950-1955.* Ottawa, Queen's Printer, 1965

TRUMAN, HARRY S. *Memoirs.* II: *Years of Trial and Hope.* New York, Signet Books, 1965

VATCHER, WILLIAM H., jr. *Panmunjom: The Story of the Korean Armistice Negotiations.* New York, Praeger, 1958

WARNER, ALBERT L. 'How the Korea Decision Was Made.' *Harper's,* June 1951

WHITING, ALLEN S. *China Crosses the Yalu: The Decision to Enter the Korean War.* New York, Macmillan, 1960

WHITNEY, COURTNEY. *MacArthur: His Rendezvous with History.* New York, Knopf, 1956

WILLOUGHBY, CHARLES A. and JOHN CHAMBERLAIN. *MacArthur, 1941-1951.* New York, McGraw-Hill, 1954

WOHLSTETTER, ROBERTA. *Pearl Harbor: Warning and Decision.* Stanford, Stanford University Press, 1967

WOOD, HERBERT FAIRLIE. *The Private War of Jacket Coates.* Don Mills, Longmans, 1966

– *Strange Battleground: Official History of the Canadian Army in Korea.* Ottawa, Queen's Printer, 1966

WOOD, JOHN C.W. 'Canadian Foreign Policy and Its Determination During the Korean War.' unpublished MA thesis, Carleton University, Ottawa, 1965

YOO, TAE-HO. *The Korean War and the United Nations: A Legal and Diplomatic Historical Study.* Louvain, Librairie Desbarax, 1965

YOUNG, ORAN R. *Systems of Political Science.* Englewood Cliffs, NJ Prentice-Hall, 1968

Index

on Formosa question 95, 97–9; relations with MacArthur 97–9, 221–3, 226, 229–30; and crossing of 38th parallel 117; and 7 October resolution 124; reaction to Panikkar's warnings 126–7; and neutralization of Formosa 125; and first reports of Chinese intervention 128; and bombing of Yalu bridges 129; defence of delegation of decision-making to MacArthur 135; later reflections on buffer zone proposal 135; and Chinese intervention 142, 145–6; and need to reassure allies 143; and possible use of atomic bomb 146–7; talks with Attlee 147–55; view of Cease-Fire Group 158; Korean War policy of after Chinese intervention 220–1; dismissal of MacArthur 229–30; and start of armistice negotiations 239–40; apparent inability to control MacArthur 330
'Truman's War' 272, 272n
trusteeship (of Korea) 3, 4
Turkey xn, 85, 98n, 122, 165, 198–9, 201

Ukrainian Soviet Socialist Republic 17, 26
unemployment, and CASF recruitment 185–7
unified command see United Nations Command
Union of Soviet Socialist Republics (USSR) 57–8, 81, 111, 148, 163, 165, 172–3, 175, 199, 233–4, 285, 327, 330–1; as instigator of North Korean attack x; and post-1945 occupation of Korea 4, 5; and UNTCOK 6–12 passim, 16, 18, 19; veto of Republic of Korea application for UN membership 27; and outbreak of Korean War 29–

30; absence from Security Council 37, 41, 41n, 46, 69, 82, 107; possibility of direct embroilment in Korean War 40, 44; communications with State Department 53–4; Korean War as action to preserve balance of power against 92; interest in linking Korean and Formosan questions 97, 97n; return to Security Council 100–2; position on UN action in Korea 100–1; Pearson's view of policies of 107, 109–10; and 38th parallel issue 116–17, 119, 121; resolution recommending withdrawal of all foreign troops from Korea 123; veto of six-power resolution 144; Acheson's view of objectives of 145; as potential rival of China in Far East 151; and start of armistice negotiations 235–7; proposed as member of NNSC 244–5; and UN involvement in POW repatriation issue 269–71; question of participation in post-armistice political conference 282–3; relation to Canadian 'systemic' capabilities 323; impact of Korean War on Canadian perceptions of 332–3; see also Soviet bloc
United Arab Republic 322; see also Egypt
United Church 259, 259n, 269n
United Kingdom xn, 68, 98n, 121, 143, 163, 165, 207, 216, 273, 277; Canadian tendency to follow foreign policy line of 55–6, 111; decision to send ground forces 84; and Formosa question 98; effort to persuade Chinese not to intervene in strength 135; and bombing of Manchurian airfields 138; and Committee of Sixteen 139; and invitation to Peking to attend Security Council 142; anxiety arising from intractability of